Ralph Towne.
Ottawa.
June 2002.

THE LAUGHING ONE

The
Laughing

One

A Journey to Emily Carr

Susan Crean

Harper*Flamingo*Canada

www.harpercanada.com

HarperCollins books may be purchased for
educational, business, or sales promotional use.
For information please write:
Special Markets Department,
HarperCollins Canada,
55 Avenue Road, Suite 2900,
Toronto, Ontario, Canada M5R 3L2

First HarperFlamingo ed.
ISBN 0 00 200062 8
First HarperPerennialCanada ed.
ISBN 0 00 638581 8

Canadian Cataloguing in Publication Data

Crean, Susan, 1945–
The laughing one : a journey to Emily Carr

Includes bibliographical references and index.
ISBN 0 00 200062 8

1. Carr, Emily, 1871–1945.
2. Painters – Canada – Biography.
I. Title.

ND249.C3C72 2001   759.11   C00-932351-1

01 02 03 04 HC 4 3

Printed and bound in the United States
Set in Apollo

The author wishes to acknowledge the generous
support of the public through the assistance
of the Ontario Arts Council, the Arts Council
of British Columbia, and the Canada Council.

The material from the unpublished manuscripts in the Phyllis Inglis Collection in the B.C.
Archives are used and quoted in this book with
the kind permission of John I.D. Inglis.

The illustrations listed below are reproduced
with permission. Those not listed are
photographs taken by the author.

View of Ucluelet, 1899, pen and ink drawing
(B.C. Archives Pdp 641)

Mrs. Wai-in-uck, 1899, pencil drawing (B.C.
Archives Pdp 00593)

Photo of Emily Carr and Richard Carr, Hall &
Lowe, Victoria c. 1891 (B.C. Archives G. 2842)

Banks of the River ("Tree by the Canal") oil
on canvas, 1910 (James C. Wilson Collection)

Brittany Coast, watercolour, 1911 (Collection
of the Art Gallery of Victoria; Gift of Major H.C.
Holmes) Photo: Bob Matheson

Skidegate (shark pole), dated 1912, oil on
card on board (Vancouver Art Gallery, Emily
Carr Trust, VAG 42.3.73) Photo: Trevor Mills

Mrs. Douse, 1928, watercolour (B.C. Archives
Pdp 629)

Totem Mother, Kitwancool, 1928, oil on
canvas (Vancouver Art Gallery, Emily Carr
Trust. VAG 42.3.20) Photo: Trevor Mills

Indian Church, 1929, oil on canvas (Art
Gallery on Ontario, bequest of Charles S. Band)
Photo: Carlo Catenazzi

Grey, 1929–30, oil on canvas (Private Collection) Photo: Michael Neill

Sophie Frank, 1907 or 1908, watercolour
(Collection of Jane Williams) Photo: Bob Matheson

Photograph of Emily Carr in her Simcoe
Street studio in October 1933 by H.U. Knight
(City of Victoria Archives)

Photograph of Emily Carr with her animals
(cat, dogs, monkey) at the door of the Elephant,
May 1934 (B.C. Archives, Newcombe Collection,
D 3844)

Scorned As Timber, Beloved of the Sky, 1935,
oil on canvas (Vancouver Art Gallery 42.3.15)

Photograph of Emily Carr by Nan Cheney,
August 1930 (B.C. Archives, The Parnall Collection H – 2812)

Index prepared by Christopher Blackburn

For Laurie

*who brought home
the West*

Acknowledgements

There are many people who have contributed to this book over the ten years I have been researching and writing it, but three individuals, Sandy Duncan, Shirley Bear, and Ed Carson, have been instrumental in their support and guidance. I have also depended on the generosity of those I met during my travels, the people who spoke to me, and allowed me into their story. Some appear in these pages, some do not. I would especially thank Douglas Cranmer and Ole Skogan of Alert Bay, Freda Diesing of Prince Rupert, Bev Anderson of Hazelton, Diane Brown, Fred Russ and Millie Pollard of Skidegate, Peter Hamel of Masset, and Abel Campbell of Gitanyow.

I am indebted to friends, artists, and colleagues, some of whom are no longer with us, who have talked with me about Emily Carr and painting, and discussed the issues that arise from her legacy: Howard Adams, Lillian Allen, Shirley Bear, Mary Billy, Fred Bodsworth, Kate Braid, Jeanne Carritt, Mel Charney, Peter Clair, Freda Diesing, Sandy Duncan, Laurie Edwards, Brian Fawcett, Cynthia Flood, Jerry Grey, Paul Hogan, Lenore Keeshig-Tobias, Michel Lambeth, Patsy Ludwick, Jane Martin, Lee Maracle, Jennifer Mascall, Robin Matthews, Doris McCarthy, Judith Merril, Roy Miki, Steve Osborne, Stan Persky, Marcel Rioux, Carmen Rodriguez, Isabel Cleland Rowe, Mildred Ryerson, John Ralston Saul, Mary Schendlinger, Joan Skogan, George Stanley, Viola Thomas, Dot Tuer, Scott Watson, Joyce Wieland, Peter Wilson, Winsom, and the Carnivores (Eve Zaremba, Susan G. Cole, Susan Feldman, Lynne Fernie, Myrna Kostash). I have also benefited from the work of countless academics and independent researchers, including artists, who have devoted their time and imagination to the study of Emily Carr's work. This book could not have been written without their scholarship. I owe a tremendous debt in particular to Gerta Moray, who shared her unpublished research with me and was willing to read my manuscript. Others who have been helpful in conversation are Marcia Crosby, Gloria Cranmer, Dara Culhane, Charles Hill, Judith Mastai, and Doris Shadbolt, as well as Daniel David Moses and Veronica Strong-Boag on the subject of Pauline Johnson.

I was fortunate to have Patrick Davidson as a bibliographic researcher, and Shereen Legault as a research assistant willing to help when it was needed. No research project like the one undertaken for this book could be accomplished without the assistance of librarians and their staff and I am grateful to those at the Vancouver Public Library, the Fine Arts Library of the University of British Columbia and the Library of the Vancouver Art Gallery. I am particularly grateful to Kathryn Bridge of the British Columbia Archives for her help in accessing the Carr Archive, and Jackie Conway for second-guessing a forgetful researcher, to Cyndie Campbell of the library of the National Gallery, and Benoit Theriault of the Canadian Museum of Civilization Archives. To Saeko Usukawa I owe the idea of revisiting the Carr journals, and to Joan Skogan critical early support and a postcard bearing a photograph of Emily Carr, grinning broadly, in the doorway of the Elephant. I have had invaluable assistance, too, from Penn Kemp (who showed me the poetry of John Barton), Terry Glavin, Heather Menzies, Arthur Gelgoot, Marian Hebb, Matthew Kassirer, Barry and Cathy Humphrey, the late Edmund Walker, Lindsay Godfrey, Bob Foley, Bernard Edwards, and Carol McIntyre.

Finally, there were those who gave me editorial advice at various stages: Don Obe at the Banff Arts Journalism program in 1993 when this book began to take form; Barbara Moon, whose recommendation was a sentence long but made all the difference; Nicole Langlois, who was trusting but asked questions; Iris Tupholme, who asked more; Ed Carson, who gave me a picture of what I had done; and Shirley Bear and Lynne Fernie, who let me hear it. All of these people deserve credit for helping me get things right. The errors that remain are my own.

The origins of this book are undoubtedly the passion for history and the written word that I learned from my late father, John Gale Crean. I wish to pay tribute to the man who offered me an education, who encouraged me to follow my own course, and first introduced me to the woods.

NOTE ON SPELLING

The old and often incorrect spellings of aboriginal place names have been kept in the fictionalized sections, and likewise the original spellings used in the titles of Carr's paintings are honoured. Elsewhere I have used the current spellings. Mable Dodge Luhan and her husband Tony Lujan spelled their last name differently.

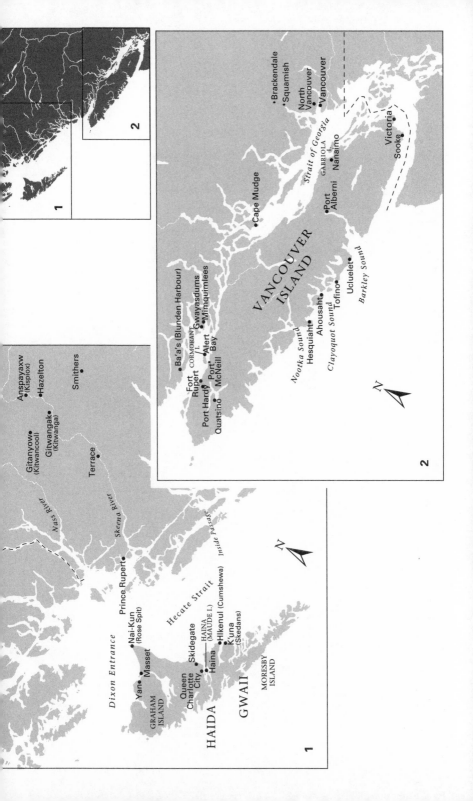

1

Dixon Entrance

Nass River

Gitanyow•
(Kitwancool)
Gitwangak•
(Kitwangai)

Anspayaxw•
(Kisplox)
•Hazelton

Smithers
•

Terrace
•

Skeena River

Prince Rupert
•

Nai-Kun
(Rose Spit)

Yan• •Masset

GRAHAM ISLAND

Queen
Charlotte
City

Skidegate

HAINA
(MAUDE I.)

Haina•

Hecate Strait

Hlkenul (Cumshewa)

Kuna•
(Skedans)

HAIDA
GWAII

MORESBY
ISLAND

Inside Passage

2

Brackendale•
•Squamish

North
Vancouver• •Vancouver

Strait of Georgia

GABRIOLA
Nanaimo•

Victoria•
Sooke•

Cape Mudge•

Port
Alberni•

Ba'as (Blunden Harbour)•

CORMORANT
I.

Tswayasdums
•Mimquimlees

Alert
Bay
Fort
Rupert• Port•
McNeill

Port Hardy•

Quatsino•

Ucluelet•

Barkley Sound

Tofino•
Ahousaht•

Hesquiaht•

VANCOUVER
ISLAND

Nootka Sound

Clayoquot Sound

Introduction

Emily Carr appeared in my life when a friend gave me one of her paintings to keep for awhile. The picture is of a house and garden beside a river in France, the composition dominated by a thick, leafy tree. You would have to know a lot about green to recognize this as an early Carr, I remember saying to Peter when he left it with me. But then, aside from being an artist trained by Europeans who taught him how to grind his own pigments, Peter was raised on the British Columbian coast and has a natural acquaintance with Emily Carr's greens. I have had to learn it. Peter's father, an affluent chartered accountant who doubted his son's artistic ambitions even while he appreciated collecting Canadian art as a relatively inexpensive indulgence, bought the painting from Walter Klinkoff in Montreal in the 1950s for a few hundred dollars. It came with a provenance, a now-brittle piece of paper affixed to the back, stating that the sketch was one of several that belonged to Alice Carr, and subsequently her niece Lillian Rae. The painting is unusual because of these associations. It is evidence that some connection between Emily Carr and her family existed through her art, minimal though that may have been. Alice was her favourite sister; Lillian Rae her favourite niece. The note reads simply: "These sketches were left to me by Miss Alice Carr who was a sister of Miss Emily Carr the artist. They are studies done by Miss E. Carr while a student in France. [signed] Mrs. Clare L.I. Rae—niece of Miss A. & E. Carr."

The painting was named *Banks of the River*, which is accurate enough as straight description, though it is not my perception of the work. I'd be more inclined to call it "Tree by the Canal," for after living with it for several weeks, I recognized that the tree and the reflecting surface of the river were its main features and the image I remembered. The sun-drenched lightness of the foliage, poised over its rippling likeness, delights me and draws me into the picture time and again. My first response to the painting was thus as a representation, as a landscape painted in the North American modernist tradition and a piece of Canadian art history. Yet I could not avoid its physical presence, given that I shared a miniscule apartment with it and given that, like me, Emily's painting imposes itself on its surroundings. The picture, a 13" x 16" piece of aged wood, canvas and oil paint encased in a gilt-edged, fabric-faced frame twice its size, sat sententiously on my wall. I looked at it, and it would stare mutely back. I began imagining its life as an *objet* and its itinerary once it left France in 1911. There was the original voyage across the Atlantic and the continent with Carr, the trip back East forty years later and its subsequent sale to James Wilson, who kept it in Montreal for nearly twenty years. Then another trip West when Wilson sent it out to storage in Calgary for a time before finally deciding to take it with him into retirement in Florida. Peter found it there after his father died, stashed in a closet with several other paintings (a David Milne and an Albert Robinson among them), which the new wife didn't care for. Back came the painting to Canada in Peter's Volkswagen van, and a few years later back it came with me to British Columbia on an Air Canada jet.

Inevitably, I became curious about the role the "Tree by the Canal" painting played in the evolution of Emily Carr's art, and where it figured in the unfolding of her life. I began reading the Carr biographies, rereading the art historical record and Carr's own published works. I had encountered her in passing as an art student, and knew that she was discussed in the same breath as the Group of Seven. At the same time, I was aware that a great deal more had been written about her than about any member of the group, and that she seemed to have achieved, all on her own out there on the fringes of British Columbia, what took seven men with private backing to accomplish in Ontario. Moreover, ever since the publication of her first book, *Klee Wyck,* in 1941 she has had a popular following.

For a time I fantasized that the painting recorded the actual moment when Carr snipped her artistic strings, moved into a modern idiom, and let go of surface reality. This may not be exactly true, but it is not far wrong. The "Tree by the Canal" was painted early on in Carr's stay in France, during her first session with Harry Gibb in the countryside at Crécy-en-Brie near Paris. As for Alice, the sister closest to Emily in age and affection, the only one of the four sisters who was ever able to summon up an interest in her younger sister's art (and, according to Emily, that happened only once), Alice was there at Crécy-en-Brie, staying with Emily in 1911. I began sifting through Carr's journals for comments, wondering if there was material left out of the published version. I thought of taking a trip to Carr country myself. I could follow her to Ucluelet and Alert Bay, along the Skeena River and perhaps to the Queen Charlotte Islands, to places where the landscape might tell me something else about her and the colour green.

There were other reasons for this interest. I grew up in Ontario where I spent summers as a teenager camping in Algonquin Park. The Precambrian north woods are imprinted on my psyche and are part of my formation, along with images of the Group of Seven and memories of paddling past Tom Thomson's cairn on Canoe Lake. I discovered the depth of this attachment when I first left Canada to study in Europe. I was surprised to be feeling homesick at the age of twenty, but there was no other word for the loss I felt; the absence of that landscape wrung my bones. I was not unhappy to be living in Italy and though I thrived on my studies, a sadness weighed me down. In the end, it made me sick. In Paris, the doctor at the American Hospital told me, "Ce n'est pas grave, Madmoiselle, mais, c'est très, très sérieux," avoiding mention of the word "tuberculosis." Like many North Americans, I had grown up without any exposure to the disease and was therefore vulnerable to it in countries where it was still widespread. I was also unaware of the social stigma it carried, so it took me some time to understand the doctor's meaning. Shades of *La Traviata,* I thought. The association of consumption with bohemian life and loose living rather appealed to my theatrical imagination, but the reality of recovery was not nearly so romantic—or (thankfully) tragic. The second time I went to live in Europe, I fell ill again, this time with anaemia, which no one winced at or bothered much about. I cured myself by returning to the familiar environment of North America, consoled by the thought that Europe was not everyone's cup of tea. Carr's memoirs had quite an effect on me when I read them then. I recognized the malaise she described and the cultural dislocation she felt as a Canadian in Europe. What struck me particularly were the physical ramifications of her emotional and social dis-ease in those foreign milieux. Later I discovered that her illness was perceived by many as a symptom of her own physiological disorder. The doctors in England in 1903 called it hysteria and the dismissive diagnosis stuck. Yet my own experience told me that the deprivation Carr described was perfectly real. Some organisms, including some people, do not thrive when removed from their natal environments. Moreover, Carr's struggle for a sense of her identity spoke to my own situation. Circumstances seemed to be pushing me to leave Canada, to pursue my life and options abroad, but my body and my dreaming mind had other inclinations. I felt a need to go home. How was I to conceive of this desire?

To complicate things, I discovered the Quebec Question at about the same time. It burst upon me in a book constructed of a dialogue in letters between two Quebec women writers living on opposite sides of the linguistic and cultural divide in Quebec. The book was called *Dear Enemies*, and the writers, novelist Gwethalyn Graham and journalist (and later Senator) Solange Chaput-Rolland, argued about history, race, and democracy instructing me as they did about that contested terrain called Canada. There were other books soon after—by Léandre Bergeron, Pierre Vallières, and Marcel Rioux, among others—but this was my first encounter with the story *les québécois* told about themselves.

Towards the end of my stay in Paris, I went down to the branch of the Royal Bank of Canada in rue Scribe to deposit some Canadian cash in my account. This was living money I'd brought back from a visit home at Christmas. However, the teller refused to take the cash, informing me in rapid-fire French that the rules on foreign currency did not permit such a deposit. The account was mine and so was the money, I protested, and what is a bank account for if not to stash your money—including cash—right? The man was unmoved. I wasn't keen on money belts or socks as an alternative, so I tried marshalling arguments for another assault on his rule. The money is Canadian, I am Canadian, and so is this bank, I tried. "Il y a des règles," he answered, sounding as if he were actually saying, "Be quiet, madam, or get out." He then shot me a look of such vile contempt that I was rocked. Where did that come from? My French promptly collapsed. In a panic, I spluttered out bits and pieces of Italian and German, any foreign language would do, knowing full well I'd just met a brick wall. At that precise moment, an impeccably dressed elder gentleman sporting a Borsalino hat, yellow kid gloves, and a beautifully kept goatee, appeared at my elbow. He nodded politely and said a few obviously pithy words to the teller whose hauteur instantly dissolved into obsequiousness. Then he turned towards me and spoke as if he knew me, though I couldn't understand a word he was saying. While trying to figure out who he was (and what language he was speaking), I watched the cash being whisked away into my account, and the teller disappearing into a cloud of apologies. I was speechless by this time. Then the teller made out a receipt, handed it to me, and thanked me for my patience. Still it wasn't until my debonair gentleman was taking his leave, tipping his hat with an "amusez-vous bien, Mademoiselle," that I also heard, "et faites attention que les parisiens n'aiment pas les canadiens" and finally realized he was speaking French. He was

Canadian like me, speaking Québécois French, and I'd taken him for a stranger. I was shocked by that realization and its corollary, the fact that my education had outfitted me with knowledge of the French spoken halfway around the globe but not the language spoken by my compatriots next door. That was when I made my decision.

I returned to Canada as Emily Carr did, and looked for ways to anchor myself here. I was clear about the choice. There was no career I wanted badly enough to exile myself for; I did not want to be stranded outside Canada, and I wanted to learn about the country I suddenly realized I hardly knew at all. I also realized that a person could be stranded *inside* Canada. It had to do with a sense of belonging. Thinking about Quebec and its relationship with anglophone Canada inevitably led me to reflect on the very idea of country and the elusiveness of Canadian culture. It also invited re-evaluation of a few inherited myths, such as the one about Canada not having much of a culture to start with. How was it possible that Quebec had a definable culture, that Native peoples had their own culture, that Newfoundland had one too, but the jury was divided on whether Canada did? Was Canada, after all, just a real estate deal? A figment of the federal imagination? The search for national identity is an old theme in Canadian history, and it concerns this matter of the collective imagination. "Where is here?" is indeed the primal question. It's as old as the arrival of the first European *habitants* who came to stay, who wanted to make a life and, if possible, a profit here. Several thousand miles and many months away from home, where the old rules and social distinctions needn't apply, there was freedom for a man to reinvent himself and, you might suspect, the country was invented to go along with that idea. The question, first articulated by literary critic Northrop Frye, takes the newcomer's perspective and the form of a denial. It does not ask "who is here" or even "what is here," but "where is here," implying the answer will come from the same place the question does, from some imagined "where" outside of here, outside of nature, and outside indigenous societies who could, of course, have answered the question. The question comes from deep within the incoming colonial culture and was inspired by the fear of having arrived in an indefinable place, a wilderness where there were no landmarks. The European settlers actually characterized this place as *terra nullius*, or no man's land, a conceit that served the immigrants' purpose when they seized Aboriginal land, but which required some fictional props nonetheless. So the story took root that the original people here weren't really "a people," or very Aboriginal given that intermarriage and modern ways were taking over their traditional cultures. My grandmother's generation believed the Indians were a dying race; mine looks on the surviving First Nations as victims; all along governments, politicians, bureaucrats, and most Canadians have refused to hear what Native peoples have had to say about our common history and their own vision of the future.

While reading *Dear Enemies,* I blessed the choice my forebears made in not stopping in Montreal but pressing on to southern Ontario where both sides of the family took up manufacturing, the Scottish side in textiles, the Irish in hat making. Both my grandfathers employed scores of men in their factories, learned to accept collective bargaining, and made money during the Depression. Whatever their sins as moderately successful capitalists (I would joke), at least we didn't have Quebec on the family conscience. When I learned more about history and about my own family, I discovered our conscience was full anyway—with the Asante in West Africa in 1900 and the Métis at Duck Lake in 1885, thanks to a single great-uncle. There are probably hundreds of European Canadians with ancestors who were soldiers or missionaries in Africa. Many of them brought back souvenirs and trophies as Uncle John did, and a surprising amount of this booty ended up in museums. A few pieces remained in my family, sifting down through the generations to my own. As children we played with Great-uncle's old pith helmet and ceremonial sword—when we could get our hands on it and Dad's back was turned. With the objects came the stories: how Great-uncle had taken himself halfway cross the continental U.S. by train, with his uniform under his arm, so he could join his regiment, the Queen's Own Rifles, fighting Louis Riel and Gabriel Dumont in what would become Saskatchewan. How, by 1900, he was in West Africa with the Gold Coast Regiment in what is now Ghana, commanding a battalion of African recruits in the fabled Asante campaigns.

Uncle John died a nasty death seven years later from the amoebic dysentery he contracted in Africa. Shit out his bowels and died, so the relatives whispered. He was forty-nine. The city of Toronto gave him one of its last military funerals, and the family buried him in Mount Pleasant Cemetery. Like all the other soldiers of his day, Captain Crean faded to flowers and was forgotten, that is until 1989, when an exhibition at the Royal Ontario Museum brought him back to life. The exhibition was called Into the Heart of Africa, and was built around the artefacts that the White clerics and military men brought home and left to posterity (in Uncle John's case, the Royal Canadian Military Institute), and which had been collecting dust in museum storerooms for the better part of a century. Although I had known about the show in advance because the curator had been in touch with my father, I wasn't at all prepared for the sight of Uncle John elevated to star status, treated as a historical figure with an entire case of "his" collection of Hausa weaponry and Asante objects (drum, quran pouch, stool, and tobacco pipe) while his pith helmet, spruced up and adorned with a shiny new brass spike, was displayed in a glass case of its own. His life was illustrated with newspaper accounts from the battlefront, and a photograph of the Hausa battalion dated 1902 was mounted on a wall nearby, with Uncle John still hale and hearty in stalwart command.

I wasn't prepared either for the public protest, the demonstrations outside the museum, or the ROM's refusal to engage in any form of self-criticism. The Black community denounced the exhibition as a glorification of colonialism and colossally bad judgement in a multicultural city like Toronto. And, in the end, the show's tour was cancelled, and the African collection was bundled back into storage after nine short months on view. Great-uncle's presence in the middle of the débâcle gave new meaning to the phrase "The personal is political." While it is easy enough to grasp the political and ideological dynamics of the world that produced Captain Crean and put him in Africa, his presence in the present was perplexing. It provoked ultimate (and unanswerable) questions about his personal role in the scheme of things. Did he rape women and brutalize children? Did he kill in anger or just in the line of duty? And it asked for a reckoning with the past. If Louis Riel could be recast as a father of Confederation, what did this make of the Great-uncle Johns of the past? None of us gets to choose our ancestors, of course, and none of us has any moral authority, really, for condemning their exploits. But if we are to claim their achievements, then surely it requires admitting their malefaction too. To be blunt about it, Uncle John spent his entire adult life in one part or another of the globe, killing Native peoples on behalf of God, Queen, and the Empire. His job was to provide the brute force necessary to keep "Pax" Britannica operating in the interests of British mercantilism. In Africa, as in the Northwest, this meant participating in the "glorious cause" of bringing European civilization, Christianity, and commerce to the continent and to Native communities. It involved alienating people from their land and destroying indigenous institutions. Curiously, one can use similar language to describe the plight of Uncle John's own people, his father Thomas Crean having taken the King's shilling and joined the British army in the years following the great famine in Ireland. The Irish had their taste of British oppression, and many fled the consequences. My great-grandfather left his home in Boyle, County Roscommon, in the 1850s and, with his wife and growing family, saw duty in a string of imperial outposts, ending up in Toronto where his ninth child, my grandfather, was born in 1865 and where the family gratefully settled.

There were always pots of shamrock around my grandparents' house on St. Patrick's Day. The Irish past was readily celebrated, though my grandfather thought of himself as unequivocally

Canadian. Gramp loved putting on the brogue and plunking out ballads on his banjo, but he was from "here," and when he went back "there" once with my grandmother when they were middle aged, it was to see the sights. This son of a displaced soldier had bound himself to the New World; within a single generation the family had relegated the past to a prologue and adopted this place as home. There were many like Gramp: born in Canada, no longer attached to the Mother Country (which in any case had ceased to exist as it was when the family left); they were focused on the future. But the fundamental questions left unanswered by their generation did not go away. They have dogged Canadian politics ever since, grabbing centre stage every once in a while, like Uncle John, to mock the whole proceeding. What was the stand-off between federal armed forces and the Mohawk of Kanasatake at Oka, what *were* all those failed attempts at constitutional reform in the 1980s and 1990s if not evidence that the concept of Canada is flawed from within? The effort to reconcile our three constituent founding societies—Aboriginal, French-speaking and English-speaking—gnaws at our entrails.

Perhaps it was coincidence that Uncle John showed up in my life at the same time as the "Tree by the Canal." Perhaps not. Both preoccupied me for months. I wrote about Carr and Great-uncle, though separately, drawing comparisons in my mind about their attitudes to the Empire and to the young country Canada. Uncle John's fascination with non-White society parallels Emily Carr's, though he did not leave behind diaries or letters to explain it, only a large number of photographs from his time in Africa, which his descendants pore over, inventing likely narratives. Into the Heart of Africa served as an object lesson, too, about the pitfalls awaiting writers and cultural historians who lose sight of who they are in relation to the story they are telling. To me, however, it was a question of the community you imagine yourself speaking to when you mount a show like Into the Heart of Africa. "Where is here" indeed. Apparently, in the various calculations about context, the curator Jeanne Cannizzo missed calculating the context in which her own creation would debut, and, save for the use of ironic quotations (in the texts mounted on the wall), she made no attempt to deconstruct the racism in the documentary imagery. Her experience is sobering and reminded me that telling Emily Carr's story, like telling Uncle John's, plunges me into the debates about cultural appropriation and racial privilege. It requires some self-examination as well as self-consciousness about my position and purpose in examining the life of someone like Carr. Is it to exonerate, vilify, or understand her? Is it to rewrite history, and, if so, from whose perspective, or is it simply to engage with the perplexities and perversions of Carr's character, the implications of her artistic achievements, and the allure of her legacy? I reread Charles Taylor's *Six Journeys*, the chronicle of the lives of six Canadians who crossed cultures in their search for identity. Carr is one of them, a woman, he notes, who styled herself as an outsider and sought out non-White society as a way of discovering herself. She rejects the garrison mentality of the eastern élites without knowing it, and embraces the Canadian wilderness as her own, finding "in an alien art, a vision she drew out of her own deepest feelings."

This is exactly what I want to know more about: how Emily Carr learned to paint the giant, vertical rainforest, how her imagination was fired by the spiritual presence she felt in the woods and in Aboriginal art. Trailing after her through the archives, through books, articles, academic theses, catalogue essays, tapes, and the like, other things tweaked my curiosity. Several people whom Carr knew and had a significant connection to are scarcely visible in the biographies and monographs—other women artists like Frances Hodgkins, Sophie Frank, and Georgia O'Keeffe, for example, and Marius Barbeau, the ethnographer who discovered her for the art world. The contact with O'Keeffe was very brief but symbolic, and though huge amounts have been written about the American painter, almost nothing is known—or was recorded— about her encounter with Carr. The same is true of Carr's time on the west coast of France, painting with New Zealand artist Frances

Hodgkins in 1911. Sophie Frank and Marius Barbeau are no strangers to the Carr record, yet very little of this touches on the intimate side of their relationship with Carr. Sophie is the biggest puzzle. There she sits at the centre of the story, Carr's one constant contact with Native culture, the mystery at the heart of a riddle, the woman whose life is just beginning to be investigated, whose work as a basket-maker has yet to be documented. These are the silent moments of history that can only be imagined, and so this is what I have done in the front section of each chapter, starting with Carr's trip to Ucluelet in 1899 and her meeting with the ship's purser, Mayo Paddon. I take few liberties in recreating these scenes in Carr's life: all of the characters are real, and most of the dialogue comes from published sources. Though the ideas may not have been expressed in the circumstances I depict, they are actual nevertheless. The exceptions are Sophie Frank and Mayo Paddon. Although the basic biographic information on Paddon is available, in both cases the knowledge and ideas imputed to them is informed speculation on my part.

Besides wanting to find a way for Carr to speak *within* her own time, I also wanted to interrogate her history with the knowledge and sensitivities of our own postmodern, post-colonial age. However, to do so focussing solely on Carr's life and achievement is to risk being anachronistic. The solution, I decided, was to introduce the present in a journalistic voice; that is, to include my travels in search of Carr as part of the narrative and my own discoveries about the past as part of the background of the book. Each chapter thus concludes with a section written in our time and in my voice. Each thus begins in Emily Carr's time and ends in ours, combining discrete sections of historical fiction and journalism surrounding a middle section of analysis and history. This format permitted a wonderful flexibility in approaching the Carr material and deconstructing her legacy. However, it was feasible only because the Carr literature is itself so extensive and diverse. With several biographies in print, this book will not be taken as a history of Carr's life; with the number of art historical treatises available, it need not be mistaken for a monograph on her art either.

My reasons for turning to fiction had only partly to do with curiosity about the gaps in Emily Carr's biography. I reached for a literary means through which I could show her struggling with love, for example, revealing her attitudes to sex and art without having to account for her ideas then or current theory about them now. While we do not know if Carr discussed the subjects with Frances Hodgkins, Georgia O'Keeffe and Marius Barbeau that my stories allege, the literature on these four individuals is large and detailed enough for such conversations to be constructed from the record, and they are not improbable. I also chose to write about Carr's mysticism and her private friendship with Sophie Frank in this same manner, drawing largely on unpublished sections of Emily Carr's journals in the provincial archives for both sections. The material on which these "fiction" sections are based is annotated at the back of the book so readers and researchers can follow up and draw other conclusions.

To me, the very fact of Carr's continuing popularity seemed to invite a re-writing of her story. Circumstances suggested writing it across the usual boundaries of time, discipline, and genre. Other things came to light as the research unfolded. I became aware, for example that there were many more convoluted side trips in Carr's life than straight paths, more myth than truth. And one truth is that there is no one Emily Carr, only a myriad of reflections of her. The other is that Carr has long since superseded the category of "important woman artist" and has become a historical figure in her own right, a well-known Canadian and perennial source of controversy. Moreover, in deciding to follow her into the woods, I am part of a long chain of unacknowledged giving and taking, borrowing and missappropriating between peoples. Inevitably, I am part of the tradition of White people writing about Aboriginal affairs, and precisely because of this problematic history, I decided to visit Aboriginal communities and speak to various people and elders as part of a personal search; and although I do not write about it in detail here, this whole book is inflected by what I learned. I decided instead to focus on Carr and the story of the non-Native newcomers here, and in doing so I began to see the outline of another story altogether.

The basic facts of Emily Carr's life are these. Born in 1871 in Victoria, British Columbia, she was late maturing as an artist. She went to England in 1899 and to France in 1910 to pursue her studies, working when she could with artists outdoors in the countryside. A trip to Alaska with her sister Alice in 1907 at the age of thirty-five originally gave her the idea of incorporating a documentary project into her landscapes by painting records of the monumental wood carvings produced by the Native peoples of the region—the poles, canoes, and enormous houses in the villages of the Kwakwaka'wakw, Gitksan, and Haida she visited. In 1913, following her first big sketching trip to Alert Bay, the Skeena River, and Haida Gwaii (the Queen Charlotte Islands), Carr mounted an exhibition of her work in a rented hall in Vancouver. She printed up handbills inviting the public to attend a talk on the "totems" depicted in her paintings, hoping for an enthusiastic response. She thought the province might purchase the series in its entirety given its historical value, and would perhaps subsidize future travels, but the breakthrough failed to materialize. Emily Carr was forty and she had come to a dead end. Her art, she realized, was not going to support her; teaching had proven a mug's game as most adults she taught were not serious and didn't want critiques. So she returned to Victoria, and built a two-storey apartment building on her portion of the family property, which had been divided the previous summer, counting on the rent to keep her in art materials. This didn't happen. Times turned sour and the war came. Carr ended up breeding bobtail sheepdogs and making pots and rag rugs decorated with Aboriginal motifs to make ends meet. She never quite abandoned painting, but for fifteen years she had time for precious little.

Then came the great discovery: the trip out of oblivion in 1927 when she was invited to participate in an exhibition of West Coast art at the National Gallery in Ottawa. She was sent a railway pass to travel east to attend the opening where she met members of the Group of Seven and finally, after long years of isolation, discovered kindred spirits. "You are one of us," Lawren Harris told her. Harris took an avid interest in Carr's work, and their discussions about art and the spiritual opened doors for her. She found the inspiration to return to work and, over the next fourteen years, painted as she never had before, producing the major part of her *oeuvre*, the paintings she is most celebrated for. She showed in galleries across Canada as well as abroad, was written about, and occasionally sold some work. It was no ride to stardom, much less to Easy Street, but it meant validation and vindication. In later years, Carr began to write and was encouraged by her friends to think of publishing her stories. When the first collection came out in 1941 and was immediately successful in Canada and Britain, it largely had to do with the subject matter (the tales of her travels to Native communities up the coast over the previous thirty years) and Carr's simple, personal style.

Klee Wyck won the Governor General's Award for literature in 1942 and made Emily Carr famous. Infamy was not far behind, and even before she died in 1945 there were accusations of exaggeration: she was unfair to her sisters in *The Book of Small*, to her tenants in *The House of All Sorts*, and to her friends in her cantankerous years. It was said by people who knew her then that she was prickly and bull-headed, a terror to deal with, and a thoroughgoing eccentric of the sort who frightened neighbourhood children. True enough, Emily did move to the margins of Victoria society where she constructed a peculiar existence based on her travels, her art, and a domestic life shared with animals—dogs, cats, birds, Suzy the rat, and Woo the Javanese monkey. Her posthumously published autobiography, *Growing Pains*, and her journals, *Hundreds and Thousands,* admit some of this ill temper and estrangement from intimacy, but they also allow her bitterness at the lack of sympathy for her work. Success was something she attained on her own without support, and she was not inclined to forget it.

The disagreements among scholars, critics, and enthusiasts over Carr's story have increased over the years along with her popularity, the one feeding off the other. Because of this, her life and her art have been under constant scrutiny. No other Canadian artist, dead or alive, approaches Emily Carr's renown. Her books have remained in print, her works are reproduced, the Carr family home has become a heritage museum, and the original House of All Sorts around the corner a shrine to a growing number of devotees. She is honoured as a pioneering woman, an important artist, a great Canadian, and a beloved character of unique (if quaint) dimensions. Dogs, cats, children, ships, and buildings have been named after her, as have projects, schools (including British Columbia's premier art college), studios, and art centres all over the country. In her own time, Carr's influence on younger artists of her day was actually slight. She did not attract acolytes, although there were artists among the admirers crowding around her in the later years. It is also true that she cast a shadow on the next generation of B.C. artists who had to wrestle with her large posthumous reputation. To artists born after her death, however, the mantle has been less confining. Poets, playwrights, songwriters, dancers, and actors have been fascinated by her persona and her story and have created works inspired by hers. A dozen plays, several suites of poetry, a ballet, a television musical, one large-scale modern dance, at least two major musical compositions, and several song cycles have been written about her or for her, not to mention the documentary films, the biographies (seven, at last count, directed to various age groups and markets), the picture books, CD-ROMs, and web sites. While one might guess this interest to be mainly female, focused perhaps in the feminist community, it is not, nor is her audience exclusively European or White. I have known First Nations women who hang reproductions of her paintings in their homes, and Black immigrant artists who read Carr's books and were inspired to come to Canada. Her appeal seems boundless.

Contemporary critical opinion has never been quite sure of the Carr phenomenon, and being Canadian is suspicious. No one contests Carr's place in the history of Canadian art or her high repute among collectors and other artists, but there are those curators and art writers who wonder at her enduring allure and growing mythic status, and who would offer worthier—in their considered opinion—candidates for artistic stardom. Even feminist critics sometimes doubt her aesthetic achievements. And those writing about postcolonialism typically view her as an agent of colonialization whose use of Native art benefited only herself and Canadian culture but never any Native community. We are unsure even as we embrace her. And which version of the Carr story are we to believe? The one about the star-crossed modern artist who prevails against the current of conformity to finally make it in the end? The one about genius tempered in pain and trapped in Victoria, or, for that matter, the one about the neurotic, sexually repressed social misfit who is hailed in her dotage despite her patently crazy behaviour? Or perhaps the more recent version featuring the lonely, depressed, postmenopausal woman, who brings about her own spiritual transformation?

People take sides over Emily Carr. Fifty years after her death you will find her being hailed as a visionary and condemned as a blissninny in the weekend papers. She is both beloved as a woman with a special connection to the land and Aboriginal culture, and condemned for appropriating Native imagery; she is hailed as a misunderstood genius, yet dismissed as a second-rate modernist, which leads to the final question. How does this woman manage to bedevil a sleek post-modernist generation like ours? What does she still have to tell us? How did she become an icon?

Chapter One

The Long Beginning

The view from Gabriola southwest over the Strait of Georgia sweeps grandly over ocean and islands, up to the mountains glimmering in a blue haze. Beyond is the intimidating west coast of Vancouver Island. As I prepare to write, I think of Emily Carr travelling that coast a hundred years ago. She was twenty-eight years old, full of life and youthful purpose, pushing off on a journey into the unknown. This is where I will begin too, on board the steamship with Carr on her first trip out of Victoria and away from her sedate British background.

I spend the day ensconced inside the cabin in a cocoon of documents. Boxes and shelves full of books, file folders thick with clippings and photocopied articles, cassette tapes of interviews and old radio programs, videocassettes, art books, piles of brochures, maps and postcards and several binders of photographs. All I can think of is the meeting between Carr and a young man named Mayo Paddon aboard the Willapa. *He is the first person to see Carr for herself, to recognize the ambitious artist she had become.*

From the outset I have realized that it will not be enough to track Carr on her journey through the landscape and through history. I must also follow her in my imagination. And that means allowing Mayo Paddon the first word.

Ucluelet, 1899

April 7th, on board ship
Sailing out from Victoria this morning, the *Willapa*
wasted no time clearing the harbour and setting her
course full steam ahead. As usual, the hold is full of mail
and provisions bound for missionary and trading posts
around the island, and the passenger lounge is practically
empty. A couple of men settled in for a morning of tea and
cards while the two female passengers aboard idled on
deck as the provincial capital and surrounding farms
dropped out of sight. It was a splendid day, the kind that
makes me love working on ships. The air crackled with
sunshine and wind, and the *Willapa* moaned with pleasure as she heaved herself into the heavy waves. She's a
sturdy vessel, but grows smaller as we advance towards
open ocean. The two women stand together silently
watching the familiar landscape melt into a lonely stretch
of coastline that will have no reprieve until Barkley Sound
is reached, a third of the way up the island's outer coast.
To port, the Olympic Peninsula slips into the distance and
the ocean overtakes the view with its undulating immensity. Even those who make this voyage regularly are
affected by the shift in mood that occurs when you round
Cape Flattery and head out into the vastness. An imaginary line is crossed, and you enter another world marked
by the appearance of storm petrels, tiny pelagic birds that
live on the wing far out to sea.
   This whole region is a paradox like the birds. The coastline is deceptive, especially to uninitiated travellers who
are startled to find that inlets can extend for miles, little
bays will balloon into sounds, and rivers turn out to be
channels. I've heard mariners tell of reefs appearing out of
nowhere, announced by the sound of shattering wood, of

Pen and ink sketch of the village at Ucluelet, 1899 by Emily Carr.

ghostly sandbars and fickle currents rendered lethal by
wild fluctuations in the weather. A late summer calm
dissolves with the suddenness of gunshot into a murderous
storm.

Mountains run the length of Vancouver Island, their
highest peaks reaching 7,000 feet. Rivers and finger-
shaped lakes line their valleys, carving the island's wind-
ward slope with crevices that leave lacy patterns on the
map. Anything but delicate in daylight, these rock faces
are awful, the terrain beneath them dense and difficult.
Even where riverbeds and sheltered coves allow a foothold
for habitation when the salal undergrowth can be
constrained, attempts to control plant life here seem ludi-
crous. Things grow with such speed and intensity at this
time of year that it is alarming. Although from the deck of
a ship the coast looks much like the coast of Ireland, ashore
everything is different. Trees attain gigantic heights, the

Douglas fir and western cedar exceeding 200 feet as a
matter of course. And the animals are similarly immense.
Bears, cougars, sea lions, and even crows are larger than
anything I imagined as a boy reading adventure stories
about the colonies.

Sometimes, I notice the mountains crowding close to the
sea, their flanks thick with vegetation which matures in
defiance of violent winds and surf, right to the edge of the
shore. Mild as the climate is, this coast is beset with ill-
tempered weather and devious winds that can lash the
seas into massive hydrodynamic displays. I've witnessed
these on occasion myself, and never without presenti-
ments of death. The weather is another part of the paradox, of course. Shielded from the arctic cold by the
mountain ranges of the mainland, warmed by the Japanese current incubated under South Pacific suns, the island
is an anomaly, a temperate rainforest in a country of ice
and snow. While the rest of Canada freezes in winter, here
it is merely dark, windy, and wet, the salient feature
being the wetness. Like the cedar trees and the salmon, it
comes in immense quantities, the price of the warm ocean
air being its moist cargo. And because of the idiosyn-
crasies of wind and geography, there are places where
rainfall reaches excessive proportions, even for a rainforest, at the end of a fiord, for instance, where compressed
rain-clouds are forced to rise abruptly, consigning tiny
areas beneath to interminable dampness. Ucluelet might
claim to be one of the world's rainiest spots for this very
reason. However, it is on the map because of the trading
post and the government wharf.

Summer is the reason people call British Columbia an
earthly paradise. The days are sun drenched like today
has been, the light crisp and transparent. All around the
abundance of life declares itself shamelessly. Salmon leap
from shallow waters, seals frolic in the harbours, and

eagles maraud herring runs, gorging on the easy catch. Occasionally I've seen sea otters floating on their backs, cracking open abalone shells on their chests, and down by the shore, in between forest and sea, lies the most conspicuous display of nature's wealth imaginable. There in the intertidal zones molluscs, crustaceans, and sea anemones flourish in brilliant colour and diversity, nourished by fifteen-to-twenty foot tides.

Winter is extraordinary in reverse; it is incubus to summer's idyll, the dark side of the calendar when the sky descends and the mountains disappear for weeks on end. Birds and animals withdraw. In forest caves the black bears hibernate while the deer and rodent populations forage cautiously and make do, hoping to avoid starving cougars. Fog rolls into the hollows of the landscape, clogging forest and village, hovering around the coastline where it muffles the din of the surf breaking over rocks and reduces visibility to the length of an arm. When it isn't raining, the air hangs heavy with mist. Moss sprouts on every available surface, including roofs and wharves, and woe betide anyone who counts on it appearing only on the north side of trees and goes into the woods without a compass. To many newcomers the winter darkness is disturbing, for it leaches more than light from the atmosphere. It dulls colour, deforms familiar landmarks, and reduces daylight to a scant six or eight hours. Winter is the season when the evil side of this grand magnificence is revealed—the gentle climate that hides hideous storms, the spectacular geography that harbours the most treacherous waters in the world.

For the two women aboard, this trip can not have been lightly undertaken. They are unmarried sisters from a proper, if not prosperous, family. I have heard the name.

One of them seems much older than the other and is, I am sure, heading for the little Presbyterian mission at Ucluelet. She has that look about her. I am not so sure about the younger one; there's a spark in her expression, and I noticed her studying her surroundings even while her blanched complexion told me she was seasick. I offered her some ginger water and tried to engage her in conversation. Were she and her sister going to stay at Ucluelet, I asked, forgetting that she'd know I knew she had a return ticket, being the purser. "My sister is visiting the mission," she allowed. "Are you spending the summer there, then?" I asked, fearing my questions were sounding forced. "I'm going to see for myself," she replied enigmatically. I didn't press her further but kept my eye on her. It was her assertiveness that caught my attention. I haven't met too many young women like her before, for I take her to be an adventurous sort despite the queasy stomach. She puts me in mind of Frances Barkley, who sailed around the world with her husband, had her first child, and buried it at sea, all before she was twenty. Miss Carr is someone interested in the country, too, I'll wager. That sets her apart from most settlers in Victoria who have raised children to adulthood and barely know the place they live in. It was the 1860s before any official attempt was made to survey the interior of Vancouver Island, about the same time gold was discovered on Leech River and a road hastily built out to Sooke Inlet from Victoria. There the push to expand westward ended, though, which is why Sooke still marks the boundary of *terra cognita* for most Victorians, the beginning of wilderness. It is, in fact, the beginning of Nootka country.

The Nootka are the Indians who live on this coast, and a reclusive people, very different from the gregarious Songhees who settled around old Fort Victoria in the 1840s. The annual summer migration of Natives from all

over the coast to trade and visit around the capital offers
instruction in such distinctions, and there are stories
enough for all to know that some Indians are feared, some
are admired and others envied, and all have reputations
among traders and travellers. Like the coast they inhabit,
the Nootka exude mystery and danger. For years after
Captain Cook's original voyage in 1778, British and American trading ships stuck to the west coast of the island,
avoiding the inside passage with its awkward tides and
island-infested channels. They were the first people the
Europeans met. Then, when steam-powered ships
appeared, the pattern changed; attention and trade
retreated to the sheltered east side of the island, leaving
the villages here on the coast distant and isolated despite
their geographic proximity to Victoria. Travel is still
mostly accomplished by canoe, though treacherous seas
make that impossible for large portions of the year. Even
so, to the Nootka, the sea is the source of all bounty. In
canoes forty to fifty feet in length, carved from single
trees, they ply these waters in search of sea lions,
porpoises, and even whales. Few other West Coast people
hazard the whale hunt, but the Nootka are intrepid; they
are also superbly skilled fishers and harpoonists, capable
of spending days, even weeks, at sea following continental foragers like the great grey whale.

Given its roughness, it is small wonder few Whites
have tried settling the West Coast. I've heard tell of the
heyday of the fur trade when the sea otter was abundant
and commanding high prices in the Orient and trading
ships came in droves, but no one stayed over until the
Hudson's Bay Company arrived, accompanied by Royal
Navy gunboats to enforce its trading monopoly. You
don't have to be Irish to see what schemers the British
are. But perhaps if you are a newcomer you have to be
Irish to see the wonder of this country.

Approaching the eastern edge of Barkley Sound, the day stays clear, and a strong westerly prevails, frothing the waves white. I know the route well now and anticipate the moment when the wooded curtain, which hugs the shore all the way up the coast, abruptly parts and a profusion of islands explodes into view—like the change of scene in the theatre. Tufted islets ringed with turquoise water, large-limbed islands straddling white beaches, smaller ones encrusted with rock, and far too many of them to count. I never fail to be amazed. Barkley is one of three giant sounds that punctuate the outer coast of the island. Nootka and Clayoquot are the other two, the latter dominated by three huge islands as impressive in their bulk as the Barkley cluster is in their number. Barkley Sound is also the largest and reaches the furthest inland, twenty miles up the Alberni Inlet to Port Alberni.

I find myself explaining all this to Miss Carr, whose name I ascertain is Emily. Her sister calls her Millie, and I'd assumed Mildred, but I much prefer Emily. The broad smile in the name suits her. I carried on with the story that McKenzie, the trader at Ucluelet, first told me about the Sound. It was named after an English sea captain named Charles William Barkley, who made his name demonstrating that the Strait of Juan de Fuca did exist, contrary to Captain Cook's assertion that it couldn't possibly. Barkley was on a journey of "mercantile speculation" when his ship, the *Imperial Eagle,* anchored here in June 1787, flying Austrian colours. He had no licence to trade from the East Indian Company, which meant that by British regulations he was operating illegally. He was twenty-three—my age—and taking a run at the rules. The circumspect description of the voyage was his wife's, Frances being all of seventeen when she married William and set off on the two-year expedition. Frances Hornby

Trevor Barkley is said to have been the first White woman ever seen by the coastal Indians, a claim that likely originated with Dr. John McKay, whom the Barkleys stumbled across when they first moored at Nootka Sound to trade for furs. One morning a canoe paddled alongside their brig and a filthy specimen in greasy otter skins clambered aboard and introduced himself as the ship's surgeon from the *Experiment*. McKay explained how he had wintered with Chief Maquinna and his people at Friendly Cove, and how dreadful the experience had been because early on he violated a taboo and so offended everyone he was ostracized and left to fend for himself. The story goes that McKay learned enough of the language to converse and was forever talking about the lily-white women with strawberry cheeks at home. So when the *Imperial Eagle* arrived, he sent out word that a White woman was on board. Crowds turned out to trade with Barkley, no doubt lured by ordinary curiosity as much as by McKay's summons. Still, he'd tell anyone who'd listen how the Natives fell on their knees at the sight of Frances's long red hair, how they thought she was something supernatural.

Miss Carr and I were seated in the lounge as I was telling her this. I looked at her dark hair, which she has pinned up in a way that frames her face most attractively. It is fine and curly, and bits keep escaping the pins. While on deck, she had let the breeze have its way; inside, she keeps them tamed. In the softer light, it is her piercing, pale grey eyes I notice. Was Frances Barkley actually the first White woman on the coast, she wants to know. I tell her I know none of it for sure, only McKenzie's story, which I'd heard from others, including someone who had read Frances Barkley's recently published diary in London. Do the Nootka tell the story, she asked. I didn't know, but pointed out that even if Frances Barkley was

not the first White woman the Nootka had seen, she was
the first White woman immortalized on British maps. Miss
Emily smiled at that, and urged me to continue.

After the traders, the missionaries came, I explained.
The Roman Catholics appeared first in the person of Father
Brabant, who now has two missions, one at Namukamis in
Barkley Sound, the other farther north at Hesquiat near
Nootka Sound. Father Brabant was here twenty years
before the Protestants arrived as neither of the two leading denominations (the Church Missionary Society and
the Methodists) were interested in the far side of the
island. It was left to the Reverend Melvin Swartout, a
Presbyterian, to set up at Ucluelet. He and his wife
arrived just six years ago, and immediately organized a
school in a building donated by a local man Swartout
describes as "more progressive than the rest—even if
more debauched." "The man's a convert with two wives,
you see," I added eyeing Miss Carr. She didn't blanch at
this, so I went on. The building is not large or handsome,
but it is pleasantly situated on a grassy knoll halfway
between the mission house and the Indian village. On
Sundays it doubles as a church. The mission house is small
and spare but comfortable. I try reassuring her about the
accommodations, but she waves her hand to stay my
concern, so I return to Father Brabant and the rumours
that he is infuriated by the Protestant incursion, particularly as the Department of Indian Affairs pays for the
school. Father Brabant has been heard dismissing
Swartout as a "schoolteacher by profession who holds
divine services on Sunday," and castigating the opportunism of the Presbyterians for placing themselves
between two communities with resident priests. "And the
poor little children so anxious to learn to read and write
will be perverted without noticing it."

Just past Cape Beale we turn into Trevor Channel and proceed a short distance up Mills Peninsula, sounding the ship's whistle. This is not a scheduled stop, but the captain always slows here. Sometimes nothing happens, but today a small boat detaches itself from the shadows by the shore and sidles up to the ship's starboard. "Hello, Archie," I call to the dishevelled individual gesticulating up at me. I have to cup my hands to my mouth and shout over the engines' clatter. "Hello, to you Paddon," he shouts back. "Any mail this time?"

A letter—I suspect *the* letter—has arrived from England along with a stout package marked "Books." I affix one to the other and drop them overboard into the little skiff. I half expect it to capsize, but Archie is incredibly agile. The mail produces a joyful whoop, and a little dance is executed in the air while his legs hold steady to the gunwales, balancing the act. No one seems to know exactly who Archie is or was or even where he has his cabin in the woods. He's one of those West Coast characters I think of as rejects and loners—remittance men, failures, and hermits who withdraw to remote places for their own particular reasons. Some turn strange with isolation. Archie apparently was strange when he got here, and always seems close to the edge. (I don't mention this part to Miss Emily when she asks about him.)

The exchange accomplished, Archie drifts back into the shadows and the *Willapa* proceeds north, heading for the trading post at Dodger Cove. This is one of five scattered around Barkley Sound, supplying canneries and sealing expeditions. Once docked, the passengers get off and stroll about. Swartout has plans for a second mission station here and some of the supplies taken off the boat are for his new school, so it would seem the Reverend's itinerant work has been fruitful, and Father Brabant's prediction accurate.

Miss Emily is eager to hear more about Reverend Swartout, so I tell her about the way he has with language, his own and several others besides, and the short time he took to master the Ucluth people's tongue well enough to preach in it. By contrast, the Scotsman McKenzie gets by on primitive Chinook. I retell the story of the Sunday McKenzie went visiting, and Swartout got him to attend church in the little schoolhouse; seated him in the front seat, he did, and then proceeded to expound on the doctrine of sin, ending with a pointed question to the congregation. "Now," he said extending his arms, "can any of you *not* show me a sinner?" The question was rhetorical. Swartout didn't expect an answer, but he got one anyway from an old woman, who rose from her seat at the back, pointed a long finger at McKenzie, and bellowed, "You see that man? He is an exceedingly bad White man." Later when McKenzie asked about the interruption, Swartout told him the truth to which McKenzie gave a shrug. "Well, maybe she's right. There are only two of us after all, and you have the corner on heaven."

By all accounts Swartout is a likeable man. Like most missionaries, he is stern, but he does not have the taste for interference that some do. Where Father Brabant has been known to deliver suspects to the police in Victoria, Swartout avoids contact with outside authority. He deals with alcohol by preaching a peaceable solution. "If you get drunk, I will not inform against you or seek to get you into trouble. Nor do I want to bring White policemen here. We are men, and we ought to know what is good and what is evil." That's his policy. Miss Emily asks me what I think. I tell her how it isn't only demon drink that has soaked the villages with despair; sickness has come in waves. Smallpox and influenza decimated the population, the worst of it thirty-five years ago when whole villages died. Daily life is far from picturesque in the aftermath,

which may be why Swartout goes through teachers like
flypaper.

The *Willapa* threads its way through the maze of islands,
across the twenty-mile expanse of Barkley Sound to
Ucluelet Inlet. An odd formation this one, for instead of
jutting inland, it runs parallel to the coast, incising a thin
lip of land that possesses remarkable features. All satiny
safe for anchorage on the inside, it is a mean stretch of
coastline on the ocean side, notorious for the scarcity of
shelter and a century of spectacular shipwrecks. Florencia
Bay, just to the west, nicknamed Wreck Bay, was named
after a 200-ton Peruvian brig that foundered off Cape Flattery in 1860 with a load of timber on board. The ship
survived, only to lose again to heavy seas when the
towboat taking her south for repairs developed engine
trouble and cast her adrift. At the eastern tip of the peninsula lies its crowning glory, a deadly outcropping of rock
and rip tides called Amphitrite Point, which is named for
the ancient Greek goddess of the seas. Wife of Poseidon or
Mother of God, Amphitrite's name is uttered in despera-
tion and in many languages by seafarers tossing out of
control in a storm or trapped in deadly fog. They call on
her to calm the elements and deliver them to safe harbour.

There is much about Vancouver Island that reminds me
of the Old Country, starting with this ragged coast of staggering beauty, which is blessed with the most dismal,
depressing winter weather imaginable. Only in this evergreen forest beside the sea do I feel hope when I inhale the
salt air and behold the wild green blanket of trees reaching to the mountains. I feel at one here, very close to God,
and emboldened in my resolve *not* to follow my father
into the ministry. Despite my strong belief and my desire
to live a good life, I do not have the calling. I *do* have a

desire to strike out on my own, and I want to stay in North America because I no longer belong back there, to County Mayo. The New World has given me ambition, if not a clear sense of where it should take me.

I am sure of one thing, though—my longing for the safe haven of marriage and another soul to face adventure with. That is what the story of William and Frances Barkley puts me in mind of, the wife I would have who would share my love of this country. I want to find work, a profession maybe, on land. Eighteen months working on the *Willapa* have been enough to acquaint me with danger and death. Twice I've contemplated the possibility of shipwreck. From what I know, the easy part would be surviving the ship's demise. The hard part would be getting past the rocks to shore without being dashed to bits, and then the truly hard part would begin. Making your way through the dense forest back to civilization would be the miracle, and it would take tremendous strength and ingenuity to survive. Only a fool would ever think this place benign.

April 8th, the Mission House, Ucluelet
We arrived here yesterday, late in the afternoon. The Willapa *steamed into Ucluelet, tooting a greeting to the crowd collecting on the shore. Dogs and children bounced about the beach as adults hurriedly made for the wharf. Evidently everyone is in high spirits on Steamer Day, but the bright blue day added to the levity. I looked at Lizzie and read relief in her face at the prospect of leaving the boat full of rough-mannered men— ruffians, she calls them. Her relief was clouded only by the thought of what lay in store here. Pretty well everyone who visits Indian country is appalled by the living conditions, and those who record their experience always comment on them with disgust. Lizzie has an inkling, having been here once*

before when she was twelve and Father took her and Alice with him on a three-day trip around Vancouver Island by steamship. I was seven and deemed too young to go, and the memory of that rankles still for, of all of us, I was the one who loved wild things and nature. Lizzie was always the pious one who could recite religious texts in reams as a little girl and followed all the rules with enthusiasm. Now she reads books about prayer in an endless stream and yearns to be a missionary. Though raised Anglican like the rest of us, she has of late taken up with the Presbyterians, who focus their missionary efforts on education and are in constant need of teachers. May Armstrong has been running the Ucluelet school for the last three years and it was she who asked Lizzie to come and see the mission life first hand. Then thinking that Lizzie would never come on her own, she persuaded me to come along with descriptions of "wild places" and the opportunity I would have to sketch around Indian villages. White women aren't permitted near the reserves in Victoria, certainly not on their own— and who would agree to accompany me? Visiting the encampments around the shore is equally out of the question, so I've only had glimpses, like the time when I was wee and an Indian family pulled up, in a beautiful carved and painted cedar canoe, on a beach near where we were staying. I watched with fascination as they made camp, ate their meal, and retired for the night. I learned things about Indian ways from Wash Mary, too, but I've never had a chance to really see for myself. Ucluelet, however, is a long way from James Bay and Mrs. Cridge's tea parties. I expect things are freer with fewer Whites around.

May was there to greet us, all smiles with the news that Reverend and Mrs. Swartout have gone to Port Alberni taking their daughters, Nina and Viola, with them. The whole mission house will be ours for a while. Looking about me, I could see several enclaves along the shore—the herring cannery opposite the post at Port Albion, and the Native villages in between, which are known as Edetsu and Kwa-Imp-ta. This I glean from the purser, an Irishman cum Canadian, who has made quite a study of the coast. He also told me about Reverend Swartout and the Scotsman who runs the post. I looked at the sky and drank in the panorama of green, thinking how glad I was to be on solid ground again, released from my fear of bad seas and evil omens. I recognized McKenzie, who was on hand to help unload supplies and mail, and watched him readying his pirogue to ferry the three of us down to "Toxis," as the mission is called. This takes quite a while, but eventually he beckoned us over, pointing to a tarred rope ladder snaking down the side of the dock. The low tide was just turning, and the boat below looked minute. The idea was to land in the tipsy little craft without falling, a task that May accomplished with astonishing ease, leaving the two of us to follow suit. With legs still wobbly from the long hours pitching and rolling aboard the Willapa, *I felt sure I'd lose my balance. Gloves, I realized, would only hinder the grip; there was nothing for it but to grab hold of the slimy ladder with bare hands. Flinching inwardly, I lowered myself down, spurred by the knowledge that it was a short trip down the shore by canoe and an arduous mile on foot.*

McKenzie is a huge, gruff man who settled into the stern with the agility of a boy and manoeuvred the boat out into the bay with a few large movements. He's a taciturn man, at least around women, so the women's talk took over—May's descriptions of the mission routine, prompted by Lizzie's questions about her duties. Up in the bow, I basked in thought, marking our progress along the inlet, thankful for the returning tide carrying us in. Smaller boats frighten me less. The sky was turning orange and the shore was deep in shadow when we arrived at a break in the vegetation where the mission house sits in an alcove of Douglas fir. The landing is neatly made, and with McKenzie's help, our luggage and May's supplies are quickly transported up the beach.

We leave the luggage at the door and set to work stowing the supplies and preparing supper. May lights the wood stove and announces baked fish and tinned vegetables in honour of our arrival. "Praise God you have come," she says. The meal ready, we sit down at the table. Candles are lit and the prayers begin, intoned with gravity while the food cools and my stomach growls. Later the three of us creak up the stairs to the sleeping room, each carrying a tin candlestick. The space above is large and occupied by a wide wooden bed with a metal cot at its foot, with up-ended apple crates for tables on either side. No carpets, no curtains, no chairs, only neat piles of devotional books stacked on the bedside apple crates. I watch the two older women prepare for bed as if performing a ritual. Without a word and almost in unison, they fold their clothes, unlace their shoes and pair them under the bed, put on stout nightgowns, and sink to their knees on the splintery floor. Their hair, unravelled into long plaits, dangle down their backs, swaying like the rope ladder to the silent movement of their prayer.

The room grows quiet. Outside the forest is hushed in a vibrant stillness, tense with life. From my cot I can see an ancient balsam towering over the trees beside it, its pinnacle pointing to heaven like the hands of the two missionaries outlined in candlelight.

May 16th
All this spring I've observed May and Lizzie tending to their missionary business, teaching school, holding Sunday services led by May in choppy Chinook, dispensing medicine along with Bible lessons, and practising a regimen of prayer and penitence. I like to spend my days on my own, exploring outdoors. At low tide, I often walk down the shore to the village and sit about sketching the children playing games.

Eventually I screw up the courage to visit one of the big houses. These, I've been told, are constructed with cedar beams that take 200 men to set in place. Their sides are of hand-hewn planks pegged and slotted together horizontally, and the low-pitched roof is held in place with stones and has a central smoke hole to provide for fires kept alight inside. Several families live in each house. I've been told not to bother knocking, but I find it awkward. Instead I clear my throat noisily, and call out "hello" upon entering. My eyes take a while adjusting to the gloom, but then I see two old women sitting by a smouldering fire with a sick boy sleeping beside them while they smoke their clay pipes and rock back and forth. With no language between us, I communicate by gesture and tone. "Dumb talk" I call it, though it is anything but dumb. The grannies let me know the boy fell off a cliff and badly injured his leg. I can see it propped up and bandaged with moss. I sit with them for a few minutes and then take my leave, nodding to them as I shake my head and touch my heart. I think they understood my distress at theirs. It was the same with the old man who yelled at me when he saw me about to circumvent a tree that had fallen across the beach. Meaning outstripped language and I knew he was warning me against going around it through even a tiny bit of forest. Panthers, I suppose. The Indians forbid their children to go into the woods, and to them I am a child, ignorant of the wild things they know so well, and can speak of with such authority about to White people.

Despite the old man's warning, I am still drawn to the trees. I patrol the periphery and am amazed by the hedges of salal growing in thick patches by the beach, six feet or more in height. The purser made a comment that struck me, about the flora and fauna—slugs, ravens, trees, blackberries— being generally bigger than anything he was used to or had seen in Ireland. He warned me about the woods, too. So I am wary, and keep to the paths.

Following one little-used trail, I find my way to the "place of the dead." May calls it that, explaining that it is not a cemetery with people buried decently in the ground but a place where they are hung in trees. She intimates I couldn't possibly want to go there, only I do. The walk winds through the forest to a clearing at the end of a spit of land. Arriving, I first become aware of objects strewn about the ground as if a troop of Alice's grade threes had spent the morning there wreaking havoc. The image lasts the few seconds it takes me to register the fact that the bones I am looking at are human. Skulls stare out of the bracken, ribs and thigh bones lie among tree roots where the coffin boxes suspended above have dropped them. High in the branches of the encircling pines, a dozen or more boxes still rock in the wind. Some have Hudson's Bay blankets tied around their middles, frayed ends flapping like flags on a ship's mast. Up there in the keen air, the bones disintegrate quickly while the sun and rain rot the boxes and ropes securing them. Something finally gives and everything cascades to earth. I notice how the lower branches of the trees have all been chopped away. I wonder if it is to keep the dead from returning to life, or to ensure that the ancestor's remains will return to earth unimpeded.

I absorb the scene, conscious of my dry throat and the sweat beading on my upper lip. I hear the screeching of trees rubbing against each other in the wind and feel terror prickling my nerves. Rooted to the spot, I listen to myself breathe, deliberately marking it—in-out, in-out—until I feel myself chanting. Before I know it, I start singing, picking out the tune of a lullaby that Mother used to play on the music box. I sing a couple of verses and when the words run out, start over. Soon the fear dissipates and I am able to look around, seeing now a strange-looking cedar across the clearing sheltered in behind some alder trees. In its bole a body has been buried. I see a scarlet blanket spread over it, bracelets and beads scattered about beside it, along with a brass lamp and some clothing. A shaft of sunlight seeps through a crack in the tree trunk and glitters off the shiny surfaces. I move closer, contemplating the phenomenon of the dead lying inside a living tree, of the woman encased with her dear things by the life racing through its shell. I squint as I bend down to see. Some twigs snap as I move, and just behind me the salal shifts, sending my heart back into my mouth. Straightening up, I start singing again, quietly, soothingly. The feeling passes and I fall silent. Ravens chortling in the trees lull me back to normalcy and I look about for a place to sit. After a few minutes I take out my sketchbook and start drawing. There is a beauty about that place despite its creepiness.

For a while, everything is calm and then I hear it again, the commotion in the underbrush. More movement, coming close, and then two dogs burst through and circle around me, sniffing intently. These are large, lean hunting animals unlike any I've seen in the village. I call to them and hold out my hand, but they ignore me, rushing back and forth. One picks up a bone and tosses it about briefly until some unheard signal causes him and his companion to turn tail and disappear. Shouldering my gear, I follow them walking slowly, thinking about the steep hill up behind Toxis where the missionaries have established a Christian cemetery and buried one lonely soul—Reverend Swartout's only self-professed Christian Indian. The man was buried in a coffin in the earth among the roots of the trees but away from his people and, I ruminate, away from the rain and the sun and the wind that he loved and which would have rushed in to help his body disintegrate speedily into dust, so the earth could be richer because he lived.

June 1st

Yesterday when I was down at the post, I met an old chief known (so McKenzie says) as a "reader of faces." He had come over to Toxis to meet the White visitors. To see for himself, I'd say. He sat on the table, puffing on his pipe; a short, crinkled grandfather who surveyed me with a hawk eye and, after a while, declared me friendly and down-to-earth. "Someone who laughs," said the Indian fisherman Joe, who loiters around the store doing odd jobs for McKenzie and acting as interpreter. I wasn't sure if that was good or bad, so I asked him to repeat the chief's words. "He say he can't understand you talk but he understands you smile," he reiterated. I was pleased with that, and wondered if it would be all right to approach the village women on my own now. May has told me many of them are frightened of White people. I resolved it would be now or never, and this morning went over to the village to seek out the mat-maker to see if she would let me watch, and perhaps sketch her at work.

I found her seated on the floor, weaving away with swift, practised hands; all around her bundles of materials made from cedar bark, spruce root, and goat hair were arranged. Mrs. Wai-in-uck is an old woman with bad legs who rarely leaves her house. May has told me that she tolerates visitors and suggested that I take some tobacco as a gift. "They all like to smoke," she explained. I arrived at the house to find the door propped open. Mrs. Wai-in-uck smiles at my greeting and motions at me to come in and sit. The house is cavernous and dim, the air thick with wood smoke and the smell of candlefish grease. Her comfortable corner, however, is lit from the doorway. She continues working as I fumble with a few words and present the packet of tobacco. She gestures at the pot on the slumbering fire and says a number of things in her language, so I take it that I am to serve myself some tea, which I do. Then I settle down close by and watch her for a while. She is tiny and swaddled in clothes.

Her round body moves rhythmically as she weaves, and her hands work the piece with nimble gestures in and out, back and forth, across its surface. I pull out my sketching pad and begin to draw. Time passes while we work quietly side by side, absorbed. Suddenly a pile of baskets topples over when a cat clambers down through the smoke hole, waking an old man who has been sleeping underneath. The place erupts. I am shooed off in a shower of angry words before I have a chance to show Mrs. Wai-in-uck my handiwork. Later in the day I catch sight of her calling across the bay to me, but I don't follow her instruction, fearing she is still annoyed. Then this morning down at the post store, Mrs. Wai-in-uck appeared, causing quite a stir. I was there with May to pick up supplies when she came in, helped by two strapping grandsons who kept her steady and upright, for her gait pitches her body at dangerous angles like a ship in a gale. Once inside she settles by the stove, takes tea, and begins talking. It sounds like a speech she'd come specially to deliver. Listening, I catch the words "Klee Wyck" repeated several times in my direction. Finally I ask what it means. Indian Joe says something, Mrs. Wai-in-uck looks at me, then pulls her mouth into an exaggerated smile using two index fingers, and guffaws. "The Laughing One," comes the translation. Old Joe winks. "The chief thought you are funny," he tells me. I laugh at that and Mrs. Wai-in-uck joins right in, slapping her thighs with glee. Her face lights up in a sea of dimples and her voice drives the whole company to laughter. She slurps some tea, and grows serious then. Leaning forward, she strokes my skirt and holds forth. She has an elaborate explanation about how her husband had mistakenly blamed the White woman for waking him yesterday when the cat was the culprit. But there is more than an apology on her mind. When prodded by May, she admits that the old Indians don't like pictures because they believe the spirit of a person can get caught in the likeness.

They can be trapped there even after death. Her husband wanted me to know.

"They have such silly notions," says May turning to me.

"Tell her that Klee Wyck will not do any more pictures of the old people," I say to Indian Joe. "Tell her I will bring over my pictures for her to see."

"Mrs. Wai-in-uck," the mat-maker at Ucluelet, 1899 by Emily Carr.

July 6th
I feel I have been given a name and a new start in life. It matters to me that the Indians accept me; perhaps they do see me differently from other Whites who come here with their questions and designs. Missionary women with their long Lenten faces, teachers with starched manners and thick rulers. I think now I know what the purser meant when he advised me. "Just be yourself," he said. "You'll not go wrong."

July 29th
I've wondered all summer if I'd see Miss Emily on her trip back. This morning she boarded at Ucluelet without her sister and, as luck would have it, she's the only passenger. The fair weather conspires further. I found her on deck sitting comfortably on some packing cases enjoying the day, her dislike for sea voyages seemingly abated. I engaged her in conversation, and I was glad to see that she remembered me. I notice a change in her. It is not just the sun in her face; there's a gaiety about her that was not there before and, in an odd way, a calmness. Together we watched a pod of sea lions lazing in an eddy of warm water, flippers dangling in the air as they rolled up against one another. The weather holds most of the day, and tomorrow looks promising. She has agreed to see me again in Victoria.

August 6th
Home again, but not for long. I've seen Martyn several times since getting back. We take walks through Beacon Hill Park and out along the Dallas Road cliffs where we continue the discussions we started on board the Willapa. *We talk about his family; we reminisce about Ucluelet and philosophize about spiritual things. He tells me he is called "Mayo" for*

the county back in Ireland where his people are from origi-
nally. It seems strange to call him that when I think of him
as pure British Columbia—straight, strong and handsome
like a Douglas Fir. So I call him Martyn. He was fifteen in
1890 when his father took up a post at St. Saviour's Angli-
can Church and brought the entire family to Canada. He says
he loves Canada and intends to stay here, though his family
will eventually go home.

I find it easy to share deep thoughts with him. We talk
about religion and I like what he has to say about atonement
and grace, so I agreed to attend services at his father's
church and twice now have gone to Bible study. My sisters
view this with sceptical approval, which makes me want to
screech. They welcome Martyn to the house, serve him tea
and blackberry wine, and cluck about him like chickens. He
doesn't seem to mind; like a true friend, he overlooks the odd
parts. He is four years younger than me, but far more
worldly and, I think, wise. I feel free to talk about inner
things, too, like my sad feelings about Mother and the regret
that I was such an unruly little girl. What he said I'll never
forget. "You were the difficult one, Emmie. You can be sure
she worried more about you than the others, and loved you a
tiny bit more."

August 8th
I fear Emily is not the marrying kind. She is older than I
thought and at twenty-seven you do not make life decisions frivolously or easily. She is determined to be an
artist and becomes animated when she speaks of her plans
for her painting. She is off at the end of the month to
England to enrol in art school. I can't expect her to
forsake that, but we could become engaged. I know I'll
have to take care when I broach the subject, but my
intentions are sure. There's no woman I've met like her

and, as grandfather would say, I'll have her to wife, if she'll have me. Sometimes I catch myself thinking that her interest in me is platonic. It didn't seem so at first, but more and more I sense a reticence.

August 16th

It's a week now since Martyn asked me to marry him, and a week before I leave for England. What sweet irony. Just when one love is denied, another appears on a platter. I gave my love where it was not wanted and almost simultaneously an immense love has been offered me. To set the story down on paper is horrifying. I look such a fool, such a stupid school-girlish thing it was, and now Martyn brings me proof that it has changed me utterly.

It happened last March, a few weeks before I set out with Lizzie for Ucluelet. I had spent most of the morning tacking up the vine over the kitchen veranda, using the sharpening stone from the kitchen as a makeshift hammer. It was late in the afternoon when I remembered I'd left the stone on the roof. There had been a tennis game down the street at the Cridges' earlier in the day, and a few of the boys had passed by our house on the way. Martyn was not among them. I suppose because Anglicans and Episcopalians, especially Reform Episcopalians, don't mix. Several of the boys hollered and waved when they saw me up the ladder at the side of the house. I waved back and thought no more of it. But I noticed Jamie's thick, wavy hair and broad shoulders among the knot of energy dashing past.

The sharpening stone is large and coffin shaped, a prized possession of Dede's who always likes things kept in their proper place. I scrambled up the ladder, hoping to have it back in place before she could miss it. The warm sun had worked its magic all day, bringing out the flowers on the vine. As I ascended, I was enveloped in a cloud of little white bells nodding gaily at the cherry tree below, scenting the air with sweet lily smell. The sky was pink with twilight, the liquid sounds of thrushes filled my ears, and at the top of the ladder, I paused breathless, transfixed with joy. My senses exploded and I broke into song. Then I closed my eyes and breathed slowly, feeling at that moment closer to the vine and the blossoms and birds than to my own flesh. I was transported, as the poets of old would have said. Or perhaps it was a daydream of unusual intensity. Whatever the case, I had the most perfect vision of the lily field I remember from childhood, full of light and white with flowers. I was flooded with the same diffused sense of well-being, and I came to not knowing if minutes had passed or hours. I felt exhilarated and fatigued at once. Then the exquisite moment was gone.

Feeling a bit disoriented, I scurried down the ladder and instead of landing on the ground, landed in a strong set of arms belonging to Jamie. He held me tight and turned me around and put a finger to my lips when I started forward to speak. Then he kissed me. I knew him and already liked him, but this was unexpected. The joy bursting through my veins was too. Love rushed in from nowhere and settled down hard. We took a walk down the back lane and he kissed me again and told me I was beautiful. I thought, I assumed . . . but he didn't return the next day, or the next. I soon found out he was a flirt. I meant nothing to him at all, was nothing more than part of the loveliness of spring and that moment. I was mortified when I realized, ashamed of my gullibility, and mystified by the fierceness of the love that had driven itself into my heart. It was torment until I resolved to root it out and starve it to death, for I do not want to be governed by feelings like that. I do not want emotions running my life and shaping my world. And now Martyn appears, as if to test my resolve.

The trip to Ucluelet gave me courage. It was not difficult to put Martyn off. I will go to London and learn what I have to, to paint what I want to here. Everything else in life, especially happiness and married love, is unpredictable and undependable. But my love of painting is not. It may be hard to imagine my life alone as an artist, but no harder than imagining myself as someone's missus, at his beck and call like Mother was to Father. I'd rather be destitute. Still, I suspect Martyn of being a good man and true to his word. I can love that in him even though I cannot love him.

August 17th
It didn't work. I talked to Emmie about making a life together and she talked about painting. She says she is not ready to think about such a thing as marriage. It wasn't an absolute rejection; a sliver of light pricks my despair. So I will have to contrive a way to get to England to visit her. A few months in a dingy London pension may change her mind, and I shall pray for that. Emily is a determined woman. It could take her a lifetime. I wonder how long I should wait.

August 20th
Departure tomorrow. I am dizzy with apprehension, and fear flutters in my gut at the thought of the ocean voyage ahead. I bolster myself with the thought that millions have crossed the Atlantic and survived. The train trip across the continent I look forward to, and I like the prospect of being on my own in a foreign country, even though it frightens me. I also like the idea of leaving town for a spell. I have been too long in the company of my sisters where I am required to conform to their habits and admire their proclivities. I grate on their nerves, and they on mine. I need time and a place to concentrate. To see for myself.
    Leaving home makes me pensive. Martyn has the same

*effect, for he forces me to think about love—and how my
heart has hardened, exactly as I meant it to. Jamie would
possess my thoughts still if I let him. What I allow myself is
the memory of that blissful moment at the top of the ladder
in the flowering vine, and what I realize now is that the
experience was familiar. I've had it before, that sense of
being in a trance, and the presentiment of being spoken to. It
is how I felt in the lily field as a baby, how I felt when I was
small and played games with Drummie, my fairy friend,
whom I never really saw, though I felt and heard him
anyway. It seems to me Ucluelet is of the same order. I felt it
better than I saw it. The fog-cloaked woods beguile me and I
know I need to go back. But, for now, there is England and
art. The forest will have to wait.*

The Making of Klee Wyck

Emily Carr was still weighing and measuring the possibilities of
life in the summer of 1899. She had studied art in San Francisco for
three years, given painting classes to children in Victoria, and was
seriously preparing herself to become an artist, yet she had not
done with the idea of love and marriage. She only knew it was
improbable that the two—art and marriage—could be combined.
She had seen it once when a European couple (he was French and
she English) turned up in Victoria in 1886 and stayed a year giving
classes and exhibiting their work. The de L'Aubinières were both
artists, which impressed her. All the other women painters she
had known in Victoria were single, either spinster ladies who had
remained at home to care for widowed fathers, pursuing cautious
careers on the side of domestic duty, or young aspirants like Miss
Withrow whose art classes she and her sisters attended as children. The de L'Aubinières' message about having to leave British
Columbia to seek serious training abroad was not lost on her. And
she had watched Sophie Pemberton and Theresa Wylde, two

slightly older art students who had attended the same classes as she, make their way to Europe. Pemberton had gone first to England and was now at the Académie Julien in Paris; Wylde was ensconced in the English countryside studying landscape. Emily Carr was still saving up to leave Canada.

The five years since San Francisco had not been edifying; Emily spent them treading water. Whatever else she was doing, society assumed she was waiting, as all women of her age and station in life were, for a suitable suitor to materialize. Her biographers describe her at this time as immature for her age, the product of a sheltered life and her position as the pampered baby of the family. She was the youngest of five girls, and although a son was born four years after her, he was frail and sickly and kept at home close to his mother, a reminder of the three other boys who had died in infancy. This left sturdy, outgoing Emily to shine as her father's favourite, whom he would say "should have been a boy." She was the one who met him and walked back home with him from work each day, the one who mollified his moods and centred his attention. She wrote about this and about her growing disenchantment with her father in her childhood recollections in *The Book of Small*. At some point, perhaps when she was as young as eight or nine, she saw through the special treatment to the autocrat behind it and from then on, their relationship was a contest of wills. Her mother, who exerted a warm and steady influence on Emily's early life, is mentioned little and, in fact, was ill through Emily's early teens, dying of consumption when she was fifteen. Years before when her mother first became ill, Edith, the eldest daughter, had started assuming responsibility for the household and for raising the younger children. "Dede" nursed both ailing parents and, when Richard Carr died in 1888, sad and despondent two years after his wife, Edith simply carried on. Not much changed, or had to. The house and garden were left to her provided she keep them as her father had in his lifetime. In addition, there was an estate of $50,000 to support the five children left at home. (Clara, a year younger than Edith, had married and moved out by

1882.) Already thirty-two, Edith did what society and her father expected, put aside her personal life to look after the family. It had been a large one; nine children born over twenty years and two continents, divided by infant deaths into two groups separated by ten years. Richard Carr and Emily Saunders had met in San Francisco during the prosperous years of the Gold Rush. They returned to England to marry in 1855 and then settled in California where their first two children were born. A few years later they retired to Devonshire with a modest fortune, intending to live a life of genteel retirement. They stayed only two years, and then returned once again to North America, arriving in Victoria with their two older daughters in 1863.

Richard Carr had not reacclimatized to the country he had left as a youth of eighteen when he had turned his back on England and his family. The son of a tradesman who afforded him a poor education and poorer prospects, he nevertheless believed in the Empire and the ideals of gentlemanly behaviour, and remained loyal to English culture all his life. He spent his twenties travelling all over the Americas, working as a seaman in winter and at whatever else he could find—in the fields, on the docks—in summer. He kept on the move, recording events in his journal as he went: saloon riots in New Orleans, the Cherokee being marched off their lands in Alabama, various near disasters at sea. He tried his hand at daguerreotype photography for a while, and made a trek from the Yucatan to Peru, which took him three years during which he lived from hand to mouth and depended on the kindness of the people he met. His notebooks reveal the mind of a typical nineteenth-century British adventurer, eager for experience and romantically detached from it at the same time.

Carr was a solitary and restless individual who had no intention of settling anywhere during those years. He was in Ecuador when rumours came of the California gold strike and he decided to head north to try his luck. If he was reluctant to return to the United States (he disliked Americans and found their society crude), he recognized there was money to be made there, and that his youth was disappearing. His timing was right, and within a couple of years he was able to transform his gold stake into a lucrative wholesale business. He was in his mid-thirties by then and ready to marry. Emily Saunders was just eighteen, on her own and unattached in North America. She had left England for much the same reasons he had, only in her case, reduced prospects included an illegitimate birth. Her dubious beginnings, along with Richard's peripatetic past and frontier fortune, did not serve them well in Britain. Like many expatriates who tried to go home after years in the colonies, they found they didn't fit in. With no family to rely on (Richard had all but lost touch with his by this time) and with Emily's ill health aggravated by the deaths of two babies, they fled England. Richard apparently missed the activity of his old life and complained of the rain in Devonshire. Surely, he thought, it would be easier to establish oneself in British Columbia.

In Victoria, Richard Carr lost no time setting up a grocery and liquor importing business on Wharf Street. Within the year it was flourishing, and he was able to buy land in the best section of town, engage architects, and build a large house surrounded by a garden planted with cowslips, primroses, and English flowering shrubs. This was where Emily Carr grew up, a short walk to the cliffs at Beacon Hill Park overlooking the Strait of Juan de Fuca, in the middle of an English country garden.

Early on, she became acutely aware of the differences between herself and the rest of her family, most particularly her four older sisters. She felt it in their reactions to the drudgery of domestic routine, to raw nature at their doorstep, to animals (which Emily was always befriending and bringing into the house), and to the rules of polite society. She was all passion and protest to their reserve and conformity, and she grew up feeling odd among them. To their horror, she loved the cow yard and didn't mind dirt. It was a clash of temperaments that became a clash of values that led her to see herself as the black sheep of the family, the one the rest couldn't account for. And indeed, she once overheard adults puzzling at her strange behaviour and whether a strain of gypsy blood might explain it.

After their parents died, the Misses Carr lived on at the house on Government Street together. Alice and Lizzie settled into spinsterhood as if it were a calling, sticking close to home and to Edith. They did what was respectable: taught, did church work, and minded one another. Edith was active with the Protestant Orphanage, and with Lizzie (called Betty by everyone but her sister Emily), she helped establish the local YWCA. Alice became a teacher and in 1899 was making plans to open a kindergarten. Emily did none of the above; she didn't teach Sunday school, she didn't do charity work, and she didn't fall in line with Edith's perspective on the seemly pursuits for young, unmarried women. Edith was a dour disciplinarian, and in *The Book of Small* Emily describes her behaviour as abusive. As Emily grew into adulthood, she resisted Edith's position of authority in the family. Biographers recount how she railed against her older sister's control over their life and the family purse strings. Far from being relieved of familial constraints by the death of her parents, it had delivered her into her older sister's fierce protection. She resented it all the more because of Edith's antagonism to her artistic ambition.

Originally the family had gone along with young Emily's fascination with art and even encouraged it. It was customary, after all, for youngsters to take painting lessons and all the Carr girls had been sent off to art class. This was not done with any hope that they would make a profession of it, but with the idea that painting was a fine attribute for a lady. Edith herself was an accomplished china painter. Still, Emily's precocious facility for drawing had caught people's attention early on. Impressed by the likeness she made of him when she was about ten, her father had it framed and presented her with five dollars. Emily was thrilled by the praise and straight away made an easel with three large sticks, and set up her paints in her bedroom, and went to work "like a real artist." All through her teens she painted and drew incessantly while performing indifferently in school. The year after her father died, she dropped all her studies to concentrate on art. But there was no place to go with her painting in Victoria, no serious art community that could nurture her career. She remembered the de L'Aubinières' advice, but her sisters, who regarded her desire to become an artist as a perversity that didn't bear mentioning, deplored the idea. Stymied by their disapproval, she finally decided to seek the help of James Lawson, the lawyer Richard Carr had appointed as Edith's financial adviser. Somehow she convinced Lawson, who in turn persuaded Edith to give Emily the money and the permission to go to San Francisco.

Thus, in the fall of 1890, aged eighteen, Emily Carr finally left provincial Victoria to begin her training in San Francisco, the fabled city of wickedness where her parents had met thirty-five years before. San Francisco had become a large port city with a population of 300,000, bursting with American energy and enterprise. Like Victoria, it was built on a gold rush and had grown quickly. Derided by some for its brashness, San Francisco was by far the most sophisticated and cosmopolitan city in the region and, judging from the theatre and opera on show, it had a flourishing artistic community. Attracted by the landscape as well as the isolation, American visual artists had come West seeking freedom from the entrenched tradition of eastern art institutions. The California School of Design, where Carr enrolled, was already twenty-five years old and was the first art academy established in the American far west with a faculty of practising, professional artists. The faculty included Alice Chittenden—or would officially by 1897—a successful floral painter who served on the school's board and awards committee during Emily's time there.

Chittenden participated in the legendary Ladies' Art Exhibition of 1885, the first show of its kind organized in the United States, which demonstrates there were serious women artists in San Francisco at the time making contributions and pursuing public careers, women whom students like Emily would have known of or possibly met. There is, in fact, some reason to think that she did meet Chittenden, who quite probably was the "woman of mature years and great ability" who critiqued her work. Carr wrote of their meeting in her autobiography, *Growing Pains*, reporting how the older woman spoke to her of the difference between naked and nude, about "surface vision" and art. She had chided Emily for letting misplaced prudery keep her from life drawing classes, where she would learn the subtleties of life and line. "Child, don't let false ideas cramp your art. Statues are beautiful, but they do not throb with life," Emily remembered her saying.

Five years later, Chittenden joined with a number of other women artists to "storm" the annual Bohemian Club Winter Show (as the *San Francisco Chronicle* put it) in an effort to break the male monopoly on public exhibitions. The Bohemian Club was the most influential art society in the city (the School of Design sublet quarters in the club's building on Pine Street near the old California market), and the exclusion was significant for women who were making inroads elsewhere in the San Francisco art scene. Compared with most other art schools, for example, women felt welcomed at the School of Design, where they were taken seriously enough to be allowed into life drawing classes and the presence of nude models. Women had traditionally been barred from such classes for reasons of propriety, but as life classes were considered essential curriculum, this exclusion effectively denied them accreditation and professional careers. So the San Francisco School of Design had a reputation, some prestige, and a large contingent of female students.

Carr immersed herself in her classes, settling into the bohemian informality of art school life, making friends with other students, but she was hardly living the life of an art student full time. Edith had "made arrangements" and Emily was consigned to the protection of close family friends. After a year, moreover, Edith decided to rent out the house in Victoria and take everyone (save Dick, who was at boarding school in Ontario) to join Emily in San Francisco. An apartment was rented for them all on McAllister Street, at some distance from the art school, which meant Emily could no longer walk to classes. That year she slowed down and lost focus as she was reabsorbed into family activities. That year, too, Dick was diagnosed with TB and sent to a sanatorium in Santa Barbara, near enough for his sisters to visit. When the year was up, Dede, Lizzie, and Alice returned to British Columbia. Emily stayed on, found rooms on her own in Oakland, and returned to work with alacrity. But within six months, curriculum changes at the school, its relocation to a fancy section of town, and money troubles at home induced her to leave. By Christmas 1893, she was back in Victoria.

Emily Carr and her younger brother, Richard (Dick), in a studio photograph c. 1891.

The time in San Francisco gave Carr a taste for independence. She discovered qualities in herself that brought a measure of self-confidence—an ability to care for other people, for example, and to hold her own with her artistic peers. She worked hard, was eager to learn, and not entirely uncritical of her teachers. But she progressed slowly and had begun to realize that even if she wanted to hurry, her artistic apprenticeship was taking its own time. She had also observed the dark side of art, the side that "steals from babies," as she put it.

If she was impressed with Alice Chittenden's success, she was equally affected by her landlady's predicament; Mrs. Tucket, a single mother with two children, was attempting to make ends meet by renting out rooms while continuing to paint. The effort to put her art first was valiant, though Emily was horrified to see the littlest one take sick and almost expire while the mother pined away for her muse and referred to her children as "encumbrances." Emily saw this as neglect and undoubtedly got the message that mixing motherhood and art was a dangerous recipe.

Back home, predictably, everything irked. Emily began to hold art classes in the house and the sisters complained about the disruption and the mess; she moved into the barn and converted the hayloft into a classroom and they fussed on the cow's behalf. She, on the other hand, disliked having the house full of people on their knees, whispering into their Bibles, and she wasn't above saying so. She thought of striking out on her own with Alice and even located a place that she thought would do for the two of them, a place with good light and a northern exposure for her studio. Alice was not entranced, however, figuring the *menage à deux* would end up with her doing the housekeeping. It is possible that Emily considered going it alone. Single women were known to live on their own in late nineteenth-century British Columbia, but rarely middle-class White women from James Bay, and certainly not unless driven to it by the ill winds of circumstance. To leave home except as a nurse, teacher, or missionary in the service of others was to stray beyond the pale of community propriety. To do so by choice, even if in the service of God-given talent, was unfathomable. To the extent that they thought about it at all, Edith, Lizzie, and Alice would have been mystified by Emily's ambition and probably sensed that if she followed through with her idea about art, she would end up out there, beyond the pale. They understood she would, in effect, be renouncing *their* way of life and were offended.

What kept Emily Carr at home through those six long, unproductive years if not fear and indecision? It was the fear of defying the rules and then having to live with the consequent loneliness and ostracism for a lifetime, and the fear of alienating her sisters. There was indecision about her project, about the huge amount of time and money it would require, and the ever-present uncertainty about whether or not she could pull it off. She couldn't imagine herself in Alice Chittenden's situation with a market at home, a reputation in Paris, and regular sales in New York. And she understood she would first have to invent art as a way of life for herself in British Columbia, and then she would have to find a way to support it.

On the face of it, it was something of an accomplishment for a woman to reach the age of twenty-seven without a husband in turn-of-the-century Victoria. The town was full of single men, a holdover from its wild beginnings as a Hudson's Bay Company fort and Gold Rush boom town. The predominance of men was a symptom, too, of the seasonal employment available in isolated spots up the coast and around Vancouver Island in the canneries, mines, mills, and logging operations that materialized in the 1880s and 1890s, and of immigration policies that prohibited Asian men from settling with their families—through regulation and a head tax, in the case of the Chinese. So despite the massive influx of people following the completion of the railway, there were still three men to every woman in Victoria when Emily Carr was growing up. It was a society where women were scarce and everyone was preoccupied with marriage. The story was often repeated of the disappointed naval officers who scoured the island for eligible young ladies to invite to a ball in 1860, only to came up with a scrawny band of girls, "most of them half-breeds." Conversely, there were tales of society mothers lying in wait for the arrival of Royal Navy ships with guest lists in their hands and brilliant matches in their heads. Even the Church of England got involved in a matchmaking scheme in 1862, the year before the Carr family arrived.

It was the brainchild of a Reverend Lunden Brown, who was stationed up the Fraser River amid the chaos of the mining camps when gold fever was at its height. Brown was particularly appalled by the prostitution of Native women, some of them prepubescent girls, and eventually he wrote the Church Missionary Society in England, proposing a solution. He suggested that Britain should send out some of its surplus women to serve as wives to the rowdy frontier bachelors. The women would infuse civility into the place faster than God, Brown reasoned, and the Anglican Church apparently agreed, for the Columbia Emigration Society was formed and a committee hastily convened to select the women. About a hundred mostly orphaned and working-class girls from the poorhouses were then dispatched to the colony with the expectation that they would marry upon landing. Officially the women were being sent out to work as servants; unofficially everyone knew what the real purpose of their journey was.

The ships were called brideships and, according to historians, there were three of them. The first seems to have arrived unannounced early in 1862 and it is assumed that several of the women disembarked at San Francisco. Only a handful reached Victoria where they promptly faded into the landscape and off the record. A second group of sixty-two women came on the *Tynemouth* three months later, the youngest of them just thirteen years old. This brideship included a contingent of older, middle-class women, many of them out-of-work governesses, displaced by the passing of an age and the advent of public schools, who were desperate for a respectable way to make a living. They had petitioned for inclusion and been so public and persistent about it that the Church hierarchy finally relented. Their euphoria couldn't have lasted long, however, for the voyage across the Atlantic and through the Panama Canal was a nightmare. The women were sequestered in ill-ventilated cabins that were never intended for such prolonged occupancy, and they were locked up whenever the ship was in port. They were issued rations, but not allowed to use the kitchen except during off-hours once or twice a week, and they were permitted up on deck once a day. They reached Victoria ill, exhausted, and filthy. But there was no question this time of the ship arriving without its cargo intact. First, the women were kept for a further two days in their cabins aboard ship in Esquimalt Harbour. Then they were taken into Victoria where they faced a city full of men who were given the day off work—some had walked in from miles away—to see them arrive. At the end of a five-month ordeal, these poor women were marched in twos, past crowds of ogling, whistling men along the quays and up towards the Marine barracks near the Parliament buildings. There they were issued pails and soap and ordered to wash themselves as best they could before entering the building where they were to be temporarily housed. At least one woman dropped out of the line and disappeared into the crowd before reaching the barracks. A few of the sicker ones collapsed; a couple of others became hysterical and were led away. Inside the rest were greeted by a committee of leading citizens and Anglican clergy, who carried on as if nothing untoward had occurred.

The women on the Welcoming Committee came from Victoria's élite, that circle of Hudson's Bay Company men, politicians, and businessmen and their families who directed the colony and controlled its affairs. The Carrs, who arrived the same year as the third and last brideship, belonged to the first generation of English-born immigrants who established themselves in their midst. Richard Carr wasn't the only *nouveau riche* resident in James Bay, but he was one of the few who didn't try to advance himself socially. Although there is reason enough to assume that some doors were closed to him (he was in trade, apart from anything else), Carr was unusual in his aloofness. Bishop Cridge lived next door and his children played games in the back garden with the Carrs'. Dr. Helmcken, speaker of the first colonial Assembly and a son-in-law of Governor Douglas, often visited the house. But the Carrs rarely "entertained"—held teas or received company. Their name wasn't on the social register, and they were known as stay-at-homes. Mrs. Carr's poor health may have necessitated this, but Richard's detachment was a factor. He disliked society. While his wife attended Cridge's Church of Our Lord (despite the Reform Episcopal designation, it was the church of the local Anglican establishment), Richard continued attending the First Presbyterian Church. Some say he did so because the preacher there spoke loud enough for him to hear, being slightly deaf; others say the Presbyterian austerity suited his temperament better. Certainly Richard Carr did not shine in the drawing room, much less the boardrooms of politics and business. As he grew older and suffered financial setbacks, he became reclusive and turned increasingly to his religion. Moreover, his moroseness was easily indulged in a family of daughters with no other relatives to intercede. Both he and his wife were cut off from family, and other than a few vague references to an Aunt Nancy on Emily's side and some siblings in Richard's boyhood stories, the family tree was blank. The Carr children were raised with a sense of familial isolation, in a social vacuum, which meant that as the daughters came of age, they had limited opportunity for meeting marriageable men. Possibly Richard and Emily discouraged suitors when they appeared on the horizon, setting impossibly high standards in an effort to protect their daughters from murky pasts such as their own. Perhaps when all was said and done and his roving were days over, Richard Carr desired a domestic cocoon, even if it cost him grandchildren. There is some suggestion that the old patriarch was quite content for his daughters to stay unmarried and at home, even after he was gone. Whatever the case, this is what they did, except for Emily, who remained unmarried but struck an independent course.

When Emily Carr finally did fall in love, she was well past prime marriageable age. By her own admission, love was unreasonable; it rushed in and settled down hard, leaving her gasping with humiliation and weak from its intensity. In an effort to expunge it and ensure that she would never be caught out again, she turned her back on love—which is to say heterosexual intimacy—and used that renunciation to fuel her creative project and her independence. In doing so, she was unconsciously repeating the pattern she established with her father, first as a child and then as an adolescent at the time of the incident she called the "brutal telling," when she turned on him and shut him out of her heart. Decades later there was still anger in her voice when she recalled his death. "I can feel the awful relief still when I stood by his grave and it was filled up. Thud, thud the clods fell on the box. . . . I was peering down into the black hole and in my heart there was relief. Nobody knew the sinking agonies of terror I had suffered when I had been alone with father. I had been his favourite trolling after him like a dog. Now I was free." The break with Richard Carr, like her first encounter with love, marked Emily profoundly. Both were experienced as betrayals and were as traumatic as they were formative, and they were the psychological backdrop to the decision she made in Ucluelet. Martyn Paddon was less an actor in the drama than an embellishment in a story already in progress.

In the 1880s, the Carr family was not the only one that kept to itself in middle-class Victoria. Many, including Governor Douglas's family, did so for fear of censure. As a young Hudson's Bay trader, Douglas had married the mixed-blood daughter of his boss, William Connolly, the chief factor of New Caledonia and his Cree "country wife," Suzanne Pas-de-Nom. "Country wife" was the term used to describe the custom of cohabiting with an Aboriginal woman without benefit of clergy. Amelie Connolly grew up speaking Cree and French and in contact with her mother's people and culture. When she married Douglas in 1828, she was barely sixteen and he twenty-six, himself the illegitimate son of a prosperous Glaswegian merchant who had interests in the sugar trade in British Guiana and a mistress there of mixed blood, who bore him three children. The sons were sent to school in Lanark, Scotland, so it is clear that their father accepted responsibility for them. In his early HBC days, Douglas was occasionally described as "mulatto" and clearly he was sensitive about colour. Young Amelie, who favoured her father with her fair skin and auburn hair, was nicknamed Little Snowbird, and when she arrived to meet her husband at Fort Vancouver, headquarters of the Columbia District where he was transferred in 1830 (she had stayed behind to bear and then bury their first child), what she always remembered of their reunion was his chagrin that her skin had tanned so deeply on the long overland journey.

This may not only have been Douglas's personal prejudice

speaking. He was aware of the growing intolerance for the old fur trade society, which had evolved out of the collaboration of Aboriginal women and White traders. Country marriages were often significant economic partnerships as well as sexual unions in which the women were essential to the enterprise. They not only knew the country and how to survive in it, they also kept the men in moccasins, cleaned and treated pelts, acted as interpreters, smoothed relations between their husbands and Natives, and occasionally prevented disaster. Amelie once did so herself in a much-quoted incident that occurred shortly after her marriage when Douglas was in charge of Fort St. James during Connolly's absence. Angry about the brutal slaying of a man in their camp by a party of Whites led by Douglas, Chief Kwah (Quah), of the Tl'azt'enl (Stuart Lake) Band, arrived with a large group of followers, invaded the fort, and held Douglas at knifepoint. The dead man had killed two employees of the company at Fort George five years earlier, but had eluded authorities while his accomplice had been caught and executed. Douglas heard he was visiting the area and had gone out to apprehend him, no doubt assuming that once he had, the incident would be closed. The man was hiding in Kwah's house, which, as a chief's house, was considered a sanctuary in Dakelh (Carrier) tradition. Douglas violated sanctuary when he entered and killed him. The confrontation was an example of the clash of cultures repeated endlessly in the West as British and Canadian officials attempted to superimpose British law on Aboriginal systems of justice. It was the typical set-up for catastrophe, but in this case, Amelie read the situation, understood the grievance, and had the presence of mind to offer retribution by presenting the chief and his men with trade goods from the HBC store.

In the early Canadian West, the Douglas' country marriage was not merely common, it was accepted practice, one that was perpetuated for two or three generations. The change, when it came, was sudden. In the late 1820s, senior HBC men began marrying White women when they were back in England or in Montreal on furlough, setting aside (as the euphemism went) their Native partners. Governor George Simpson led the trend by marrying his eighteen-year-old cousin, Frances, and bringing her back with him to the Northwest. There were always men who regarded their mixed-blood liaisons as illicit and impermanent, designed purely for sexual gratification, and Simpson had been one of these. He had children with at least two Native women before he married, and he treated both with callousness. There were other men, however, who thought of themselves as husbands and fathers, who provided for their wives and children in their wills. For these, the moment of truth usually came at retirement when they considered returning home with their mixed-race families, and when they began to see the material advantage in acquiring White wives. William Connolly was apparently one of the latter, a man who regarded marriage as a matter of expedience, although he had originally been critical of Simpson's behaviour, maintaining it was "a most unnatural proceeding" to desert the mother of one's children. He changed his mind once he was posted to Eastern Canada in 1831. Suzanne and their younger children had accompanied him, but within the year he married his pretty cousin, Julia Woolrich, and repudiated Suzanne, although he continued to provide for her and eventually arranged for her to live out her days in a Catholic convent in Red River.

By the mid-1830s, a mixed-blood marriage was no longer a wise choice for an HBC man with ambition. True, the first European women who ventured into Rupert's Land had a hard time adapting to rough pioneer conditions and found themselves constitutionally unable to withstand the isolation from home, from family, and from other women. A few died trying, but slowly their numbers in the settlement increased, and as they prevailed, so did the values and mores they brought with them. At Fort Vancouver, Amelie encountered the prejudice of White immigrants for the first time, and it came from the clergy, who were usually the first to make a fuss about the old-fashioned, out-of-wedlock unions. Some priests were willing to be conciliatory about it, pressing couples to formalize their marriages according to the rites of the Church, characterizing the ceremony as a "renewal of their mutual consent of marriage." But then there was the odious Reverend Herbert Beaver, one of those who was inclined to such vitriol in his condemnation of local custom that the remarriage ceremony seemed more like a public humiliation.

Beaver was the Anglican minister sent out to be Fort Vancouver's first clergyman in 1836, and a more self-satisfied and recklessly ignorant man would be hard to imagine. Stunned to find that Chief Factor John McLoughlin was allowing the largely Catholic population its own religious services and a non-denominational curriculum at the parish school, Beaver set out to subsume everyone into his congregation, insisting on teaching the Anglican catechism at the school. When McLoughlin put a stop to it, Beaver started attacking McLoughlin personally, accusing him of having a "kept mistress." In dispatches to London, he described Marguerite McLoughlin as a "female of notoriously loose character" (she and John had been together twenty-five years at that point) and recommended denying rations and medical attention to such women. Jane Beaver, the reverend's wife, did her part by refusing to associate with the HBC women, deeming them beneath her class and her English dignity. What would twenty-seven-year-old Amelie have thought of such hardened prejudice? Marguerite McLoughlin had befriended her when she first arrived, and helped her through the dark days of four baby deaths. She must have reflected on her father's desertion of her mother, on her mother's exile, and her own vulnerability, and perhaps that was reason enough to consent to a church marriage. The ceremony, which took place in February 1837, may also have been intended to alleviate tensions between Beaver and McLoughlin who, by this time, had come to blows—on the street with McLoughlin wielding his cane. The old trader bitterly resented the chaplain's intrusion in his private affairs, but he, too, thought it prudent to marry legally, and did so a few months later in a civil service conducted by Douglas.

When Amelie and James Douglas moved to Victoria in 1849, there were other Beavers to contend with. As the settlement grew, so did the pressure on mixed-blood women to conform to English codes of dress and behaviour, to educate their daughters to be ladies, and to sever ties with their Aboriginal relatives. The European women who settled the colony erected a social barrier between themselves and Native peoples and refused any traffic across it. They thus became agents of a heightened class-consciousness and the reintroduction of racial discrimination to the domestic sphere. As fur trade society disappeared, women like Amelie were expected to bury their past and assimilate quietly, yet even when they did, they remained vulnerable to slander and their legal status as wives and children was often uncertain. After William Connolly died, for instance, Amelie's brother sued his father's estate for a share, claiming that the marriage to his mother Suzanne had been real and legitimate and her children by Connolly were rightful heirs. The judge actually agreed, perhaps cognizant of who he would be labelling a bastard if he didn't, for James Douglas had been knighted in 1865, and Amelie was now Lady Douglas, the one woman in Victoria that etiquette required everyone to address as Lady. As it happened, this was the first time a case had hinged on the validity of a country marriage in a Canadian court. Other judges had other opinions, but Chief Justice Coram Monk concluded thus: "Can I pronounce this connection formed and continued under such circumstances concubinage and brand his offspring as bastards? I think not. There would be no law, no justice, no sense, no morality in such a judgement." He was agreeing, in other words, with Connolly's youthful opinion. The ruling was made in 1867, three years after Douglas had retired from public life.

Throughout James Douglas's twenty years as chief factor and governor of Vancouver Island and British Columbia, Amelie was the most reluctant of chatelaines. She did not participate in her husband's career, and almost never appeared with him in public on formal occasions or at society functions. Her difficulty with

English may have been a factor, as was her preference for family and private friendships in the face of the prejudices of White society. Whatever the reasons, her reserve was a means of conserving space in the recesses of family where the heritage supposedly "left behind" could still be savoured. As Douglas wrote to his youngest daughter Martha when she was eighteen and in school in England, "I have no objection to your telling the old stories about 'Hyass' but pray do not tell the world they are Mamma's."

Lady Douglas was part of the world Emily Carr grew up in, the known and socially prominent part, as well as the little-mentioned and covered-up part. A diminutive figure draped in widow's weeds after her husband's death in 1877, Amelie was the invisible figurehead of Victoria society. Her social standing was no small irony given the insult she was treated to by British women in the early days. Historians and biographers often remark on the city of Victoria's straight-laced character in those years. They note how emerging English-Canadian society modelled itself on the most conservative custom prevailing in Britain at the time, without the contending visions and voices of reform, which were part of the public debates there. So it was a rather dated version of English womanhood to which the Carr sisters and their Victorian peers subscribed, one that was supremely unsuited to living conditions in the Northwest. Elsewhere in metropolitan centres, the emancipation of women was being advanced, sometimes in the streets; the New Woman smoked cigarettes, appeared in public astride bicycles, and demanded the vote. Lady Douglas had been equally daring in her youth, but she would never have said so, certainly not to the blue-blooded ladies like Mrs. Cridge or Mrs. Joseph Trutch, who served with her on the Brideship Welcoming Committee. Nor would she have talked about her Cree grandmothers and the independent way of life lost when Métis women like herself crossed over into White society.

The 1880s and 1890s were, in addition, decades of intense pro-British patriotism in Victoria. British connections were assiduously tended, and the appearance of anyone titled or moneyed in the city's midst was cause for great pomp and social display. People followed the exploits of the Empire with rapt attention and the Queen's birthday on May 24th became the civic event of the year. Nothing stirred this sentiment more than the visit in 1882 of Queen Victoria's daughter, Princess Louise, who arrived with her husband, the Marquis of Lorne (the then governor general), for two weeks and stayed three months. The city and its citizens turned themselves inside out to show the princess their appreciation and to demonstrate their enduring British fervour. "Loyal Hearts and English Homes," read the inscription on the arch erected for the occasion at the Point Ellice Bridge.

This identification with everything British was an attitude that James Douglas and Richard Carr shared. Although neither had been dealt any favours by their background, both managed to make a great deal of themselves in the colonies. The New World created them and inevitably they became "of" this place themselves, but neither felt any particular allegiance to the population they lived with or the country they were engaged in building. Their distant, nostalgic attachment to the Mother Country and a future already past was more than mere sentiment, it was a primal commitment. It made them both exiles. Douglas's disdain was perhaps most explicit in his preference for hiring British immigrants over Canadians. Richard Carr's was reflected in his voluptuous English garden that, to his daughter's mind, denied the very existence of the soil in which it grew. Native plants were expelled, and fast-growing poplars were planted at the periphery, as if to block the view of all the evergreen beyond. It was this anti-Canadian side of her father's professed "Englishness" that Emily came to disparage, feeling that he shut out beauty along with everyday Canadian reality.

No doubt Emily, the family rebel, had some sympathy for her father's dislike of society functions; she, too, despised them. However, while his was a rejection of the form and formality of it, she was offended by the hypocrisy and the pretended interest in people that drove it. Long before she went to Ucluelet she had started looking for other standards of behaviour and other values than the ones she inherited. The childhood jousts with the mores of polite society are recorded in *The Book of Small,* and in her autobiography, *Growing Pains,* she gleefully bares her distaste for English snobbery and the shallowness of rote custom as she encountered them during her 1900–1904 stay in England. "I had not dreamt social obligation could be so arduous," she wrote about one family she stayed with. "After breakfast we marched soberly into the library to write notes, notes of inviting or of accepting. Every dinner, tea, house-party, call, must be punctiliously returned. I was rather sorry for these rich, they could so seldom be themselves; even their smiles were set, wound up to so many degrees of grin for so much intimacy. Their pleasures seemed kept in glass cases out of reach. They saw but could not quite handle or feel their fun, it was so overhung with convention." This experience of the wealthy upper classes came via her friendship with another art student, Mildred Crompton-Roberts, whom she meet at the Westminster School of Art. Carr's response was not admiring. Although she tended to be harder on middle-class pretension than upper-class arrogance, she set herself up as separate and "other" in both cases. Similarly, her disaffection for missionaries is thinly veiled in *Klee Wyck*'s description of the Ucluelet mission. The Greater Missionary—presumably May Armstrong—is almost a parody. In *Growing Pains* she is introduced thus: "Life at the Mission House was stark, almost awesome, but you could not awe our Missionary, she had no nerves. She was not inhuman, there was earth underneath. It was just her crust that was hard and smooth." Carr disapproved of the missionaries' effort, noting that while they refrained from giving medicine out in one large dose, they yet "expected to give the Indians the whole of religion at one go." Undoubtedly her alienation from her own cultural background fed her curiosity about Native culture and her openness to it. Her heart was loyal, but not to her father's English home—to her own Canadian one. This was the home she was looking for when she went to Ucluelet. In the face of Christian zeal, she notes, "the Indians held back," and she admired them for it.

Emily Carr took her newfound confidence with her to London where three significant things happened to her. She became a serious art student, if not an immediately successful one; she rejected Martyn Paddon's offer of marriage; and she suffered a physical and emotional breakdown. This last was grievous enough to land her in a sanatorium for eighteen months with a diagnosis of hysteria and instructions to relinquish all creative activity. Paddon, who visited her in 1900, three years before her collapse, was never a serious contender for her heart although he signalled a major passage in Carr's life, which no doubt contributed to the stress that put her in hospital. The account in *Growing Pains* makes it clear that she understood the effort to set her course in art required turning down marriage and, further, that the struggle to be taken seriously as an artist was connected to this choice. She turned him away, saying that she didn't love him and was worried about her work. "Hang work; I can support you. Love will grow," Paddon replied, to which Carr said, "It is not support; it is not money or love. It's the work itself. And Martyn, while you are here, I am not doing my best." The choice of spinsterhood and celibacy therefore was, at least in part, a bid for control of her life, for possession of her own identity. All the same, she left England feeling that she had failed.

More English than the English; more proper than the Queen. This was the image Victoria had fashioned for itself by the end of the century. Having ceded economic leadership to Vancouver by the 1890s, the city had retired to the somnolent role of picturesque provincial capital: part government offices, part tourist attraction, and the perpetual symbol of British connectedness. The stamp of English culture was visible in the architecture, in the political system inherited from the Hudson's Bay Company and the British North America Act, and in the English language, which dominated public life. No one lived the stereotype more assiduously than the wealthy and privileged who measured social success on

Crown Derby china at high tea. However, the image they curried is deceiving, for the city was hardly homogeneous. There had always been an indigenous population there, for example, and (after the Gold Rush) a continuous flow of polyglot speculators, itinerant workers, and renegades from all over. The disadvantaged came looking for opportunity and an escape from the past; the advantaged came to exploit the situation. There was also a substantial Chinese population in Victoria that almost equalled the White community in size until the mid-1880s and which created a Chinatown to rival San Francisco's. Being a port city, people congregated on the waterfront, drifting into bars where they fought and gambled and got arrested for drunkenness as they did in colonial outposts everywhere. No matter how vociferous local opinion was on the evils of drink, the fact of the matter is that Victoria was built on the whiskey trade. Denial came in the form of unenforceable laws prohibiting the sale of alcohol to Native people, which also served to assuage any guilt for the misery the trade produced along with the lucre. Polyglot Victoria was there to be seen in the streets anyway. On one side of James Bay sat the new Parliament buildings, which lit up like a Ferris wheel each evening when 3,000 electric light bulbs outlining its shape were switched on. On the opposite side flourished a rough and raunchy downtown, alive with dance halls, gambling dens, opium parlours, and bawdy-houses. Victoria had its derelicts and criminals and a seamy side where the unfortunate took shelter in shacks. Moreover, across the Johnson Street bridge in the other direction lay the Songhees reserve, which was also visible by night when fires were lighted.

During the day and all year long, the Natives were ever present in the city. Their canoes could be seen in the harbour and up the Gorge, slender horizontal shapes slicing through the water with elevated prows riding high above the waves, familiar forms pulled up on the beach. In the early years, the Songhees far outnumbered the White population, so the sights and sounds of their activities, language, songs, and ceremonies were inescapably impressed on the settlers. Right into the new century they were a visible part of the city's life. When major events took place on the reserve, like the great potlatch of 1895, non-Natives streamed across the inner harbour to watch the dancing and costumes from the bridge above. Emily Carr quite likely was part of the crowd.

The Songhees' situation had deteriorated over the fifty years since the White people arrived on Vancouver Island. Disease had taken a terrible toll, the most dramatic event being the smallpox epidemic of 1862, which was carried up the coast in canoes when the authorities in Victoria expelled all non-resident Natives from the city. It killed an estimated 20,000 people, a third of the Native population in the province. Many Songhees took refuge on Discovery Island, but the isolation did not help and they, too, died in devastating numbers. Immigration and industry also played a part in altering the racial balance, which, by the mid-1880s, put Whites in a majority. Carr was thus raised in a house full of women, in a small town full of single men where White people were initially outnumbered and by 1899 had become dominant. She belonged to the first generation of native-born European Canadians, a White child who grew up around Chinese, First Nations, and Black people who were not part of her family's social circle except as servants. (She relates a story in *The Book of Small* of being rescued by a Black man when she was a small girl and had wandered away from her father's store into the path of some wild cattle.) As a youngster, Emily Carr would have seen the Natives who came into Victoria to sell fish, berries, and baskets to towns-people and tourists in the streets, or to work at occasional jobs. She saw men and women competing in the Indian canoe races at the May 24th holiday regatta held at the Gorge, and she saw them at her father's store where she once observed him give a group of women a batch of maggoty raisins, explaining to her later that "the Indians love raisins and don't mind the maggots at all." At home Wash Mary came to do laundry for Mrs. Carr every Monday, working outside across the yard in a wash house that Emily would visit to announce the noon dinner in carefully rehearsed Chinook. There she found diminutive Mary standing on a block of wood so she could reach into the tubs, up to her shoulders in soapy water. Mary was apparently not local Salish; she lived on her own in a little house on Fairfield Road, which Emily visited with her mother once when Mary was ill and dying.

Carr's early experience with Native peoples was thus bound by barriers of class and race. To her kith and kin, Aboriginal culture was something entirely foreign, even though it was actually indigenous. It existed all around them but in the background, and was a mystery at best. Nevertheless, she heard her father's stories of the Aboriginal peoples he had seen in his travels to the southern U.S. and Latin America. He had witnessed the Cherokee in Alabama setting off on the Trail of Tears and remarked on how healthy and presentable they were. He had seen how the Ojibway and Chippewa shared their fishing grounds with Whites and even taught them elementary survival. He admired Native technology and wrote in his journal in 1839, "I have always found [Indians] civil and obliging and very honest, much more so than their white neighbours who never miss an opportunity of cheating them." Such views were unusually sympathetic, though tinged by an antipathy for Americans. Yet if they were part of Carr's early environment, so was the free-wheeling racism building in Victoria during those years. Young Emily heard the slurs and slanders about Indians' filthy habits and heathenish ways, and she must have known, too, that the Songhees across the harbour were a source of civic controversy despite their supposed weakness and decline.

The history went like this. When the Hudson's Bay Company was given charge of Vancouver Island in 1849, it was on the condition that it arrange for colonization. Governor Douglas realized he would have to clear title to the surrounding area if settlement were to take place. He turned first to the Lakwammen people who occupied the region where the fort was built, and who had helped supply pickets, particularly the giant ones, which stood twenty to forty feet by three feet across. They had acceded to the fort's construction with a view to forming a home guard and benefiting from the control of access to the post, an ambition Douglas moved quickly to block. Nonetheless, the relationship with the Songhees, as the British called them, was friendly and Douglas was able to conclude a series of agreements called the Fort Victoria Treaties, which are unique to British Columbia. These were negotiated with eleven groups in and around Victoria, Sooke, and the Saanich Peninsula (and three others later at Nanaimo and Fort Rupert). The treaties set compensation and stipulated that Aboriginal fishing and hunting rights would continue while the land itself became the "entire property of the White people for ever." Shortly after, two reserves were set out in the vicinity and almost immediately agitation began for the removal of the one situated in Victoria's inner harbour.

The pressure from the White community was relentless and ultimately, in 1911, the Songhees gave in, accepted a settlement, and were removed to the present site on Esquimalt Harbour. From a historical point of view, they were brushed aside by the wave of in-coming White settlers and entrepreneurs sweeping up the coast. Emily Carr was part of that wave, as was Governor Douglas. The popular story concerning Douglas, corroborated by most historians and writers over the years, is that Old Square-toes was a compassionate administrator of Indian affairs whose attempts to clear title were foiled by the British who refused to foot the bill, and whose liberal policies on the size of reserve lands were abandoned by his successors. The real story is rather less heroic and principled. Douglas tried to forge other treaties with the First Nations, but failed mainly because they were unwilling to negotiate. The question was not one of money, for the colonial Assembly repeatedly voted funds to purchase lands in Chemainus and the Cowichan Valley. In the end, Douglas ordered and then organized the occupation of the Cowichan Valley by a group of settlers in the summer of 1862—in the midst of the smallpox epidemic, as it happened. Relations between Whites and Native people worsened in the ensuing decades, as did the economy; popular prejudice against Natives hardened as the settlements grew. Douglas's generation was replaced by men with little sympathy and less understanding of Native ways, possessed of a desire to see Native peoples disappear in the name of progress only they tended to speak of doomed cultures and disappearing races. Elsewhere in the province, land was being appropriated without acknowledgement. Legal arguments were constructed afterwards, the justifications usually having to do with the idea of the land having to be exploited, improved, or in some way "used" to demonstrate ownership. Where the Songhees were concerned, moral arguments were constantly being invoked. The motivations were twofold: the City Fathers wanted the valuable commercial property the reserve was sitting on, and they wanted to remove the unhealthy and dangerous presence of the Aboriginal population, which was blamed for prostitution, crime, and the dissolute behaviour of anyone who looked Indian, including rowdy visitors, as was pointed out. The Church agreed and lent its voice to the refrain. Everyone would be better off if the Native people went elsewhere.

Offers were made, but the Songhees resolutely refused to budge from their reserve. A sticking point was the fact that monies derived from the rent and sale of their land concluded by the authorities (as permitted by the treaty agreement) had never been paid over to them. They also had reasons for wanting to stay close to Victoria as they had built up a life around the city and depended on it economically. Moreover, they had come to suspect White men's promises. What guarantee had they that the same thing wouldn't happen again if the place they moved to turned out to be valuable—that is, if settlement and industry were to move in and make it so? In 1885, the Songhees had had to go to court to prevent the government from constructing immigration sheds on reserve land without permission. Their first inkling about the project had come the day lumber was delivered to the site. There had already been encroachments on the reserve by this time (some land had been leased to farmers and a naval hospital built), but the band was not inclined to cooperate because, as Chief Skomiax stated, the reserve was too small as it was. The man behind the project was

Joseph Trutch, at the time the lieutenant-governor of the province and not a man to allow Native peoples the last word on anything. He rarely used the word "Indian" without the epithet "savage" attached. Trutch treated the clause in the Fort Victoria Treaties requiring the band's permission for any use of their land as if it were nothing more than a diplomatic gesture, something that had to be said in order to secure an agreement. The denial of permission was not envisaged as an option. Nevertheless, he had consulted the Department of Indian Affairs, which condoned his scheme, and he presumed the courts would fall in line if it came to that. When it did come to that, however, the judge did not fall in line. The Songhees cited their agreement with Douglas, the judge agreed with them, and construction was halted.

This was happening, it might be noted, while the Métis uprising was taking place in Saskatchewan. The court case against Trutch actually occurred the same year that the Canadian government hanged Louis Riel for high treason and buried the dream of a Métis nation in the West built on an accommodation between Whites, mixed-bloods, and First Nations people. In British Columbia, the dream, if it ever existed, evaporated on contact with political reality. Douglas's liberal legacy did not prevail, but his resort to the autocratic disposition of Native land rights did.

When Emily Carr stepped outside the White world for the first time in 1899, perhaps she thought about her father's youthful wanderlust and insatiable desire for new places and people. She had always had the urge to seek solace in the woods and as a child had often gone there on her pony. She was certainly aware of artists who had gone into the countryside to paint. Alice Chittenden, for one, travelled into the desert and High Sierra mountains of California by packhorse and stagecoach to find and draw the region's wildflowers. Chittenden's accomplishment was to catalogue 250 plants in exquisite renderings, but her project hardly fits the cliché of the delicate female flower painter waiting for life

74

to happen to her. Emily was seeking adventure, too, when she went to Ucluelet. She was looking for a way to cast herself in the world that was not framed by her family, and she was seeking access to Native culture, or at least Native society.

There is tremendous creative power in the human ability to communicate across the barrier of language and culture and when Carr experienced that in 1899, it was freeing. It was a lesson in trusting her instincts while being prepared to admit mistakes. However, it didn't occur to her to try sketching the forest when she was at Ucluelet. She notes this about herself later in her auto-biography, and it is indicative that the original attraction to the woods was thus more spiritual and visceral than aesthetic. She had not yet settled on landscape as her subject and *métier*. The trip whetted her appetite to see more and to travel further afield in her investigation of the land and the people indigenous to the place she was native to, which is to say, born and raised in, herself. At Ucluelet—who knows exactly why?—several threads of her life and experience came together. Emily Carr began to imagine the independent woman, the dedicated artist, and free social spirit she could be. She became Klee Wyck. In England she would adopt the name as a sobriquet and use it as a way of asserting her non-English, North Americanness, as well as her sympathy for Aboriginal cultures. Klee Wyck became an emblem of that special connection.

For us today, Klee Wyck is the Laughing One, the historical figure who laughs with us and at us: at the confusion her story has engendered, and the contradictions it straddles. She taunts and teases. And she makes demands.

Tofino, 1997

A hundred years ago the road to Ucluelet didn't exist. When Emily Carr visited, the only way to get there was by boat, which was also the only way to get logs out if you were interested in selling them. The timber industry was fully fledged by the 1890s and was already a leading generator of revenues in the province, but its activities were limited to more accessible trees and it was decades before companies turned their attention to the coastal forests. Even so, the work of loggers in the woods was largely invisible to ordinary citizens at the turn of the century, whereas today it is hard to miss. This is because of the road, constructed in 1957, connecting the West Coast villages of Tofino and Ucluelet with the towns of Port Alberni and Nanaimo. Highway 4 crosses the island at its middle, snaking its way west from Alberni alongside Sproat Lake and the Kennedy River to Kennedy Lake and Clayoquot Sound.

All these names are redolent with meaning and my head is full of history and current events as I drive the narrow switchback route over the spine of the island one February morning. The water on Sproat Lake is smooth and dark, and an orange-pink mist hangs over its surface. I am tempted to stop to take photographs, but dissuaded by the piles of crusted snow beside the road, leftovers from the blizzard last Christmas. Gilbert Sproat was the man who pioneered a logging operation at Port Alberni in the early 1860s, an endeavour he was forced to abandon after two years because of difficulties in hauling the wood to market. Sproat published an account of his adventures in the woods in which he paints the geography and the Native peoples as equally barbaric. Of all the declarations of racial superiority, which were expressed frequently in the newspapers and magazines at the time, his have haunted me most, perhaps because he went on to become an adviser on Native affairs to Sir John A. Macdonald in the 1880s. Writing about the period of the smallpox epidemic, he expounded on the "tendency to extinction" of the Indian races, which seemed to wilt and decline by their very proximity to stronger, civilized White races. "Habitual contact with a superior people render the bodily system of savages specially subject to diseases," he theorized. The susceptibility of Native peoples to European diseases he interpreted as a confirmation of his own culture's vigour. To him, and men like him, the mass deaths seemed to be God's way of emptying the continent for their benefit.

The lake named after Gilbert Sproat is a favourite summer vacation spot today, and in August it is full of speedboats towing water-skiers, families picnicking on the beach, and children playing in its sandy shallows. This morning the sun is out, but few people are, and the lake lies lush in quiet. Beyond it is the well-tracked wilderness claimed by forestry giants (MacMillan Bloedel, Fletcher Challenge, and Weldwood), which have been systematically logging the coastal watersheds for the past two decades. The highway follows the trail of the Kennedy River, one of several river systems that drain into Clayoquot Sound, down to Kennedy Lake where the highway turns west and heads towards Tofino. To the left lies Ucluelet. During the drive across, I come to understand something of this territory. The roadside signs are the clue. They start appearing every so often, announcing the beginning of a new "forestry management division" or the state of the adjacent forest's cultivation. Placed there by the logging companies operating in the vast reaches of the surrounding Crown lands, they are simple and unadorned; they could be for-sale signs in expensive Vancouver neighbourhoods for all their studied understatement. However, the facts and figures they present—the date of reforestation, of "thinning," of the projected "harvest"—could be notes for a novel, for there is a lot more going on out here than a spot of grain farming. By the looks of the terrain, tree planters reforesting the area would have to be rock climbers. Another clue is no clue at all but the real thing: clear-cuts visible in all directions from the highway as it winds towards Kennedy Lake and the area where the huge blockades have been staged to protest MacMillan Bloedel's plans to log Clayoquot Sound. The homemade signs that sprout up as the highway nears the Tofino-Ucluelet junction is the final tip-off. This is a PR campaign with a different tone. Here the voices are spontaneous and urgent. They are the voices of the disenfranchised—the loggers, teamsters, fishers, millers, and ordinary citizens who live in the communities nearby, who have turned Highway 4 into a democracy wall with their protests.

This road is living irony. Constructed in the 1950s and paved in 1971, it both facilitated the expansion of the logging industry and hastened the transformation brought on by new technologies and machines with names like feller-bunchers and grapple-yarders. The global economy, pushing for maximized profits, made clear-cutting a widespread and desirable practice by the 1980s. This is a technique whereby great swatches of forest are razed to the ground, usable logs removed to market, and the rest (as much as 25 percent of it actually usable) left behind as waste until platoons of planters are sent in to reforest the debris. The timing of the road's arrival meant that as loggers and their machines pushed farther up mountain slopes, claiming more and more of the old-growth forest, the public was able to travel farther and farther inland by car and then foot. Citizens and tourists began to see what the forest hinterland really looked like and they likened it to the dark side of the moon. Driving Highway 4 in the winter provides incontestable evidence that nothing, not even a gentle snowfall, can make a clear-cut look pretty or like anything other than what it is—a scar on the earth's surface. Sometimes the cut, with its tumble of stumps, reaches right to the road; sometimes it is visible across the valley, girdled by thick red lines carved into the earth by logging roads, gigantic patches fringed with messy blow downs. Even the forestry industry has had to recognize these for the PR disasters they are.

You notice the graffiti almost at once. The black paint on the white company sign demanding "Job Loss or Jobs?" in jagged letters. There's a war going on in the woods about jobs, about logging practices and the environment. The current skirmish involves the NDP ("No Darn Paycheque") government's policy on commercial fishing, too, which, the slogans say, abandons communities and working people. Up and down this last stretch of highway I track the debate, noting the banner at the Ucluelet turn-off reading, "Welcome Visitors. You May Be Our Last Resource." Another proclaims, "Forest Renewal B.C. Isn't Working and Neither Are We," taking aim at the first pronouncement I noticed on the way through Sutton Pass assuring the public "The Working Forest Welcomes You." Out here it is a war of words, where language is deployed to package perception at the source. The bid to normalize clear-cuts by representing forests as horticultural farms, and the effort to colour the situation with warm feelings is met with outspoken dissent and plain talk. "Experience Life on the Edge—Ucluelet–8 km" reads the last sign.

Ucluelet is a logging and fishing community fighting for its economic life. A working-class town with modest amenities, it fronts onto a beautiful marina, which is its main tourist attraction. On the opposite shore, the village of Ittattsoo straddles several bays in a mirror image of Ucluelet, only Ittattsoo lacks Ucluelet's view of Mount Ozzard rising up behind it, naked and bruised as MacMillan Bloedel left it. Sitting in Smiley's Family Restaurant and eating a bowl of home-made turkey rice soup, I ask the server, Connie, how people feel about the view. "No one's complaining," she retorts. Across the aisle a quartet of teens are tucking into mounds of fries and onion rings. Two older guys sit at the counter in two-day-old beards and sagging jeans. Behind me a table of young bloods pull at their Pepsis and assess the girls, talking in code. The restaurant doubles as a bowling alley and there is a low wall separating the eating establishment from the bowling lanes. People drift back and forth between the two and the air is spliced with the clattering of pins. I sense that Smiley's is a community hangout and not just for kids cruising. On the way out I discover an information rack and bulletin board, both recently stocked and copiously used. The literature promotes the vision of the industry-sponsored Forest Alliance, which calls on people to "share the forest"—a bit of a non-starter if you are an environmentalist battling for the habitat of the endangered spotted owl. The material is credible and well produced; the articles sound almost eco-friendly with words like "stewardship" and "cooperation" on display, but they are highly critical of citizens' groups and protestors, who are seen universally as irresponsible urbanites and job killers. A notice on the board offers $1,000 for information leading to the conviction of those responsible for destroying the Kennedy Road logging bridge.

I can't help but feel it is significant that my contemporary retracing of Emily Carr's footsteps through British Columbia begins in Ucluelet and at the foot of a mammoth clear-cut. Such phenomena were not unknown to Carr, who wrote about felled trees as if viewing the remains of a massacre. "There's a torn and splintered ridge across the stumps I call 'screamers.' These are unsawn bits, the cry of the tree's heart, wrenching and tearing apart just before she gives that sway and the dreadful groan of falling, that awful pause while her executioners step back with their saws and axes resting and watch. It's a horrible sight to see a tree felled, even now, though their stumps are grey and rotting. As you pass among them you see their screamers sticking up, out of their own tombstones as it were." It is not surprising then that Carr's name is invoked by environmentalists, and it would not be even if there were no passages like this to quote from her journals. For two generations now she has been considered the quintessential painter of the West Coast forest, her images so familiar that people coming to the region for the first time frequently report seeing her trees everywhere they look. This forest, these trees, and Emily Carr have indeed become synonyms for each other, and the forest, in the meantime, has become a major player in the provincial economy, the hinge on which prosperity swings, according to the polls and the politicians. In 1995, it was worth $18 billion, three times the value of tourism, which was the next largest source of provincial income.

On my first visit here in 1991, I found little to remind me of the past. The town and its relationship to the land seemed totally removed from the missionary outpost that Emily Carr knew. The Native community, small and disabled though it was then, surrounded and dominated the White enclave. Now the reverse is

View of the Pacific Ocean from the beach at Ampitrite Point (He-Tin-Kis Park), Ucluelet, August 1991.

true. Moreover, the entire area is now dominated by the ravaged visage of Mount Ozzard. Everywhere you go in town, it accuses you like the quizzical stare of a portrait that follows you around a room. There are some glimpses of the vanished landscape at He-Tin-Kis Park, located at the tip of the peninsula where a carefully tended boardwalk leads you through the woods, along a cliff, and down to the beach. From this vantage point, the rock and tree formations of Amphitrite Point appear through the mist as ethereal as Chinese watercolours. The beach tells another tale, of course. Beside the rotting seaweed and the broken shells, it is littered with giant logs that have been shredded and mangled by the rocks, and tossed onto shore like so many pick-up sticks. The human detritus, which arrives daily with the tide, fares little better. It comes in minute pieces, most of it plastic, such as a length of nylon rope reconfigured into a mop with only the dayglow yellow surviving the trip in. Along the shore a small group of least sandpipers pick at the decaying kelp. With them is a lone semi-palmated plover, which spies me spying her and stands quiet for some time in exquisite camouflage. Few birds are about at this time of year, but the sandpipers make up for the absence with their light-winged acrobatics. Looking up and around the little cove, I feel mist tickling my cheeks and wonder how something so delicate can muffle the din of the sea. The plover comes within ten feet of me, still wary, still eyeing a choice piece of seaweed. I cede to her foraging instincts and move off down the beach into the fog.

Six years later, on another lonely beach up the coast towards Tofino, I am again watching the birds on their endless search for the perfect morsel. This time I am not entirely alone. From a distance I see a young woman, standing by a pile of logs, Ray-Bans shielding her eyes as she studies the breakers rolling in one after the other. Behind the iridescent lenses her eyes focus with an intensity that absorbs her whole being and holds her limbs taut. I follow the gaze out to the surf, which is coming high and rapid, the waves baring their watery green backs to the sun before breaking into a thousand patterned pieces like a Hokusai print. The sound silences everything but the shrieks of gulls and crows; gesture is all that is left to humans.

I had seen her arriving earlier, striding along beside her young man dressed in camouflage trousers and runners, and a warm jacket against the winter chill. I see now she has come to stand watch as he takes to the sea with his surfboard. In his wetsuit, he seemed strangely naked beside her, every muscle outlined in neoprene, and they laughed at the touch of her hand on his ass. Just getting out far enough to ride the waves in Cox Bay takes nerve as well as muscle power. A hundred yards from shore and you are still waist high in the sea, surrounded by moving walls of water twenty to thirty feet high, being pulled and pushed from below by a tricky system of tidal currents that suck at your extremities. Out there her young man disappears from view for minutes on end, and then mysteriously reappears. He turns, catches her eye and waves, thumbs up. A few seconds later the big one thunders in and he catches it, works it, easy, through and up like a kite taking wing.

I offer her my binoculars. "I'm Megan," she says. Her boyfriend is a pro, she tells me. A local hero, I gather, and one of a family of athletes. "He competed in California last year and came second; his brother came first, but that was a year ago and Jeff has improved a whole lot since then." She spins it out like a pro herself.

"Have you known your boyfriend long?" I ask, noticing the pale complexion and the sore on her lip.

"We both grew up in Tofino," she says. "And he's three years older 'n me." Obviously significant information, this.

"And you?"

"I'm fourteen," she says with exquisite assurance, looking straight at me, woman to woman. And then, quizzically, "How did you know he was my boyfriend?"

From Megan I learn that this beach is a Mecca for surfers, though extremely dangerous. The entire coast is famous for its long sloping beaches, warm water (the warmest you'll find north of San Diego), and waves, which are ridable year round. The signs confirm it, out here you can "live to surf." For the last four days, moreover, it has been unseasonably sunny. Already a year of extremes, which began at New Year's with the epic snowstorm, now we are being treated to gentle winds, cloudless skies, and roseate sunsets worthy of the South Seas—only this is the Northwest Coast in February. Just a week ago, a rare specimen of whale washed up dead down the shore, a blue whale, I'm told, which normally dwell hundreds of miles out to sea. But that wasn't a day for walking two yards down the beach against the sleet prevailing at flesh-eating speeds, so even the curious stayed home. Just the kind of tempest people come here expressly to see at this time of year. Summer in February is lost on them. The surfers, of course, pray for storms, especially the kind that happen somewhere else and bequeath a glorious swell here. Earlier on I watched a couple of surfers testing their prowess, tiny, black-hooded figures paddling their multicoloured boards towards Mount Olympus, hoping to catch and keep a wave. None succeeded for more than a few seconds, unlike Megan's young man, who seems to understand the music well enough to dance.

"Rough stuff," says Megan. "The waves are coming in close and the current's bad."

I ask her how she feels about growing up in a place everyone else thinks of as paradise. She doesn't seem to mind; she likes the view from Duffin Cove where she lives, although she wants an animal, which is something her mother's bed-and-breakfast operation apparently precludes. "I'd really like to have a lynx," I hear her saying. "Without its claws." I try to visualize Megan in her rural grunge, pacing the back paths of Tofino with her declawed lynx on a leash—and can't without also imagining the rude objections of neighbours and passers-by. This is Tofino, after all, spiritual centre of British Columbia's environmental movement.

The beach at Long Beach just south of Cox Bay and the Estowista peninsula, February 1997.

It goes back to the 1970s when the logging practices of forestry companies became conspicuous and plans to log Meares Island in Clayoquot Sound made it a flashpoint of public protest. Cradled in the southern arm of the sound, close to the village of Tofino and shielded from the pounding Pacific by the Esowista Peninsula, Meares is a mountainous 22,000-acre forest of ancient, moss-draped spruce, cedar, and fir trees. Clayoquot is fed by no less than ten mountain river networks that have deposited quantities of silt into it over the millennia, creating extensive mudflat systems that ooze with life and have the bioproductivity of an estuary. Five of these rivers spill directly into the waters around Meares Island, which was (re)named in the eighteenth century for an English seafarer who sailed into Nootka the same year as William Barkley. You could say John Meares was the province's first freelance capitalist, for it was he who conceived of establishing a local base for trading fur. In 1788, he purchased land (or so he construed the arrangement) from a local chief and built a house. The following year, when the Spanish sailed up from San Francisco to exercise their presumed sovereignty over the area, they encountered ships arriving from China with craftsmen to construct Meares's post. An international crisis erupted and played itself out at eighteenth-century speed, producing the Nootka Convention of 1790, which spelled out the surrender of Spain's claim to the Pacific Northwest in exchange for British recognition of its holdings elsewhere on the continent. Britain and France agreed that Nootka Sound would be left open to all European trading nations, and Meares got his land back. No one mentioned the Nootkans who, in any case, were (and are) the Nuu-Chah-Nulth.

Meares Island happens to be the home of the largest known cedar tree in the world, the Hanging Garden Tree, which possesses a girth of sixty-one feet and is thought to be over 2,000 years old. It is also the home of the Tla-o-qui-aht people who have lived in the village of Opitsaht beside this forest forever. Anthropologists can attest to at least 5,000 years of continuous habitation on Meares, a huge island studded at its curved ends by two mountains, Mount Colnett and Lone Cone, which are visible from the beaches on Esowista's outer edge and as far away as Cox Bay. From the dock at Tofino where the Trans-Canada comes to a dramatic end, Meares stares back from every direction, although the eye sees something more like a flock of small bays and islets than the sprawling arm of a single island. A *trompe l'oeil* set in bucolic splendour, Meares Island has been the cause of unpleasant and acrimonious debate.

This conflict began in 1979 when MacMillan Bloedel, whose

Tree Farm Licence #44 includes close to half of Meares Island, announced its intention to start logging it. By then, the tiny population of Tofino had become dependent on the fresh water supply piped in from Meares, the one good local water source. More than the physical beauty was at stake, in other words, and there were land claims to consider as well. In fact, the Nuu-Chah-Nulth's claim was accepted for negotiation shortly after MacMillan Bloedel's announcement. That same year, a group of residents decided to fight for the Meares Island forest. They wanted to be part of the process that would decide on the usage of public lands (as they assumed Crown land to be), to have their views and expertise considered, and, ideally, to instigate a rethinking of industrial logging methods. They called themselves Friends of Clayoquot Sound, and their campaign to protect the world's largest remaining coastal lowland temperate rainforest (to be specific about Clayoquot's designation) was unusually effective. It brought environmentalists and First Nations together in an effort to change the assumptions of logging companies and governments. After two years, however, in 1983, the public process was rudely pre-empted when MacMillan Bloedel pulled out and the government announced a "compromise" that would permit logging on ninety per cent of the island while setting the other ten per cent aside for twenty years. Native and non-Native residents were appalled by the blanket rejection of their arguments and concerns. When company boats arrived loaded with loggers ready for work, a flotilla of protestors greeted them. Chief Moses Martin welcomed the visitors to his "garden" and asked them to leave their chainsaws in the boat if they wished to come ashore. The blockade went on through the winter of 1985 until the Tla-o-qui-aht declared Meares a tribal park and went to court to get an injunction against all logging pending settlement of Native title.

After MacMillan Bloedel came Fletcher Challenge, intent on building a road through Sulphur Passage to reach the unlogged recess of Shelter Inlet and the Megin Valley in the further reaches of Clayoquot Sound. Blockades reappeared; protesters placed themselves behind the blast safety zone, interrupting dynamite crews day after day; injunctions ensued, then arrests that resulted, by summer's end, in thirty-five jail sentences. As the news caught fire, reporters from all over North America were wondering how to pronounce "Clayoquot" and learning that it consisted of over 642,000 acres of prime ancient forest, and was the location of the last seven (of sixty) unlogged principal watersheds on Vancouver Island (watersheds over nineteen square miles, that is), and the home of the fabled marbled murrelet. For decades this common little seabird baffled ornithologists and naturalists who watched it flying in from the ocean each twilight, headed for its nest somewhere ashore. Eventually, just a few years ago, its nesting grounds were discovered in the canopy of old growth forests. Under the glare of publicity and the moral suasion of the diminutive bird, Fletcher Challenge abandoned Sulphur Passage for another less visible route into Shelter Inlet. The Megin Valley was left, too, and is now a protected area. But this protest at Sulphur Passage in 1988 brought renewed attention to Clayoquot Sound and in the spring of 1993, another government produced another decision, which led to another summer of non-violent civil disobedience, only this time the numbers were staggering and the media came from around the world. Every morning at dawn, several hundred people would gather at the Kennedy Lake bridge on the MacMillan Bloedel logging road. There they would stand quietly singing, holding hands or holding their children, with banners silently declaring "No Trees, No Fish, No Jobs." A preselected few would then lie or sit down on the rough gravel road waiting for the Mac-Blo trucks to rumble through. Each morning the dusty convoy would arrive, groan to a halt, and wait, engines rattling, while the RCMP arrested and removed the protestors who were herded off to jail in an old school bus. Then the trucks would rev up and head on into the rain-forest. Eight hundred and fifty-nine quite ordinary people came to Clayoquot to be thus arrested. Hundreds more came from all over the country to lend support, and millions saw it on television.

When it was all over, more than 800 protesters were charged

with contempt of court for disregarding the injunction forbidding any obstruction of MacMillan Bloedel on a logging road. The
mass trials and jail sentences that followed constitute the largest
criminal prosecution of peaceful dissent in Canadian history. In
other times or places such strife might be taken for civil war;
certainly it plays on fundamental civic values and revolves on the
question of land, which pragmatists and idealists both claim to
understand. The attachment to principle is passionate on all sides.

And as a result, all through the fall of 1994 I would see people
at the post office and on the ferry that crosses to Nanaimo from
Gabriola Island where I live, sporting the tell-tale grey ankle
bracelets. Some of them were kids barely out of their teens, others
stolidly middle class and middle aged, and several were seniors,
members of the Raging Grannies. They had become local celebri-
ties, electronically shackled to their parole office for all the world
to see. They were the Clayoquot vets, the environmental movement's radicals, the antithesis, one would suppose, of Megan and
her declawed lynx. Yet, there is something similar in the desire
they share to hold close to the wild, to befriend the strange and
fearsome, and in the need to protect both the reality and the
mythos of nature.

Meares Island, Clayoquot, the Carmanah; Sulphur Passage, South
Moresby, the Stein. The names roll off the tongue like an incanta-
tion. A hundred years ago these places were scarcely known
beyond the Native community; today they are recognized all over
the globe as sites of environmental protest. They have become
symbols in a long debate that rarely admits the battle is about
meaning and metaphor as much as machinery and corporate strategy, and the human environment as much as the physical one. It
concerns the land, it concerns ancient trees, and it concerns something called nature, or rather something human beings conceive of
as nature, which, predictably, has multiple meanings and a basement full of baggage. Our experience of the natural world is not,

strictly speaking, natural for we perceive it through a prism made up of the stories we assimilated as children and the attitudes of the culture we live in. Consider the shift in the basic assumptions about the environment over the last thirty years. No longer does anyone seriously maintain that the environment is inexhaustible and the planet indestructible or that industrial development is divinely inspired for everyone's (including nature's) own good. This is not a cue for me or you to moralize about the conspicuously wasteful habits of developed nations (like Canada), which collectively hog most of the world's energy and wealth while contributing most of the pollution. That would be to narrow the point. And the point is that human societies always conceptualize and ritualize their relationship with the physical surround. We are constantly arranging and rearranging the landscape to suit us. Canadian society is no exception, try as some might to rise above the nitty-gritty of our technological selves.

The period since World War II, spanning what has been called the high summer of industrialism, produced spectacular renovations to the North American landscape. This was the era of superhighways, strip malls, motels, and drive-ins (restaurants, movies, and, latterly, cappuccino bars), the "Paved Paradise" Joni Mitchell sang about in the 1970s, which was created by the automobile in association with franchise marketing. The car was at once the emblem of postwar affluence and mobility, and the agent of the new consumer culture and its expansion to the suburbs. And just as suburbia was the counterpart to the mall, so the suburban lawn—a contrived monoculture of grass sustained on a diet of pesticides—became the homologue of asphalt. After the war, populations that had crowded into the cities earlier in the century flooded back out to these newly created subdivisions. They bought station wagons and took their nuclear families on holiday in the summer to see the country. The once sharp distinction between urban and rural began to blur as the suburbs sprawled in all directions as tourism grew and as agribusiness drew farming into global networks of marketing and advertising, detaching the operation from its local base.

Meanwhile, a generation of Canadians was growing up in the fifties on news stories about the construction of the St. Lawrence Seaway and the Aswan Dam in Egypt, engineering feats that entailed moving square miles of earth, rerouting rivers and shifting mountains of rock with machines the size of buildings. (In the latter case, this included the relocation of the ancient rock temple of Abu Simbel.) It was taken for granted then that nature was man's for the taking—and the remaking. At the same time, my generation was watching Walt Disney's "Wild Wild World of Animals" on Sunday night television and reading books like Fred Bodsworth's *The Last of the Curlews* in which we discovered there was something much worse than death—there was the extinction of a species. Nature was presented to us alternately as a force to be reckoned with and tamed, and as an artefact to cherish. The messages were mixed, but nature was always talked about as something Other.

Concepts of nature and human nature have altered radically over time. In prehistoric times European peoples thought of animal and plant life as the fabric within which they lived themselves. Nature wasn't always understood as a set of laws to be deciphered, secrets to be divulged and treasure extracted. It was the Greeks who forged the division between body and soul and nature. Then Christendom recast the ancient identity of nature as nurturing mother, transforming the dominant metaphor from an organic cosmos that unites the self, society, and the universe in a single world view, into a great chain of being with man sitting just below God. Then, at the very time Europeans were colonizing the New World, modern science conceived of God as the great clockmaker and nature as a machine which was man's duty to use and improve. The dualism invented by the Greeks—heaven and hell, body and soul, mind and matter, male and female, culture and nature—now dominated the European mentality to such an extent that nature's sole role was to be tamed. Nature, once seen as abundant and fruitful as well as wild and uncontrollable, extremes associated with women too (nature invariably being a feminine word in Indo-European languages) was reduced to wild-ness. Like women who were also dismissed from intellectual life, Lady Bountiful had bleak moods, moments when rational behaviour yielded to wanton impulse, when base nature revealed herself in the chaos beyond the garden wall. As the eighteenth century waxed into the nineteenth, the positive aspects of female nature receded in the collective imagination and popular parlance in favour of the idea of unruly, disordered, "raw" nature, which invited (required?) human intervention and patriarchal guidance. This in turn called forth the modern notion of conquering nature. It was no coincidence, historians suggest, that this philosophic shift, which had its roots in the Renaissance, occurred just when Europe "discovered" the Americas and declared them a possession. As writers like Carolyn Merchant have noted, the wilderness tales from the New World sparked the European imagination. "The savages of the new lands became symbols of the wildness and animality that could gain the upper hand in human nature," she writes in *The Death of Nature*. Aboriginal culture thus represented a side of human nature that was thrilling and ominous at once. Nature and human nature, though separate and distinct, were to the European mind both meant for mastery and domination.

Industrialization did not come about in Europe without an upheaval either. It coincided with the alienation of large numbers of people from the land they had lived on for centuries, and triggered a mass migration to cities and towns, and to jobs in factories and mills. The process had been going on for a long time by the nineteenth century, if you consider the enclosure of the commons, the draining of the fens, and the cutting down of forests as part of it. In the British Isles and elsewhere in Europe, the peasant classes who had subsisted on public lands up until the Elizabethan times were driven off as the arrangement of common ownership and the collective use of resources was eliminated. The Tragedy of the Commons has been mythologized as a moral and mathematical dilemma illustrating the flaw in the concept of collective use—the conflict between the individual desire to put more cattle out to graze in the common pasture, and the finite capacity of the commons to support animal life. However it is theorized, though, the privatizing of land in Europe was a tragedy of body and spirit, breaching the relationship of individuals with communities, and societies with their traditional territories. It also challenged long-standing moral indictments. Today we forget that there were the widely held proscriptions against the new techniques of resource extraction when they were first invented in the Industrial Revolution, and that the discussion of how far science should be allowed to go did not begin with the atomic bomb, much less Dolly the cloned lamb. Those who mined the earth for metals in the eighteenth century had to overcome the widespread conviction that to do so was to invade the womb of Mother Earth. The best European minds of the day, notably Francis Bacon's, were applied to find a justification for the new techniques, and, in the end, the sanction against them dissolved into its opposite—approval of all manner of environmental interference for the sake of improving the human condition. Passive, permissive nature became the crucible of the great scientific experiment, and, in their fashion, so did the colonies.

A hundred years ago, Emily Carr took her culture's idea of nature with her on the trip to Ucluelet. It was an idea that encompassed both the drive to dominate the physical world and biblical notions of the power enshrining the superiority of Man over animals, nature—and women. It embraced her father's garden, steeped as it was with nostalgia for an eighteenth-century pastoral approach to nature cultivated as an extension of art appreciation, and it embraced her father himself with his cold discipline and domineering gaze. Thomas Hardy wrote novels lamenting the passing of the old ways on the land, and painters like Constable in England and Corot in France similarly eulogized a vanishing landscape. Landscape painting flourished in nineteenth-century Europe as never before, creeping out of the background of history painting and religious panels to fill the canvas on its own. By Emily Carr's time, landscape painting was a subject worthy of contemplation in terms of pure aesthetics, but in the colonies such pictures were constructed for other purposes too. Etchings and small watercolours of familiar *belvédère* were brought out as souvenirs or personal mementoes that doubled as signs of refinement and good connections. Not surprisingly, they bore little resemblance to the forest that greeted their owners when they stepped outdoors. In Carr's day, European settlers had barely overcome their horror of the wilderness they encountered on this continent, which was unlike anything they knew, and which struck them as irredeemably gloomy, forbidding, and "awful in its solitude." It was mid-century before the Rockies were seen as anything more than a grotesque pile of rock. Ugly was the word. Nature was an unsightly wasteland. There was, moreover, a tendency to moralize about place in terms of scenery, and in the hierarchy of landscapes, Canada's ranked as extreme—unkempt and savage, they called it.

Not everyone was repelled by the difference, though; some newcomers were ineluctably drawn to it. Some, like the painter Lucius O'Brien, were able to devise romance out of the ragged terrain. His ode to Precambrian magnificence, called *Sunrise on the Saguenay*, bathes the river scene in a nostalgic glow and sets time adrift with the brigantine under sail in the middle distance. The painting has political significance, for it was O'Brien's diploma piece for the Royal Canadian Academy of the Arts, donated with other founding members' works to form the nucleus of the National Gallery's collection in 1880, and it demonstrates an appreciation of Canadian geography reconfigured as serene and monumental.

By the decade of Carr's childhood, perceptions had thus mellowed to the degree that wilderness was no longer irrevocably equated with menace. It had come to be regarded as a valuable resource, for one thing, and much more of it was becoming known to the White world, primarily the result of fishing, mining, and logging ventures. For another, the unpleasant side effects of industry had spurred movements in the larger European cities to reclaim despoiled land and create public parks. In England as well as in Canada and the United States, these campaigns for living green spaces had been clean-up efforts that were in part intended to infuse a bit of bucolic grace (*à la* Capability Brown) into the urban landscape. In part they were memorials to a lost landscape. Somewhat later, there was a similar move to create national parks outside cities whereby whole chunks of geography would be preserved in a "natural" state for the benefit of posterity. The first in Canada, established at Banff in 1870, was intended as a recreation spot, and thus the connection between nature and tourism was made at the outset and attached to a national purpose.

It is not possible to travel far down this road discussing Euro-Canadian attitudes to nature during the early settlement of British Columbia without confronting the question that won't go away. The history of land rights and expropriation demands an accounting for what happened when the European ancestors arrived. This means recognizing there was nothing to warrant or justify it. Polite White society might like to call it trespassing save for the fact that the perpetrators moved in permanently, but the European settlers were no innocent squatters. They occupied lands as they wanted and filled the place with immigrants so the original occupants were, in effect, held hostage in their own country. Whatever you may think of Aboriginal rights as a legal or moral issue, the Europeans had no *a priori* right to the land they occupied, and now we know the old arguments will no longer stand up under honest scrutiny: not the one about the land being empty, or inadequately utilized; not the one about the superior needs of the newcomer society, or the inevitability of progress; and obviously not the argument about indigenous peoples disappearing. Not even the pseudo-scientific claim that Aboriginal nations weren't fully fledged societies in an anthropological sense will hold water, although some Canadian judges refuse to notice the puddle on the floor. It was the reasoning of B.C.'s Chief Justice Allan McEachern in his decision denying Aboriginal title to the Gitksan-Wet'suwet'en in 1991: "It would not be accurate to assume that even pre-contact existence in the territory was in the least bit idyllic . . . there is no doubt, to quote Hobbs [*sic*], that aboriginal life in the territory was, at best, 'nasty, brutish and short.'"

After Governor Douglas's negotiations in the 1850s, there were no attempts by provincial authorities to negotiate with the local Native peoples, and once British Columbia joined Confederation and responsibility passed to the federal Department of Indian Affairs, the province simply took the position that there was nothing to discuss. Meanwhile, the project of staking out reserves was initiated across Canada and proceeded haltingly in B.C. because of the province's peculiar legal position, and because of Native resistance to the process and to the exceptionally stingy allotments being proposed here. As a result, the process took four decades to complete.

From the very beginning, the indigenous peoples of British Columbia protested the settlers' incursions into their territories. There were never-ending conflicts that Whites have endlessly written about, but from the testimony of recent years we can only conclude that the basic experience from the Native point of view was invasion. What else do you call the slow appropriation of your lands and resources by visitors who come and displace you from your home? The newcomers profited from the displacement and made no official accounting of it, yet at some semiconscious level, Canadian culture has always been aware of this original sin, this ill-gotten title. Only in the last decade have governments agreed to sit down to discuss it, forced by court decisions other than McEachern's. In 1899, though, the denials were in full swing. Nature and landscape were loaded topics, shot full of subtexts and assumptions about the right way of seeing things.

Emily Carr was not ignorant of all this when she went to Ucluelet. She knew about the clash of cultures and at some level understood the tendency of her culture to arrogate all knowledge and excellence to itself. In *Klee Wyck* she told the story of Tanook, who arrived late for church one Sunday, his legs bare and shirt-tails flapping, though the missionaries had declared it mandatory for men to wear trousers in church. Mortified, Tanook's wife passed her shawl up the rows of seats to her husband, who grasped it around his middle and stormed out. Wrote Carr:

> The service was over, the people gone, but a pink print figure sat on in the back seat. Her face was sunk down on her chest. She was waiting till all were away before she slunk home. It is considered more indecent for an Indian woman to go shawl-less than for an Indian man to go bare-legged. The woman's heroic gesture had saved her husband's dignity before the Missionaries and shamed her before her own people. The Greater Missionary patted the pink shoulder as she passed.
> "Brave Woman!" she said, smiling.

Unlike most Whites at the time, Carr was aware of the contradictions between the two cultures, but, like most, she believed that Native culture was doomed, and that she was witnessing the end of an era and a civilization. Although it would have seemed improbable to someone standing on the Ucluth Peninsula at the turn of the last century, there were people who worried similarly about the wilderness disappearing. When the buffalo vanished from the prairie, they saw that a way of life went with it and, in effect, so did a landscape. It was not beyond the realm of possibility that such a thing might happen in British Columbia, and in fact it was already happening. By the early nineteenth century, the sea otter had been hunted past decimation, almost to extinction, and by Emily Carr's time, the slaughter of the forests was underway, though it was certainly not often depicted in those terms. Yet if it is true that the settlers had a vested interest in the idea of the original occupants' disappearance and if, in hindsight, we can read their prediction of the Natives' demise as something more like a prayer, what was the psychosocial function of parks, which also made their debut in this period? Alexander Wilson, in his examination of the culture of nature, offers the explanation that they were a method of normalizing the ecological damage occurring elsewhere. In his book, *The*

Culture of Nature, he points out that conservation springs from the same intellectual precept as exploitation, a concept that posits nature as requiring humans to decide what should be tended, what preserved, what sustainably developed, or what torn up and turned into cities, farms, and car parks. Nature still ends up as passive, pliable, and Other to our human effort.

There are several sticky issues lurking beneath the surface of this discussion, the main one being the idea of wilderness itself. In a sense, it is a thoroughly artificial and self-referential concept; nature is wild to whom, you have to ask. It is a matter of opinion, you must conclude, as in "my wilderness may be your grandmother's trap line." Or, as Poncas Mo-chu-no-zhi (Luther Standing Bear) is reputed to have said, around the time Emily Carr paid her visit to Ucluelet, "To us it was tame. Earth was bountiful and we were surrounded with the blessings of the Great Mystery—when the very animals of the forests and fields began fleeing from the approach of the settlers, then it was that for us the 'Wild West' began." Wilderness also conjures up images of nature in a pristine state, before the downfall and the loss of innocence associated with the advance of human culture—a powerful narrative in the parks movement which seeks to reconstruct the lost Garden of Eden. Again the idea of wilderness objectifies nature, implying that humans exist outside her sphere and are antithetical to her by definition. The process of taking private possession of the New World was therefore a cultural as well as a physical and political undertaking and it required reinventing and renaming nature. The irony is that the same alienation of indigenous populations from land once held in common had happened in Europe too.

You could say the fight over B.C.'s forests began a long time ago. It began with John Meares and has scarcely abated in two centuries. While finding expression in concrete struggles over ownership, land use, and public policy, it has rebounded on philosophic issues. For the newcomers, this has had to do primarily with the problem of belonging. What happens as the generations lengthen and the newcomers cease to be new? When does "here" become "home," for example? When does myth catch up with reality? The Canadian quandary—"Where is here?"—began with the land and always goes back to it.

Nowadays, tourists trek across Highway 4 to Tofino in their thousands, stopping off along the way at the MacMillan Bloedel Park, which is commonly called Cathedral Grove. In actual fact the park is a copse of old growth forest that the company ceded to the province in 1947. Just 330 acres in size, it stands as a relic of what once was; a glimpse of a forest primeval in its optimum state, which, from the human vantage point, is mainly an experience of colossal size and of trees almost too tall to see. The largest one stretches up 250 feet, is 9.5 feet thick, and was already 300 years old when Columbus set sail from Cadiz looking for the Orient. It began growing almost the same year Abbot Suger invented Gothic architecture at the abbey church in St. Denis near Paris, the system of pointed arches and flying buttresses construction that enabled twelfth-century masons to build straight up 150 feet, filling the walls with stained-glass windows instead of stone, making the soaring walls of light at Chartres possible.

The trees have the same effect as the churches. People wander about the feet of the giant columns, speaking in whispers. Curiously, it was in France, not very far from St. Denis, in the little town of Crécy-en-Brie, that Carr's next transition occurred.

Chapter Two

Casting Off

Paris, 1911

She sits staring at the colours floating on the wall. Slabs of
green and mauve, patches of blue and orange shimmy and
shift, and then resolve into perspective as a picture
emerges. In the centre a lush and bushy tree grows in a
garden behind a house with a tiled roof, hanging over an
old stone wall and reaching its branches towards the canal

*Banks of the River ("Tree by the Canal") painted
at Crécy-en-Brie by Carr when she was a student
in France, 1910.*

running alongside. Everything is silent in the hot summer sun, engulfed in the thick atmosphere of midday. Even the river holds still, fixing the wavy reflection of leaves and masonry on its slippery surface. She crosses her arms and leans back against the far wall of the narrow hotel room, her mind drifting back to the women in the village she'd seen doing their washing in the canal, kneeling on large wooden trays perched out over the water, slap, slapping their wet linen against the stone. She had painted them, too, a bit later.

From the portfolio on the bed she draws out a sheet of paper, turns it right side up to reveal a spray of bright blues, ochres, and pinks and tacks it up beside the oil painting. Bookends, she thinks. The second, a watercolour painted a few days ago on the coast of Brittany, shows a cluster of fishing boats at their moorings, described with broad strokes of liquid colour and not much else: shape dissolved into evanescent light. The courtyard garden by the canal was painted in May at Crécy-en-Brie, back at the beginning of this process when she first began allowing detail to play second fiddle to the structure of things. She notices now how water features in both pictures. A sure way to let go of the literal image, she smiles to herself. Having come to France looking for clues, she had finally found them. The evidence of the transformation stares back at her from the wall.

This she would not have dared imagine a year ago when the miserable headaches returned. Paris had closed in on her as London had, and in the end she lost four months to illness and spent a fifth with Alice convalescing in Sweden. In May she returned ready to try again, and luck was with her. Harry Gibb was leaving Paris for Crécy to teach a class in landscape, and she joined up immediately. Gibb was the first artist she contacted upon arriving in France; he was the one who urged the Académie Colarossi

*"Brittany Coast" painted at Concarneau when Carr was
studying with Frances Hodgkins, 1911.*

over the Julien where classes were segregated and the fees
higher. But his reason was that she would benefit from the
stronger work of male students, which didn't thrill her as
a reason, although she actually agreed. She wanted to be
taken seriously. She would be forty in December, which
meant the journey was now twenty years old. And where
exactly had it taken her? First to England where she had
also enrolled in an art school in the city and suffered
through two years of figure drawing and studio instruction before finding her way to art colonies at St. Ives and
Bushey. There classes were held *en plein air* and Emily
thrived. In the country, a couple of individuals had
shown her something about painting forests, about the
sunshine to be found in shadows and the constant

"coming and going of crowded foliage that still had breath-space between each leaf." This had carried her a certain distance in the search for a way to paint the western landscape. But not far enough. As she saw it, the five years in England had ended in failure. She had neither advanced her career as an artist, nor found a style and artistic *raison d'être*, and she actually spent the last year and a half laid up in the "san." Another nasty pocket of memories she shoves to the back of her mind.

She had dreaded a repeat performance in France, but this time she didn't succumb to the lassitude and ennui. Furthermore, the artists she has worked with have had a lot more to offer. Without any French, she didn't last long at Colarossi, so, on Gibb's advice, she went to study with another expatriate, a genial Scotsman named Fergusson. Through him she first approached the moderns, absorbing the techniques of *les Fauves* who were called wild beasts when they originally exhibited together at the Salon d'Automne of 1905 because of their loud colours and riotous forms. At Crécy, she put these ideas into action, producing a number of landscapes using planes of colour to suggest form. Once or twice she sketched the little village straddling the Morin River, too. Alice, who came to visit from Paris on weekends, would look down from her window over the canal and declaim her enchantment. "It's the closest thing I'll get to Venice," she'd sigh. After a few weeks Alice left for home, and Emily followed the Gibbs who had decamped for a resort town on the coast.

At St. Efflam she buckled down to a schedule, sketching in the fields behind the village where Gibb would come late in the afternoon each day to instruct her. Twice a week she took her work to the Grand Hotel where he was staying and he would critique it. She had agonized while waiting for the first one, but was rewarded by his interest and acumen. Later, on the hill, he took a fresh canvas and sketched the scene in front of them, "realizing" rather than copying the woods. The colours, she remembers, did not match; they jarred. And it was as if they were mixed with air. "You go through space to meet reality," she says in wonderment, starting at the sound of her own voice. Once roused from her reverie, she sets about readying herself to go out for tea. It is past four in the afternoon, but everything starts later in Paris.

Gibb had been terse, but his "crits" were awfully good. He seemed ambivalent and vaguely disapproving, perhaps because he was remembering their first meeting, when she and Alice had appeared at his studio and both been nonplussed by his work, especially the distorted nudes on the wall. She had appreciated the still lives, though, noting the inventive design and luscious colour, but she felt gauche. Alice, on the other hand, kept her eyes glued to the floor and said not a single word. Studying with Gibb, Emily was irked by the fact that he never showed his own work to her as he did to the male students. When she questioned him, he retorted, "Don't have to. Those others don't know what they're after. You do. Your work should not be influenced by mine." He'd gone on to say she could well become one of *the* women painters of her day. Flattering, she thought, if hedged; but should she believe such a compliment? Mrs. Gibb had once remarked that she'd rarely seen her husband so absorbed with a student's work as he was with Emily Carr's. For her part, Emily had never seen a woman so ably and unobtrusively manage her husband's atelier as Bridget Gibb.

"Every artist should have a Bridget," she informs the two parrots perched on the lone chair in the room. Josephine, the jocular green one, had been purchased when Emily and Alice first arrived in France and thus "knows the language better than I do," as she likes to say. Rebecca, the grey one, comes from England, is shy, and says little while Josephine chats with everyone. This was an enormous help in Brittany with the children who came to watch her painting and then eagerly agreed to take her home to meet their mothers. (She painted them, too, bottling preserves or knitting in their kitchens.) "Worth your weight in birdseed, you are, when it comes to bridging language," she tells the parrot. Mrs. Gibb helped with another sort of bridge, over the gaps in Emily's knowledge about the art world. Mrs. Gibb talked about money, a subject that her husband kept close to his chest. He never said so, but Mrs. Gibb did, that things were not going very well for them, and that a return to England was likely in the new year. Emily was floored by this information, having taken Gibb, the consummate francophile, as a permanent fixture in the *quartier latin*. Although of an age, she thought of him as far more settled and established than she. Certainly he was in a position to take two of her canvasses under his arm to the Salon d'Automne, the boisterous annual exhibition that welcomes students, foreigners, and interior decorators as well as the avant-garde. He was a quantity on the scene, a *sociétaire* of the Salon, a man who knew the local milieu well and counted himself part of the expanding circle of iconoclasts who had broken the spell of impressionism, and with it the romance of naturalist rendition. So, apparently, even in Paris making a name for oneself was not to be equated with making a living.

Amazingly, her two pictures, both Brittany landscapes, were accepted at the Salon and this very morning she had taken herself to the Grand Palais to see them rubbing shoulders with the best and most rebellious. Granted, Fergusson was on the selection committee; granted, the exhibition was huge and participants numbered in the hundreds, but this at long last was some success—measurable, visible success.

Emily finishes fixing her hat, gathers up her satchel, her purse, and the walking-stick with Josephine attached and heads out the door. Over her shoulder she coos to Rebecca, who's settled in a cage on the bureau, "Your turn next, sweet girl." She figures on a stroll down to the *quais* along the Seine, past the *Dôme* to see if Frances is there. Frances was the denouement to the story in France, for when Gibb returned to Paris and her intense five-month study with him ended, Emily had cast about for alternatives. Miss Frances Hodgkins was slated to give watercolour classes at Concarneau on the Brittany coast in September. A woman, another colonial and, according to Gibb, a comer. Being the first woman to teach at the Colarossi had brought her some renown, as had the exhibition prize from the American Women's Artists Association, which included the free use of a studio for herself and for her classes. This past year Hodgkins had returned to private teaching, but had done something unusual: opened her Paris studio to women only. Gibb admired Hodgkins's work, was seized by her original touch with colour, and her intuitive approach. Bridget Gibb admired her as well, thought her a card, and told stories about her. Both Gibbs predicted it would be a good match.

This is why Emily Carr found herself once again on the West Coast of a continent facing into the ocean. For the first time since she was a child, she was studying with another woman and, furthermore, someone in a situation very like her own. Hodgkins came from Dunedin, New Zealand, a British colony at the opposite end of the Empire from Victoria, British Columbia, and, like Carr, was a single woman attempting to make a career in art. Two colonials at court, you might say, or two women on the loose from convention.

At Concarneau, Emily met a prepossessing person, a
small woman with a large presence, with strong features,
sharp eyes, and a breezy manner, who was formal and
down-to-earth all at once. She had never known another
woman so single-minded about her purpose in art, so
direct in her comments and yet so benevolent an instruc-
tor. Miss Hodgkins entranced her students, brightened
their colour boxes with cadmiums and *vert émeraude*, and
urged their efforts on while leaving them to *feel* their own
way. She was neither pretentious nor precious, which
Emily appreciated, and she worked with staggering assurance. Standing well back from a student's easel, she
would paint in a few decisive sweeps, her whole body
moving with the motion that flowed through her brush,
like music through a violinist's bow.

Hodgkins spent time with her students, often taking
meals with them at the *pension* where they lodged. She was
willing to talk endlessly with them about art and the
changes taking place in the making of it. In the city, she
said, she always advised students to take an afternoon a
week to look at the new work in the galleries. She talked
about the *enfants terribles* (Pablo Picasso and Henri
Matisse) and all the others breaking with the academy and
taking painting into uncharted territory. The thing about
Paris, she kept saying, was the constant bubbling of new
ideas. "The French are so eager for them, they give them
such a welcome. And progress must come with new ideas,
musn't it? We can't go on with modern minds painting
like Old Masters." She always talked as if they were part of
one great experiment, mentioning this new work, her
own, and the students' in the same breath. "France is the
only place to be if you are serious about art," she would
add. Emily sympathized with what she said about modern
minds and Old Masters, but declarations like this set her
reflecting on her own desire to paint the Canadian West

and her impending trip home. Her painting had gone from
strength to strength over the months in France, and
Hodgkins's class was the topping. Having worked exclusively in oils with Gibb, she returned to watercolour with
alacrity and was entranced by the airborne lightness she
felt. What had been a constraint in painting realism
before—the transparency of the medium and the speed it
demands—was no longer. And colour became pure
ecstasy. The leap required the courage of her conviction,
but she found it was there when she needed it. The days
rolled into each other like butter into warm bread; she was
supremely happy and felt fit as she never had before.
Leaving Concarneau, she realized she was finally ready to
push off on her own. Her only turmoil was about the
future: not about her resolve to paint her own country,
but about her decision to paint the totem poles.

Emerging into a narrow street abutting rue de Rennes,
Emily surveys the hustle and crush of people and vehicles
for a moment and then sets off in the direction of Boule-
vard St. Germain. The afternoon is rapidly approaching
evening and the October twilight has washed the sky
indigo. She is intimate with French skies now, and with
the French custom of working late; she scarcely thinks
twice about taking a glass of wine with supper, and regularly stops for tea and a bun at the *Dôme*, which also
serves liquor and would pass for a saloon in Victoria. A
big barn of a place, it has tables and chairs outside on the
sidewalk as well as inside in tiers where anyone can sit
alone and not be noticed, man or woman, with or without
parrot. Still, she feels exposed walking through the place,
scanning the tables, glancing at faces. Blessedly, she spots
her company in the rear; Frances with Betty Rhind,
another student from Concarneau and a family friend from
New Zealand who was there with Hodgkins at the Grand
Palais this morning.

"Well, there you are," exclaims Frances. "We've saved you two chairs." Emily perches Josephine on one and settles herself on the other.

"Jo-Jo mange du gâteau!" rasps the parrot as a short, dark waiter with a spiky moustache appears to take the order. He vanishes and the next thing Emily sees is her tea and lemon sailing down the aisle on a tray held high above people's heads on elegantly outstretched fingers. She pays the man, puts sugar in her tea, and offers Josephine a morsel of biscuit.

"I must say that I was a bit overwhelmed by the exhibition, but I am glad I went," Betty says after they renew their acquaintance and conversation resumes. "I was there four hours and missed your paintings entirely, Miss Carr. And much more besides I am sure. I know it was the last day, but the crowds were staggering. Imagine all those people clamouring to see the ugliest paintings in the world!" She stops to catch her breath. "What did you make of it?"

"If the Fauves are called wild animals, I can't think what this group will be labelled," Emily answers. "Cubist sounds altogether too tame. They break all the rules I ever knew in art, although I've noticed the French seem to love breaking rules."

"Almost as much as making them up," quips Frances. They all laugh, thinking of the habit of concierges to post rules everywhere. Josephine squawks and beats her wings, causing people at nearby tables to turn and look. A little girl sidles over, eager with questions and the desire to touch the red feathers on the parrot's wingtips.

"We were talking about Betty's departure for New Zealand," Frances says. "I was confessing that New Zealand no longer supports the painting I do. The last pictures I sent back to Dunedin didn't sell at all, and I have to accept that the buying public there is not prepared to follow me into newer styles. The more one improves in that direction, the narrower the circle becomes. Actually, for a time I seriously puzzled over ways to pamper them with cheap attractive work."

"And did you try it?" prompts Emily when Hodgkins pauses.

"It's hard to remain true to yourself doing that. You try because it's that or come to terms with exile."

"Do you mean to say you have moved too far ahead of everyone back home?" asks Rhind.

"That's one way to put it."

At least Dunedin has an art world to be ahead of, Emily jokes to herself silently. She had quit Victoria for Vancouver in 1906, shortly after her return from England, when she realized there was no living to be made there as an artist. Hodgkins left New Zealand the same year, after two years of teaching and exhibiting in Wellington (where her mother and sister had gone to live), convinced that New Zealand would never satisfy the artistic side of her, and that art was leading her elsewhere.

"What is it like in Canada?" she asks Emily. Both New Zealanders turn to her expectantly.

"It's rather hard to describe," Emily says pursing her lips and looking pensive. "Victoria, where I grew up, is so cut off—a ferry ride from the mainland, which is separated from the rest of the country by several ranges of mountains. It hasn't any art clubs, or galleries, or a professional milieu to speak of. Vancouver, where I live now, is only slightly further advanced."

"What will people think of your new paintings then?" Hodgkins asks.

"I don't expect too many will like what I am doing right off, and some are sure to take offence. They take offence here, too, after all, and in British Columbia there is no avant-garde to take refuge in."

Emily had wanted to ask, but it's Betty Rhind who does. "Whatever did you mean, Fanny, when you said just now that it's that or come to terms with exile?"

"Well, when the place you have grown up in offers no promise for you to develop, and if you take the step of swearing your life to your *métier*, then sometimes it becomes a choice between the two. Home and art. Country and exile."

"And for you?" asks Emily, thinking now of the story Rhind had told her about coming upon Miss Hodgkins in tears at her easel. Both women had been acutely embarrassed and Rhind retreated, but it confirmed her sense that Fanny was unhappy. By September, when she met Emily and told her the story, the cloud had lifted. Hodgkins seemed like her old self again and Betty wondered if perhaps she shouldn't have said anything.

"My decision?" A look of weariness crosses Hodgkins's face. "I suppose I knew when I left New Zealand the last time that I was leaving for good—although I do plan to return for a visit soon. It's been six years since I've seen my family. To be frank, it isn't art history that brings me here and makes me want to stay. I am not terribly impressed with artists of the past. It is not that, I want to find out where this experiment is going. If I'm going to measure myself against the moderns, if I want to excel, then this is where I should be. And that seems to mean exile."

"To me the very word is frightening," protests Rhind. "Even if Europe is 12,000 miles and five weeks away from home, it shouldn't require exile. How can you be expected to spend your life in someone else's language, in someone else's country? What if everyone did that?"

"Distance makes for extreme choices," Emily offers, looking at Hodgkins.

"Well, I think it may be easier to remain alone and unencumbered here, which is what painting demands after all. Perhaps there is more room to be different in a foreign place. Certainly it is unusual for a woman to live on her own without children or family pretty well everywhere, never mind the obsession with art. But in Paris you can live as you like; few questions are asked."

Emily thinks about Fergusson and how he always says art is "a quality of being" rather than something he does, how it is necessary to ignore the world and all its damn silly rules and regulations and get on with it. Easy for him to say. Home is across the Channel, and he has a wife and so doesn't face this tug and pull of the heart. She does understand Hodgkins's need for the freedom to concentrate, though.

"The day-to-day difficult part is scraping together the money to keep going," Frances continues. "The teaching is always getting in the way of my painting. If you are any good at it, it leaches the creative juice from your own work." She and Emily have talked before about the fortunes of art teaching. In New Zealand during her first return visit, Frances had taken it up seriously, recognizing it was unlikely that she would ever be able to support herself on sales alone. After three years of uninterrupted study in Europe, her painting had grown, and so had her reputation. She easily attracted students, although in nothing like the numbers that flocked to her classes in France (most being English-speaking foreigners like herself). Back in Europe, luck now seems to be running with her for a change. She has begun exhibiting with the French watercolour societies and the more exclusive salons, and the possibility of establishing herself here at the epicentre of the modern art movement is actually taking shape, so she has written her mother once again, pleading for time and postponing the departure for home. "Don't you want me to find myself permanently and definitely an established niche in the Art

World? I wish you were as terribly ambitious for me as I am myself," she wrote.

Emily's experience of teaching was not as positive as Hodgkins's. She had despaired of the group of amateurs in the Vancouver Ladies' Art Club who originally hired her to teach them, and she had eventually given up on adults. Instead she had concentrated on classes for children, which in the last few years had turned into quite a success. About seventy-five youngsters traipsed down to her studio on Granville Street each week, though often she organized sketching trips to Stanley Park or—to the horror of parents and the eternal delight of children—down the back alleyways to see all manner of marvellous things. (Garbage cans and manure, the mothers worried.) Children loved her unorthodox ways and her menagerie of pets—Billie the sheepdog, Sally the cockatoo, the rats called Peter and Peggy, and the squirrels in a cage. She did well, saving enough to buy five small city plots in a new part of Vancouver and to finance this year in France, but even at the best of times, teaching was an insecure living and "the buying public" more fancy than fact. So while working at some sort of job was a necessity, she wished there was an alternative.

"I don't think the two can be made to suit," Emily says. "Teaching takes extroverted attention, a sociable disposition, and, of course, dependability. Painting wants the opposite: introversion, unsociable manners, and unreliable behaviour." She ponders the insatiable appetite of art for time and attention and her own aversion to the self-promotion that teaching requires. She returns to the subject of painting abroad. "Living here has its advantages, I can see that. Yet it makes one dependent on an alien landscape. I think of places as having temperaments. Some seduce you into painting them, and some don't appeal and never will. Some put you—or me anyway—right off. It can be visceral."

"I don't disagree. Yet I always find it interesting to learn a new place, to find ways to make a landscape familiar that was originally alien to me," Frances offers. "In any case, it is the luminescence, the light and action that interest me. These are special qualities but ubiquitous ones."

Betty Rhind makes motions of leaving at this point, excusing herself to go back to the hotel to dress for dinner with her parents, with whom she is travelling. The conversation drifts into pleasantries. Frances seems fond of the young woman, but declines the invitation to dine with her family on the weekend. She does not embrace her when she leaves, but waves Rhind on her way, almost as if she were resisting the temptation of friendship.

Emily finds herself drawn to Frances and repelled by her at the same time. She respects her, admires her *savoir faire* and figures that many of the same debates over the troublesome choices that art foists on women roll about in her head. Hodgkins seems years ahead in art, but the semi-nomadic independence, fabulous in the telling, is terrifying to Emily. Hodgkins's quest obviously takes stamina and breeds detachment. This spurs the realization that it's not a route she herself could ever take. As far as Emily is concerned, life's choices do not include living in exile from British Columbia, or, when she gets down to it, from her sisters. Given that she might not survive European winters on a permanent basis and, more to the point, given her conviction that the landscape of the Northwest is the subject she *must* paint, living in Europe is not possible.

Emily lingers over a second cup of tea. Frances orders a Pernod and when it comes, toys with the glass for a time, and then drops a thin stream of water into the clear liquid, watching it cloud. "This is not something I usually do, Miss Carr. Once in a while, though, I like the liquorice taste." Hodgkins is the sort of woman who dresses with theatrical flare on almost no money. Her broad-brimmed felt hat has a rakish tilt to it and is complemented by a stylish set of silk scarves, which give her the air of a *femme du monde*, hardly the look of an absinthe drinker. Moreover, her not-to-be-fussed-with demeanour commands respect, the achievement, no doubt, of years sketching in public places where the curious and the obnoxious always show up to test an artist's concentration.

"Well, perhaps I'll join you in sin," says Carr, casting an eye around the café where women of all ages can be seen adding to the blue cloud of smoke hanging in the air. She fishes out her cigarette case and a packet of matches from her bag. Frances nods and waits for the ritual to conclude before asking her own question. "How do you see your future, Miss Carr?"

As if she'd been waiting for the question, Carr launches into an answer. "I have talked to you a lot about my country and my desire to paint it, haven't I? And I have told you about sketching in Native villages on Vancouver Island and up the Fraser River. But I've not said much about the huge carvings you see up and down the coast. To tell you the truth, it is the art of the Indians that entices me as much as the land and the forest. I find the sculpted and painted house fronts and posts, the totem poles and burial boxes strangely beautiful, and they visit my dreams. I have painted a few poles as historical records, and my thought is to paint as many as I can while they are still in place and before they become a thing of the past."

"Would your purpose be artistic?" begins Frances. "Let me ask that another way. How do you think such a project would build on the breakthrough you have experienced with your painting here?"

"I don't exactly know how it will relate, not until I try it. I just know there is some connection between the expressive form artists are experimenting with here and the Indian carvers' approach in representing bears and frogs and ravens. My objective would be to make accurate renderings of the poles, yes, but I see them as belonging to something larger. They belong to the landscape, to the spirit of the place, really, and that is the same quality I am after in my work."

"Do you think people in Victoria will be interested in such subjects? Do they like the Indian motifs or find them hideous?"

"Well, I have met artists who make a living painting Indian themes. I came across an American in Alaska who had been doing it for twenty years, selling his paintings successfully in New York, though they didn't seem very Indian to me, come to think of it. He told me museums sometimes commission historical paintings, which they mount in exhibition halls to accompany the objects on display. Richardson—that was his name—often travels on his own; he hires a canoe and Indian guides to take him into far-off places where he lives with the Natives while he makes his sketches. That is something I want to do myself, and intend to next summer. So I am curious to ask you, Miss Hodgkins, I know you have painted the Indians of New Zealand . . ."

"The Maori."

"Yes, the Maori. I wonder if you found the travelling too difficult, or if the pictures didn't sell, or if they caused a stir. Why is it that you stopped painting them?"

"Stopped?" Hodgkins is taken aback for a moment. "It is rather more that I left New Zealand. I always enjoy spending time with Maori women, watching them as they gather mussels or sit about with their children doing their handwork. I'm not so comfortable with the men, so I have painted mainly women and children. They sell well enough, it isn't that. And it isn't the facial markings either, if that's what you are wondering about because most people do," she adds, gauging Carr's response. "The tattoos aren't very popular with young women any more, anyway. But I think the *moko* is rather like your Indian poles. It takes European eyes a while to adjust to the beauty in it."

"I have heard tell of a New Zealand artist here who keeps a collection of preserved heads for his study of tattoo designs."

"That would have to be Horatio Robley. He is an older artist who wrote an entire book on the subject. He is not alone in this fascination, though. Most Maori painters are preoccupied with dress, ceremonial objects, the tattoos, and so forth, and treat their subjects as scientific curiosities. My interest is the faces. I wanted to paint them as people without any accessories."

"What of the villages you visited? Are they hard to get to? Were you welcomed when you arrived?"

"The travel can be rough, but then I'm from the South Island and rather used to it, and I always travelled with a party anyway. I have to say I was struck by the beauty of the Native villages, especially in Rotorua. The Maori I sketched were people we happened on along the way. I never made a project of painting them, though, from an artistic point of view, their faces are wonderful. And the women always seem happy to model."

"What did you see in them?"

"In their faces? The most amazing blues and purples and an undercurrent of light. Or perhaps you mean . . ."

"No, what did you think of them?"

"As a race of people, they are gentle enough and pleasant to meet. Yet I could tell you some hair-raising stories, like the time I was almost trampled to death along with the baby I was drawing because some men inexpertly shot a cow in an open yard, causing a stampede. Mostly I'd say the Maori are a degenerate lot."

It is Carr's turn to be surprised.

"To come back to your question, though, I haven't really stopped painting the Maori. I expected to do more on my last trip. I remember writing my mother from France, enthusing at the idea of going back to an island full of Maori, remarking that they were still so much more beautiful to me than anything I'd seen on this side of the world. And I did make a trip to Rotorua in 1904 with Dorothy Richmond. She is another New Zealander who studied in Europe for some time, by the way, and then returned home to a career in teaching. Only a few small Maori studies came of it. I produced very little during my stay, actually. Most of the large pictures I did were concocted in my studio with my sister's laundress dressed up for the figure in the *Dutch Housewife*, and a local girl in Moroccan costume holding a mandolin for the one I titled *Ayesha*, a name I know from my travels in Tangiers—that sort of thing." She glances at Emily, who is listening intently, rolling a cigarette.

"Maybe when I finally returned after the year-that-turned-into-three years' absence, I was reluctant to leave my mother and go off travelling. She suspected I wasn't home for good. But we keep to the story that I will eventually quit Europe and make a home with her." Frances sips her drink and adds more water.

"Would the Maori fit into your current work if you were living there?" Emily asks.

"Probably not. Unlike some moderns, I am not very keen on primitive art as a source of formal inspiration. Anyway there were other things going on that were pulling me away from New Zealand back then. However, I was asking about *you*," Frances asserts, hauling the conversation back onto a more comfortable track.

"I leave for Canada in a couple of weeks, " Emily reminds her. "I can't say I'm looking forward to the

Atlantic crossing one bit, but I will be happy to get back
home. I felt compelled to come to Europe to study, and I
shan't ever regret it, but for me living here is something
of an ordeal."

"You know, I share your aversion to cities, Miss Carr.
That's why I moved to Concarneau last year, to get away
from the noise and frantic activity. And, of course, the
sickness."

"It's more than that with me and cities. Even without
the threat of pestilence, I fall ill. I am not cut out for the
life of the exile either."

"Well, I have to admit I do lead a wayward existence.
Partly it is the eternal search for fresh subjects; partly, it
is to save money and escape the northern chill; but partly,
too, it is my innate restlessness. I *am* anxious to get wherever it is I am going."

"Oh, my! I know all about that impatience," says Emily
shaking her head ruefully at Frances. To herself she is
thinking how different their experience of Europe is. Hers
nurtures an appreciation of her Canadianness, and deep-
ens her aversion to British snobbery and French charm;
Hodgkins's seems to stoke her fondness for Europe and
reinforce her estrangement from New Zealand. How
contrary their response to Native life is too: Hodgkins's
lack of interest compared to her affection for Native
culture. She thinks of her closest sister, Alice, and decides
with a rush of affection that perhaps she should give her
the painting of the garden beside the canal. Alice just
might like it.

The skinny waiter reappears with a flourish at this
moment to inquire if the *gentilles Mesdames* wish to order
anything else. The two women decline, pay their tab and
leave. Outside on the sidewalk the evening crowds are
beginning to gather. Street performers, jugglers, flame
throwers, and acrobats who work the boulevards at night

are in evidence. No one notices two middle-aged women passing by with a noisy French parrot.

"M. Emily Carr"

Emily Carr went back to Canada in October 1911 and never returned to Europe. Frances Hodgkins went back to New Zealand the next year, stayed a scant ten months, and never returned home again. She saw her immediate family and her country for the last time in 1913 and she lived the rest of her life at no fixed address in rented rooms and studios, or in digs borrowed from friends in England and France, cobbling a living together and dreaming occasionally of going home. She wrote regularly to her mother, her sister, and, latterly, one brother, grasping familial affection through the mail, but she never saw any of them again. Her letters home (she left no journals) describe the practical side of the painting life as she studied, worked, travelled, and slowly built up an artistic reputation. One gap occurs in the correspondence over the decades. Between the summer of 1911 and the fall of 1912, save for a few letters written in November and December, there is a yawning absence. A family story exists about Rachel Hodgkins burning her younger daughter's letters and for years it was assumed that the entire correspondence had thus perished. In fact, only this brief period is missing, the period when mother and daughter were undergoing a painful transition, which happens to coincide exactly with the period when Emily Carr and Frances Hodgkins met at Concarneau.

We don't know if Hodgkins ever mentioned Carr in her dispatches home, and Carr left few clues about Hodgkins in her journals and letters; only an oblique reference in *Growing Pains* to having studied once with a fine watercolourist who was Australian. "Change of medium, change of teacher, change of environment refreshed me. I put in six weeks of good work under her." Following Carr's death and the publication of her autobiography in

1946, several people made the connection with Frances Hodgkins. Early in 1947, National Gallery officials approached her dealer in London with inquiries, but before anyone could ask Frances Hodgkins what she remembered of Emily Carr, Hodgkins died, leaving the mystery to us. There were those at the time (including Duncan Macdonald of the Lefevre Galleries, which represented Hodgkins latterly, and Harry McCurry, then the director of the National Gallery) who saw a powerful resemblance between the two artists' work and believed Carr to have been deeply influenced by Hodgkins. Yet Carr and Hodgkins were artists with radically different sensibilities who were headed in different directions. Hodgkins was a figure painter who came from an artistic family. Her father, an avid amateur and devotee of J.M.W. Turner, created romantic images of the New Zealand countryside following the well-worked formulas of British water-colour painting. William Hodgkins was active in Dunedin's art society all his life and believed that landscape was the natural theme for New Zealand art. Frances's older sister Isabel painted in the same vein and was considered a precocious talent, which meant that Frances grew up under her shadow. Some have speculated that it was perhaps for that reason that she gravitated originally to figure painting.

Unlike Carr, then, Hodgkins grew up in a house full of art and art talk where there was ample opportunity for her to learn. Although largely self-taught, she went to Europe with some training, some clue about European art history, and a mounting ambition, which, in 1911, seemed to be coming to fruition. Had she remained in France she might well have become a French artist, for she was participating on the periphery of the modernist movement there when the war intervened, forcing her to retreat to England and start over. In England she was destined to become associated with a group of artists half her age who opened British art to the ideas that would dominate twentieth-century Western art. She would become known for her unique combination of landscape and still life, which somehow intertwined interior and exterior spaces through a flattening of perspective, but, most of all, for her colour. "Hers is twilight colour. It's queer and surprising," wrote Eric Newton, the critic at the *Sunday Times*. "She can make certain colours 'sing' as they never have, in particular a certain purplish pink, a most unpromising colour. She makes greys and browns look rapturous." Henry Moore once said that he could tell a Frances Hodgkins at any distance by the colour alone. Hodgkins was in her sixties when she came into her own and a modicum of fame in the 1930s, and she did so in association with painters like Winifred and Ben Nicholson, Cedric Morris, and Graham Sutherland—and sculptors like Moore. The story popular about her then was of the enigmatic artist appearing out of provincial obscurity, producing work of astonishing modernity but in association with no particular school or movement. As Sutherland recalled in the 1960s, "She had without question a moral effect on artists of that day, far more than any other woman artist. She was virtually the only one who was artistically emancipated and already speaking the language which gradually spelt freedom in art. Away from the Academies and the academic tradition." And away from her native land too, he noticed. "One was not conscious at all in her painting that she was a New Zealander. She just seemed to know exactly what she wanted to do."

In England, Hodgkins was certainly accepted, though as a woman and a New Zealander she was the exception to prove the usual rule of exclusion. As she once said, New Zealanders like her could not help becoming denationalized. "It is one of the tragedies of leaving home. New Zealand is too far away; it ceases to be real." In any case, the role of resident outsider in English society suited her purpose, for it gave her a measure of freedom. And the persona she cultivated did seem to transcend nationality. It was not just imperial ignorance speaking in Sutherland's comment; there was a way in which Frances courted ambiguity about her age and background too. She made an art of defying categories. To her fellow artists in England, she seemed to belong nowhere and everywhere; her provenance was ambiguous, just as geography was in her painting. Yet, although she relied on physical surroundings to inspire an ambience, it was people and peopled places she was really drawn to, not the great outdoors.

As an expatriate, Hodgkins became addicted to the foreignness of her adopted continent. As New Zealand art critic Linda Gill has written, the unfamiliar produces a dislocation, which has its own rewards and often lends poignancy to one's vision. Hodgkins always said a change of environment gave her "fresh impulse and new courage and heart," which suggests that her itinerant ways were a strategy for renewal and artistic revelation. Eventually she devised a visual language that captured a sense of the extraordinary hidden in the mundane, recreating the visual innocence of childhood. This is the quality of amazed delight she conjures at the sight of simple things, such as a desiccated tractor rusting in the yard, or cut melons on a table. These later works, says Gill, arouse in the viewer "sensations that are as difficult to describe as the atmosphere of a dream." In them people tend to disappear in favour of crafted objects, which are kept in the foreground, framed by a landscape backdrop. These landscapes elude the stamp of the particular, and cunningly use symbols to do the work. A self-portrait painted in 1941, for example, consists of an arrangement of personal objects—scarves, a beret, a shopping bag—which allowed Hodgkins to avoid describing her physiognomy altogether.

Carr's relationship with the land was, by contrast, unequivocal and her allegiance to it the motivation for her isolation. She felt compelled to live her life on Vancouver Island, which she characterized once as the "edge of nowhere" but which she considered the centre of her psychic universe. If she were to paint, she knew in her bones, it would have to be there. There she waited for the Canadian avant-garde to find her (which it did eventually), and for her creative process to gel. Like Hodgkins, Carr was largely self-taught, although she had a smattering of formal training from her studies in San Francisco and England. Still, she arrived in France a neophyte, lacking Hodgkins's sophistication and self-confidence (not to mention her colonial connections through a banker brother and brother-in-law politician). Perhaps Emily was intimidated by Hodgkins, who was not a person often described as "nice" by acquaintances; strong-willed and sharp-tongued, more likely, which rather describes Emily Carr, too, and therein may lie a story. Perhaps Emily was put off by Hodgkins's self-assurance even while the life her extreme choices produced validated Emily's own. In other words, the memory of Frances may have been more remonstrance than reassurance; a reminder of the path not taken, of the years lost to art. It could have been that Emily liked Hodgkins and aspired to a friendship with her. Their artistic differences might have accommodated a connection; perhaps their temperaments disallowed it. Nevertheless Carr evidently profited from her time with Frances Hodgkins. The art historians suggest it produced a facility with watercolour and a certain dash to her style. If she promptly displaced the memory of Hodgkins, the fact that Hodgkins had committed herself to modernism and to following her own path through to it would in itself have been encouragement to "M. Emily Carr."

However dissimilar their creative impulse and their ultimate destination as artists, Hodgkins's and Carr's stylistic paths did converge in 1911. Hodgkins was the senior artist, but she would have taken Carr for a serious painter and an independent seeker like herself. Carr, who by this time had begun signing her work "M. Emily Carr" to distinguish herself from her mother and her elder sister, presented herself with a certain gravity as the name with its titular "M" implies. She could only have been enchanted by Hodgkins's version of French impressionism, by the canvases that glowed with suffused colour. It wasn't just the ingenious combination of hues that caught people's eye; it was the way Hodgkins seemed able to colour the atmosphere, as if the daylight of Impressionism had been infused into the smouldering shades of Fauvism. "What are the qualities of a good watercolour?" she would ask students. "It should be liquid; it should be transparent and luminous; it should flow."

Carr would indeed have appreciated Hodgkins's intuitive approach, and the fact that, while conversant with contemporary art, she did not preach a theory or ground her own art in one. "My chief aim is not to be beholden to any school but to work out my own salvation in my own way," she told an Australian journalist in 1913. And likewise she shied away from exerting too much influence on students. "Where original talent shows itself, it should be nurtured, not stamped out as often happens from the teacher insisting upon all work being more or less an imitation of his own." She met Carr during a time of intense activity when she was painting with energy and conviction, and her financial affairs were propitious. It was a good time in her life, but it was also a time when her path was becoming clear, and the consequences of her choices coming home to roost. Carr was in the same position, coming to grips with the trade-off she had made between family, art, and social convention. If the encounter between the two women left only a faint trace, it nonetheless occurred at a main juncture in both their lives, during the turbulent passage from apprenticeship to maturity. The fact that both were forty and single is significant, as was their choice of uncompromising independence. By the time of their meeting, they had each resolved to pursue a professional career without the aid of male protection or the comfort of family.

For Hodgkins, the emotional tension revolved primarily around her mother and the expectation that as the unmarried and otherwise unoccupied second daughter in the family, she would come home to take care of Rachel Hodgkins in her dotage. In 1909, Frances was still talking to her mother about plans to take up housekeeping together. She had been writing weekly letters with news of her peregrinations, which were always construed as an adventure that would end some day and bring her back to New Zealand. Two years later, the charade was over. In one of the few letters surviving from 1911, Frances wrote in November telling her mother that upon her return "I will not tag on to Colonial life after staying away so long—surely you don't expect & want me to settle down into a Maiden Aunt do you & throw up career & ambition & lose the precious ground I have gained—you are too dear & unselfish for that I am sure. I am coming out merely to see you & Sis & the children to be with you for a while & then to return to my work like any man of business." It took her years to get to this stage of frankness, and to articulate the obvious but forbidden truth. "But *do* realize Mother that it's on this side of the world that my work & future career lie."

Like Carr, Hodgkins had also had a brush with marriage. His name was Thomas Wilby and Frances met him on the voyage from England in 1903. They courted by mail and agreed to marry in Europe in 1905—and that is all that is known about the engagement, besides the fact that it was broken off and the whole affair suppressed by Hodgkins, who never spoke of it to friends or family. (She did, however, keep Wilby's first letter written to her after he disembarked in Cairo, enclosing a scarab dating from 4000 B.C.) Whatever caused the breach, the emotional tangle undoubtedly taught Hodgkins something about the value of detachment. Historians tell us she thought of herself as unattractive and did not seem to have expected marriage. In her mid-twenties, writing to her sister Isabel, who had recently become engaged, she spoke of "slowly settling down to an oldmaidship" with one prominent idea in mind, "that nothing will interfere between me and my work." Perhaps the attempt to commit herself to wifehood at the age of thirty-seven sobered her into realizing that this really was too narrow a choice for her. She had a future in art, and it looked like that was something she would have to go after on her own. "It must be alone. A woman has no future otherwise," she told her mother in 1907. Six years earlier she had lamented to the contrary, "my art is everything to me—at least at present—but I know it is not the higher life or the right life for a woman. The older I grow the more convinced I am that after all love is everything and one's own people become more precious than all else in the world. To be without ties seems to me to be awful beyond words." Yet now she was repudiating ties, or at least the possibility of creating new ones.

After 1905 Hodgkins never lived closely with other people again, although she had many friends whom she visited and sometimes travelled with. Like everything else in her life, her friends revolved around her art. Most were artists (former students, occasionally patrons) and most, but not all, were women. Surviving letters reveal these friendships as intense and lively, a source of affection and connection. However, Hodgkins's friends were scattered about, often did not know of each other's existence, and frequently slipped out of touch with her when she would heave to and cut herself off in order to turn inward towards her art again. This aspect of her story, the chosen solitude and the refusal of intimacy, is what originally struck biographers. E.H. McCormick, in his book *The Expatriate*, tells the tragic tale of competing demands, the pull of two hemispheres, and the strain of living from hand-to-mouth all her life. There is much talk of Hodgkins's courage and discipline in the face of prolonged adversity. She set her sights on a European career and, by 1911, had successfully established herself in exhibiting circles in London and Paris, showing at the Royal Academy and the New English Art Club on one side of the Channel, and the Société des Artistes Français, the salon of the Société Nationale des Beaux-arts, and the exclusive Société Internationale de la Peinture à l'Eau on the other. Her work had received recognition to the point where real success was not beyond the realm of possibility. And she had, in the meantime, adapted to the rigours of expatriate life on the continent. She spoke the language, knew the customs, and in general felt herself advantaged by her hardy colonial upbringing and robust constitution. Delicate English women, she judged, would hardly be up to the hardships she endured as a matter of course.

A great deal more is known about Emily Carr's romantic history, or at least her rejection of marriage. Emily was happy to see Mayo Paddon when he turned up in England in 1900, a fresh reminder of home, but implacable in her refusal to marry. The story has Emily asking Paddon to forsake her, and because he did love her, he complies. She herself was forsaking respectability in exchange for the freedom to create. She knew that marriage and motherhood would sap the life from her and subsume her art. She was ambivalent and adamant about her choice at the same time, just as Frances Hodgkins was torn about her duty to her mother and her need to stay in Europe. Occasionally Carr worried about the price she paid. "Maybe if I had not killed love I would have had more intensity for the love side in my painting," she wrote in her journal in 1934. But she doesn't question the basic deal with society. She may have missed motherhood, but never marriage. After France, she essentially dropped out, conducting her life with only oblique reference to social norms. She had her own standards and she kept to them. She lived in close proximity to her sisters, who resolutely refused to acknowledge the existence of her art, so her "choice" to make it the centre of her life was not something they were inclined to comprehend or notice. Emily's reaction to their active lack of interest was to "make myself into an envelope into which I could thrust my work deep, lick the flap and seal it from everybody." The origins of Emily Carr's solitude lay with her family, and in the emotional strategy she developed to cope, which was to shut herself off and keep to the margins. Whereas Hodgkins had to do without kin, she had to do without the companionship of other artists or the stimulation of an artistic milieu.

Frances Hodgkins's trade-off with respectability took her to the epicentre of modern art. This was Paris in the twilight of the Belle Époque when Edith Wharton's salon at *18, rue de Varenne* was still in full flower and Alice B. Toklas had just moved in to *27, rue de Fleurus* with Gertrude Stein. It was Stein who once remarked that the twentieth century began the day the Great War started, but in 1911 the forces of modernism were already gathering. A year earlier *Le Figaro* had published the Futurist Manifesto, which called for the destruction of museums and galleries and the eradication of "imprisoning traditions and stultifying formulae." Cubism burst on the scene in its wake, disrupting forever the concept of beauty in Western art, sending critics on the rampage for even worse things to say than they had six years earlier at the debut of the Fauves. The investigations of these iconoclasts led away from nineteenth-century naturalism and romanticism and towards expressive, symbolic, and impressionistic representations of the world. The very terms of art history were contested. History painting, for example, would not survive the turn of the century as Art's most valued genre. Subject matter was de-emphasized as artists became preoccupied with painting itself. And now, for the first time, the image was actually being fractured, dissected, and reassembled before the viewers' eyes.

Despite the declared machismo of the young moderns and their cohorts—the writers, artists, and intellectuals who lived on the Left Bank—the movement included women. Besides Picasso and Braque, there were Laurencin and Valadon. Suzanne Valadon, the illegitimate daughter of a laundress, became an artists' model and from there a self-taught artist and painter of nudes herself; Marie Laurencin, who was associated with the Bâteau Lavoir artists, exhibited with the cubists from 1907 until 1913 and was a lover of the poet Guillaume Apollinaire, who also promoted her work. And besides Eliot and Joyce, there were Stein and Wharton. Gertrude Stein was the great American modernist, and Edith Wharton the self-made woman of letters who, if not in the avant-garde for her writing (*The House of Mirth* was a bestseller in 1911, which Frances Hodgkins recommended to her mother), was definitely part of it for her life as a divorcee and a bohemian. Much was permitted in the *quartier latin* where the *haute monde* and the *demi-monde* intermingled, where foreigners were accepted, and a large expatriate community flourished. Artists and intellectuals who migrated there came for the free society as well as the intellectual ferment; the loosening of taboo and familial tradition permitted sexual and social relationships that would never be tolerated at home. In Paris there was freedom to be homosexual and, just as significantly for women like Frances Hodgkins, there was freedom to be asexual; to be celibate and single, and to refuse traditional feminine roles.

Life in the colonies bred an independence and resourcefulness in women, which won them the vote early in New Zealand (in 1893). At the same time, settler society was too hidebound to afford the margins to accommodate single women living as professional artists. The same was true of Canada. And Edith Wharton left the United States to escape the puritan mind-set and, as she put it, the perversity of American women who refused their freedom. Frances Hodgkins left New Zealand in search of a cosmopolitan milieu and the liberty to paint without interruption. Emily Carr left Canada to find the technique she needed and the moral support of other artists. Unlike Hodgkins and Wharton, it did not occur to Carr to stay on because she did not find Europe personally emancipating. Aesthetically invigorating, yes, but on a personal level she felt constrained and restricted by European social custom as well as cultural difference. If Hodgkins could find a way to pursue her solo project in the middle of France, Carr might well have reasoned that she could pursue hers up on the Skeena River or at Alert Bay.

In the final analysis, Hodgkins was able to adapt to Europe in a way Carr couldn't. This had to do with aesthetics and attitude. Hodgkins was willing to embrace European art and adopt the modern movement as her own; Carr was willing to be influenced by European art, but she kept something of herself back. She retained an oppositional stance to European and English culture, thinking always of herself as an outsider. This may have derived from a cultural and social critique, but it was affected by other concerns, including physical ones. Carr's dislike of cities has always been taken as slightly potty. Though the doctors at the time corroborate the physical symptoms she experienced in London and Paris, scholars and biographers generally represent her illness as psychologically based, the result of hypochondria, if not neurosis. In this she has probably been maligned if only because the possibility of cities being hazardous to ordinary health has not been considered. In fact, while Carr was in France the region around Paris and all through the Loire was afflicted with terrible rains and floods, which led to catastrophic crop failures in 1910 and 1911. This unleashed disease and dislocation; there was mass suffering and fear of an outbreak of typhus. Carr was well advised to leave France in the winter of 1911. Nevertheless it seems to be true that she also experienced a discomfort and disorientation in European cities that others did not. Psychically, as well as physically and culturally, she felt out of tune as well as out of place. In some measure, this stemmed from her attachment to the land in British Columbia, her need for it, and her sense of alienation without it. In this she was quite unlike Frances Hodgkins.

But in another way the two were quite similar, for both were painfully slow starters—plodders, you could call them—who required years to make the transition from student to serious professional. Biographers have often pointed out that Hodgkins did not begin her major work until after her mother's death in 1926. And in Carr's case, they point to 1927, the year that ended the fourteen-year-long interregnum during which she all but withdrew from painting. That year Carr resumed painting with creative fervour, and the following spring she returned to the Native villages, to the art of the Kwakwaka'wakw, the Haida, and the Tsimsian and their great cedar forests. As her work evolved over the ensuing decade, however, she began to focus more and more on the natural world alone, much as the Native carvers did, groping for its essence, intuiting its spirit. So whereas it might be said that the search for modernism galvanized Frances Hodgkins's life and took her from her natal landscape, Carr's connection with her native land took her to modernism. The motivation differed, as did the result.

There is, too, the perennial question about whether Hodgkins belongs to New Zealand or English art history. The answer is unclear. Although an absentee New Zealander for much of her adult life, she remained a foreigner wherever she lived. Moreover, once she abandoned the effort to stay in touch with New Zealand by sending back pictures for exhibition and sale, she dropped out of sight in the art world there, and was not heard from again until after her death. Then she came to public notice in the blare of controversy over a painting called "The Pleasure Garden," which the art gallery in Christchurch refused to accept when it was donated by an anonymous philanthropist. Posthumously Hodgkins became engaged in a fight for modernism against the forces of provincialism. Though initially forgotten in her homeland, Hodgkins's story so symbolized the conflict inherent in New Zealand's cultural history, it was inevitable that she be patriated as a hero. Meanwhile, the woman who helped birth British modernism, who was a legend in her own time in England, vanished from the British record and does not even appear in Germaine Greer's important history of women artists, *The Obstacle Race*. Despite modernism's reverence for individualism, Frances Hodgkins's identity as an artistic loner was and is problematic. As a woman and a colonial, she could make art in England, could even contribute to the advancement of English art, but recognition was fleeting and in the end she was not allowed to make English art history at all.

With Emily Carr there is none of this paradox or confusion. Her connection to Canada is unmistakable and unchallenged, and her posthumous reputation has waxed without interruption. Ultimately, of course, she, too, discovered a language with which to translate her vision, creating images that today are icons. Her renown is rooted in the land, but it is also linked to Native culture. This is perhaps the most significant difference between the two women, for while Frances Hodgkins had likewise turned to the Aboriginal world around her for subject matter early on, she was not rooted in it. By the late 1890s she was exhibiting studies of Otago Natives, which won praise and sold briskly. These were somewhat unusual among contemporary renditions of the Maori by European New Zealanders, being completely devoid of ethnographical detail. Other painters produced portrait studies, focusing on the figure alone without background or setting, but never to the exclusion of all the accoutrements of Aboriginal identity, including the face markings, the *moko*. Divorced from any context, Hodgkins's models float free and anonymous in time, for although they focus on character and expression, they are not portraits of individuals; they are genre pieces in which the subject-individual is rendered as artefact. The women become performers. As McCormick suggests, Hodgkins may have seized on Native women as substitutes for the peasant figures so popular in European art at the time. Whatever the case, her "Maori Madonnas" are of a piece with the theme of mothers and children she was exploring then. And it is easy to see that her artist's eye was seduced by the sumptuous skin tones, which inspired her to experiment with blues and sepias. As simple observations of human life, her Maori women are striking for their vitality, yet they are obviously Europeanized and viewed through a prism of conventional Victorian sentiment. Her interest in the Maori was not entirely casual for all that; she made sketching trips to Moeraki in 1899 and to the Maori heartland of Rotorua in 1904. Yet she did not become curious about the people she was painting, or their culture. Hodgkins remained the tourist and the Maori, incidental subjects she experimented with. They were not an obsession as Native culture was for Carr, much less a key to her vision. The same can be said of her response to the New Zealand landscape, which did not seem to figure in her make-up as an artist. Her attachment to the place she grew up in was not compelling, and it did not hold her. She was wistful about the Maori. Her family she mourned, but New Zealand she scarcely missed as she embraced her self-imposed exile.

The Vancouver Emily Carr returned to in 1911 was a lusty city, prosperous, new, and filled with dreams. Built on the green-gold of the forest and the strength of the thousands who came at the sound of opportunity knocking, it had burst into being. In the space of twenty-five years following the arrival of the Canadian Pacific Railway, the population quadrupled; the city quickly outstripped Victoria, establishing itself as the business and industrial centre of the region. As it did, the polyglot character of the old mill town was radically altered. Women arrived in large numbers with their men, and families replaced the shifting population of unattached transients. Asians and First Nations peoples, originally significant minorities, were further marginalized in the workforce and segregated, at times through legal pronouncements such as the 1893 by-law restricting laundries to the Chinatown district. And after 1887, when an angry mob ransacked the shanties of Chinese workers in Coal Harbour and the chief of police ordered the Indian rancherie at Hastings Mills cleared, there were repeated attacks on these two communities by the White majority. You could say the city was built on the CPR and racism. B.C. politicians clamoured for an end to Oriental immigration, newspapers decried the "Yellow Peril," and in 1907 a large and angry mob smashed its way through Chinatown and Japantown. In March 1913, after years of pressure from the ever-expanding White population, the Squamish "agreed" to leave their village on Kitsilano Point at the south end of Burrard Bridge, much as the Songhees in Victoria had, but with a major difference—the complete absence of due process. Eying the waterfront property and the growing affluence of the adjacent residential communities, the provincial government under Premier Richard McBride took action, summarily ordering Natives to gather their belongings and report to the dock at a certain hour on a given day. There each family was offered a cash settlement as they boarded a barge to be taken across the bay to North Vancouver. Only eighteen families accepted the money, but the government took over all the land and torched the houses and barns left behind anyway. That year Vancouver's population passed the 100,000 mark, and the tide of economic prosperity peaked.

With rapid urbanization came homogenization, and with development capital came respectable society—Anglo-British, Anglican, and White. These were the golden days of the *cartes de visites* when corseted matrons in plumed chapeaux chaperoned a city otherwise preoccupied with speculation and easy money. As the settlement put down roots, it put up barriers along class and ethnic lines, clearing the shack dwellers off the foreshores in the 1890s, restricting relief to "proper" citizens, treating all non-Whites—and even some Whites, such as the Italians—as "foreigners" and "outsiders." Vancouver society became status conscious and civic minded with a vengeance. The stately architecture of edifices like the marble-columned Dominion Trust building at Hastings and Cambie—a fourteen-storey, steel-framed structure completed in 1909 and briefly the tallest building in the British Empire—proclaimed its self-assurance and high-minded public ethos. Likewise the beautification movement, which held sway among the city's middle classes, mixed civic pride with a dollop of reformism, promising to clean up the industrial blight while civilizing the general public. The City Beautiful movement's moment of glory came in 1912 when a plebiscite was called over a proposed electric tramway through Stanley Park, the 960-acre wilderness expanse at the edge of First Narrows on Burrard Inlet. The City Beautiful Association, along with the Local Council of Women and the parks commissioners, opposed the tramline and championed a vision that would keep the park "as natural as possible," excluding commercial sports but providing tennis courts, a bowling green, and a children's playground. The blue- and white-collar workers who had originally petitioned City Hall for transit to the park were outflanked; their affluent West End neighbours were more concerned about what would happen once they got there, fearing rowdy behaviour and overcrowding. They argued for a park with limited access, and they carried the vote.

The same public spirit shot with self-interest marked the inauguration of the arts in the city. The first effort to establish a civic art gallery was made by a group of prominent citizens who appealed to City Hall in 1890 for space to house it, only to be rebuffed with the comment that "art was for the rich." The alderman who said that had a point, as most members of the group were wealthy and well connected. And the same could be said of several other arts organizations that were founded at the time: the

Vancouver Operatic and Dramatic Society, the Women's Musical Club, the Vancouver Museum (which opened in 1905), and even the Studio Club, which hired Emily Carr to teach its members in 1906. As Carr discovered, the arts were organized more for social than for artistic or cultural reasons, and usually with the edification of the masses in mind—as in "We, the educated and refined, will set standards by patronizing the right art in the name of the public." And just like other Canadian cities, the right art in Vancouver was the theatre, opera, art, and music of Britain and Europe, not the work of local playwrights or composers. It would be decades before Canadian artists were given credence or attention. Moreover, as the flood of immigrants into the Lower Mainland was mainly British, public life in Vancouver emphasized British custom more and more, and continued to harbour an aversion to things Canadian, including Canadian art. There was, of course, a predilection for music and art practised as social graces, so the city was not without its cadre of amateur musicians and painters working in derivative styles with conservative techniques. It was one of colonialism's ironies that in order to escape the hold of the Old World in the New, Carr and others like her found it necessary to return to the Old.

In those days, few serious artists garnered any success without patronage. A partial exception to that rule was the poet Pauline Johnson, who lived the last three years of her life in Vancouver, having built a career as a recitalist touring back and forth across Canada, performing in costume and dramatizing her Mohawk heritage for non-Native audiences. In 1909, Johnson gave up the circuit and settled into an apartment on Howe Street within walking distance of Stanley Park. She began writing for the local newspapers, collaborating in the retelling of stories of the Squamish people with Chief Joe Capilano, whom she first met while she was on tour in London in 1906 and he had led a delegation to petition the King over land claims. But the income from writing was scarcely enough to keep her, and when she fell ill with breast cancer, her situation became perilous. A group of friends in the

Women's Press Club discreetly raised money and facilitated the publication of *Legends of Vancouver* in 1911. Ultimately, the Women's Canadian Club and the Imperial Order of the Daughters of the Empire (which renamed theirs the Pauline Johnson Chapter) took up her cause, and for the last months of her life, Pauline Johnson was nurtured by the good ladies of Vancouver's upper crust. When she finally died in March 1913, flags flew at half-mast in the city. There was a huge public funeral at Christ Church Cathedral attended by the city's most prominent men and women, including the mayor, who followed the funeral cortège through hushed streets. By special arrangement, and through the intercession of the governor general, the Duke of Connaught (who had met Johnson when she was a seven-year-old and he was made a chief of the Six Nations in a ceremony led by her father), the federal government allowed her ashes to be buried in Stanley Park.

Pauline Johnson was a literary celebrity, but she was also a cultural conundrum. As a child she had watched her father moving between two worlds and two cultures with ease and dignity. He spoke English, German, and French, as well as six Native languages, and she was proud of his renown beyond the reserve. Pauline herself grew up the consummate anglophile, yet by Canadian law she was a full-blooded Indian. Unlike Amelie Douglas and the vast majority of Métis children whose mothers were Native and fathers were White, her father was Native, so the entire family was considered Indian, including her mother, who came from Bristol. Emily Howells's bourgeois family was appalled by her marriage to George Johnson, but Johnson faced the opposition of both his mother and his community. "Marrying out" meant he forfeited the right to pass on his title to his son. "Marrying in," from Emily Johnson's vantage point, was marrying not only a man of means and experience, but an aristocrat in his own society.

Pauline inherited many of her mother's class aspirations, but at the same time she was her father's daughter. Although she lived among Whites all her adult life and ardently cultivated her appearance as an English lady, she never denied her Native origins; on the contrary, she celebrated Native life in her poetry, and was lionized in the White world as "the Mohawk Princess," Tekahion-wake. She spoke for her father's people, explaining and representing them to her mother's, and she took on that interpretative role consciously. In her day-to-day life, though, she did not evidently participate in Aboriginal affairs, and counted few Native people among her close friends and colleagues. The men she was associated with, her managers and collaborators, and the man she wanted to marry, were all White. Caught up in this world, a Native woman trying to make a career in a White man's world, her attitude towards Indians was predictably ambivalent. Her reason for opposing enfranchisement, for example, was that Native people were not yet ready for it. In retrospect, it is obvious that she fulfilled the longing of mainstream White Canadians for a romantic, guilt-free and safely distant image of Native peoples to embrace. And she was undoubtedly trapped by the public's desire. According to the Toronto *Globe* in 1892, listening to Johnson was like listening to "the voice of the nations that once possessed this country, who have wasted away before our civilization, speaking through this cultured, gifted, soft-voiced descendant." She became the embodiment of the imaginary Indian.

A month after Pauline Johnson's funeral, Emily Carr rented the Dominion Hall on Pender Street and held a week-long exhibition of her Indian paintings. It was a major undertaking that involved framing and hanging close to 200 works, arranging publicity notices, and greeting the people who showed up. Some of the paintings, which included both oils and watercolours, dated from her early trips to Ucluelet and Alaska, from her forays up island to Campbell River and Alert Bay, and inland to Lytton and Hope in 1908 and 1909. Most were painted after France and based on her first trip back to Alert Bay and north to the Skeena River and Haida Gwaii in 1912. There had also been excursions to Native communities on the Sechelt Peninsula, and in and around Victoria and Vancouver before 1911, so obviously the prohibition against lone White women visiting reserves no longer held her back. In one sense, Carr was following Pauline Johnson's lead in looking to Native culture for a subject and a setting for her art, and she, too, worked within a thoroughly European idiom. Her paintings were poems of a different order, but they likewise appealed to a sentimental taste for the primitive, which deracinated Native culture. Carr would have known about Pauline Johnson and probably read her stories in the *Province*. She would have felt some sympathy for Johnson's purpose in retelling old legends as she herself was embarking on the project of documenting Aboriginal culture and presenting it to the White world. Yet there is no evidence she paid serious attention to Johnson or read her poetry, although we know Carr was an assiduous reader of verse. Carr's journals and notebooks reveal her infatuation with Tennyson and later, Walt Whitman, whom she habitually quotes. Although she was not a wide reader, the absence of any reference to Johnson is interesting and possibly indicative of Carr's attitude. On a personal level, she would have disliked Johnson's ingratiating attitude to society, but Johnson would equally have found Emily rough, and, were she to overlook the eccentricities, rather common. Would Native art have been a shared interest between them? Would Johnson have approved of Carr's project? Did Carr's doubts have something to do with her lack of interest in Johnson's poetry? Johnson had a huge following and was ardently admired as Carr was to be. And yet, despite their differences, Canadian culture has absorbed the work of both women in much the same way and for the same reason, treating the Aboriginal content as folkloric expression and the art as fodder for the newcomers' creation story.

Ucluelet started something that evolved slowly in Carr's imagination. Even before she left for Paris, her journey as Klee Wyck had begun. When she returned to Canada in 1911, she rented a studio apartment on West Broadway in Vancouver and started planning to resume her travels almost immediately. She was also eager to find an audience and invited the public to an open house to view the work she had done abroad. The response was mixed, but from Carr's point of view, discouraging. The *Province* carried a genial notice with quotes from an interview with her in its section on women's activities and interests, which was par for the course. Then a few days later, it published a long, anonymous letter damning Carr's work and the impertinence of her attempt to improve on the Almighty (and, it would seem, the almighty canon). Carr countered with equal conviction. "Pictures should be inspired by nature, but made in the soul of the artist," she wrote, noting that no two individuals could behold the same thing and express it the same way either in words or in paint. She defended modern art with her own experience. "A casual glance at exhibitions of paintings is not enough to form an opinion; one must live amongst it, give it serious study before one can understand the whys and wherefores of the newer work. I did not take to it at first. It was only after months of careful deliberation and comparison that I found in the new work what I had long been seeking." Accused of having betrayed her talent for a style that was "nothing but the work of an excited and vitiated imagination," she answered: "Contrary to my having 'given up my inspirations' I have only just found them, and I have tasted the joys of the new. I am a Westerner and I am going to extract all I can . . . out of the big, glorious west. The new ideas are big and they fit this big land."

She seemed to enjoy the debate, though the anonymity of the author (whom the paper would of course have known, and whom she addresses as "he") may have rankled. The unsigned letter, easy to dismiss as cowardly, she may have found ominous. She was stung, say the biographers, but hardly because of this single letter. More probably it was because she had heard the same criticism on the lips of others, friends and strangers alike, and sensed it in the silence of those, like her sisters, who pointedly avoided the topic. The paper's response to Carr's work in this period was

generally positive, although art was usually covered as an extension of society news and the *Province* was as likely to comment on
Miss Emily Carr's health and her travel plans as her paintings. The
criticism she felt the most—and remembered the longest—was the
informal variety that came from her peers, artists, and cultivated
people. Not that she was alone in her modernist proclivities; there
were a few other artists travelling the same road away from the
traditionalism and realism, and she had moral support from a
handful of women like Statira Frame, Ann Batchelor, and
Margaret Wake. The senior artist in their midst was Sophie
Pemberton, who had scored great success in Europe and been
voted an associate member of the Royal Canadian Academy of the
Arts in 1906. But by 1911, Pemberton was long gone. She married
in 1908, left the country, and abandoned painting.

Meanwhile, as sales and private students dwindled, the old job
Carr had teaching at the Crofton House School for girls failed to
materialize as she had expected. According to her biographer
Maria Tippett, Carr also ran afoul of the British Columbia Society
for Fine Arts at this juncture. In April two of the ten pictures she
submitted for the spring exhibition were rejected. Carr rightly
suspected that her non-representational leanings were the cause;
in the eyes of many, she had gone "violently modern," and some
of her works were too much for the hanging committee. Although
she was a founding member of the society and had exhibited in its
first three shows (with the largest number of works on view in the
first and the second), she reacted instantly to the rebuff, withdrew
all her work and resigned forthwith. The society had been set up
in 1908 by a small group of twenty artists who saw themselves as
professionals in need of an organization that would exert some
standards as well as mount exhibitions to promote art to the
public. Unlike the slightly older Studio Club, which catered to
amateur artists and held open shows, the society's exhibitions
were juried. To Carr, the insult of having her paintings judged and
found wanting merited treatment in kind, and she is reputed to
have included a nasty note to the executive along with her resig-

nation. No doubt the gesture seeded her reputation as a testy character, given to extremes. In any case, it served notice to other artists that she was prepared to go it alone rather than to be held to account by people "whose ideals and views have been stationary for the past twenty years." As spring progressed, Carr became absorbed with her plans and preparations for an extended trip North. She was eager to get back to her "silent Indians." In early July she set off with her dog Billie, a portable easel, and a pack full of materials, heading for the Skeena River, Haida Gwaii, and Alert Bay, just off the northeastern tip of Vancouver Island.

The journey she was now undertaking was arduous and accomplished by a combination of conveyances—steamboat, motor launch, cart, and train. Mainly she travelled via standard routes; only at the far reaches of her itinerary did she rely on Native canoe, and only when she went to the old sites and abandoned villages was she was alone with Native peoples. There were Whites pretty well everywhere she stayed, although they were often a minority, and at various way stations she was helped by family connections—a niece in Port Essington and missionary friends of another niece who had taught at New Masset. Nevertheless, for most of her trip Emily was on her own. She was accompanied by guides, drivers, and other passengers as she made her way, but she worked alone. And the work was hard that summer; it meant braving bad weather to get to places where she could see the old poles and then battling slugs, nettles, and mosquitoes to sketch the carvings in detail. Back in Vancouver her pace didn't slacken. She set about painting a series of oils based on her fieldwork; about three dozen new paintings were completed in anticipation of the April exhibition. At the same time, the project committed her to educating herself about the carvings and what they represented, so she visited the ethnology collection at the Vancouver Museum and consulted books explaining the meaning of totems, and she may have talked to Native peoples she met along the way. In those sketches executed on-site with time breathing down her neck, Carr tended to restrain her expansive

French manner, sticking close to detail as if recognizing the new style wouldn't always suit. She kept the vivid Fauve palette, however, and these early works stand out as a group for their chromatic brilliance, as well as the fact that they focus on the giant carvings which are often depicted in abandoned villages where the flux of community life has been replaced by the chaos of nature reclaiming her own. Though the emphasis was reserved for the poles and the landscape surrounding them, human figures were occasionally included in the middle distance when she sketched in living villages.

Carr conceived of her endeavour as a preservation project that she had undertaken for others—for history, for the Indians, for posterity—but now she was faced with the question of what to do with it. In the fall of 1912 she approached the provincial government through the minister of education with the proposal that the collection be purchased for the new Legislative Library being built in Victoria. She had heard that an art gallery was being planned as part of it, and she saw her Indian collection as a natural addition. The story is a curious one, for her suggestion was not dismissed out-of-hand. C.F. Newcombe, a well-known collector and dealer in Native artefacts, was detailed to visit Carr and make a report to the curator of the Provincial Museum. Dr. Newcombe was a retired medical doctor, an amateur botanist, and a self-taught ethnologist who had fashioned a career as an expert on Northwest Coast culture. At the time he was in the midst of amassing a collection for the Provincial Museum as well as being a buyer for several other institutions. Newcombe's experience with Native culture was thus as part of the trade in artefacts, which coincided with the great age of museum building in Europe and North America. As Maria Tippett suggests, the minister and his officials were curious about Carr and took her for a likely collector, perhaps assuming, with some justification, that any White person travelling through Native communities to look at poles and carvings would surely acquire some artefacts for themselves if not others. Newcombe's opinion of the paintings, however, was not

"Skidegate" (shark pole), dated 1912 and painted by Carr following her first trip to Haida Gwaii.

particularly positive. They were accurate renderings, he reported, but Carr's painterly qualities got in the way of the documentary purpose. The scale of the poles was ambiguous, the impasto technique crude at close inspection, and the colours too brilliant to be real. His report allowed that these "deficiencies" could be corrected "under proper supervision," and that Carr might produce backdrops for museum collections, like ones he knew of at the Brooklyn Museum and the American Museum in New York. He referred to these as "decorative wall paintings," and seemed unclear about the difference between a diorama, which is meant to be a reconstruction of the past, and Carr's paintings, which were painted directly from life. Without knowing it, Newcombe put his finger on the central tension in Emily's work at this stage. Although he mistook the impressionist brush for ineptitude, his assessment that the paintings were half art and half illustration was nonetheless valid. She was mixing genres. But his assessment was telling for what he *didn't* mention, and that was Carr's grand concept of the project. In her mind it involved more than reclaiming the monuments of a "passing people"; it also meant claiming them as Canadian, and it was because of this that she sought provincial backing.

Taking stock of her situation that winter, Emily must have realized her work would not command the requisite scientific credibility for a public sale. Neither the purchase nor the funding to help her complete the task were forthcoming, and she would have to look elsewhere. Meanwhile, Dr. Newcombe became a friend. He purchased three sketches and told her he admired her drawings, presumably keeping the advice he'd given the museum to himself. She may never have known his true opinion. We know she herself worried that the documentary demands of the project were eclipsing her artistic purpose. (Interestingly, this issue was raised in connection with Pauline Johnson, whom critics and other writers accused of sacrificing art in pursuit of an audience.) If Carr did perchance have conversations with Frances Hodgkins about the issue, and if Frances Hodgkins pressed her about it, those words would have come back to Emily in these months. It is known that she showed some "Indian sketches" to Harry Gibb, who encouraged her to use the motif, making the comment one day when the discussion turned to the critics, "Your silent Indian will teach you more than all the art jargon." The avant-garde had discovered the formal properties of African art by this time, so there was precedent among modernists for what Emily Carr was doing. It remained a question of the balance she could strike between the contrary purposes of history and art. It is easy to see that Carr's motivation came in part from a desire to have a legitimate artistic purpose, it being easier to paint for history than for herself, and easier to justify a socially acceptable art to herself as well to her sisters. It is also true that while she continued exhibiting with the Studio Club through 1912 and attracted the friendship of a handful of sympathetic artists, there was no rush of public support from other artists for her or the new ideas she was expressing. The debate ended before it began. Meanwhile, sales were negligible. Newcombe's interest in her work, it seems, was an anomaly, just as his appreciation for Native art was. Few people in Victoria and Vancouver would have given house room to a Van Gogh or a Gauguin at this time, but no one was ready for the sight of totem poles on the parlour walls. An evening of Pauline Johnson reciting "The Legend of Qu'Appelle" at the Pender Auditorium was one thing; living with "Indian grotesques" was something else.

From Carr's notes for the "Lecture on Totems" she presented to the public, it is clear that she wanted to counter such convictions and was conscious that her depiction of Indian country differed from the norm. She spoke of the people she met as individuals and recounted her experience with them in positive terms, although her interactions with Native peoples were not clear of misunderstandings. She was, for instance, accused of stealing poles by painting them and asked to leave two villages. Still, she found the people approachable and honest. She could leave her painting gear about without fear that anything would be swiped, and she said she could never do the same with White children around. She told her audience that she considered it a privilege to be taken into the confidence of a Native person "for they are and have good reason for being suspicious of the whites." In describing her travels to Native communities, moreover, she spoke as a visitor who assumes the best of her hosts and attempts to suspend judgement about their odd ways. She shows herself more willing to be critical of White behaviour in the Native world than of Native custom, strange as it was to her. She refers once to a scene of people sitting around the fire, dipping their spoons into some "disgusting concoction," but otherwise steers clear here of the popular subject of Native hygiene and living habits. And in what would have been most singular for the time, she describes the passing relationships with local Native people in terms of friendship. When her presence or her sketches gave offence, she reports "with a little tact and jollying on my part and even, at times, a present of a duplicate sketch we have always become best of friends." She was both exaggerating and speaking in code here, for these people did not become friends, except in the sense of displaying good faith and accepting her genteelly. She established cordial relations by ingratiating herself and displaying a willingness to be open about what she was doing so that she was allowed to remain and even to join their company. Moreover, Carr had also experienced cross-cultural friendship by this time. Apart from casual acquaintances she made while visiting reserves, she had formed a friendship with a Squamish woman named Sophie Frank, whom she met in 1906 when she moved to Vancouver. They visited back and forth, Emily taking the motor launch across Burrard Inlet to visit Sophie on the North Vancouver reserve where the two would drink tea and tell stories. From the time they met, Emily felt a special attachment to Sophie, and they remained friends until Sophie's death in 1939.

To say that Emily Carr was more tolerant and solicitous towards Native peoples and their culture than her own contemporaries is not to say that she was unscathed by the racial prejudice present in her own background, nor did she leave all of her opinions behind in Victoria. There is an air of condescension in her language, in the repeated use of the word "dignity" to describe Native custom and character, for instance, in her constant use of the word "Indian" to prefix Native names, and in the assumption that civilization marches to an evolutionary drum such that the fading of some cultures and the disappearance of others is projected as part of the natural course of events. "The poles behind me are relics of the West's first primitive greatness," she told her audience, suggesting that they ought to be venerated by Canadians as relics of an ancient civilization, like Stonehenge is by the Britons. Far from being treasured, she continues, the ancient poles lie rotting in the woods, or are being hauled off to museums. The people know not what they have achieved, and White people don't recognize their own part in the story. "Native people are becoming ashamed of them fearing that white people whom they are anxious to resemble will regard them as paganish and will laugh at them. They are threatening to burn them."

By 1913, Carr had become conversant with the basic approaches being used by museums and anthropologists in the study and classification of ethnographic materials. In her lecture she liberally quotes Charles Hill-Tout, a well-known ethnologist who was then president of the Vancouver Museum, drawing on his and Newcombe's knowledge of Native culture. Her text follows the already established conventions of ethnographic writing, describing artefacts and elaborating on the legends and practices associated with them (as reported usually by the family owners). The anomaly was her addition of personal anecdote alongside the scientific account. Here, for the first time, she publishes the story of Klee Wyck, a nickname she had adopted in England among friends whom she had regaled with her "Indian tales." Here, too, she recounts experiences she had staying in Native villages: how, for example, people became fascinated by her drawings, having seen photographs before but never someone making "real" images by hand, and how, before leaving, she would tack up all her pictures on the wall of a house so everyone could view what she had done. While displaying uncommon interest in and respect for Native peoples and their cultures, she had nevertheless absorbed the prevailing concept of Aboriginal societies as "primitive" in comparison to the achievement of White culture. The term appears on the first page of her text and thus frames the whole of it. This was not a new concept, of course, nor was it the invention of anthropology and art history. It was as widespread as colonialism. What was novel, at least in Canada, was her alliance of Aboriginal art with modern art. Gauguin had introduced the motif of primitivism to European painting in the 1890s, removing himself to the South Seas (Tahiti) in pursuit of the subject and the full-scale experience of the exotic, erotic Other. Then came Picasso's discovery of African sculpture as a source of modernist form and stylistic inspiration in 1906, his epiphany recorded in the faces of his *Demoiselles d'Avignon.* Carr's work reflected these cross-currents, and it distinguished itself from the "Indian" paintings of earlier artists who recorded Aboriginal art as detail, and part of the subject matter. To her, Aboriginal art was a source of artistic inspiration.

Although the documentary project began to take shape after her 1907 trip to Alaska and before her trip to France, there is no question that Carr's concept of it was altered by her second, and successful, experience in Europe. She came back with an appreciation of primitive art, heightened by the desire to incorporate the techniques of modernism and her own artistic sensibility into her "Indian" work. As she also pointed out in her lecture, she did not work from photographs but studied the poles in their original settings and was, as it were, personally acquainted with each of them. Despite the physical difficulties in getting to the sites and the constraints that required that she work with dispatch, she had striven for an artistic dimension, a "something plus," which distinguishes art from mere reproduction.

Carr's 1913 exhibition was an extraordinary event that might have been a landmark in Canadian art history had the public risen to the occasion and her lecture been seriously considered. This is the case made by art historian Gerta Moray in her study of Carr's early work, the so-called Indian paintings, which comprised the painted record of Native villages and carvings. It was the largest and most ambitious show ever staged in Vancouver by a single artist. Individuals did occasionally exhibit solo in those days, but this was usually in storefronts like Bishop's Art Store, or Hicks & Lovicks Pianos. Never before had anyone rented a hall—in this case, the same one the Studio Club rented for its annual show—to mount a professional-scale exhibition of his (never mind her) own work. At the same time, as Moray points out, the sight of a White woman artist inserting herself into the debate about Native affairs, challenging received opinion on the basis of her own experience and expertise, was unprecedented. It was all the more daring because Native/White relations were then in flux. Indeed, several of the places Carr visited in 1912 were hotspots in the ongoing resistance of Native peoples to the imposition of reserves and the reduction of their entitlements. In the circumstances, there is reason to imagine that Carr could have had some influence on her contemporaries. However, her exhibit demonstrates the opposite. It seems not to have made any impact at all; neither the art nor the lecture stirred up any controversy or instigated any debate. This must have been a devastating anticlimax, considering the enormity of the effort and expenditure. More than anything else, the silence of her colleagues hurt; it would have felt like repudiation, which is more cutting than dismissal. Carr had begun advancing herself as a fully fledged professional artist before her departure for France in 1910. Just as she adopted the name Klee Wyck and used it both as a mask to hide behind and as a character to enact, so she had taken her signature "M. Emily Carr" as a sobriquet and invested it with larger meaning. It stood in for her public self and artistic persona, and she wrapped herself in it. Writes Moray, "In the face of what she managed to do, the failure of local professional and governmental circles to endorse her project, accompanied by the public's inability to understand her vision, were severe blows to her self-esteem and her prospects of earning a living as an artist." Still, the failure does not seem to have caught Carr by surprise. Although she scarcely mentions the event in her writings, it is apparent she was devising a backup plan all winter, having decided to build a small apartment building on her share of the family property in Victoria. As the inevitable failure loomed, she soured on Vancouver. Shortly after the exhibition came down, she packed up her paintings, her animals, and belongings and turned her back on the city. But the question lingers: What was the world Emily Carr eulogized in her paintings and why was it an anathema to White people? What was the real history of the "disappearing Indians"?

Alert Bay, 1991

The ferry from Port McNeill docks at the government wharf on Cormorant Island, right in the centre of the community. The town of Alert Bay lies to the right as you get off the boat, the reserve and the Native community to the left. Following instructions, I take the road to the right to find the Nimpkish hotel. I find it past the cemetery, rough and weather-beaten and looking its age, which is pushing seventy. I also find Phil, the manager, who gives me a room with a view over the moss-covered roof of the hotel bar. I had called ahead to make a reservation, which seemed to surprise him. "Sure there'll be a room for you," he coughed into the phone. Phil looks like the place: angular and rustic, edging towards seedy, your basic one-star establishment with a heart of brass. He hands me two keys—one for the room and the other for the outside door—after telling me to stay as long as I like. "In case I'm not around, you can let yourself in," he explains. Management is informal, I guess, especially during fishing season. I soon discover that management is usually good for a cup of Styrofoam coffee, too, and often to be found in the bar below where a stream of people pass through the day to shoot pool, croon with the jukebox, or drink beer. It doesn't take long to figure the place for a landmark. A photograph on the wall records the day in 1925 when the building was barged over from the reserve end of the island, where it originally stood opposite the Indian agent's office. Liquor laws prohibited a beer hall on reserves, *ergo* the entire hotel was moved, or so the story goes.

After dinner I descend to the bar to make some calls. The rooms aren't equipped with phones, although there is satellite-fed cable TV and, when I return to my room, a space heater the size of a refrigerator, which Phil has rustled up. (I had asked for an extra blanket.) Next morning I drop around to thank him and find him holding court. To meet Phil, first of all, is to meet Max, a large and placid black-and-tan Dobermann pinscher who occasionally acts as security. Mostly he guards Phil. After Max comes Ken, the town's retired druggist, and Hector, one of its many taxi drivers. Ken shows up early, ready for the day of drinking coffee and trading barbs with Phil. He is affable and full of stories and in no time I hear how he homesteaded in Saskatchewan before the war, took vets' pay to study pharmacy afterwards, and then came west where he had a helluva time getting someone to apprentice him even though the salary was subsidized. "Go back to the Prairies where you came from!" he was told. But he didn't, and in the 1970s he migrated to Alert Bay. His great folly is gambling. "Dropped about eighty grand on the ponies over the years and still dabbling," he tells me. And his great chagrin is not having planned for retirement. "It's too easy to sit around here and do nothing." Ken isn't the only one I hear that from. Alert Bay is full of people who came to visit and forgot to leave. Phil says he came to help out a friend doing night-duty at the hotel twenty-five years ago.

I head over to the café for bacon, eggs, and coffee, and then pass by Leo's boat to see if he's there. I've come with introductions from a friend who was once married to him and lived here in the bay. Instead of waiting, I take a long walk along the beach where the kindergarten kids from the Native school are combing the foreshore for treasures left behind by the tide. The broom along the banks is in fragrant flower and birds are everywhere; a loon fishing thirty feet from shore, eagles hovering about like gulls, comfortable with human proximity as they never are farther south where I live. I watch a pair of violet-green swallows building a nest in the eaves of the U'mista Cultural Centre, the community museum newly built in the old tradition with huge cedar beams and boards. The front end facing the sea is painted with the images of a killer whale and a thunderbird, which are visible as you round the corner of the island and head into the deep bay formed by its crescent shape. Here, in the most beautiful setting imaginable—and a strategic one, you can't help noticing, with its commanding view of Johnstone Strait—Natives and newcomers have lived next to each other in roughly equal numbers for most of the century. Looming behind the centre is the old residential school, a depressing monstrosity built in regulation red brick that has been painted white in an effort to brighten the mood and perhaps placate the ghosts. The band office is located there now and the school is housed in temporary buildings ranged alongside. An old-fashioned school bell rings the end of recess and the children scamper up the shore into class.

Late in the morning I return with a picnic lunch and the small telescope I use for watching wildlife and the sea. Some older children are out collecting seaweed. Their teacher tells me this is the time of year to gather and dry it to eat with clams and such throughout the winter. I take turns with them watching a great blue heron through the 'scope. Carefully, as though the rocks were hurting her feet, the heron stalks up the beach with an eel squirming and twisting in her beak; she drops it, pokes at it, lifts it up and finally angles the creature into position. Whoosh—down the long neck it disappears. Then back she goes at a stately gait for another. The children chatter in English and tell me they learn Kwakwala in school, and at the U'mista Cultural Centre where the elders teach them to sing and dance.

There is, I know, a story to the centre beginning with the name, U'mista. As the Kwakwaka'wakw explain in the centre's brochure, "In earlier days, people were sometimes taken captive

Beach beside the U'mista Centre at Alert Bay, May 1991.

by raiding parties. When they returned home, either through payment of ransom or by retaliatory raid, they were said to have *u'mista*. The aims of the U'mista Cultural Society are the *u'mista* of our history, our language and our culture." So *u'mista* is about the captives' return, about restitution. Moreover, it seems things can have *u'mista* as well as people. Inside on display are objects that were captured and held for ransom for sixty long years until they were returned—the masks, rattles, and whistles of the Kwak-waka'wakw of Alert Bay and their relatives in neighbouring communities, artefacts that were confiscated during the infamous potlatch trials of 1922. They are the reason the centre was built. A law had been on the books banning the feasts since 1884, but what the Indian Act intended the courts could not deliver until 1922 when forty-nine people were convicted for participating in Dan

Cranmer's potlatch on Village Island the previous December. The word "potlatch" is actually a misnomer even though it is still widely used today. It derives from the word "to give" in Chinook—the lingua franca used on the coast until well into the twentieth century, which was an amalgam of several Native languages, French, and English—and it refers to one aspect of traditional feasting, the extravagant giving of gifts. However, the term is now used indiscriminately to refer to a vast array of ceremonies, events, and transactions. In the White world these would roughly correspond to the justice system, the treasury (banks), government, the public archives, social services, the Church, and Christmas. Yet such a list is barely accurate, save as an indication of the centrality of the potlatch and its character as a social register and cultural institution. It was certainly a great deal more than a huge party thrown by a man for the purpose of giving away all his wealth, which is how the feast was generally characterized by settlers. The White authorities, such as the Indian agent and the Anglican minister in Alert Bay, understood it little better despite their claims of expertise. Nevertheless, they were correct in sensing that it lay at the heart of the culture. "All their ideas centre on the potlatch," proclaimed Indian Agent William Halliday of the Kwawkewlth district. "Break it and you break the hold of heathenism on the people."

The reasons marshalled against the potlatch by the authorities were all over the map. The damage alleged was economic, moral, and sanitary, as well as religious. The feasting, it was said, encouraged sloth and dissolute behaviour, the ruinous expenditure of money, the neglect of children and the old (while the festivities were going on), and the prostitution of women to acquire potlatch goods. "In my time about fifty women under twenty-five years of age have died, all of them sacrificed to maintain the potlatch," wrote Reverend A.J. Hall from Alert Bay to the *Victoria Daily Colonist* in March 1896. The purpose of the 1922 prosecution thus was unequivocal. The Department of Indian Affairs termed the seizure of the objects a voluntary surrender, secured along with an undertaking by the defendants and their communities that they would renounce the practice. This was arranged by the lawyers and White officials as a kind of plea bargain, where the objects were relinquished in exchange for suspended sentences. Not all the Kwakwaka'wakw could be persuaded to cooperate, though, so twenty-two men and four women served two to four months in Oakalla prison in Burnaby. Dan Cranmer's wife, Emma Cranmer (Zoh-la-lee-tlee-louq), for whom the feast was called, fed and cared for the prisoners before and after the trials; she followed the convicted to jail and, when they were released, put them up and paid their expenses back north. She even attempted to serve the prison sentences of the women, particularly Florence Knox, who was an elderly grandmother with a sick husband.

Meanwhile, the Indian agent, William Halliday, took a scow and rounded up artefacts from Cape Mudge (on Quadra Island), Village Island, and the communities in between, including the Namgis (Nimpkish) community in Alert Bay. He itemized the 450 pieces, which were eventually packed off in seventeen crates to Ottawa, though not before he sold thirty-five items for $290 to a seasoned American collector named George Heye, the man who founded the Museum of the American Indian in New York. Halliday was reprimanded for this, ostensibly because his superiors did not want to see more ethnographic material leaving Canada. In reality, they had other plans. Halliday's mistake was to assume the artefacts would be sold for serious money. The bulk of the collection was deposited without sale in the Victoria Memorial Museum in Ottawa and the Royal Ontario Museum in Toronto, neither of which had much Northwest Coast material in their collections at the time. In addition, a few items were kept by the deputy superintendent general of Indian Affairs for his personal use. A token $1,495 was then paid in compensation for the objects, although it appears the monies were never paid out to the owners and may have remained in the Agency's general fund. Fifty years later, which is to say twenty years after section 149 outlawing the potlatch was dropped from the Indian Act, and eight years after the first request for the return of the artefacts was made, the National Museum (as the Victoria Museum had become) agreed to relinquish its holdings. Its only stipulation was that a suitable place be built to house them. Two community-run museums were subsequently constructed, one at Cape Mudge and the other in Alert Bay. It was another decade before the Royal Ontario Museum came around to the idea of returning the objects in its possession, but the collection is finally home—what remains of it, that is, for the elders remembered what had been taken. And they understand that what was returned came back as relics, objects that have acquired significance not only of modern *u'mista* but of old-fashioned injustice. They are symbols of Aboriginal strength and White insecurity.

Eventually someone recommends that I look for Leo's red-and-white three-quarter-ton truck around town. I do and discover him at B.C. Packers. I have messages and parcels for him, and a chair to be delivered (with his help) to Doug Cranmer, the artist. He suggests a coffee in the café and then he takes me down along the shore on the non-Native side of town. We park and take a crooked path to a tiny cottage perched on the beach with a majestic view across Broughton Strait to the greening clear-cuts on the opposite hills. A sweet-faced dog inside lets us know that no one is home. Tomorrow, Leo proposes, we should try again. All the same, I retrace my steps to the U'mista Cultural Centre, thinking I might still catch him there. Douglas Cranmer is a senior carver of his generation, a successor to the great Mungo Martin, who was his step-grandfather, and to Willie Seaweed, the 'Nakwazda'xw master who lived close by in Ba'a's (Blunden Harbour). Seaweed's masks are masterpieces of baroque invention, his Dzunukwa poles at Alert Bay and Fort Rupert unforgettable and unmistakable. Cranmer is a contemporary of Haida artist Bill Reid, and his work can be found in many of the same collections across Canada. He and Reid carved one of the house frontal poles at the Museum of Anthropology in Vancouver, and he helped with the construction of the bighouse erected here in 1963, as well as the U'mista Cultural Centre in the 1970s. Just as the great cathedrals of Western Europe were designed by the masons who built them, so architecture in Kwakwaka'wakw culture is the *métier* of carvers. Four cedar panels grace a sliding door at the entrance to the centre with images carved in Cranmer's distinct, attenuated style. Commissioned originally for the B.C. pavilion at Expo 1970 in Japan, they have acquired a pride of place here. When I meet Cranmer, he explains two of the reliefs, which are more difficult to recognize than the killer whale, thunderbird, and the Dzunukwa on the other panels. One shows a tiny wren in a bear's stomach lighting a fire, and the second a large mosquito and three teeny men—cannibals condemned to repeat their lives as mosquitoes.

The name Cranmer is synonymous with Alert Bay, Leo tells me. The café where I had breakfast and where we sit drinking coffee is owned by Doug's brother, and his mother Agnes lives in the house up the hill. From the history books I have learned that Agnes Hunt of Fort Rupert and Dan Cranmer, along with several other Kwakwaka'wakw couples who had agreed to legalize their unions according to Christian ritual, married in a public ceremony at the Anglican church in 1935. Agnes was Dan's second wife and the mother of several children whose status under the Indian Act was thereby legitimized. Just as Governor Douglas and Amelie Connolly bowed to political pressure a hundred years before, so the Cranmers went along with the authorities, only theirs was not a mixed marriage in which the Native partner married into the non-Native world; both husband and wife were First Nations and the pressure to assimilate came entirely from outside their culture. After years of admonition from missionaries, Indian agents, and police to change their religion, to abandon their marriage customs and give up feasting, direct intervention by the police was apparently having sway. But only apparently; beneath the surface the tradition carried on.

Since the early days of European occupation of the West Coast,

Alert Bay has been the focus of White interest. Named after yet another British naval vessel (a screw corvette with seventeen guns whose crew christened the bay some time in 1858), its large protected harbour made it a natural port of call for steamships. In the 1880s a cannery was established here and the Anglican mission in Fort Rupert was persuaded by its owners to relocate. At the same time, the Kwakwaka'wakw from the Nimpkish River area were induced to take up permanent residence here in order to provide a steady labour force. Today we would call it a planned community; to Reverend A.J. Hall, it was God calling. Along with a new mission house, he acquired a captive flock for whom he immediately established a school and, within a decade, built a sawmill which was meant to give Native men a trade as well as lumber for housing. He brought to the job tremendous energy and an industrious wife who was also a teacher. Added to this was his determination to enforce the potlatch law, which he and other missionaries had petitioned government for. In 1892, Christ Church was built, a diminutive, clapboard structure with an unusual crenellated roof, and a frieze of wrought iron along its peak outlined against the green forest behind. By that time the headquarters of the Indian Agency had also moved to Alert Bay, and the German-American ethnologist Franz Boas had met George Hunt (Agnes Hunt Cranmer's father), commencing the collaboration that would lead to Boas's publications on the Kwakwaka'wakw people, which have drawn generations of anthropologists and collectors to the area. Not long after Reverend Hall arrived, William Halliday turned up to teach trades at the Boys Industrial School. In 1906, he took over as Indian agent, a post he held until the early 1930s. With these two individuals in residence representing the Church and the Department of Indian Affairs, Alert Bay was bound to become the centre of the campaign to end the potlatch.

In 1979, the year the first lot of potlatch artefacts returned from Ottawa to Cape Mudge, the Nu-Yum-Baleess Society published a document called *Prosecution or Persecution?* compiled and written by Daisy Sewid-Smith. In four sections, the book tries the case of Dan Cranmer's potlatch and the role played by Agent Halliday in the prosecutions of 1922. Following the charge, which provides background on both the law (English), and the custom (Kwak-waka'wakw), the prosecution takes up half the book. Without any commentary, the words of the original prosecutor are reproduced, culled from letters and memos that passed between him and other key players, mainly Department of Indian Affairs people: Duncan Campbell Scott, the deputy superintendent general, J.D. McLean, the department secretary, W.E. Ditchburn, the chief inspector of Indian agencies, with brief appearances from the local MP (H.S. Clements) and the RCMP officer (Sgt. D. Angermann) who obtained the evidence from Native informants at the Village Island feast. The defence, which takes up the other half of the book, comprises the accounts of the arrests and imprisonments of three of the princi-pals: Agnes Alfred (Ack-koo), Sewid-Smith's grandmother whose sister was Florence Knox, Herbert Martin (Me-Cha), the brother of Spruce and Mungo Martin, who was Dan Cranmer's ceremonial assistant (*hamatsa*), and Chief Henry Bell, who was called upon by his aunt Emma Cranmer to be the head official at the feast. Bell was arrested but released when his people, the Mamilillikulla of Village Island, gave up their potlatch items. From this testimony we learn that people understood the seizure of their regalia as a temporary measure, in the nature of a fine, or as security for their agreement to abandon feasting; nothing was surrendered willingly or in perpetuity. Further, we learn that Halliday did not assist the fami-lies of the convicted as he said he did; that the prisoners were ill-treated, strip-searched upon arrival, and the men's bodies measured. These witnesses speak of the humiliation of seeing the chiefs forced to feed the prison pigs, of fire hoses being turned on the women by the guards, of Florence Knox coming back changed. "She developed a nervous disorder and a bad heart and the same thing happened to many others. . . . Some obtained injuries from the prison guards and were never the same," her sister says.

Finally, we learn that the feast in question was called to witness the completion of Emma and Dan Cranmer's marriage contract. This entailed the repayment of the marriage security, known as *gwalth*, paid by the groom to the bride's family at the time of the marriage. Hall and Halliday took particular exception to marriage practices such as this, which they designated as the "chief evil" associated with potlatching. They complained that young girls were being paired up with old men and married off without their consent while young men were thus forfeited their choice of women (i.e. young nubile women). They charged that the system of marriage investment was nothing more than a market in which women were bought and sold. Sewid-Smith's response is to quote back a bit of English history, instances when royal babes in arms were married off, for example, and the quite ordinary practice of arranged marriages among the European nobility. Hall and Halliday had similar objections to the lavish gift-giving accompanying the feasts, though this was hardly an alien concept to Christians. In part, it was the sheer quantity of goods and valuables distributed that offended their sensibilities; in part it was the inverse form of capitalism they disliked. People like Halliday and Hall and the settler society they represented could not understand a value system that deemed hoarding a vice and the giving away of possessions a mark of distinction. In 1915, Halliday remarked to his superiors, "The system nearly approaches socialism in many of its ways as the desire of every Indian is to get something to give away to his friends." In 1918, he went on to advise them, "As you may be aware one of the difficulties and troubles I have with my lot of Indians is their frequenting the potlatch. During these gatherings they lose months of time, waste substance, contract all kinds of diseases and generally unfit themselves for being British Subjects in the proper sense of the word." To the chiefs in his agency, on the other hand, he was typically terse and patronizing. Justifying an amendment to the Indian Act in 1914, which prohibited the wearing of ceremonial dress without permission from the superintendent, he wrote to them: "The law against the potlatch has been passed because it has been seen that where the potlatch exists there has been no progress and the Government wants to see the Indians advance so that they are on the same footing as the white men, and this can not be as long as the potlatch continues."

The facts presented in Halliday's evidence tell the story of justice being manipulated by those in charge of administering it. After years of ineffectual skirmishes in court where charges would be thrown out or sentences suspended (the minimum was two months in jail), the Department of Indian Affairs finally had the rules changed so potlatch convictions could be assured. Nineteen people were indicted for potlatching between 1884 and 1918; 135 were charged between 1918 and 1922. So 1918, the year the "War to End All Wars" ended, was also the year the campaign against Canadian Native peoples recommenced with Duncan Campbell Scott at the helm in his capacity as deputy superintendent general. The new amendment to the Indian Act empowered agents to prosecute and judge section 149 cases (now designated summary offences) as justices of the peace. Thus Halliday and Hall could finally have their way. The prosecution file gives us an idea of how this was done and, incidentally, a glimpse of an extraordinary moment in history when single individuals can be observed affecting its course by force of their own prejudice. The alliance of William Halliday and Duncan Campbell Scott, the *major domo* of Indian Affairs who served nine ministers and ruled the department with little interference from his bosses and virtually no public scrutiny for two decades, was the crux of it. If Hall and Halliday were zealots of the Herbert Beaver order, D.C. Scott was the thin-blooded bureaucrat who believed that the assimilation of Native peoples was inevitable and essential. Rather perversely but not atypically, he wrote lyric poetry that idolized the very vanishing race whose affairs he was governing. The dialogue preserved in the correspondence between Halliday and Scott was obviously not meant for public consumption, and just as obviously it never occurred to either man that justification for their actions might someday be sought.

The activity of Hall, Halliday, and Scott, undertaken in the name of God, country, and the Canadian people, can only be seen as flagrantly racist today. It was also foolhardy as they were pitting themselves against traditional knowledge systems and the experiences of elders and medicine people, which they could not hope to duplicate, much less surpass. They assumed that Aboriginal cultures were about to disappear and constructed policies predicated on that assumption. They curried schisms in the community, used converts as informers, and promoted suspicion and ill will. Then, when they could not achieve the change they wanted through persuasion, they turned to coercion as they had before, only in this case they used the law in lieu of fire power. Not coincidentally, the Kwakwaka'wakw had a reputation for resisting White civilization. Boas was attracted to the area because of this vitality, having discovered that missionary work, as he said, "got in the way" and worked against the preservation of the traditional cultures he was interested in. So in Alert Bay the potlatching continued after 1922 even when other groups were said to have stopped. The truth is the potlatch went underground and was practised clandestinely, under cover of Christmas, for example. It did not die out any more than its practitioners did.

Prosecution or Persecution? never answers the question in its title. After a brief summation, the judgement is passed on to the readers. We are meant to learn the history and do the understanding; we are left to explain the feat of delusion that made this story possible.

Back at the Nimpkish, Phil spies me returning from the day's roving and asks me in for a drink. Ken is there, and the two of them are well on their way, accompanied by a sandy-haired character called Scuba, whose sentences are as splintered as his mind seems to be, and another fellow called Peter, who was born in Borneo, fought in the Philippines during the Second World War, and was all of twelve years old when he first took up arms. "I sure have a biography to write, if I could write," he declares when the subject comes around to what I do and why I'm in Alert Bay. A short man with a gimpy leg and a grin to light up next Friday, he teases us with some gruesome memories, flashes of split limbs, and smashed brains. I've seen Pete around town and like many other people in the bay, he waves and says "Hi" whether he knows you or not. As I walked down the road from the Nimpkish yesterday, a man slowed his car beside me and smiled, nodding to the passenger seat. I surmised he was inviting me to hop in for a ride. Right, I thought; you don't see people out walking much. Those who can't manage a bicycle or a half-ton pickup take taxis, which is where Hector and his taxi come in when he isn't around here doing a shift or shooting the breeze.

Ken launches into a story about how he got into the RCAF on ground crew during the war when he didn't know which end of a screwdriver to grab. I watch Phil getting edgy as the story gets windy. He starts jutting in with *sotto voce* commentary, shoving his cap back and forth over his thatch of hair. I consider his baleful appearance: the dark, bushy eyebrows curling up his face like briar on a cliff, the grey complexion and stubbled chin, thinking of the anecdote of one grandmother I'd talked to on the reserve who threatened a trouble-making grandson with being sent to see Phil and his dog. (The threat apparently worked.) Phil, on the other hand, describes himself cunningly as Alert Bay's oldest bachelor, "oldest *virgin* bachelor," he emphasizes.

Scrounging around in a drawer, he comes up with a 1991/2 Nimpkish Hotel pocket diary with the wrong telephone number and Albert Bay, instead of Alert Bay, stamped on it . He can't use it for customers at New Year's, so he keeps them for special occasions, he says, handing me one with another beer. Some time after that, the conversation heads into choppy waters when Oka is mentioned. Phil is suddenly talking about Crown land having been given to the government to do with it what it wants, and warning us that he's read a bit of history. I offer a platitude about it being time to settle with the Aboriginal peoples, and he mutters something else about taxpayers paying for it and gets up to leave, asking us if there are any Athabascan in Ontario. I'm not sure if that's a brand of beer or a bad joke, but while he's gone, Ken is at me to drop the topic. "Yeah, I agree we have to settle. But not here. Phil's bad on this topic." Ken's personal beef with history is that he doesn't see why, if the Native women used to dress up and perform for tourists who came in on steamers, they won't do it now. At this point Phil reappears with a photo of himself as a young navy recruit, decked out in uniform and "HMCS Athabascan" written on his hat.

Next morning I run into Hector at the supermarket buying a Mother's Day plant for his ex-mother-in-law. He tells me in a stage whisper that he is on a tear and usually does it up good when he does it. "But I'll be sober on Monday, though, for sure," he lisps, fixing me with blue, bleary eyes. As soon as we're outside, he lights up a Players. At the Nimpkish he smokes these non-stop, punctuating his conversation with deep orange fingers and off-colour expletives. On Monday he was still at it, though, which means that Phil had to cover his shift and was up all night. Even Max is cantankerous.

I decided to take Ken's suggestion and drop in at Wong's General Store. It is a wondrous place, as I've been told, chock-full of shoes, work clothes, toys, and candy, stuff for school and the house piled high on counters. No frills and no production. Mr. Wong is sitting in an armchair strategically placed where he can see everything. His legs are a bit creaky and he has just had a cataract operation in Vancouver. I introduce myself and find he is happy to chat. He tells me he has been in Alert Bay for fifty years; came in 1940 or so when there was no road and one Model T. He was working in a mill up the coast when someone suggested coming here, and for a time he worked in another store. Then he opened his own. He has been back to China (Canton) once, to marry Mother with whom he's raised five children here in the bay, one of whom owns the electrical store next door. A couple of grandchildren weave in and out through the aisles, searching for Grandmother, who has disappeared into the back. Mr. Wong is a roundish man with a merry smile and an easy way. Some kids clatter into the store with after-school money clutched in their fists. He greets them and shuffles to his feet to help. One little girl hasn't enough money for the candy she wants, so Mr. Wong waits patiently while she chooses something she can afford. Each time he gets up, he excuses himself, and comes back wondering out loud if he is talking too much. Then he climbs back into the conversation, picking up where he left off. No, he never fished. The Chinese didn't get into that, and weren't allowed to at first. One man he knew almost drowned when his boat foundered on rocks and sank; he climbed up on the mast and was picked up, but after that his wife put her foot down. "I like the life here," he tells me, tapping the floor with his foot. Then he talks about the Native people, what good people they are and how very hard it has been for them. "In the old days they wouldn't let them potlatch; then they did, and now it's coming back." He shakes his head. Mr. Wong has had the honour of being invited to one feast, but you can tell he's no groupie. "Been to one, been to them all," he says in inverted commas.

My next visit is to the Anglican church, which lies back down the shore past the café. I stop and take a few photos of it gleaming in the May sunshine in a new coat of yellow and white paint, contemplating the message its builders thought to convey. Power and splendour, no doubt, but that would have been a hard sell, dwarfed as the church would have been by the bighouses in the 1890s, a pale imitation beside the ornate Kwakwaka'wakw poles. I knock on the door of the rectory to ask permission to see the church. A young man dressed in sweats and socks answers. He is Reverend David Dingwall, thirtyish and balding, sent here directly from divinity school about three years ago. He offers to show me around and tells me about a building very similar to Christ Church in Hawaii, and the theory that this building was shipped out from England in numbered pieces and reconstructed the same way. Dingwall doesn't think so. More probably, he figures, the lumber was donated and the design of local invention. He takes me inside and points out the church's features, which include a contemporary painting on the back wall of John the Baptist baptizing Christ by Tony Hunt. He continues, telling me how he came here knowing nothing of the place or its history, thinking Alert Bay was somewhere in the Arctic when he first heard the name. Since then, of course, he's learned a lot, about synod land, for instance, which is the land the church sits on and owns even though it is actually part of the reserve. A few years ago, the church decided to sell a portion of it. The buyers were White people, which caused tremendous ill feeling on the reserve. "Some people considered it stolen," he tells me, explaining how it is now, that the band has the right of first refusal. Moreover, when there is negotiating to be done, the church sends in higher-ups. Young Dingwall has come to appreciate the strategy. "I am the one who has to live in the community," he explains. It's better not to be the responsible party.

What I learn from listening and talking to people in Alert Bay is just how conscious the memory is, and how conspicuous the presence of the potlatch trials still is despite the amnesia of the Anglican Church. The legacy festers among the Kwakwaka'wakw and in the adjacent non-Native community, though both speak of their long history of peaceful coexistence. For one thing, the potlatch persecutions have never been acknowledged by the authorities or mainstream Canada. When the Indian Act was changed in 1951, section 149 was dropped silently. It was not repealed and therefore never formally repudiated. For its part, the Anglican Church has yet to acknowledge the role it played in promoting the law and its brutal enforcement.

On Mother's Day, 1991, there are half a dozen people at Christ Church in Alert Bay. Nowadays the religious flock to Glad Tidings, the Pentecostal church off the reserve where the music is better and the clergy don't carry such heavy luggage. It was the young Anglican minister who explained to me that the Christian denominations had long ago abandoned the old "spheres of influence" arrangement they had observed in settled areas like Alert Bay in the nineteenth century. Is this free trade in souls or poetic justice, I wonder. Unacknowledged history and unanswered questions lie around here like toxic waste. I am reminded of the collections taken up at the Anglican church school I attended in the 1950s for food for the unfortunate at Thanksgiving, presents for needy kids at Christmas, and coin offerings on all occasions for the missionaries up North. Now I hear from Native women my own age how it felt to be forbidden to speak your language as an eleven year old, to hear it condemned as primitive by people who didn't speak it, to see treasures like the chiefs' coppers ridiculed and devalued, to see the pain of the grandparents accused of doing wrong by doing good. I hear how the sun died when the feasting stopped. And I rue the day Hall, Halliday, and the others ignored the words of the chief, who greeted Franz Boas in 1886. "We want to know whether you have come to stop our dances and feasts as the missionaries and agents who live among our neighbours try to do. We do not want to have anyone here who will interfere with our customs. We were told that a man-of-war would come if we should continue to do as our grandfathers and great grandfathers have done. . . . Do we ask the white man to 'Do as the Indian does?' It is a strict law that bids us dance. It is a strict law that bids us distribute our property among our friends and neighbours. It is a good law. Let the white man observe his law; we shall observe ours."

The opinions of the missionaries and agents acting in this drama were immensely potent, but not unopposed, as might seem at first from the history books. It is true that the early witnesses and missionaries whose views dominate the record were unremittingly negative. However, settler society in early twentieth-century British Columbia was not of one mind or the same experience when it came to Native peoples and outlawing the potlatch. There were those like William Dwyer, who wrote the Vancouver *Province* in 1896 to press one clerical ideologue—Hall, possibly—to defend his position. "Will the reverend gentleman give the public some idea what he would propose to offer the Indians in exchange for the pleasure they all experience at these gatherings? Will he contradict the police when they say that there is seldom a case of drunkenness at a potlatch? Can he claim that we have any just right to prevent Indians from meeting together even if it does interfere with mission work?" Dwyer contended that the majority of the people in the province "were opposed to any forcible interference with the harmless customs of the native, knowing as we all do that these customs are rapidly dying out." In 1910, a coalition called the Conference of Friends of the Indians of British Columbia was organized to support the cause of land rights and Aboriginal title, drawing together a number of radical clergy and reform groups, including the Trades & Labour Council. It was spearheaded by Arthur O'Meara, a one-time Ontario lawyer and lay Anglican minister, who went on to become a key figure in the Nisga'a campaign to bring their petition on land claims to the Privy Council in London. The effort was genuine, though it garnered little public support and its impact was negligible. To all intents and purposes, Hall and Halliday spoke for White British Columbia.

The potlatch's most ardent defence was made in private by the White Community and is contained in a series of letters solicited from the experts of the day by Edward Sapir, the chief anthropologist at the Victoria Memorial Museum in 1915. Sapir wrote Duncan Campbell Scott in February of that year to advise him about the value of coppers, having heard that the deputy superintendent general was seeking information about them. (Coppers are ceremonial objects and at the same time were part of a credit system in which they carried symbolic and ascribed value like currency.) Sapir also knew of the department's policy on enforcement and was aware that more stringent measures were on Scott's mind. He decided to intervene. Outrage seeps through the formality of his bureau-correct prose as he informs Scott about the relationship of coppers to the coastal system of credit and the custom of conducting all important business transactions in public. To set these aside, he warned, "could mean the complete demoralization of their business system and the consequent bankruptcy of the most prominent and respected among the Indians." Then he lets Scott have it: "It seems to me high time that white men realized that they are not doing the Indians much of a favour by converting them into inferior replicas of themselves. . . . I have always failed to understand why we pride ourselves so much on tolerance in dealing with European foreigners, and so conspicuously fail to apply the same tolerance in dealing with our own aboriginals."

The Sapir testimony came from all the influential names in the field: Boas from Columbia University, John Swanton of the U.S. Bureau of American Ethnology, Harlan J. Smith from Ottawa, Charles Hill-Tout, James Teit, and C.F. Newcombe from British Columbia, all of whom unanimously advocated abandoning the effort to suppress the potlatch. Boas: "the abolition of the potlatch would mean as great a hardship to the Indians as the wiping-out of all credits in our community would mean to us." James Teit from Spences Bridge: "It is a serious matter to destroy suddenly and by force the social economic and other institutions of a people. You are aiming a blow at their life, and if the blow is effective it will mean their demoralization. Any white race powerful enough would fight to the bitter end against this." Charles Hill-Tout: "The rigid enforcement of the present laws is neither wise nor humane as it is carried out in utter disregard of the experience and wisdom gained by our government . . . of the native races of our Empire elsewhere, and also of the most deep-seated feelings and prejudices of the Indians themselves." Newcombe endorsed Boas's views and added, "How is it that on no single occasion can [the Indians] recall a refusal of presents at potlatches by Indian agents and other authorities? When the Duke of Connaught was here a year or two ago the Royal party was conducted to a potlatch at Alert Bay and accepted some valuable objects from the Indians. The law has for a long time been a dead letter & it is wrong to enforce it now without any special reason."

According to historians, this protest was wasted on Scott.

"Against the determined opinion of the deputy superintendent general the Kwakiutl and other potlatchers were powerless. Their allies—retained legal counsel, a handful of anthropologists, a sympathetic fisheries inspector, some local merchants, one or two backbench MPs and a vague but entirely unmobilized public opinion—were impotent," write historians Douglas Cole and Ira Chaikin in *An Iron Hand Upon the People.* "Department views were solid and intractable; contrary opinions were ignored, even suppressed. Native opinion meant even less." Scott was operating in a political vacuum, the authors maintain, drawing a parallel to the Department of Immigration during the Second World War under H.G. Blair, who had much the same latitude in implementing policies derived from personal conviction, particularly in the exclusion of Jews. "In an area where few cared very deeply an entrenched bureaucrat had the liberty to do as he pleased. Indian affairs concerned few people, most of whom were not even voters." Cole and Chaikin suggest that Scott's poetic image of the noble savage and doomed culture merged with official policy. On the subject of the potlatch, he was implacable. "The efforts of the Department have been directed to the promotion among Indians of industry, progress and morality, all of which are greatly hindered by indulgence in the potlatch," he wrote to the Indians of the Kwawkewlth Agency in 1919. The warning about economic havoc hadn't moved him and, perhaps even more damning for the poet, neither had the admonition about spiritual loss.

In the mid-mornings when the air is still, I take to the marshy highlands at the centre of the island where a cacophony of ravens and crows greets the solitary visitor. The walk takes me through a forest of tall cedars decorously draped with moss, like furniture in a Victorian parlour, to a clearing where the swamp squats in its primal juice. The change of scene is jarring. Husks of dead trees rise from the murk; scrappy bushes and shrubs grasp at land beneath the shallow water as earth and water tussle for domination. The place is eerie and pregnant with death. In life the trees danced and swayed with the rhythm of the wind; in decay they become still and grey, needing the raven's throat or artist's adze to speak again. I find a spot to rest on the boardwalk someone has

The swamp on Cormorant Island, May 1991.

constructed across the boggiest sections, reminding myself that while a swamp may not be much to look at, it is nursery to all kinds of birds, insects, and amphibians that crowd the ecosystem, filling the air with their noise and their brilliance, and my nostrils with their fetid smells. I sink into the echoing sounds of the crows and their raven cousins, cataloguing the cries, yelps, clicks, chortles, and squawks. It strikes me that these shaggy corners of the island, not the town or the reserve, are the parts of Alert Bay that Emily Carr would recognize today. According to old photographs, the waterfront in 1912 was dominated by a line of longhouses, interspersed with numerous carved and painted poles, which appeared elsewhere around the settlement as well. There is one old-style house left, built in modern times as a community ceremonial space or bighouse, and only a few old women in the village remember living communally in the old way. These days, the poles are sequestered in the cemeteries and ceremonial places. Then, it would have been impossible to avoid them. And it would have been equally hard to avoid the fact that the carvers were practitioners of an illicit art in the 1920s. It may never have been construed that way by White commentators, yet when the potlatch was banned, carving was effectively criminalized so intricately connected was it to the feast. Coincidentally, a market for the old poles, masks, and traditional regalia developed in the White world. In 1912, museums were still buying Aboriginal material and Canadian institutions, which had been slow off the mark compared with their German, American, and French counterparts who began seriously collecting in the 1880s and 1890s, were chief among them. This provided a tremendous incentive for families to sell their heritage, and perhaps gain favour with the priests into the bargain. Significantly, there was no market for contemporary carvings, which were regarded as "replicas" and eschewed as inauthentic by collectors. It was decades before Kwakwaka'wakw carving by living artists would sell as art.

So Emily Carr's perception, expressed in her "Lecture on Totems" and elsewhere, that the poles were disappearing was not wrong. The poles were being moved. We know from her writings that she criticized the missionaries' efforts to change Native peoples and their culture. What we don't know is how closely she connected the disappearance of the poles with White attitudes and government policy. The potlatch laws, after all, were created by Parliament. When she came to Alert Bay for the third time in 1912, carvers were working, but she would not likely have heard of them from her hosts. She had arrived with an introduction to Reverend Hall who assisted her during her stay and provided a chaperone for her trip across to Gwayasydums, Mimquimlees, and Tsarsisnukomi. This was Emma Cook whose mother, a mixed-race child, had been raised by the Halls. Jane Cook married another mixed-race convert and protegé of the reverend's whose white father likewise had left him to the care and education of the Church. Emma was one of sixteen children born to the Cooks, and she grew up in the embrace of the mission. Her parents were active in the church, and her mother was an influential figure in the reverend's campaign to eradicate the potlatch. Two of Jane Cook's letters petitioning Scott and Halliday for enforcement of the law appear in Daisy Sewid-Smith's *Prosecution*. Emily would later complain that young Emma was more hindrance than help on that trip—not surprising, given the youngster's lack of knowledge about or interest in Native ceremonial life. This was the last time Carr allowed herself to accept "help" of that sort. As an old woman, Emma Cook Kenmuir remembered Emily Carr as reserved and preoccupied. "She wasn't the type for saying much and I was just a girl," she says. Emily was quite prepared to make the trip alone, apparently, but the Indian agent insisted. "So did Reverend Hall who asked my mother if I could go with her for there was no one else in the village at the time. They were all out potlatching I suppose!" The two spent two nights together at Gwayasydums, camping in one of the longhouses where they lit a fire and cooked tea. Emily paid little attention to Emma, leaving the girl to amuse herself. But she was forced to pay attention to Hall's and Halliday's views on Native culture.

The work Carr did in the years leading up to the 1913 exhibit has been given short shrift by the experts over the years. Gerta Moray re-examined the paintings as a group and has set them in a political and social context. She points out that Carr would have been aware of Arthur O'Meara and his activities as an advocate for the Native peoples through her own church, Bishop Cridge's

Church of Our Lord, which had given support to radicals like William Duncan of Metlakatla in the past. Carr read missionary memoirs and consulted anthropological texts in her research, so she had access to the scholarly opinion of the day. Moray believes Carr used the documentary project to enter the debate on Native affairs, her position being both deliberate and dissenting. Given the public malaise about Aboriginal claims, coupled with its entrenched apathy towards Native peoples, it is apparent how peculiar her public declaration of love for the Native people must have seemed. People were used to Pauline Johnson, the safely assimilated Indian, reciting poetry about her lost ancestors. But the sight of Emily Carr, the oddball and unpredictable spinster, embracing Native culture and proposing that it be accepted as part of Canada's heroic past was close to ridiculous. Even if her perspective was in perfect harmony with current anthropological thinking, which saw human civilization as evolutionary (and some cultures therefore more evolved than others), Carr's intervention clashed with the missionary rhetoric and the popular conception of Aboriginal culture. Even though her message was essentially placating, for she challenged no policy or law, no one wanted to hear it. The polite sounds from the press, which reported on the exhibit but not on her lecture, indicate that the newspapers were willing to record the event as having taken place but were not prepared to consider what Carr had to say. Her attempt to make a public statement was sidelined and ignored.

Carr was making a statement in more ways than one with her 1913 show. The project was a complex undertaking, and the exhibition a bold act by which she presented her paintings and her ideas to the public under her own aegis. As well as challenging the missionaries, she was distancing herself from the art establishment, such as it was. There was more than pique involved in her scuffle with the Fine Arts Society. There was genuine disaffection, which had only partly to do with aesthetic difference. Carr had proposed a vision of the country that included Native culture as ancient 'found art'; she was also proposing a vision of art making that included participating directly in the public debate on political and social affairs. Neither idea was popular with her peers.

Who was Emily Carr in 1913 when she staged her exhibition? At forty-two she was an emerging artist who had found a subject, an approach, and the makings of a style that had come together in a compelling idea. Unquestionably, the Vancouver exhibition and the "Lecture on Totems" were part of an effort to establish her identity as an artist, as M. Emily Carr, and to find her own audience. When that audience failed to materialize, and her search for public sponsorship fizzled because experts like Newcombe did not accept her contribution (or return her professional respect), Carr retreated to Victoria and life as a landlady. Moray's research suggests that the 1913 exhibition signalled the collapse of Carr's career, and that this was an event of much larger proportions than people have so far comprehended. The struggle was professional and artistic as well as personal, she emphasizes. Maria Tippett sees Carr at this stage in her life as a loner by default, bossy and difficult to like. She suspects Carr's affinity for Native culture of being a romantic projection, the invention of a lonely, middle-aged woman who was neurotic and fat, and had an axe to grind with authority. Biographer Paula Blanchard, like many others, views Carr's enchantment with Native peoples as an expression of disenchantment with her own, as a substitute for mature friendships, and as a crutch for her own rebelliousness. In short, Carr's connection to Native culture has been seen by the scholars as a symptom of her personal problems. Furthermore, they have tended to dismiss the work of this period as inferior, worthwhile mainly as a prelude to what was to come. As a result, both the work and the project itself have been overshadowed. Writes art historian Doris Shadbolt: "Hers was an art, at that point, of painterly seeing but not of feeling." Carr herself acknowledged the tensions in the work, writing some time later that she feared she had hugged the historical side too closely in the documentary paintings. However, Moray proposes we take another look, for she perceives an evolution in Carr's struggle to match her style to her subjects, which was resolved in the paintings of the Haida poles in the middle of her trip in 1912. The lessons learned in France were not forgotten or set aside. By the time she got to Skidegate in late July 1912, the old mauve and green patches were back.

Carr had negotiated an accommodation between precepts acquired in France and the Northwest Coast reality. European landscape tradition depended on a geography that could be viewed from a short distance, taken in with the human eye, whereas Carr faced painting a huge and half-imaginary place that she could often sense better than she could see. Painting the forest from the inside out was her task. Early on she associated this—the forest, her beloved West—with the First Nation's cedar carvings. Now she began to read the poles as abstractions, reductive representations of nature, and to understand their creators as proto-modernists. Some of her canvases focus on this quality by highlighting single figures from the poles in close-up treatment. This disposes of their original formality in a way that must have been startling to 1913 audiences. Paintings like *Skidegate* or *Indian Raven* push the images right up to the picture plane and into the viewer's face. What rivets attention then is the expressive quality of the shark's visage, tongue protruding through his teeth, and the deep, brooding raven augmented by a high-key, high-contrast colour composition. Such passages bring Frances Hodgkins to mind with her tough, expansive colour.

So Carr was looking for more than subject matter when she visited Native communities, she was looking for artistic insight. Her writings on that score are clear. France, it would seem, made her realize she had something to learn from the Kwakwaka'wakw carvers whose images belonged irrevocably to the landscape around them. Knowing how their stylizations captured the essence of a bear might help her divine the essence of cedar and forest. "Indian art broadened my seeing, loosened the formal tightness I had learned in England's schools. Its bigness and stark reality baffled my white man's understanding. I had been schooled to see outside's only, not struggle to pierce. I was as Canadian-born as the Indian but behind me were Old World heredity and ancestry as well as Canadian environment. . . . The Indian caught first the inner intensity of his subject, working outward to the surfaces. His spiritual conception he buried deep in the wood he was about to carve. . . . Indian art taught me directness and quick, precise decisions." Carr's interest in this direction makes it hard to imagine that she would not be interested in meeting its creators. By the time of her second big trip north in 1928, Mungo Martin and Willie Seaweed were into their maturity and were leaders in their communities.

In Alert Bay I ask the Native peoples I meet about Carr and Native carvers and the answer comes back "impossible." The old men didn't speak any English, they say, and I surmise that Carr's attentions would not have been welcome. The Cranmer trials had happened just four years before, and even today, I am told, there are people afraid to open their doors to Whites. I bump into memories of Emily sketching down on the beach, but no stories. There are no lasting impressions, save for Emma Cook Kenmuir's oft-quoted remark that Emily Carr must have been standing behind the door when God was handing out looks. What might the impression have been? Historically speaking, Carr was part of the advance guard of White people and institutions who pushed themselves on Aboriginal society with increasing insistence. Like the rest, she came to their communities for her own reasons, took her pleasure, and left. She would protest such a characterization, saying she was giving something back in the record she was creating for posterity. Posterity, however, had other ideas. While her writings may be used as primary source material by historians who routinely quote passages from *The House of All Sorts* and *The Book of Small* as original descriptions, her paintings have never been valued as documents by Natives or non-Natives. And her art has never been very popular in First Nation communities. Whatever her personal motivation, whatever her actual experience,

Carr was speaking through a tradition that was already well established by 1928—the tradition of White people writing about Native peoples, representing their ideas, telling their stories, and speaking for them on the one hand, using their technology and exploiting their art on the other. It started with Captain Cook, continued with the missionaries, the Indian agents, the anthropologists, and the journalists, and carries on today. This was done without a second thought in Emily Carr's time, but cannot be in ours.

I take my leave of the Nimpkish early one morning, bumping into Ken, who proposes a cup of coffee before I go. He scouts about Phil's office, but finds it locked tight and quieter than a morgue. Hector has the keys and lets us all into the bar, then disappears up to his room to fetch some "Juan Valdez." It takes the big coffee machine days to warm up, the plug-in kettle only a few minutes. We sit around chatting for a bit, and then unavoidably it is time to beard the lion. No one is eager. Hector hands the keychain to Ken and we follow him up the stairs and down the hall.

Phil is out cold on the couch, legs stretched over Max, who doesn't take kindly to anyone, not even Ken, tapping his master on the head. "Nursing a woolly one from Sunday," Ken says. The three of them had shot pool and tied a serious one on, but that was two days ago and I'd seen Phil upright yesterday afternoon. Ken tells me Phil was actually in the middle of it then, and just carried straight on drinking all day. He leans over towards the head on the couch and announces firmly, "Sue's checking out now, Phil!" Astonishingly, Phil wakes, bolts into gear, and immediately sets to making me up a bill. He seems almost chipper. When I arrived he'd said that the rates go down the longer you stay. True to his word, the bill for the week comes to $105. If you stayed long enough, I figure, it'd be free. Like the land once was.

Chapter Three

River of Clouds

Kitwancool, 1928

There were plenty of people who said not to go, and they all said the same thing. The Gitksan at Kitwancool are a fierce, unfriendly lot who keep to their village buried in the hills miles above the river and dislike uninvited guests, especially Whites. I heard that sixteen years ago when I first came up the Skeena. I also heard of the unusual poles at Kitwancool, particularly old Methuselah, the "Hole in the Sky" pole with the large, ornate oval carved through its middle. In 1912, I travelled up river from Prince Rupert on a flat-bottomed paddle-wheeler; this time the train dropped me at Kitwangak where I waited for chance to deliver someone in a cart heading up the trail and willing to take me, my gear, and my little dog along. Last time I was persuaded to leave without seeing those poles, and I'll admit that part of me was glad to avoid finding out how accurate the warnings were. This time no one was going to dissuade me.

It helps to talk to someone who knows about the place and the people. When I was in Ottawa, Mr. Barbeau told me more about the poles he has studied and photographed and the Tsimsian people he works with. He talked to me about his book, too, and asked if he could include a repro-duction of the Bear and the Moon totem I painted at Kispayaks in 1912. The book, he says, is quite different from the writing he does as a government anthropologist, this being an attempt to retell the story of Kitwancool Jim in the style of a traditional storyteller. The account is his own imagining of the events as told to him by the old Indians. Fanny Johnson, for instance, whose other name is Hanamuk or Sunbeams, is still alive to tell the tale of how her husband Jim was shot dead by the police when they came to arrest him for murder. That was over forty years ago, Mr. Barbeau explains. In the aftermath of the measles epidemic that had killed their son and many other children, Fanny urged her husband, whose Native name was Kamalmuk, to take revenge on a local wizard called Neetuh. Fanny held firm with the old ways, while Kamalmuk had fallen in with the new, but he carried out her wishes nevertheless. Later he regretted the killing and paid retribution to Neetuh's relatives, according to Gitksan custom. Native law was appeased, but Canadian law wasn't, so a posse was sent out to bring Kamalmuk to trial. When it returned with a corpse, everyone knew there would be trouble. The captain of the posse met with the Kitwancool chiefs at Kitwangak and promised justice and redress, saying that the man who pulled the trigger had disobeyed orders; the advance party was not supposed to capture the suspect. Meanwhile, Billy Green was claiming that Jim, who was shot in the back, had fired first. In fact, Green had grabbed the dying man's pistol, fired a shot into the ground, and then tried to persuade his companions to corroborate the story. Jim's last words, they say, were uttered in protest.

Soon afterwards a court was convened, though constables had to be temporarily discharged from the force to form a jury—a jury that proceeded to acquit Green and everyone else on trial that day for lack of evidence. The news ripped through the valley, dragging anger and fear with it. Relations between Whites and Natives became tense and the militia was sent to the mouth of the Skeena to protect the White population should anything happen.

Nothing ever really did. Over the next several months there were disturbances, but nothing amounting to open rebellion. There was no resolution either. Peace was never made between the Canadian authorities and the people of Kitwancool, and the Kitwancool have shunned outsiders ever since.

That is how Mr. Barbeau tells the story. According to him, Jim and Fanny were separated by conflicting ambitions, she for her son to become a chief, he for a life in the White world. They were both caught up in a larger tragedy that didn't spare individuals. As Mr. Barbeau says, "their history forms a chapter in the obscure annals of Native Canadian races struggling against fate without a ray of hope."

I was surprised at first by the title of his book, *The Downfall of Temlaham*. It doesn't refer to Kitwancool or Jim, but recalls instead the ancient city said to have flourished in prehistoric times in the Hazelton area. Temlaham is like the fabled lost Atlantis, and when Mr. Barbeau gets into the story, it is as if it all happened yesterday. Time collapses and history invades the present, stands right there in solid form in front of you as Mount Stekyawden, the giant mountain we know as Rocher de Boule, where the legend of the painted goat and the lost city originate. Mount Stekyawden fascinates Mr. Barbeau, enough for him to have climbed it once, and he says it shadows the book. Jim's story is folded into the retelling of the old legends, which all have a moral. Mr. Barbeau lists them and one in particular strikes me as plain wise: "Do not abuse animals or ridicule them. Their lives are not unlike your own." Another one was quite convoluted, so I wrote it down and have thought about it a good deal since: "The man who never seeks restraint shall never know endurance and fortitude; he shall never have visions of the spirit world, never grasp the dictates of unseen wisdom." There is more to wilderness, I know now, than meets the five senses. The old stories speak of deep and unseen things that I sometimes sense but can't really imagine, and, oh, how I wish I could.

Mr. Barbeau has been to Kitwancool and knows the dangers. Two years ago he encountered such strong local opposition that he and his guide Beynon left early. The tribe was constantly in council discussing his work, and there had been a howling debate the night before. This didn't augur well, so he rose at first light, photographed all thirty poles and skulked off to Kitwangak where, he said, he and Beynon would have the peaceful atmosphere they required, and privacy for the informants who came down to see them there. Despite this trouble, Mr. Barbeau urged me to go to Kitwancool. He gave me names and suggested I visit in the early summer when few people are about the village and I would be able to sketch the poles with little interruption.

Mr. Barbeau is full of this idea of getting artists to visit Native villages. He believes Indian crafts, especially West Coast carvings, are a natural source of inspiration for modern designers and artists. He has arranged sketching trips here for several eastern painters, which rather made me feel beaten at my own game when I first heard of it, but not when I thought about their passing acquaintance with the Skeena and the people compared with my own long connection. I feel Mr. Barbeau and I share that. I said as much when I wrote him last winter, for I can understand more than most the saintly patience and perseverance against odds and discomforture one must have to get such stories out of the Indians. I like the book, but I wonder why he doesn't write about the people he has met. He is much like Dr. Newcombe in the way he seems happier in the past. I wonder if he doesn't see the *Downfall of Temlaham* as his own contribution to the artistic movement he champions.

Distress draws some people out like salt draws water from raw vegetables. My anxiety about Kitwancool induced Mr. Barbeau to reveal something about himself I didn't expect—and neither, I suspect, did he. It was when he was trying to explain why he might not be welcome at Kitwancool where others would be. He told me about attending a medicine man's ceremony for two very ill people some years ago. Although he was not welcomed by everyone present and was invited to leave before it ended, he knew he was witnessing something extraordinary. He was practically whispering in my ear as he talked, saying that no one had heard what he was telling me. The performance deeply impressed his senses. The din was tremendous, the singing and drumming absorbed every inch of space, and his internal emotional self was gripped to the core. Afterwards he reasoned that the old-fashioned fishing lodge where it happened added to the primitive effect, but there was no explaining the dreadful power of what he had experienced. He hated to leave before it was over, and so, instead of departing when he was told to go, he snuck behind the lodge where he could hear and see the goings-on through chinks in the wall. Huddled there, he scribbled notes furiously into the night until everything suddenly halted—he was discovered. Shaking with fear and remorse, he instantly confessed his regret for the ruse, pleading his obligation as an ethnologist to witness something so rare, a custom that had disappeared everywhere else. On the wings of Gallic diplomacy, he left the village unscathed and only now when I recall the anxious look on his face do I wonder which admission caused him the embarrassment—the deceit he was caught at or the intense physicality of his response to the ritual. It is not hard to lose one's bearings here, I know. It is not hard to be frightened.

Who am I kidding? This journey is an exercise in terror,
and a test of human endurance, or at least of mine.
What's hard is not *panicking at the idea of panthers in the*
woods nearby, not *fleeing from the enormity and*
anonymity of nature, not *spurning the strangeness of*
Indian ways. If I were asked, I would have to say the
primary activity up here is waiting: waiting for boats to
arrive, for the mail to come, for meals to appear or for
trains to depart. Or disaster to strike. Always there is
waiting. And always fear licking round the edges. Physical
fear of the elements, and the weather. Apprehension about
tomorrow's voyage, about the mood of the woods. Will
they be sheltering or threatening? Terror at the thought of
getting lost, or being found by ghosts.

Mr. Barbeau is an odd man. Not much of a man's man, I
wouldn't say, despite the rugged conditions he works in
and his obvious love of the outdoors. His effect is
anything but brawny, though he has a shy strength about
him and a formality that women appreciate. They overlook the Bohemian style for the courtly manners and
beautiful English. They do not seem to notice the suits
made of cloth woven by artisans in colours like green and,
bless me, mauve. Barbeau's passion for the songs and
stories of the Indians is matched only by his love of the
songs and stories of the French Canadians whom he also
studies and records. Sometimes I forget he is French Canadian himself, from a place he calls The Beauce where the
people are renowned for their tenacity and sharp nose for
business. He actually spent much of his childhood in the
United States where his father hoped to make his fortune
in gold. So he grew up speaking English, was a Rhodes
scholar, and, following Oxford, got a job with the Geological Survey in Ottawa where he has lived ever since. I
visited his home on MacLaren Street when I went east for

the National Gallery exhibit. It is full of objects and materials made by people he has met on his travels, and artefacts collected during long seasons in the remote regions
of Quebec and British Columbia. He is drawn to the artistic side of human activity; that is obvious. He values what
people make with their hands and surrounds himself with
art. I have never seen anyone quite so lyrical about ordinary crafts—my pottery included. These I have always
thought of as frauds because our Indians did not pot and
the designs I used were not made for clay ornamentation.
But Barbeau was thrilled to have them for the exhibition,
saying they are wonderful examples of what Native art
and contemporary craft can accomplish together. He has
bought several pieces for himself and commissioned a set
of bells.

Sometimes I forget he is a museum official too. Although
he says he distrusts his own opinion about art and usually
asks the advice of painters he knows like Jackson or
Arthur Lismer, he sounds more like an artist than a
scholar. When he talks about his work, he doesn't quote
books or bring up theory; he is more likely to pick up a
drum and accompany himself in a few of the old songs.

I have met very few French Canadians in my life;
though I always like them and enjoy their company, I
always promptly forget their names. I didn't remember
Mr. Barbeau's at first either. He heard about me from
Beynon, his half-breed interpreter, who is also something
of an assistant to him, who comes from the Skeena and
knew of my trip in 1912. Barbeau first visited my studio
in 1920, looking for an illustrator to furnish visual records
to accompany his work on Tsimsian and Haida poles. We
deduced that my work was not comprehensive enough for
him to rely on. A year or so later, he returned and stayed
longer. I liked his talk and I liked him and was pleased
when he bought a couple of small sketches. I gave him a

third. Still, I didn't connect my gentle visitor with the eminent professor who came to the University of British Columbia in 1926 to lecture on West Coast Indian art. Friends in Vancouver sent me the cutting, which reported his speech and I wrote the man to tell him about my collection of Indian paintings and invite him to my studio. The next October, Mr. Barbeau turned up on my doorstep again, and we pieced the story together. His memory had faded too; he hadn't immediately associated the woman who wrote him with the woman he'd dug up in Victoria or for that matter with the woman Harold Mortimer-Lamb had raved about in a letter to the director of the National Gallery. Mr. Mortimer-Lamb's letter to Eric Brown had been forwarded to Mr. Barbeau's department at the Museum on the assumption that the work in question would be of more interest to a museum than an art gallery. Last summer when he came across some of the paintings I'd left behind with people in Hazelton, his memory jogged. On the strength of what he saw there (and the praise of the artists he was travelling with at the time, Jackson, Anne Savage, and Holgate, I believe) he urged Brown to seek me out, setting in motion the events that brought me back here, and shook out my life like a dusty carpet.

Here I am, fifty-six going on fifty-seven and I can't even explain to myself where the last fifteen years have gone. Or how I ended up enslaved to domestic duty, allowing my life to be consumed by household chores when I turned down marriage to escape that very fate. Landladying has had the last laugh on me all right, and the artist in me is revolted. I was right to think such a life the ruination of art. It drains the life from you, and flattens the soul. Now, out of nowhere, comes this recognition and I am aflame again. How quickly the fog lifts when the sun comes out. Knowing

*there are people who can see my work has changed me. I
feel invigorated, sure of my purpose, and eager to paint.
Can it really be so simple? Was all that doubt merely
pride eating away at itself for lack of attention? Where
did art go?*

The trip up to Kitwancool took hours. The wagon
creaked and jerked over the bumps, heaving its load of
lumber and passengers back and forth like flotsam in an
angry sea. We arrived late in the day, but there was still
enough light to see the forest of poles facing the village.
They are taller than I expected and deeply sculpted.
Several are crowned with three-dimensional figures—here
a large-beaked bird, there a man with a bow in his hands
and a duck settled on his head like a hat. They are whim-
sical compared to the poles at Alert Bay (the bow is
strung, for instance) and besides stacking animals,
monsters, and humans on top of one another in the usual
fashion, characters are often allowed to run free. Up and
down the poles they race, acting out their stories in
pantomime.

Sketching them has been difficult because of the
weather. It has rained, drizzled, and hailed for three solid
days. Everything is soggy and rank. When the mist lifts,
the mosquitoes descend. I've managed to work anyway,
taking shelter in a broken down community house with a
pack of Indian horses. The first day I was down on the
grassy flats between the main stand of poles and the little
river, which runs past the village on its way to the
Skeena, when I was surprised by a thunderstorm. Looking
around for shelter, I crawled through a broken picket
fence into a squat little house I took for a shrine of some
sort, Ginger Pop in tow. I thought I could draw from
there. Once inside I began beating down the nettles with
my easel and came upon the wooden head of a bear,

which stared at me through streaked red paint. About the same moment, my foot struck an object, which turned out to be a rattle. It dawned on me I was sitting on the grave of a medicine man, and the presentiment of that body a few feet away spooked me, just as the cemetery at Ucluelet did years ago. This time I made myself sit tight for a few moments, heart thudding, listening to myself breathe. Instead of singing, I thought of Mr. Barbeau, of shamen who work magic to keep evil spirits away, of Kitwancool Jim and Fanny Johnson. Then I released the little dog and clambered out.

So much of this enterprise involves the unknown that I have come to see dread as normal. I won't say character building. There are times when I can go into the forest and see nothing, and other times when I am amazed at the birds and animals I come upon—or who come upon me and allow me see them. The barrier is awareness, and to be aware I've come to see you have to be willing to feel that fear, to face the fact that you are out of your element.

Just a few weeks ago the Kitwancool chased three surveyors out with axes, so I knew it would be folly to arrive unescorted. Following Barbeau's advice, I looked for a ride in with someone from the village, and found a young man named Aleck Douse, who assured me I could sleep at his father's house when we arrived. I wondered if his father would be so generous, not realizing until we got there that his father was one of the men travelling with us. An old fellow, he seemed quite content to walk part way beside the cart over the rough patches in the trail. That night I set up my bed on his veranda and slept fitfully, tormented by the bugs, cursing my stupidity for coming at all. Travelling alone like this, I have learned to expect the unexpected and to make do with whatever

accommodation is available. But I am not above complaining to myself or muttering to the little dog. It is a great
boon having Ginger Pop along. He made such an amusing
spectacle of himself when he first arrived, running after
the Indian dogs and taunting them, and then running
back to hide behind me. He had everyone laughing. Food
is the problem. When rations run short—as they are
now—I have to guard against my hosts knowing so I
won't have to eat what they inevitably offer. It takes more
grace than I have not to retch at the smell of candlefish
grease. It is trial by ordeal much of the time. I count the
days and practise restraint.

Drenched to the skin after the downpour, the dog and I
returned to the village to find my belongings had been
removed to a corner inside one of the bighouses. First
thing this morning, before I started out, Mrs. Douse
summoned me—no other way to put it—to account. Why
had I come to the village and what did I want with the
poles? I spoke through her son-in-law, who had also come
in on Aleck's wagon, explaining that I wanted to make
pictures of the poles for the young and for White people
so we would see how fine the poles used to be.

Mrs. Douse is a tall woman with a distinctive face that
gives nothing away when she talks. She did not smile, but
she was not unfriendly either. I was told to carry on with
my painting, that she would see. In Kitwangak I had
learned that Aleck is the son of a chief, and that the chiefs
of Kitwancool are particularly revered, said to possess the
powers of the old medicines. I wonder where Mrs. Douse
fits in. I do know she is giving me a taste of what it is like
to be judged for myself, accepted or no on my own merit.
There is no mission house to hide in here. Worse, there is
bad blood between her people and mine going back
decades. How will she separate me from other Whites, I
wonder? What have I got to recommend me?

Portrait painted by Emily Carr of her host, Mrs. Douse, at Kitwancool in 1928.

For reasons of her own, Mrs. Douse takes me into her house. It is an old-fashioned house built of new logs, with a gabled roof, two doors, and seven windows, each propped open with an empty blue castor-oil bottle. Her two daughters, their children, and husbands live here, as do Aleck and an orphan girl called Sally, whom everyone admires for her berry picking. Yesterday she beat soap-berries in a pail, creating a frothy pink goo called "soper-lallie," which old and young licked off their fingers with delight. People come and go as they please in this house-hold, eating and sleeping as the spirit moves them, mind-ing the little ones and rocking the infant hanging from the rafters in its cloth cradle as they pass. Behind the main house is an old cabin where Mrs. Douse and her husband

sleep. Less modern, it has an earthen floor and cedar
walls, but is cosy and well lived-in. Every surface is decorated with Indian designs—boxes, blankets, and baskets,
which are everywhere.

To be invited to stay is to be invited to live with the
whole family, a far more intimate gesture than I might
first have imagined. I am issued a corner, and the stove
there is kept lit. I am also given a rocking chair, and after
the orphan girl spies me down at the river brushing my
teeth in the early dawn, Mrs. Douse appears bearing a tin
basin and small pitcher so I can wash inside in the
warmth. The next morning my miniature sponge bath has
an avid audience.

After four days, I decide to show my host what I have
accomplished. In the afternoon I approach with a clutch of
sketches. She welcomes me into the cabin, pokes the fire
with a stick, releasing a shower of sparks up through the
smoke hole in the ceiling. I show her my sketches one by
one until she stops me at the view of two poles that belong
to her. She picks this one up and touches its surface gently,
and motions for Aleck. She wants to know how I get the
colour, he tells me, so I offer to show her my paints and
quickly retrieve my box of watercolours. I begin explaining what each pigment is made from, and as I look around
for a subject, I ask if I can paint her. She looks at me and
turns her head to one side, asking her granddaughter for
something. More tea, it turns out. I lapse into silence as I
launch into the task, building up the image with washes of
colour, forming planes to indicate forehead and cheek and
the folds of her clothing. I am enthralled by her face,
cheekbones high as the mountains surrounding us, eyes
sharp as a hummingbird's beak. She sits with her arms
folded against her chest, a countenance of conviction and
calm. Every few minutes, I show her what I am doing, and
when I finish, I immediately begin another, thinking to

"Totem Mother, Kitwancool," a portrait painted by Carr in 1928.

leave the first with her. She takes up the completed one, studies it for a long while and then starts to talk, gesturing at the portrait and herself with apparent pleasure. As the painting is handed back, I fumble and a blob of green paint splashes onto it. Mrs. Douse shakes her finger at my dismay and calls for Aleck again. This is good luck, she says.

Watching Mrs. Douse with her family and with the visitors who drop by to see her in a steady stream, I catch the humour in her voice and the deference in theirs. I see she is the one in the family with the influence and the following. I also see the resemblance of the totem pole mothers to the women in the village. I have been overcome with emotion sketching the great cedar mothers holding their babies in hands as large as bear paws, so huge they can scarcely contain the tender feel of it. They express all that is female to me, the force and magic of womanhood.

Last night I dreamt that I was deep in the forest, shafts of sunlight filtering through a canopy of leaves to the cool silence below. A silence filled with sound, I realize, becoming aware of the animal noises around me. A bear lumbers into view heading directly for the tree where I am standing, wondering to my astonished self if it is not time to flee. Instead I notice that the she-bear—I can see her now—looks familiar. I know as certainly as I know it cannot be true that I recognized her.

Since I have been in Kitwancool I have noticed how my sense of the forest has changed. Perhaps because I no longer have to hug history when I paint the poles, because I am free to paint them as part of the woods, I have started thinking about the forest as a mythic place. Ever since I saw the D'Sonoqua figure for the first time at Guyasdoms, fell at her feet on ground made slippery with slugs, and looked up to see those giant pursed lips and pendulous

thick-nippled breasts, I have understood that the poles
belong to the forest. I had no idea why she was hiding in an
overgrowth of nettles, and once I had recovered from the
fright of her, I set to finding out who and what sort of
being she was—is. The Cook girl, who was with me on that
trip, clammed right up when I asked, said she knew nothing, so I surmised something unpleasant was involved.
Then for a while D'Sonoqua was everywhere I went. There
are many stories about her, frightening ones and fantastical
ones. Her reputation is rather like the witch in Hansel and
Gretel who also has a fondness for snatching children, only
D'Sonoqua roams around looking for prey, and carries
them off to a secret lair. She is a gigantic creature who
inhabits the woods and turns up in stories of naughty children, a wild creature who is sometimes male and whose cry
is like the wind screeching through the trees. To me she
represents the primeval force of the forest, and has become
attached to my desire to delve deeper into it, to leave
Indian themes behind and go into the woods myself. Half of
me wants desperately to run into her, the other half hopes I
won't. I am not at all convinced she doesn't exist.

*I lie. I lie when I say I half hope to meet the D'Sonoqua for
I have met her. I don't mean the encounter with the effigy
in the woods, or in the ruins of the old community house
where she stood heavily atop a squatting bear, dangling
two human heads at her sides, fingers stuck into empty
jaws. Those figures spoke to me about the awe she
inspires. And now I have felt it too.*

The answers to my questions are always elusive.
Indian Tom's wrinkled face could not hide his resentment at White folks prying into wholly Indian matters.
"Sometimes bad, . . . sometimes good." This is all he
would tell me.

I am at home now in D'Sonoqua's forest. In love with
the trees and the mystic green space they create. Occasionally I have tried painting the seashore, but I cannot
withdraw inside myself there as I can here. Inside the
forest, the cedar trunks stretch to the skies while their
branches reach down to earth offering shelter, inviting
intimacy. They stand like ageless stoics defying the
seasons and whispering to those who sleep below: "Life
comes, life goes, the dream shall never vanish." I find
myself transported in the company of these beings.
Expectant. Unsure and sure of myself at the same time.
If I were to say I found Jesus here in the woods no one
would think me mad. My sisters would be surprised
but take it I had had a religious experience and was
speaking metaphorically. Even atheists would be polite.
Were I to mention D'Sonoqua's visit, no one would
understand it. They would badger me for specifics, and
I have little to offer besides the wail of the wind on a
windless August day.

They'll think me touched, which might be a good way
to describe it—touched, blessed. There are no words, no
paints to express this acquiescence of the soul. My
painting has changed too. I have lost interest in surface
work and find myself depicting carvings and trees alike
in thick, fleshy three dimensions. My palette is driven to
a deep sombre green, an awkward colour that invites
monotony—in this case a lethal heaviness, so I simplify.
The forms take on an expressive force, which matches
the change in myself. I am not the woman I was sixteen
years ago. It would be easy to note the departure of
bright colour and the idealism, and the mood of sober
reflection in my recent work. Despair has roughened my
edges, allowed me to see into the nether regions of the
soul, to admit that horror and fear are a part of wisdom.

*

I have begun cultivating a receptiveness, an open alert-
ness when I visit the woods. Sometimes their mood
depends on the weather; always it depends on my own
mood. I take a small campstool with me and select an
auspicious spot and sit down for a time watching the
trees, listening to the birds and animals rustling through
the leaves. I sniff the scented air, roll a cigarette, and take
out a small notebook to write down my thoughts and
sensations as the picture comes to me. Wording it into
existence.

There is much in what Lawren Harris and the Group of
Seven say about landscape and its connection to the spirit,
both the spirit of a nation and the spirit of a place. I think
we are searching for the same thing, and it might be called
atonement—a coming together with the "god" in nature
around us. In us, too. Harris understands this; his religion
and his painting are one. I often wonder how the rest of
them see me, though. I was a late addition to the West
Coast exhibition, visited by Eric Brown in September
when it was due to open in late November, yet more of
my paintings were hung than anyone else's. I was a bit
taken aback when I realized that, though I haven't any
illusions either. It was mainly the subject matter that led
to my choice. Mr. Barbeau's theme is clear. He sees the
poles as ancient masterpieces (as do I), and Native art as an
artistic resource. Few artists have used that motif as much
as I, it seems. So my work formed a link between the two
elements: Native and Modern Art. I can't say I regret the
attention, but it leaves me unsure of Mr. Brown. He does
single me out in his preface to the catalogue, but it is only
to observe my use of Native images. Does he see artistic
merit in my work is the question.

Mr. Barbeau is an ethnologist and it is he who
welcomed me to Ottawa and who has tried to arrange sales
of my paintings, not Mr. Brown, who is well known as the

champion of the Group of Seven. Then there was that sad
fizzle of an opening, the conflicting stories about the invitation list, and the awful dawning truth that hardly
anyone was going to show up. It was excruciating to
watch and if I were to speculate, I'd say there was rivalry
behind it. The exhibition was arranged by the National
Gallery, but the show was clearly Mr. Barbeau's and it
was he who wrote the catalogue, spoke to the newspapers,
and gave lectures about it. The opening should have been
his triumph, and the thought crosses my mind that the
invitation muddle might not have been an oversight. Mr.
Brown's forced gaiety was uncalled for and embarrassing.
I could see Madame Barbeau go rigid with indignation.
Several times during dinner beforehand her husband had
told me these affairs at the gallery are always packed, all
sorts of professional people, politicians, and society
women would come. Back at his home afterwards, Brown
carried on as if it had all been wonderful, and merrily
asked how we'd enjoyed it. Who can he have thought he
was fooling?

And who do I suppose I'm fooling with my out-of-place
bravado? Where do I get this sense of confidence, this
conviction that I am on the right track? There have been
moments of ecstasy this past year, followed by flashes of
blind panic. I worry that my technique is shaky, that my
stamina will not hold. I know praise and attention can
steer a person oV course.

I also know Lawren Harris's friendship has retrieved me
from a pit of loneliness. Some old maids like me hanker
after family, but I have never wanted that. Not really, not
in terms of everyday affection, which I've had in quantity
from sisters and all sorts of creatures. No, the intimacy
I've longed for is that of like minds, the delicious

exchange that comes from discussing art with someone who is doing the same thing. In the East they talk about me as if I had been lost to civilization and am now discovered. British Columbia *is* a long way from the art world and when I returned from France, I knew I was choosing isolation even if I was unaware of what it would mean.

I can't imagine things would have been better for me in Ontario though. I was swept away by Harris's insistence that I am one of them, his group, but that is not really true. I cannot see myself on one of their expeditions into the North woods and don't think for a minute that they would want me along. Jackson in particular seems dubious about women artists from what I can gather, and although the group has asked women to exhibit with them, only men are invited to join.

When I put that on paper and think idly of the "what ifs," I remind myself that I do not need travelling companions. I prefer to travel alone because I want to work alone and because this journey is one I *must* take on my own. I choose my own guides and now I never count on agents or missionaries being much help. Some days I suspect it may actually be better this way. Travelling alone as a White woman I have felt able to go places the men never could. I felt that especially at Kitwancool, where womanhood is strong.

"You Are One of Us"

Nineteen twenty-seven was the year that everything changed. The legend of Emily Carr begins there, with the story of her trip to Ottawa to attend the December opening of the Canadian West Coast Art show at the National Gallery and to meet members of the Group of Seven. She began keeping a journal on the train as it passed through the Rockies on the way east, aware that she was heading towards some sort of destiny. It was enough that perfect strangers had sought her out to include her work in the show and arranged a railway pass. She wrote in pencil in a small lined notebook, recording events in a free flow of description and candid remarks. Her voice is pensive and critical, the eye alive to the sights of the country as she passed through it, and to the foibles of the other passengers on the journey. She kept to herself and seemed edgy.

In Toronto, people were expecting her. She had looked up Fred Varley in Vancouver where he was teaching and he had wired ahead. Now she met Jackson and Arthur Lismer and felt she knew them. She wondered sheepishly if the men felt a common chord struck between them as she did. "No, I don't believe they feel so towards a woman," she answered herself. "I am way behind them in drawing and in composition and rhythm and planes, but I know inside me what they're after and I feel perhaps, given a chance, I could get it too." In the immediacy of discovery, her response was modest—she reminded herself of her shortcomings. She was dismayed, but essentially positive when she exclaimed, "Ah, how I have wasted the years! But there are still a few left."

All reservations melted with the praise and acceptance from the artists she met, especially Lawren Harris. Carr burst onto the page after meeting him in his studio, dazzled by his painting, *Above Lake Superior*: "Oh God, what have I seen? Where have I been?" When she saw Jackson's paintings of the Skeena, she declared herself ready to "go off on a tangent tear" the next time she painted Native themes. Harris inspired her on a deeper, emotive level. She perceived a spiritual dimension in the "silent awe-filled spaces" of his stripped-down images, a serenity she longed for. "Something has called out of somewhere. Something in me is trying to answer," she wrote. Next there was J.E.H. MacDonald's work and an afternoon with Bess and Fred Housser, whose apologia for the group had appeared the year before. Carr had read *A Canadian Art Movement* on Eric Brown's recommendation, so she was familiar with the Group's story. She was heady with delight to meet the people behind it. "Surely a movement that has such men for its foundation must prevail and live and become an honoured glory to our land," she wrote in her journal at the end of that unforgettable first week. Bordering on ecstatic, she added, "If I could pray, if I knew where to find a god to pray to, I would pray, 'God bless the Group of Seven.'"

For Carr, validation and vindication came together; validation for her work, not only for her portrayal of the forest and totem poles but for her identification with the land, and vindication for her belief in the documentary project. After all, the paintings that had buried her career in Vancouver were now resurrecting it in Ottawa. Through the intervening years, she had remained choosy about who she unpacked her collection for. Approached a year earlier by the British Columbia Art League to exhibit her Indian paintings and give a talk on the subject in Vancouver, she had refused, offering instead a show of her recent landscapes with the stipulation that all expenses be met by the league. The invitation was stiffly withdrawn. On the other hand, Marius Barbeau, a respected ethnologist with the National Museum who had spent several seasons in British Columbia doing fieldwork, was above suspicion. Carr considered his interest in Indians genuine and informed; she could talk to him as she had with old C.F. Newcombe, who died in 1924. Barbeau's interest in her work was backed by the National Gallery as well as the National Museum, which was official approval, if ever there was—just what Carr had sought so earnestly in 1913. Thus when Barbeau asked her to ship a portion of the collection (forty-six were sent to Ottawa and twenty-six were hung in the exhibition), she complied. She even agreed to send some pottery and hooked rugs.

Everywhere Carr went during that first trip east, studios and drawing-rooms opened for her. She was squired around Toronto, Ottawa, and Montreal, given teas, taken to dinner, and made welcome. She became an overnight sensation in art circles, was written about in the dailies and weeklies, paid special attention to by the critics, and issued invitations to exhibit. More than anything else, though, she was buoyed by contact with artists. Harris asked her to make suggestions if she had any when he brought out his paintings to show her. Carr was surprised. "Me? I know nothing," she told him. "You are one of us," he replied. Carr looked at their work and found herself instantly animated, fired with the desire to get back to her own painting.

Nothing like it had happened in years. Not since France had she had the opportunity to interact with other engaged artists. Not since France had she seen modern painting that challenged her own. The fact that she gained acceptance from these people with old work perturbed her and stoked her desire to paint new things. And indeed, she made her name and historical reputation on what she went on to produce, work that was fundamentally different in conception and style, so that 1927 can be seen more as a departure or a metamorphosis than as a culmination of anything. This artistic catharsis came with a spurt of energy that propelled her back up the coast to the Native villages she had visited before, and to new ones Barbeau introduced to her on the Nass River. With encouragement from Harris and the others, she took off on her "tangent tear" all right, but not one that led to any further investigation of Native art. Released from the demands of the documentary, she followed her intuition into the forest and allowed the Aboriginal motif to become one with the landscape—and sometimes to fade completely from view. Part of the change was unquestionably Harris's doing, for he counselled her to leave the poles behind. More important was what "called out to her" in his mountains and icebergs—his mysticism. Her inquiries led to discussions about the spiritual in art and Harris's devotion to the practice of Theosophy. It was a line of thinking that precipitated a realization that the power she felt in the presence of Harris's mountain was the same cosmic force she sensed in the company of the carved poles.

Nineteen twenty-seven brought Emily Carr the breakthrough of a lifetime. She found the impetus to put art back at the centre of her life, and a way to cut through the impasse of the past. The breakthrough had everything to do with her art and her understanding of its origins, but it was not, strictly speaking, an aesthetic passage; a good part of it was emotional. The change in circumstance permitted her to break free of the depression that had engulfed her over the previous decade. "Have the carps, and frets and worries that have eaten my soul since I returned from Paris full of ambitions and then had to struggle out there alone, [have they] made me small and mean, poor and petty—bitter?" she asks herself in a moment of frankness, perhaps incited by the unaccustomed happiness. The paintings would seem to confirm the alteration, for the woman who depicts the Great Raven at Cumshewa in 1931 as an apocalyptic vision is not the same one who sketched it in 1912 as a wooden giant. There is a brooding strength in the new painting, a sense of sorrow that can sometimes rock the soul.

She says very little about the "wasted" years and what happened to her, although she wrote about the period in her autobiography in a chapter titled "Rejected." There she spoke of running an apartment house during the war when low rents forced her to act as agent and janitor as well as landlady, and of being saved from financial ruin by breeding Old English sheepdogs and decorating pottery with Native designs to sell to tourists. "Clay and Bobtails paid my taxes," she quipped. The dogs she adored; the pottery operation, on the other hand, was cause for self-reproach. It was "prostituting" Indian art to apply it to candlesticks and ashtrays. What made it worse, she claimed, was her success. "Because my stuff was sold, other potters followed my lead, and knowing nothing of Indian Art, falsified it. This made me very angry. I loved handling the cool clay. I loved the beautiful designs, but I was not happy about using Indian design on material for which it was not intended and I hated seeing them distorted, cheapened by those who did not understand or care as long as their pots sold." Curiously, the only allusion Emily made to the loss of her desire to paint comes directly after this passage. The subject at hand is dropped (although I will return to it) and we are given these words: "I never painted now—had neither time nor wanting. For about fifteen years I did not paint." Carr does not elaborate, except to imply a descent into a misfortune of some kind with the next phrase: "Before I struck bottom it seemed there was one lower sink into which I could plunge." This was her ladies' boarding house scheme. Carr resumes the narrative about her commercial endeavours, concluding that the only thing they proved was that an artist could cook and keep house. But "that an artist could paint honestly and keep boarders simultaneously, I did not prove." When Eric and Maud Brown visit her in September 1927, she informs them she stopped painting because nobody understood her work. She tells us how the call from the director of the "Canadian National Gallery" (which she hadn't known existed) was initially unwelcome: "To be reminded that I had once been an artist hurt."

And this is how legend remembers it, even though historians have assiduously pointed out that Carr did not actually stop painting, that she produced some thirty canvases during the period, approximately two a year. Nor did she stop travelling, although her purpose altered. In 1916 and 1917, for instance, she spent eight months in San Francisco, a much-needed respite from the travails of running Hill House. She did some painting, but the sojourn was memorable mainly for the chance encounter with Mayo Paddon. Neither one pursued the reconnection, but thereafter Emily received a card at Christmas from him every year with pressed flowers enclosed. There were also regular forays in the summers to visit friends in and around Vancouver Island— Cowichan Bay, Duncan, and Ahousat on the West Coast near Ucluelet. These were family holidays rather than serious excursions, and sketching trips were taken only when weather permitted. Art had ceased to occupy the core of her daily life, and she had become absorbed with the unheroic task of making ends meet. Carr detested the drudgery of being a landlady and the interaction with tenants it foisted on her. She recorded her experiences in *The House of All Sorts,* which leaves the reader in no doubt as to her feelings for most of the people sent her way looking for lodgings. In addition to the drain on her time and energy, she resented the encroachment on her art (the boarding-house operation necessitated moving her studio into the attic, for instance) and she began to feel estranged from it for the first time in her life. If she never completely stopped painting, she did stop exhibiting, and for a time she withdrew entirely from the public sphere. In other words, what began as a withdrawal from the Vancouver art scene turned into a full-scale retreat from art. When she painted, moreover, she painted local landscapes, using the open, brightly coloured patterns she adopted in the Paris year.

What can we conclude about this hiatus? Whether it was from fatigue, resignation, despair, or a combination of all three, Emily Carr went through a creative crisis in the prime of her life when she all but gave up on the artist she had become. She lost the "wanting" for art and later referred to herself during those years as a quitter. What happened cannot be precisely known, but her biographers tend to relate it to the physical breakdowns she experienced in England and France when she was a student. They differ drastically in the interpretation of how it came about. Maria Tippett doesn't say it in so many words, but she treats Carr's account of her illness as the ravings of an hysteric. Hysteria was, in fact, the diagnosis given when Carr was admitted to the East Anglia Sanatorium in 1903, a condition reinterpreted by Tippett as conversion-reaction, or the extreme physical reaction to stress. The stress, in Tippett's opinion, was largely psychological, the result of conflicting neuroses which she identifies as Carr's sexual frigidity, insecurity, and paranoia that led to her childish, attention-getting behaviour and made for tortured and short-lived relations with people her own age. The rejection of Paddon is taken as evidence of the said frigidity, or Carr's inability to respond sexually to anyone. According to Tippett, Emily refused to grow up and the trouble she experienced after 1913 came from being thrust into the world of adults for the first time. The apartment scheme foundered and her painting, which she had elevated into a historic mission, ceased to function as the justification for her life. She submitted to loneliness and frustration; her *joie de vivre* faded, she hardened and turned nasty. Relationships deteriorated along with her appearance, and the dynamic with her sisters left her feeling resentful and guilty. In her twenties and thirties, Carr's art and life had had one purpose. Everything dovetailed, even sexual feelings could be sublimated to the cause. Her forties and fifties were not so easy, but, Tippett maintains, it was not because she was scoffed at or her work disparaged. The tale of rejection is concocted, she says, for approval and encouragement most emphatically did come Carr's way. She concludes that Emily was simply influenced by Fredrick Housser's romantic tale of the Group of Seven's struggle against public misunderstanding and poverty and wove it right into her own life story. She did not actually have much to struggle against, beside her own *naïveté* and neurotic delusion.

Paula Blanchard, writing eight years later in 1987, rejects Tippett's Freudian analysis, although she, too, reads Carr's collapse in Europe as connected to her immaturity and sexual repression. She sees the "bitter years" of 1913–27 as the last and longest of the dark periods in Carr's life, a time when the artist was overtaken by depression, so she accepts Carr's account and credits her with some self-knowledge. Indeed, it does not require a flight of fancy to imagine Carr's depression, not if we take the failure of her 1913 exhibition seriously, and not if we credit her distress and self-contempt at having to give up painting for the petty job of everyman's landlady. Hints surface in Carr's correspondence with Lawren Harris and Ira Dilworth, in which words like "despair" and "depression" appear and reappear. Her sisters' hostility to her art was something a person could live with, like the weather, but in the face of her apparent failure to succeed as an artist, Emily must have felt the absurdity of her quest in their eyes. What reason *was* there for continuing to paint? Like Tippett, Blanchard reaches into Carr's childhood for explanations and encounters the spectre of the man who appears in *The Book of Small* and is the subject of so much latter-day gossip—the patriarchal father, the author of the "brutal telling." The phrase comes from a letter Carr wrote late in her life to Ira Dilworth, a teacher and broadcaster who edited her books and became a trusted friend she addressed as "Eye" in letters she signed "Small." *The Book of Small* was just out and she commented on the fact that so much of her father appeared in the chronicle of her childhood, and so little of her mother whom she loved best. "I feel *Small* has sort of squared me with father . . . Of course, all of her [*Small*, the book] is stories before that brutal telling and the horrible crack-up of Small's lovely world which broke the fond devoted relationship between us. I was bitterly unforgiving. It must have been dreadfully hurtful to father." Evidently Carr had spoken of the incident to Dilworth and the conversation was helpful to her. "Small's being able to tell the deepest friend she ever had, and that friend's understanding seemed to smooth away the old scar." Septuagenarian Emily confessed that hers was the heart that had turned to stone. "If I have made people respect and honour father through the book of Small perhaps it in some way atoned for all my years of bitterness." She was contrite and the voice had softened since the angry comments she recorded in her journal in 1935 about the "cross gouty sexy old man who hurt and disgusted me." In an unpublished section, she goes into some detail about the incident. "I resented his omnipotence his selfishness and I was *frightened* of him. He knew he had hurt me, telling me things a happy child should not hear and telling them to me in a low and blatant manner. . . . I couldn't forgive father for spoiling all the loveliness of life with that bestial brutalism of an explanation filling me with horror instead of gently explaining the glorious beauty of reproduction, the holiness and joy of it." There were lifelong repercussions, Blanchard suggests, and at this moment, in addition to spurning her father and her father's church, she turned away from her own body, which suddenly repulsed her.

This interpretation is of a piece with the story of anonymous "Jamie" in the kitchen garden and the campaign to harden herself to love. And it corroborates the idea that Carr had switched herself off. Carr made the connection herself between the anguished relationship with her father and her later losses in love. Early in 1938 when she was destroying papers and letters (there being no one left who was interested or able to look after them, she reasoned), she reread letters from old friends and reflected on love. "My love had those three deadly blows," she said, wondering if she ever fully recovered from those massive hurts. "I have loved three souls, passionately passionately. Two relatives and a lover." The lover would have to be "Jamie so part of the story makes sense." Richard Carr betrayed her and she turned against him; the young man betrayed love and Emily turned against love. If nothing else, we can detect a pattern of Emily turning off at the sight of emotional trauma. The second "relative" is a mystery and Carr could possibly be referring to her brother, Dick, who died tragically young during her first year in England. However, there is precious little in her writing about him. The strongest evidence of their special affection is a couple of studio photographs of the two of them, dated 1891, in which the body language and relaxed expressions indicate a high degree of familiarity and comfort between them.

The vagueness of the reference to the "brutal telling" in the published literature on Carr has led to speculation about incest. Blanchard and Tippett describe it as merely a clumsy attempt to convey the facts of life, an ill-conceived effort to frighten pre-teen Emily (by far the most alluring of Richard Carr's daughters) into more circumspect behaviour. But Tippett opens the door to further speculation with the comment that "her expression of revulsion makes one wonder if it was caused by a misguided attempt to illustrate the explanation by some action." This is not what Emily said, but she nevertheless suggested something callous and cruel in her father's behaviour towards her. The bond between them was Manichean, and the feelings of relief she reported having at the time of his death clearly indicate that what passed between them was profound and never resolved.

Denial may have been involved, but it does not require the presence of sexual abuse to credit Emily's hard feelings; even a face value reading of Carr's memoirs indicates that the Richard Carr she knew as a child was abusive in his insensitivity. He was also the keystone that kept the hierarchy in the house in place, the primary source of her struggle with gender and privilege. At the time she wrote about the incident, almost fifty years later, she, Alice, and Lizzie were meeting each evening after supper to read from their father's diary. This had given Emily a whole new slant (as she said) on her parent. "I can see he must have been a fine young man, strong and honest and kindly and energetic. And brave. Plenty of perseverance and plenty of pluck." It may be, in fact, that Emily's own eloquent anger had obscured Richard Carr's positive contribution to her formation just as it obscures her battle with patriarchal values. The rupture affected his daughter, but so did his early benevolent interest in her drawing. And though it was not to last into adulthood, for a few years as a young child, Emily was the beloved of her father, the child given special access to his affection and his world and, incidentally, the world of men. The confidence born of that position, together with her native intelligence and spunk taught her to assert herself, to brave dissent. It may also be true, as Blanchard proposes, that her mother gave tacit approval to Emily's violation of the rules by which Richard Carr dominated the family's life. Whatever the case, it was the same spirit that led Carr to stake everything on the exhibition of 1913, and to return to serious painting in 1927.

It may not be necessary to pathologize Carr in order to understand her withdrawal after 1913. At the same time, there is much in Tippett's description of her character that rings true. Carr did become crusty and turned people away. With distance you can see her behaviour—the short temper and the tendency to be judgmental—as defensive. Her propensity for kicking against the pricks put a price on shins nonetheless. This was the side to her that had a hard time being happy, that held her back until it was almost too late to let go. For Emily Carr, 1927 was the year that knocked her on the head and reversed the proposition that it was pointless to paint. "I must get back to it and let other things go," she chides herself now. "If not, my chance is done . . . Perhaps it will be easier after this trip and the girls may not feel it quite such a waste of time, and a useless quest." Emily loved her sisters in spite of their straight laces and long noses, and at some level she desired their approval. One side of her admired their goodness and industry, the other side felt they dismissed her unfairly and she resented them for it. It was a relationship full of contradictions, just as hers had been with their father. And it is clear that Emily's sense of familial duty and her awareness of the family's opprobrium played a major role in her psychology.

It is also true that the re-emergence of "M. Emily Carr" had been coming quite a while. It was not an overnight achievement. She recommenced showing at the annual Island Arts and Crafts Society show in 1924, the same year she met Kate Mather, who began marketing her pottery in Banff and Vancouver as well as Victoria. A couple of American artists who frequented Hill House as paying guests took an interest in Emily's work in these years and encouraged her to exhibit in Seattle, which she first did in 1924 as well. When 1927 came, she was ready for opportunity. Nonetheless, the transformation in the aftermath of the trip east was abrupt and extraordinary. She would call it miraculous and, at the same time, proof that patience can win out. Yet, there is something missing in Blanchard's and Tippett's portraits of the artist and the breakdown, and that is the positive elements in the choices Carr was making. Paddon was no failure; he was a decision not to marry, and possibly part of a decision against heterosexual love. Her break with her father, which was self-propelled, was also liberating, for it framed her departure from middle-class conformity and comfort, and it initiated her quest for an identity of her own creation. Furthermore, the stress she experienced in England owed something to the social pressures she was sorting out and the physical strain of the urban environment she was in. Her later depression was inevitably an expression of her restrictive circumstances and her artistic stasis as well as deep-seated and self-destructive fear. She struggled with loneliness and isolation despite friendships with other (usually) single women. She became a loner, preferring always to paint in the woods by herself. The anguish that radiates from her journals may be directed at her sisters, may express the torment of her endless search for a core and the key to her art, but the subject is her own gloom, her preoccupation with her own soul, and the spiritual meaning of life. The paintings of the immediate post-1927 years are large and imposing in keeping with the seriousness of her mission. There is a sombre tone, and often a foreboding in canvasses like *Vanquished* and *Old Time Coastal Village*, which both depict the aftermath of the smallpox epidemic on Haida Gwaii. The landscape emptied of people. The carved figures now assume a gravity that is mirrored in the dense, curvaceous, foliate forest closing in around them, as in works like *Big Raven (Cumshewa)* and *Nirvana (Tanoo)*. The series includes *Indian Church, Indian Hut—Queen Charlotte Island, Potlatch Welcome*, and the *Guuyasdoms' D'Sonoqua*, which are all based on sketches she made during her first trip in 1912. These are followed by several paintings depicting carvings almost completely engulfed in green. *Strangled by Growth* is one such example and *D'Sonoqua and the Cat Village* is another. The period culminates with *Grey*, which represents both the nadir of Carr's descent into despair and the light she found flickering at the end of the tunnel. I see the work as symbolic and expressive, and imagine that the experience of depression opened her to the dark side of herself, which, in turn, gave her the courage to confront the dark side of nature. At least by now she had lost the fear of being herself. She could let go of her crutch and paint the forest alone.

If 1927 was Emily Carr's year, it was Canada's, too. It was, in any event, the Diamond Jubilee of Confederation, which was celebrated with a zest and self-confidence unimaginable at the time of

*The Catholic church at Friendly Cove painted by Carr in 1928 and known as
"Indian Church."*

the country's fiftieth anniversary ten years earlier. Everyone was preoccupied with the war in 1917, and that experience became the crucible of the age and of a generation; it changed people forever and it transformed Canada. As the cliché says with some truth, the country went to war a colony and came back a nation. For those who believe that nations are forged through civil war or revolution, this was Canada's requisite bloodbath. As historian Ramsay Cook has explained, the shift in attitude was both a revulsion for the gory battlefields of Europe and a disenchantment with imperial rule, having observed Britain's conduct of the war. The result was an assertion of Canadian autonomy in relation to Britain and within the Commonwealth, and a general realignment of sympathies over the next decade. With this came a preoccupation, at least in certain circles, with national consciousness and the definition of the emerging country. It never had been a forgone conclusion that the mere fact of Confederation would produce a nation—which is to say a place and a mythos that Canadians would claim and cherish as theirs. Emily Carr grew up in an era that hardly questioned the British foundation of Canadian culture, but the subject of Canadian nationalism was continuously debated nevertheless. (The question became critical, of course, in relation to defence policy during wartime when costs were calculated in human lives.) The theme of this history, this *anxiety*, was the search for Canadian roots. The dawning realization during these postwar years was that these could not be dug up like truffles in the woods, that they had to be cultivated. The dilemma, then, was whether the future of this nation-in-the-making was to be found "in its inherited Europeanness or its developing North Americanness." The political reorientation after the war was decisive. Cook styles it as the withdrawal from the Empire and Commonwealth into fortress North America. Moreover, politics were only following trends in other arenas that were taking Canada in the direction of integration with the U.S. In 1926, the same year Canada sent its first representative to Washington, American investment exceeded Great Britain's in Canada for the first time. The die was cast, economically speaking, and the era of the world's longest undefended border was upon us.

During the postwar years, Canadians' sense of themselves and their country continued to evolve. Interestingly, Cook singles out the publication of *A Canadian Art Movement* as a watershed event in advance of a new self-consciously Canadian and pro-North American perspective. He quotes Fred Housser: "For Canada to find a complete racial expression of herself through art, a complete break with European traditions was necessary; a new type of artist was required. . . The message that the Group of Seven art movement gives to this age is the message that here in the North has arisen a young nation with faith in its own creative genius." Writing the following year in a book called *The Growth of Canadian National Feeling*, Stewart Wallace repeats this last sentence of Housser's in making the argument that there had grown up a "strong and insistent" national consciousness in the arts as in other facets of Canadian life. Wallace contended that with a maritime flag of our own and the germ of a diplomatic service (not to mention our own envoy in Washington), Canada's new found independence had been recognized by the rest of the world. Previous generations had spoken of national unity in the future tense; well, the future had arrived. "In a thousand ways in matters of speech and dress and diet and amusements and even thought, Canadian national feeling is still being moulded day to day by the stubborn facts of geography." And there it was, the great Canadian common denominator, geography. The point of connection between the emerging concept of an indigenous, made-in-Canada Canada and the Group of Seven was the land, and the new significance attached to it was a metaphor for the nation.

Wallace and Housser were not alone in their ruminations. The Diamond Jubilee was a moment of high sentiment for Canada, but also an occasion when the focus on Canada's role in the world of nations provoked discussion about her shortcomings as one. Peace and prosperity had returned following the war, but so had the movement to unionize workers and secure the vote for women.

And in addition to the reformers and radicals who addressed matters of social justice, there were those who raised doubts about Canada's ability to pursue her independent purpose in any event. The country lacked the institutions and the informed citizenry, and, it was feared, the courage. Some charged that dependence on English standards and ideas was merely being replaced by a dependence on American culture and know-how. A burgeoning community of English Canadian poets, artists, and scholars began debating their views of Canadian culture in the pages of *The Canadian Forum* (founded in 1921) and in publications such as Bertram Brooker's *Yearbook of the Arts in Canada 1928/29* where they confidently articulated a determination to reimagine Canada.

Brooker's expansive anthology included essays by Fred Housser, Lawren Harris, and Marius Barbeau, among many other artists, writers, and scholars. His own introduction was a *cri de coeur* in which he confronted the fact that Canadian society did not possess the cohesion and experience to support an art of its own. "Historically we have no past as a people. . . . We are *not yet* a people," he writes. He then goes on to describe the mechanization of contemporary culture, which had introduced all kinds of new products and activities into daily life but had left art behind, mired in the predictable. People had taken to the movies like ducks to water, but in literature and painting "We permit ourselves to be greatly disturbed by ingenuity, originality, and the invention of new contrivances, new moods, new modes. . . . The artist is the last person on earth who is granted the right to originality." Writing from the point of view of a practising artist, he also describes the constraints of a population too small to provide an adequate audience, and an art establishment inhibited by a conception of art that hinged on antiquated notions of connoisseurship borrowed from another age. "The artist, seeking the living sustenance of *togetherness* with an audience, loses heart here, lacks incentive and impetus, and either hurries to Europe or the States, or turns sour and cynical in the shop or the counting-house where he is forced to work." The description could have been of Carr, and she actually would have concurred with Brooker's ideas about the need for a *rapprochement* between audience, critic, and artist. Noting the role that George Bernard Shaw played in the reception and recognition of Ibsen and Wagner in England, Brooker endorses the idea that a critic's business was not only to judge the work, but to create an audience for the artist. He skirts the issue of the colonial consciousness, saying only that he awaits a time "when we no longer regard ourselves as exiles and everybody else as foreigners." Lawren Harris, on the other hand, greets it straight on, castigating the English attitude. "So many people in North America cling to the European attitude and its traditions because it has attained to its expression in an intricate culture and because the comfort of its immense background of tradition is almost the only security they know. They view the strivings and directions of the new, now adolescent race, their race, with disdain or misgiving."

In 1931, another collection of essays appeared addressing the same theme. Called *Open House,* it was meant as an open challenge to complacent readers and newspaper editors who refused to circulate new or unconventional opinion. "Canada is youthful in every way but its national mind," wrote Wilfred Reeves in his introduction to the volume. "We must develop in this country an intelligent, open-minded sceptical attitude towards our thousand and one problems and perplexities. We must let down the barriers on radical opinion. It must no longer be considered a sacrilege to doubt our gods of Finance, Big Business, Politics, Advertising, and so through the long list." Contributors included civil servants, librarians, professors, poets (Charles G.D. Roberts and E .J. Pratt), and painters (Charles Comfort and Bertram Brooker). In his article called "Nudes and Prudes," Brooker took on the provincialism of the Toronto art establishment, which had recently removed a canvas of his displaying nudes in a landscape from the annual Ontario Society of Artists' show. He blamed the bland conservatism of the Canadian mainstream. On the other hand, writing about the still controversial topic of modernism, G.D. Roberts targeted the popular objection to its ugliness, a quality he referred to as violence. Canada's slow reaction to modernism can simply be explained by our aversion to extremism, he contended. Modernism crept into Canadian poetry "by peaceful penetration rather than rude assault," he said, implying that the approach was unwelcome and the experience unpleasant nevertheless. He then declared the Group of Seven "essentially sane" and in the main preoccupied with beauty. "Beauty they not only see with new eyes but show to us with a simplicity and truth." Roberts, a traditionalist of the older generation, insisted the militancy of the young rebels was misconstrued, that they had, in fact, little to militate against.

One could take this as evidence that the Group of Seven had arrived, that the open antagonism between the art societies and the new independents had mellowed, but it was revisionist all the same. In his re-evaluation of the history of the group for the National Gallery's 1996 exhibition *Art for a Nation*, art historian Charles Hill makes it clear that the battle for acceptance by the elder generation in the Royal Canadian Academy of the Arts and the Ontario Society of Artists and other artists' associations that commanded access to the country's art institutions was a bitter one. As a result, artists as a group lost control of the galleries they had created and were replaced by professionals, a process that may have been inevitable but which was acrimonious nevertheless. Roberts's remarks indicated that the modernist urge, particularly its individualist and anarchist tendencies, was being normalized. They also reveal an antagonism to the story of the Group of Seven's struggle against backward opinion that would feed into the myth still current today—that this story was concocted for public consumption.

As well as debating the issues of nationalism, an expanding coterie of artists and intellectuals were pouring their energy into the development of cultural and civic associations with avowed national aspirations. The Royal Society of Canada, for example, brought together scientists and humanists outside their universities and disciplines to encourage Canadian research; the Canadian Authors' Association promoted Canadian literature, while the

League of Nations Society, the Canadian Institute of International Affairs, and the Canadian Club all promoted discussion of current affairs. The Canadian Club's speakers' circuit even acted as a springboard for a citizens' lobby in support of a publicly owned radio system in the 1930s. There was ferment in the air, and a network of people in place whose ties were personal but whose links were formalized in organizations like the Radio League and the Canadian Historical Association. These were people who did not aspire to political office but to influencing those who did. They were the architects of a nationalist ideology, an élite prepared to foster a movement, though not necessarily a mass movement. As cultural historian Mary Vipond observes, "they were not social critics so much as social leaders who hoped to mould public opinion." And they did.

The view of Canada that survives in their writings is of a tentative nation that had nonetheless found the bedrock of its identity in the earth beneath its feet. There is an assertiveness in the tone, an idealism in the passion, and (with the benefit of hindsight) a certain *naïveté*. The matter of Quebec is usually overlooked, although Wallace speaks of a supranationalism that would allow the two "races" to evolve separately but together. Minimal attention is given to the First Nations, who are still presumed to be disappearing, just as the new Canadian nation is presumed to be appearing. Native culture is given a place as source material for contemporary art, a practice that Barbeau eulogizes in his piece on Canadian music, but is otherwise overlooked. Brooker mentions Native peoples in passing. "Back of all this [diversity as a result of immigration] is the Indian, supplying occasional motifs for our art and subtly tincturing the national admixture in ways that we mostly ignore." The consternation about national unity, thus, did not have to do with fear of the home-grown divisions so much as of influences from abroad, which were thought to be inhibiting development here. It had nothing to do with Quebec or Aboriginal Canada, rather, it was all about English Canada and English Canadian dreams. The picture presented is of a people who have yet to take the leap of faith in themselves and North America that these artist-interlocutors have. They are, of course, a select few, highly intelligent, publicly spirited men well placed in institutions such as museums, universities, and governments, with the freedom to pursue their political cause. The Canada they speak of, and attempt to will into existence, was intentionally unitary, and their concept of nationhood homogeneous. While envisaging a Canada independent of British or American direction, they clearly thought the nation would become a country only if ethnicity and difference were subsumed in a White, English-speaking, central Canadian ideal.

The identity that this élite embraced had antecedents in late nineteenth-century ideas about hardy northern peoples. This was first coherently articulated by Robert Haliburton in the 1870s, a man whose ideas historian Carl Berger has depicted thus: "Lamenting the fact that Confederation had been created with as little excitement among the masses as if a joint-stock company had been formed, he asked, 'Can the generous flame of national spirit be kindled and blaze in the icy bosom of the frozen North?' Convinced that the indispensable attribute of a nation, a 'national spirit', was the product of slow growth unless stimulated by violent struggle, the memory of a glorious past or the anticipation of a bright future, Haliburton added to the Canada First spirit the contention that Canada's future as a dominant nation was secure because of its northern character." We are the northerners of the New World, Haliburton cried, in effect declaring the Canadian climate a national asset, and, as Berger elucidates, reconfiguring it as a creative force in the national identity. "Since the days of Voltaire's famous dismissal, [the cold climate,] the symbol of sterility, inhospitality and worthlessness" has become "a dynamic element of national greatness." Such ideas spawned a plethora of maxims and notions. The frosty climate gave Canadians their dour character and puritan frame of mind; it provided insulation against lax morality and was conducive to mental improvement; it was the source of the superiority of northern White races who display greater inclination to liberty than their southern brothers; it was equated with self-reliance and vigorousness. From this platform a rationale for distinguishing between Canadians and Americans was deduced, as were theories of racial unity, which saw French and English Canadians coming from common Norman stock, and Native peoples, thanks in great part to Marius Barbeau and Emily Carr, thrown into the mix as "ancient Canadians."

From the beginning, the national identity project was cast in terms of race as well as gender. Wrote Harris after a trip to the Arctic with Jackson in 1930, "We know that it is only through deep and vital experience of its total environment that a people identify itself with its land and gradually a deep and satisfying awareness develops. We are convinced that no virile people could remain subservient to and dependent upon the creations in art of other peoples. . . .To us, there was also the strange brooding sense of another nature fostering a new race and a new age." Gender was perhaps a more explicit dimension of the Group of Seven's activity than it was in other nationalist expressions. Their practice and public personae cast them as he-man artists, woodsmen, and explorers who were prepared to experience the wild without the usual props of civilization. They camped out on the rocks, travelled by canoe, and sketched the country through the thick and thin of black flies and bad weather. They projected an aura of tobacco and sweaty socks, of masculine motion. So when Harris told Carr, "You are one of us," he could not have been more wrong. Carr did share a connection to the land with these artists and an ambition to be accepted, but her sources of inspiration were quite different, deriving not only from another part of the country, but from another non-European artistic tradition. Moreover, her instincts were female—one could say womanly, as she did. In several essential ways she was not one of them.

At the centre of this story is the enigmatic figure of Marius Barbeau. From the distance of over half a century, he cuts a figure that could be compared to Archie Belaney, the Englishman who

made himself over into an Indian called Grey Owl and fooled many
people for a long time with his impersonation, or perhaps Burl Ives,
the avuncular American troubadour who charmed three generations with his folk songs. Barbeau was no impostor and no musician, though he did cross cultures and loved performing. He was a
Beauçeron who became part of the Anglo-Canadian élite and spent
most of his working life engaged in the creation of an official
Anglo-Canadian culture, his fieldwork being an investigation of
the culture of the other solitudes in the Canadian equation: French
Canada and the Aboriginal nations of the continent. He was one of
this country's first ethnologists and an avid folklorist who worked
all his life for the Victoria Memorial Museum—renamed the
National Museum in 1927 and now the Canadian Museum of Civilization. Barbeau collected reams of material from Native elders and
from French-Canadian artisans, travelling to tiny, remote communities to obtain it. He produced quantities of magazine articles and
several monographs, including the three on the totem poles of the
Northwest Coast Native peoples, a biography of the nineteenth-
century painter Cornelius Krieghoff, and a book on French-Canadian painting. He was prodigious, prolific, and nothing if not an
enthusiast. In the 1920s his interests began drawing him into activities outside his job at the museum. He was already active in the
Royal Society of Canada, having been elected a fellow in 1916 (he
held several offices and was treasurer between 1920 and 1925), and
he was deeply involved in the business of acquiring artefacts for
museum collections, his own and others as well. (The mammoth
memorial pole of Nisga'a Eagle Chief Sagawe'n that sits in a stairwell at the Royal Ontario Museum was secured by him in 1929, for
example.) He was a keen collector himself, and was frequently
prompted to buy for friends. On occasion he acted as an artist's
agent, performing this function for the sculptor Louis Jobin and,
after he had purchased an Emily Carr painting and brought the
artist to Ottawa, for her as well. The selling of Carr's work was
done informally and the results sporadic. Barbeau's bid to secure a
major purchase for his own institution almost came to nought; only

one painting of the eight he proposed was bought. As he reported back to Carr, echoing Dr. Newcombe's sentiments of 1913, her work was too artistic. "We have to deal here with puritans who are very suspicious of anything that has any contact with art," he informed her.

As part of his program for popularizing French-Canadian folk culture, Barbeau also began organizing public events in the early 1920s. It started with the Montreal concerts, the *veillées de bon vieux temps*, and culminated in the two Canadian Folk Song and Handicraft Festivals staged at the Château Frontenac in Quebec City in 1927 and 1928. These were elaborate affairs sponsored by the CPR, which owned the hotel and whose interest undoubtedly lay in the extra custom generated during the slack season. Working with the railway's publicity agent, Murray Gibbon, Barbeau produced a series of performances, demonstrations, and exhibits using professional artists, artisans, and "genuine" folk performers. The following year, the Canadian Club toured a smaller version of the festival across the country. Further collaboration with performers and artists followed quite naturally. When Barbeau was invited to give public lectures he often engaged folk singer Philéas Bédard to perform with him, and he helped vocalist Juliette Gaultier organize recitals that regularly featured traditional music he supplied. It was she, for example, who performed at the opening of the Canadian West Coast Art show at the Art Gallery of Toronto in January 1928. Barbeau was in his element in this impresario role and there was no pretence about his association with the CPR or about his conflation of professional and private affairs. He seems to have had a free rein so far as the museum was concerned. Canadian anthropology was in its early days and Barbeau was inventing his methodology as he went along; he was inventing himself at the same time. In the 1920s he was at the height of his success; his articles were everywhere, his books were winning awards, and he was sought after as a speaker. His profile, however, was mainly among English Canadians, who were fascinated by the stories and songs of Old Quebec, the Indians and the

Eskimo, and were entranced by the lively and equally exotic Barbeau. (To his credit, it has been noted, a generation of Canadians grew up knowing the first lines of "Alouette.")

Meanwhile, his friendship with A.Y. Jackson brought him into contact with the Group of Seven. Jackson and Arthur Lismer joined Barbeau on a trip to the Île d'Orléans in 1925, and Jackson spent the summer of 1926 painting along the Skeena with Edwin Holgate and Anne Savage. For several years, artists came west at Barbeau's invitation on passes supplied by the CPR, which underwrote the project in return for a set of paintings to use for publicity. The railway's objective was purely commercial—more passengers for its northern route to Prince Rupert; Barbeau's was purely ideological—to promote the region and the culture he was studying as part of the national identity. His first project with the railway in the West was *Indian Days in the Canadian Rockies*, which the CPR hoped would create a popular interest in "the Indian" and publicize its annual Indian Days celebration at the Banff Springs Hotel. The book was designed around a series of portraits painted by the American artist Langdon Kihn on the Stoney Reserve in Alberta. Barbeau's text and the gallery of solemn elders in traditional dress evoked a bygone era reminiscent of Pauline Johnson's world, set with a romantic gaze that renders the real into folklore. Published in 1923, *Indian Days* was probably Barbeau's most popular book, and it won him the first English language Prix David for literature in 1925. Equally important, Kihn's visit was the beginning of Barbeau's program of connecting contemporary artists with Aboriginal culture. This heritage he considered a "national asset" that all composers, artists, and writers could use, and he became convinced that indigenous subjects and themes were essential to the development of a distinctively Canadian art. To him the Skeena and the Gitksan cultures were exemplary; the tradition was still visible and contact a matter of living memory; the poles at Kitwanga and Kitwancool vivid evidence of a sophisticated indigenous patrimony. *The Downfall of Temlaham*, Barbeau's next literary effort, was a celebration of the great river and her people. It was of a piece with his 1924 proposal for a "Indian National Park of Temlaham," which he imagined would be located near the site of the ancient city (as he figured it). His strategy was to claim the legend and, by extension, Gitksan culture, and to insinuate them into the national narrative, much as Emily Carr did in her "Lecture on Totems." It would have been Canada's first theme park had he had his way, a cross between a national monument, a tourist attraction, and a public service ad promoting the beatification of the lost Indian past. The theme, of course, was the Imaginary Indian.

As an ethnologist, Barbeau tended to follow his own rules. Early in his career he had abandoned the odious practices associated with the physical study of people, substituting the measurement of people (anthropometrics) with the examination of the artefacts people make with their hands. His philosophy was based on a veneration for art, and his methods were shaped by that. His delight in uniting carving, painting, singing, and fabric art as he did in the folk festivals illustrated his ideal—a society where art is closely associated with daily life and woven into the artistic expression of a people. The Canadian West Coast Art exhibit emphasized the integration of Native and European traditions across a diversity of media in much the same way. It was born of Barbeau's desire to introduce Canadians to their heritage. This heritage was not limited to the ballads and reels of the French-Canadian *habitants,* who were the first European immigrants to put down roots in Canada. It thought to encompass the Aboriginal world.

Barbeau was engaged in a process that we, in our own time, have labelled "indigenization." Like many others of his generation, he felt that Canada's cultural growth lagged behind her economic development, but he was also convinced that the national consciousness Canadians lacked could be anchored to the continent's Aboriginal past. This assumption of indigenous history was the key to the dilemma of belonging on this continent, and in Barbeau's hands the means of converting the newcomers—immigrants and their descendants—into Natives. As *The Canadian Forum* remarked in its review of the Canadian West Coast Art show, "Perhaps all good Canadians are bound to have something of the Indian in them having inherited this country and so put themselves in contact with that earth memory of hers at which our mystics hint." Barbeau himself waxed sardonic when commenting on the Group of Seven's denunciation of the old fashioned overfondness of Canadian collectors for Dutch landscapes: "Should we be so bold as to disclose to the world the news that the land we live in is not France or Holland but a virgin continent where man was reborn, grows into manhood and is now groping in the dark for self-expression?"

In the end, Barbeau's view of Native culture was as distorted as it was self-serving. In his estimation, neither the culture nor the people had a future. "There is little left now of the wild tribes that once roamed naked in the virgin woodlands or on the prairies," he wrote in an article entitled "Our Indians—Their Disappearance" published in *The Queen's Quarterly* in 1931. Moreover, "The majority of the people along the Saint Lawrence never have seen a real Indian in their lives, if indeed such still exists." As he saw it, Native peoples were on the road to extinction and this was demonstrated by the fact of assimilation; "real" Indians were becoming a thing of the past as Native peoples intermarried and adopted White ways. His concept of race privileged the old ways and precontact times, and implied that Native peoples' capacity for adaptation was a sign of failure and weakness. While it is unlikely that he stopped to wonder if, by the same token, he was any the less French Canadian for the Anglo-Canadian ways he had acquired, Barbeau did have an idiosyncratic view of things. He was aware, for instance, of the danger inherent in Aboriginal life: the impact of disease, the influence of missionaries whom he felt did more harm than good, and the "false promises and rank injustice" of the authorities and their infliction on Native peoples of "the most painful experience of the century"—their "exile" to the confinement of reserves. Barbeau understood the resistance to the potlatch laws and in the months prior to the 1921 crackdown wrote a report, "the nearest thing to an inquiry," as historian Douglas Cole puts it, which sympathized with the Native position, although it stopped short of making firm recommendations. Based on Department of Indian Affairs files, Barbeau also spoke at length in its preparation with E.K. DeBeck, the Vancouver lawyer who took up the case of the prosecuted Kwakwaka'wakw, and travelled to Hazelton where Barbeau was doing fieldwork that summer to represent his clients' cause. This is not to imply that Barbeau was an activist; he did not speak out publicly or become involved with the campaign of White support. But he kept a correspondence with DeBeck, who wrote him in 1922 saying, "I also object to having an Indian agent try a matter of this kind," referring to Agent Halliday's handling of the Alert Bay arrests. DeBeck (whose father has been an Indian agent and Halliday's predecessor) had come to realize that those in authority intended to "Wipe out Native traditions by attacking its core elements." Barbeau agreed, though by his lights the only action called for was the salvage of the material goods. Could the disintegrating parts of these doomed cultures be saved in time for them to be studied? Could they be preserved for posterity? Could they be made Canadian?

Marius Barbeau's view of Aboriginal Canada embraced more than one blatant contradiction. While he valued aspects of Native culture, he still judged Native society as primitive and uncivilized. He celebrated its past achievements, but did not extend that acceptance to contemporary Native artists. For example, there were two paintings included in the Canadian West Coast Art show by Frederick Alexee, an artist Jackson had come across in 1924, and who is described in the catalogue as "an old Tsimsysn half-breed of Port Simpson." Alexee's scenes of old houses and poles and the famous battle between the Haida and the Tsimshian at Port Simpson were listed by Barbeau in the West Coast Indian section along with Emily Carr's rugs and ceramics, while all the other paintings by living artists are found in a separate section called Works of Canadian Artists. The Native works—poles, canoes, drums, bent-cedar chests, painted root hats, robes, carved and painted masks and boards, argillite sculptures, Chilkat blankets—are listed generically in their section, and the only individuals mentioned or alluded to (besides Alexee and Carr) are "the famous Haida Chief Edenshaw and his faithful Tlingit slave," who were reputed to have carved some of the very finest argillite pieces. The note on the Alexee paintings classifies them as primitive art, akin to the work of the *naif* painters of Europe, and on that basis Barbeau categorizes them as folk art rather than fine art. The exhibition gave Barbeau the opportunity to present Native artefacts for their aesthetic value, a radical departure from convention. Yet there were differences to be maintained and sharp racial boundaries to be observed. Along with Eric Brown, Barbeau used the occasion of the exhibition to lament the decline of Native culture and to plead for its preservation in museums. The fact that he was actively participating in marketing Aboriginal art and profiting from it personally robs his words of credibility today, but in Carr's time, his altruism was unchallenged as hers was. The government had created a situation in which the creation of new masks or rattles was criminally suspect, and the incentive to sell any artefacts left from earlier generations over-whelming. The cost of preservation to the Native communities was the loss of their visual heritage.

There is no evidence that Barbeau thought of such things or took stock of his own involvement in the disappearances. Undoubtedly he did understand the depressing effect the anti-potlatch laws had on West Coast carving. Like many non-Native experts, he also denigrated contemporary renditions of traditional carving, seeing them as inauthentic at best and debased, along with the society producing it, at worst. He was not moved to try to preserve this, nor did he exploit his friendship with Duncan Campbell Scott in an effort to influence changes in departmental policy. In a letter to Scott from the Skeena in 1924, Barbeau deplores the unresolved land question, which he calls a permanent sore in the region, but otherwise he steers clear of political affairs and rarely comments on them. Interestingly, *Indian Days* ran afoul of CPR's Murray Gibbon, who thought Barbeau's criticisms of missionaries inappropriate (and these comments were modified by Barbeau), but no such indis-cretions were ever registered when it came to the Department of

Indian Affairs. Scott and Barbeau may have held different positions on the potlatch, but they were able to associate because Barbeau was willing to keep his opinions to himself. Their professional lives certainly brought them together. For example, Scott was the secretary of the Royal Society of Canada the year Barbeau was elected. Moreover, he was a well-known man of letters and part of the Ottawa milieu to which Barbeau was attracted. In 1924, the two worked on the committee appointed in Ottawa to oversee restoration of the totem poles along the Skeena, which the railway and Department of Indian Affairs both recognized as a natural tourist attraction. Barbeau and his colleagues were called in to persuade the owners to allow the poles to be repainted, realigned, and, in the case of Kitwanga, turned towards the train tracks so whistle-stop passengers could conveniently take their pictures. Permission was not easily accomplished and the project eventually had to be aborted. Nevertheless, for a time Kitwanga was the most photographed spot in the country next to Niagara Falls. This delighted Barbeau as he schemed to make the Skeena into a national landmark, but it horrified Emily Carr, who saw the conservators' paint and bemoaned the ravages of tourism.

Not the least of Barbeau's paradoxes was his relationship to Quebec and his own roots. Even while celebrating French-Canadian culture, he largely abandoned it personally, building his life in English and in Ontario. The view of French Canada he proselytized did speak to some Quebecers, but it was essentially nostalgic and the next generation repudiated it along with the reduction of Quebec culture to folklore. For just as Barbeau would claim Gitksan art as history for the newly created nation called Canada, so the folklorization of Quebec culture served to rationalize Quebec as colourful, old, and endearing. In the view of many Quebecers, including Barbeau's own son-in-law, the sociologist Marcel Rioux, it was a way of keeping Quebec safe and powerless within Confederation. Rioux was the heir apparent to Barbeau's movement, and he followed Barbeau's lead into anthropology. However, he turned his attention to the present, becoming a Marxist and an early *indépendantiste*. He was a passionate student of Québécois culture in all its modes and moods. One of Barbeau's fondly held beliefs was that crafts, including his own, should be passed down from one generation to the next. Rioux admired his father-in-law and understood that the old man saw his choice of working for a modern independent Québecois culture as a defection, but, if so, it was a betrayal that was never spoken of. According to Rioux, Barbeau was a hard man to know, a man who found intimacy with other men almost impossible, and whose attitude to his profession was quixotic. "I considered Monsieur Barbeau a romantic erudite," said Rioux. "He was very knowledgeable but the only things that interested him were artistic matters; he was not interested in social structure or sexuality and not at all curious about theory. I recall when he gave me his set of *American Anthropologist* I found them unread, *vierge*, the pages had never been cut. In all those years I don't think I ever saw him reading a book. He was interested in *his* work and his collection, period." And every Saturday afternoon, Monsieur Barbeau would dress in formal attire, descend to the drawing-room, and tune in to the Metropolitan Opera with Milton Cross on the radio. To the young Rioux, the house on Maclaren Street was a museum, the living room resplendent with its Chilkat blanket over the piano, the scrimshaw on the mantle, and the Emily Carr painting over the divan beside the fireplace. It was, in fact, a monument to Barbeau's conception of Canadianness.

Marius Barbeau was a complex man and if his legacy seems odd and contradictory, it is because it is. He has never been claimed by Quebecers and his status in Anglo-Canadian culture has undergone a reversal since his death in 1969. He has ceased to be venerated either as an expert or a folk hero; if anything, he has become an object of opprobrium. His anthropological work has been critiqued and his theories largely discounted, notably his contention that the bigger and free-standing carvings of the Northwest Coast were the result of postcontact affluence (which is to say the introduction of the cash economy), and his argument that the area was originally settled by people from the Far East. Similarly, his methods of acquiring information have been discredited. His racial attitudes have been reassessed in the light of postmodern theory and his relationship with William Beynon, for example, the assistant who produced thousands of pages of material for him and was indispensable to the project, is seen now as essentially exploitative. However warm his feelings may have been towards some individuals he came to know, Barbeau's basic attitude to Native peoples was patronizing and distanced. He assumed an ignorance and innocence on their part that made it easy for him to take on the role of expert on their behalf. And, of course, he had no compunction about appropriating Aboriginal culture for his own purpose. His motive in exhibiting Native and Euro-Canadian work together was in part an effort to dignify historical Native work and a bid to open up the storehouse of Native patrimony to non-Native artists. In doing so, he had a seminal influence on the Group of Seven, introducing them to a new perception of Canadian culture and history, which they subsequently incorporated into their own definition of Canadian art. In *Art for a Nation*, Charles Hill elucidates how Barbeau's Skeena project planted these ideas in receptive soil. If Housser supplied a narrative for the Group of Seven in *A Canadian Art Movement*, Barbeau supplied them with a past and dignified their attachment to the land with a quasi-scientific rationale. The identification with place and environment is a common source of national feeling, but rarely does a country rely on geography as the source of shared experience to the extent Canada has. It is a characteristic of colonies and young countries, though highly problematic in a case like Canada's where the geography and climate are so varied. Barbeau's contribution and probably his most lasting achievement was to offer nationalists a way to imaginatively possess the land that acknowledged that the wilderness was not vacant, but was replete with the images and stories of Northwest Coast culture.

This is the terrain where Emily Carr and Marius Barbeau met. Because of their friendship and their obvious sympathy, it may seem odd that Barbeau did not include her in the Skeena project once he discovered there was an artist who was already painting

Native subjects in British Columbia. The confusion on the record about their first meeting, usually characterized as a debate over "who discovered Emily Carr," is probably symptomatic. Talented women are routinely and repeatedly "discovered" by men and Carr was no exception. In her case, Barbeau, Eric Brown, and Harold Mortimer-Lamb all claimed to have found her or put her on the map, though Barbeau was the only one to make the claim publicly—at the time of the Canadian West Coast Art show and repeatedly thereafter. The confusion comes in the letter she writes to Barbeau in 1926, as if he were a stranger, in the several and sometimes obviously erroneous dates he gives for their first meeting, and in the testimony from someone present to the effect that Barbeau had never seen any work of Emily Carr's before encountering her paintings in Hazelton in 1927. This has led some scholars to conclude that he did not meet Carr until after Brown's visit, while others prefer to believe Barbeau's account, garbled though it is. The truth may lie somewhere in between. Barbeau and Carr could well have met several times before they each knew who the other was. What is interesting, though, is why they made the friendship they did. Carr's journals make it clear that her main connection in Ottawa in 1927 was Barbeau. She visited his home and was welcomed by his two daughters, his wife, and the sight of three of her own paintings on the walls. She ate several meals there with the family and friends like A.Y. Jackson, whom she had just met in Toronto. Apart from the love for the Skeena, she shared Barbeau's romantic disposition and love of Native culture. To him, of course, she was the illustration of his theories and, not surprisingly, she became a subject of great interest to him. This didn't change, though their friendship lapsed over the years, and he often said he was intending to write about her. (He was approached in the late 1940s by Ryerson Press to do the book, but never did.)

Perhaps Barbeau's reason for not inviting Carr to the Skeena was the same one that the Group of Seven had for not inviting her to join them: he didn't think of it. He didn't think of it because he didn't really recognize her as a professional artist at first. Before he met Jackson and (through him) became familiar with avant-garde art in Toronto, Ottawa, and Montreal, Barbeau had little contact with the art world, so it is probable that he lacked the aesthetic judgement to "see" what Carr was doing. He may originally have taken her for a *patenteux*, a Sunday painter or hobbyist. When he went to visit the second time and found her stoking up her kiln to fire a batch of pots, what he saw was a mad eccentric. He describes her living in the middle of chaos, not unlike some of the folk artists he interviewed in rural Quebec, with plants and animals all over the place. Her paintings were mostly stashed away out of sight and the house was full of cobwebs, birds flying in and out of cages, and small animals, which Barbeau disliked but recognized as important to her. "They were a link between herself and nature. . . . When in the bush she wouldn't feel alone if a little rat was around and the monkey to tap her hand." Emily Carr was quite an eyeful in 1926, never mind the domestic arrangements with chairs pulleyed up to the ceiling and a monkey clinging to the bookshelf. Conventional male eyes would have seen her as frumpy and unlovely, a decidedly crude figure of femininity. Barbeau might not have been much more imaginative, but he was not repelled as other men were. The attraction was simple, Rioux attests. "Finding an English woman painting on her own about Indians explains it all. He was very much at ease with women to begin with, and I think he often reacted rather like a woman himself. He was a very delicate person, and possessed many qualities we would spontaneously attribute to women. And, you see, he was enamoured of those three things: women, aboriginals, and art." Rioux does not suggest anything sexual, only that Carr's femininity was a bridge for Barbeau, and that he could see in her what other men could not. Besides colleagues and professional connections, there were very few men in Barbeau's life but a great many women—friends and confidantes, as well as lovers. His womanizing was notorious; Madame Barbeau, it was said, had a hard time keeping a maid. When she finally confronted him with his philandering, he stopped speaking to her; they remained married, but he never addressed her directly again. So Barbeau's reputation as an eccentric and remarkably difficult person is every bit as well earned as Emily Carr's.

The day Carr lunched with Jackson at the Barbeau home she wrote in her journal, "I feel as if I have met the `worthwhiles' on this trip, people who really count and are shaping a nation." That is exactly what she was doing. The Canadian West Coast Art show was a chrysalis, not just for Emily Carr, but for Canada. It enshrined Barbeau's perception of Canada in Ottawa, and provided the missing ingredient in the current construction of the "Indian problem," making it possible to recognize and even celebrate the Native fact in Canada without having to concede anything to contemporary land claims.

In February 1927, while the Canadian West Coast Art show was still in the planning stages, H.H. Stevens, the Conservative member of Parliament for Vancouver Centre, stood up in the House of Commons to ask the government to approve the establishment of a select committee to hear the petition of the Allied Indian Tribes of British Columbia, which had been submitted to Parliament during its previous session. Stevens allowed he had little sympathy with the views of those who were "agitating," but he thought it desirable for Parliament "to satisfy and quiet the Indians" by listening to the petitioners. Parliament should settle the land question instead of allowing it to drift on any longer. On March 8, Charles Stewart, the minister of Indian Affairs, responded with the government's solution—a special Senate-House committee to investigate the claims of the Allied Indian Tribes. A committee of seven MPs and seven senators, including Stevens and four senators from B.C., was quickly convened, and hearings began immediately. By the first week in April they were done, and five days later a report was sent to the Commons and the Senate where its recommendations were quickly endorsed. An amendment to the Indian Act was then drafted and enacted before summer was out. Rarely in its history before or since have the two chambers of the Canadian Parliament acted with such dispatch and singleness of purpose. "After a thorough investigation of the whole question," wrote the deputy superintendent general of Indian Affairs in his annual report, "Parliament concluded no such thing as aboriginal title ever existed." To ensure that no more time or resources would be squandered on the idea, a provision was added to the Indian Act to make it illegal for anyone to raise money from Indians for the purpose of prosecuting any claim of benefit to them or their band—without permission in writing from the superintendent general. The entire process was accomplished and concluded before Emily Carr stepped on the train to go east for the opening of the Canadian West Coast Art exhibition in early December, before any invitations to the opening went out to the Ottawa community from the National Gallery. Had they been sent, as was customary, D.C. Scott would likely have received one. He was known as a connoisseur of music and the theatre, and his house on Lisgar Street was famed for the art on the walls and the literary evenings hosted in the music room at the back. Scott came to know Carr through Barbeau; he owned two Carr paintings, one he purchased and another said to have been given to him by the artist, and the archives hold a slight correspondence between them from the mid-1930s. In 1927, he was at the zenith of his career as Canada's chief administrator of Indian Affairs. He would retire in 1932 at the age of seventy, after fifty-three years with the department, nineteen years in charge.

Whether Scott was at the gallery opening in December or not, he was definitely in the committee room during the Joint Committee hearings in April. An account of the event in Paul Tennant's history of the land question in B.C., *Aboriginal People and Politics*, begins with Scott's testimony as this is how the proceeding actually commenced. Scott's carefully modulated presentation was designed to discredit the petitioners and lay blame on their White advisers, who were depicted as self-interested and money grubbing. Deploying numbers and statistics in dazzling display, Scott set about convincing the committee members of Ottawa's magnanimous and completely generous attitude towards B.C.'s Native people. Tennant's narrative is an exposé of such claims. It is a litany of denial and neglect ringed with malevolence, and the story builds up over sixty years to this committee and this very moment. Scott is listened to with respect and deference, and the committee allows him to remain in the room, commenting as he sees fit on the testimony that follows, even though he is a witness himself and not a member of the committee. Any pretence to objectivity is tossed to the winds when Peter Kelly and Andrew Paull of the Allied Indian Tribes appear with their counsel, Arthur O'Meara, to make their case. Stevens, who began the day by suggesting that Scott's testimony be given *in camera* (Native representatives would then have been excluded and thus prevented them from hearing the government's position on the matter they were there raising), could hardly contain his antagonism. Though his *in camera* motion was rejected, his hostile cross-examination of the witnesses and his barrage of abusive remarks were tolerated by his colleagues and duly recorded. If Stevens sounded even-handed in Hansard when he called for the establishment of the committee, his politics were well known. He was an Orange Order imperialist and pro-British down to his suspenders, an opponent of Asian immigration who played a key role in the refusal of Indian immigrants aboard the *Komagata Maru* in 1914, and a disbeliever in Native rights. "Rot" and "rubbish," he hooted at statements he disagreed with, reserving particular venom, as did other committee members, for the White advocate. "I've had twenty years of your nonsense, O'Meara, and I'm tired of it," he exploded at one point when O'Meara again quoted from documents that he was unable to produce in evidence. Stevens accused him of deliberately misquoting, which led to an extraordinary exchange in which it became apparent that the compendium of documents known as *The Papers Connected with the Indian Land Question*, the authoritative record of the land question between 1850 and 1875, could not be found or accessed anywhere and had, in fact, been deliberately withheld from Native leaders. No less than three copies were actually in the room at that moment.

Scott and W.E. Ditchburn, the Indian commissioner for B.C., each had one and Stevens had a third in his possession. Not one of them would relinquish his copy to Paull and Kelly for submission as part of the evidence, even though it would have remained in the safe-keeping of the committee, as it would have entailed making the document generally available. Instead, O'Meara was forced to read his citation into the record from Commissioner Ditchburn's copy.

Reading the transcripts seventy years later, you do not have to know what the government's agenda was to understand there was one, and that it was not on the table. A child could tell that the situation was rigged and the hearings a charade. The committee and its report were serving the purpose of keeping land claims out of court and, in particular, away from the Privy Council in England, which had recently ruled in a southern Nigerian case that Aboriginal title was a pre-existing right that "must be presumed to have continued unless the contrary is established."

As Brian Titley reveals in *A Narrow Vision,* his book on Scott's civil service life, the deputy superintendent general advised against the strategy of having a Joint Committee. For once he was not heeded. However, he came around to see the advantage in submitting the land question to a final resolution, partly because he saw it as a way to target the root cause of the protest, which, in his view, was the work of mischievous White men. Like Paul Tennant in his book, Titley recites the history of Aboriginal dissent which led to the events of spring 1927 and which met with nothing but disingenuous stalling and hostility on the part of federal and provincial authorities who were at loggerheads with each other over the disposition of reserves. The encroachment of White settlement and the attempt to lay out reserves in the 1880s had initially provoked organized Native resistance. The Nisga'a of the Nass River valley sent a delegation to Victoria as early as 1881, and in 1907 they formed the Nisga'a Land Committee, which was the first instance of political organizing to deal with the White system in British Columbia. Since the days of James Douglas, the province had simply refused to negotiate Native claims. Time and again Native peoples raised the issue in relation to the surveying and the readjustment of reserves, and time and again they were told to take their grievance elsewhere. This led to the Nisga'a Committee's decision in 1913 to petition the Privy Council, then the highest court of appeal in Canadian justice. A document outlining their territories was drawn up, and, while acknowledging British sovereignty, it argued that a treaty was required by virtue of the Royal Proclamation of 1763 and the fact that their lands had never been surrendered. This land had been theirs since time immemorial, the chiefs stated. They sought recognition of Aboriginal rights and of the illegality of the province's exploitation and sale of their lands without permission. The petition went to London and was immediately referred back to Canada, ending up on Scott's desk where it languished until repeated representations from the Nisga'a and their allies—for in the meantime the Allied Indian Tribes of B.C. was formed—pushed it onto the cabinet's agenda in 1914. The Nisga'a strategy had not wavered; the leaders were convinced that a judicial decision could succeed where persuasion hadn't, and that by bringing the government face-to-face with their claim in court, justice would win out. Scott drafted the terms for the government's cooperation, which the cabinet accepted, but the Nisga'a naturally didn't. The case would only be allowed to go forward, Scott proposed, if the Nisga'a renounced whatever rights the court might find they had (for which they would be compensated in accordance with current arrangements), if they agreed in advance to the findings of the Royal Commission then determining the size of reserves, and finally if they accepted counsel "nominated and paid for" by the government.

Following the war, the Allied Indian Tribes resumed their efforts to move the government to reconsider, and when the Liberals were elected in 1922, they had reason to believe that Mackenzie King's modest support in opposition might translate into sympathy in office. By 1925, persistence brought the issue back to cabinet where a subcommittee was struck to consider it. Scott wrote a comprehensive report, asserting that the Indians of B.C. had been fairly compensated for their Aboriginal title by the provision of reserves and the services of his department. He blamed the unsettled situation in B.C. on Victoria's intemperate attitude in their policies and their endless stalling over reserves; he warned of the repercussions a court case could have on negotiations for the surrender of the reserve title, not to mention the validity of land titles currently being issued by the province. The subcommittee idled while considering Scott's advice. Another general election came and went, followed by more representations and more government stalling until finally the Allied Indian Tribes were induced to sidestep the government and appeal directly to Parliament.

Parliament's response was brutal by any standard, and was meant to be. That is to say, its position was consciously taken and not merely dictated by Scott, who was deft and effective but not running the entire show. He may have fashioned the arguments the committee used and the tactic of citing the Nisga'a rejection of the 1914 terms as grounds for declaring the matter closed, but he did not invent the perspectives that their recommendations reflected. What was the meaning of these extreme measures then if not to halt a political movement in its tracks, and to silence the cry of injustice? Scott, it seems, did persuade the Joint Committee members (those who needed persuading) that Aboriginal rights were a figment of Arthur O'Meara's imagination. "The Committee notes with regret the existence of agitation, not only in British Columbia, but with Indians in other parts of the Dominion . . . by which the Indians are deceived and led to expect benefits from claims more or less fictitious. Such agitation, often carried on by designing white men, is to be deplored . . . as the Government . . . is at all times ready to protect the interests of the Indians and to redress real grievances where such are shown to exist." You can hear the emphasis on the words "real" and "shown to exist." It is the sound of the truth being bent out of shape to construct a master narrative characterizing land claims as a recent invention, and unnecessary in any case. Scott had a definitive hand in devising this face-saving device, obviously part of his job as deputy superintendent general. But in a more general sense, through his influence as a poet and an intellectual of his day, he had a hand in shaping the emerging idea of the nation.

Scott's not-so-double life has been the subject of much curiosity and speculation in recent years. The increasingly autocratic nature of the Department of Indian Affairs policy under his rule and the conflicting interests of the situation, which placed him in control of the lives of 100,000 Aboriginal Canadians whose stories and suffering he used to fuel his poetic imagination, have conspired to make him infamous today and remembered more for his villainy than his verse. Among scholars, there are widely differing views about his ideas on race; for instance, whether these can be deduced from his poetry, or should be read from the prose pieces written in his professional capacity, or whether his real opinions are forever hidden behind his many masks. There is little doubt, however, that he was an assimilationist. He considered Native cultures inferior and destined for dissolution as Aboriginal individuals intermarried and moved into White society. On this he and Barbeau agreed. Of the Cree and Anishnabe he met as a treaty commissioner in northern Ontario in 1906, he wrote, "They were to make certain promises and we were to make certain promises but our purpose and our reasons were alike [to them] unknowable. What could they grasp of the pronouncement on the Indian tenure which had been delivered by the law lords of the Crown, what of the elaborate negotiations between a dominion and a province which had made the treaty possible, what of the sense of traditional policy which brooded over the whole?" The process of civilization—the stated objective of the original Indian Act—was intended to change this, so that in the end the Indian would be indistinguishable from other Canadians. When the transformation was completed, the Indians would be taken off the band rolls and given the vote. In practice, very few Native peoples wanted enfranchisement; most saw it as being asked to renounce their race in order to vote in Canadian elections. So in the early 1920s, Parliament actually entertained a law and kept it on the books for two years, giving the government leave to grant enfranchisement *without* an individual's consent. Scott was asked to address the parliamentary committee reviewing Bill 14 in 1920, and his comments that day have lived to be his most quoted lines. "I want to get rid of the Indian problem," he said. "I do not think, as a matter of fact, that this country ought to continuously protect a class of people who are able to stand alone . . . that has been the whole purpose of Indian education and advancement since the earliest times . . . our object is to continue until there is not a single Indian in Canada that has not been absorbed into the body politic, and there is no Indian question and no Indian Department."

In the history of Indian affairs, the period from 1913 to 1927 is marked by the increasing resort to coercion in the face of the refusal of Native peoples in Canada to either assimilate or disappear. The laws regulating Native society and culture proliferated as the twentieth century advanced, while at the same time the Native population was dwindling because disease and ill health were becoming institutionalized, most pathetically at residential schools where tuberculosis was rampant. In 1908, towns and cities with populations in excess of 8,000 were given the right to expropriate reserve land without the consent of the occupants. Wherever they were located, reserves in B.C. descended into poverty as the federal and provincial governments bickered about which of them would gain ultimate control over the extraction of resources on surrounding Crown lands. As things progressed, the conundrum deepened, for instead of increasing self-sufficiency, such policies fostered a dependency that affected everyone. Not only was Native life subjected to more rules and conditions every year, a growing number of White people—missionaries, Indian agents, bureaucrats, anthropologists, health care professionals, teachers, and even poets—became equally dependent on the arrangement that provided them with jobs, careers, and intellectual material. Enforced assimilation became its opposite, enforced segregation. There was constant pressure to remove Native peoples from sight in the cities, and to marginalize them from mainstream society, politically and socially. Natives were isolated on reserves and school-age children were removed to residential schools for months and years on end where, it was thought, they could be "civilized" more effectively away from the temptation of their native language and their grandmothers' ways.

The intention of these laws was to speed up the process of acculturation. They culminated in the 1920s with the potlatch trials and the decree against land claims of 1927. The appearance of the Canadian West Coast Art show at the National Gallery within months of the Joint Committee's report may have been happenstance, but the timing is symbolic nonetheless. It meant the issue of ownership was settled politically and legally, and it was now safe to admit that the land in British Columbia was not empty but full of history and ancient artefacts that could be represented as primitive art and exhibited with deference. In the exhibition catalogue, both Eric Brown and Marius Barbeau wrote about Indian culture in the past tense, and Brown went on to praise Aboriginal art for being entirely national in origin and character, an echo of Barbeau's "It is truly Canadian in its inspiration. . . . sprung up wholly from the soil and the sea within our national boundaries."

Into this context danced Emily Carr with her paintings. Greeted by an ideology that saw them as the quintessence of Canadianness, her paintings found a receptive audience. They were praised and so was she. The first feature articles about her in publications like *Saturday Night* and *Maclean's* focused on her "travels among the Indians," and invariably quoted Barbeau. She was treated as an adventurer who had been there and seen the real thing, as an authority on her subject as well as an artist. She might have wondered at Brown's zeal (and the entirely fanciful note in the catalogue stating that she had "spent many years among the Indians and succeeded in getting them to revive many of their native arts"), but there is no indication that she was aware of the larger political picture. Still, it was clear, even to her, that some sort of élite was welcoming her and making way for her contribution. This had not been the case in 1913 when her work matched no one else's idea of

Canada and challenged common notions of beauty and decency.

Upon arriving in Ottawa in November 1927, Emily Carr went up to the museum and asked for Mr. Brown. She was ushered into his office and "there they all were"—Barbeau, Brown, Edwin Holgate, and Pegi Nicol, who had works in the show, and Harry McCurry from the National Gallery. She was given a royal welcome and then they all descended to the exhibition hall on the lower floor where the works were assembled and hanging had begun. The opening was in two weeks and the catalogue was just being completed. Carr was asked to design a cover for it. She was thrilled, staying up half the night to complete the art, painstakingly reproducing a thunderbird in Native design as a frame for the lettering, readying it for the printer the next day. She signed it Klee Wyck, reclaiming her Indian nickname as an honorific denoting her special intimacy with Native peoples. Carr was not the first or the last White person to adopt a Native name, nor was she the first or the last to invest the gesture with her own meaning. There is a long tradition of Native groups conferring names and sometimes titles on non-Natives, be it to honour a visiting dignitary or to mark someone's special contribution. (Occasionally it is for the adoption of an outsider into the community.) Any number of politicians and visiting royals have been so named, and it is common for artists, curators, and academics working with Aboriginal subjects to seek Native approval through some sort of naming ceremony. In Carr's case there was no investiture; the naming was completely informal. The significance attached to it thus was more a projection of her desire for acceptance than any recognition from the Native community. The irony is that while Carr was consciously identifying with Native culture and drafting it to her purpose, she herself was being taken up by the eastern establishment as the mascot for their idea of Canadian nationalism. Of this she had some inkling, but no apparent curiosity. The task has been left to the present generation to uncover and confront this history.

Skeena River, 1991

Getting there takes fifteen hours on the *Queen of the North*, which sails from the northern tip of Vancouver Island up the Inside Passage to Prince Rupert. It is pelting rain at 6:30 a.m. when we board at Port Hardy, and all day the clouds play tag with the sun and the mountains teasing the trees with their tails of mist. The route takes us behind a chain of large islands, which hem the mainland coast, leaving a long, narrow channel protected from the ocean swell. The ship is not as I remember from my first trip two years ago. Humble coastal ferry has morphed into a colour-coordinated tourist liner with thick carpets, soft lighting, and reclining chairs, though not enough of them for everyone on board, I discover too late. Walking around the passenger decks, I marvel at the no-name decor, the only hint of local colour being a lone reproduction of Emily Carr's *Somberness Sunlit* stuck in a stairwell. I take refuge in the cafeteria (green carpets, pink tablecloths) and contemplate the passing coastline. The lighthouse on the southern tip of Sarah Island was built the year Emily Carr first travelled up the coast on her way to Alaska. The brick smokestack rises above the decaying wharf at Swanson's Bay to announce the ruins of another sawmill. At various times over the century, Whites have discovered indentations along this coast, hacked campsites out of the underbrush, and tried to hang on. Not everyone who came here was looking for converts or profits; some were looking for seclusion. There are stories of hermits and hippies and back-to-the-landers who arrived with their idealism and driftwood architecture to face the elements on their own. Most gave up and departed, just as the trading posts and canneries did. The region is famous for archaeological sites for good reason, and I muse over the fact that the Europeans have left a string of their own abandoned villages.

The voyage is disorienting. Outside, the vast mountainous panorama slips silently by, while indoors it sounds like Amsterdam or Paris in high season, a chorus of voices and accents from everywhere but here, Canadians being a distinct minority. The foreigners come mostly in groups: young people backpacking, middle-aged couples on exotic holiday, and preseasoned retirees, all of them enraptured with the idea of wilderness. German, British, American, Australian accents blend behind Japanese cameras. There is the man from the Isle of Man who's never seen so much water "and not a few trees either"; the two from Florida who are infuriated to catch sight of a pair of dolphins riding the slipstream of a troller when they'd left the camcorder below; and a droll ex-duck hunter from Michigan who says he prefers to watch nature now rather than eat it. The locals are easy to spot. They are the ones who make straight for the best seats in a small secluded section aft where they can snooze through the day. I recognize a family in transit, one or two Native faces, and the odd older woman from Owen Sound visiting relatives. In the floating world of the *Queen of the North* there are afternoon and evening screenings of popular American movies, video games galore, and live entertainment with dinner in the dining-room. The menu posted on a neon crayon board hardly does justice to the hotel-style buffet on offer: roast red meat, grilled seafood, and a groaning board of sugar confections. You can sip wine, lean back in the green-and-pink upholstery and listen to Chantal Morin singing "Yesterday," followed by Piaf's "Je ne regrete rien." The clientele has obviously been slotted as Sixties Nostalgia, but the real subject of this scene is the cultural salad bar down at the global village. A Quebecer sings Beatles' songs in French-accented English to Germans, while Asian Canadians clear the tables. Outside on deck, the air smells dank and it seems darker than it should be in mid-August. Approaching Prince Rupert at dusk, the coastal grain and coal depots on Ridley Island and the Tsimpsean peninsula appear through the rain in an orange tungsten glow, as surreal and disturbing as a nightmare.

Downtown Prince Rupert is small. Three streets of it encompass the requisite mall, liquor store, Zeller's, and a Famous Players theatre. I follow 3rd Avenue past McBride Street to the less kempt section of town where the Pioneer Rooms is hard to miss, even in the dark. The entrance is ablaze with light and colour; fuchsia and geranium blooms burst out of pots and hanging baskets set off by the bright turquoise facade. A large, handsomely lettered sign offers travellers showers, telephones, and pop machines. Rooms are available nightly and weekly, "small, cosy and clean." On the front door I read "Welcome to: PIONEER ROOMS Walk in . . ." in yellow letters, so I do, and quickly identify Mary Ellen, who is surprised the ferry is already in as they usually call to let her know when it arrives. She is wearing slacks and a blouse over thin legs and a somewhat lumpy torso; her reddish blond hair frames fine features and a good-natured grin. A couple of people are sitting in the front room watching an ancient TV set, one of them wearing a long wimple arrangement over her head. Mary Ellen

Entrance to the Pioneer Rooms, Prince Rupert, August 1991.

shows me around and reads me the rules. TV off by midnight; no guests past eleven; no drinking on the premises or smoking in the rooms. A single without a window costs $15 a night; with a window, it's $20. And everyone's welcome to use the communal cooking facilities tucked in behind the desk downstairs. (I'd noticed the fridge, but not the microwave, kettle or electric skillet.) Guests are required to wash up immediately, she rattles on, and there's a sink and soap upstairs on the landing all ready—and signs on the wall to remind the forgetful and admonish the shirkers. The bedroom she shows me is spare, furnished with functional relics from the 1940s, and, I notice with relief after the pink-and-green orgy of the ferry, nothing matches. From the mix-and-match patterned bedsheets to the candy-striped curtains to the scent of old wood and floorwax laced with Ajax in the corridors, the Rooms are obviously special.

Overall presides Mary Ellen, proprietor and reluctant host, who bought the place ten years ago from a couple of elderly Poles. They were the ones responsible for the marine enamel covering the walls, the red-and-white-checked tiles on the floors, and the seascapes on the walls, the work of a friend who was paid in instalments with bottles of rum. Mary Ellen has changed none of it. "Sailors and fishermen come back each year, and it's the only regular thing in their lives," she explains. The building is actually two, I see next morning when I reconnoitre in the daylight, built cheek by jowl by Japanese carpenters at the turn of the century, and are now among the last remaining old wooden buildings in Prince Rupert. Unlike the Nimpkish at Alert Bay, the Pioneer Rooms stand out. Free of termites, dry rot and aluminum siding, they seem built to last forever. "Matched treasures," Mary Ellen calls them. She had walked past one day when "something clicked" and she knew she had to have them. The story is repeated in a newspaper clipping pinned to the wall downstairs. A local reporter, who describes her as a "frizzy haired woman whose mind is as active as her hair," explains that she had wanted to preserve the buildings, and was willing to try running a rooming-house to do it. It was easier at first, Mary Ellen tells me when I ask her how it worked out. Most guests were weeklies and several bunked in for the entire season. Still, she had to get rid of a few regulars, including a couple of Quebecers. "People talk about the Natives being bad characters, but I tell you," she says, launching into an invective, keeping her voice hushed even while her dander rises. That was when she imposed a few rules.

Mary Ellen keeps the coffee brewing all day, and her guests keep the TV going so the soundtrack drifts through everybody's conversation. Young men come and go; a trio of Scandinavian women show up with bulky backpacks, wanting to rent a single for the three of them. Mary Ellen's having none of that, so they pressure her to find a fourth person to share a larger room. The presumption annoys her. She's not running a hostel, she declares frostily. No, I think, more like a makeshift commune. The reception area triples as a lounge and a kitchen and is always full of people cooking, eating, or sitting about waiting to use the phone. That's how I meet Mel and Robert. Mel is quite the blade; curly haired with a queue and a gold earring, he's into Native politics and still excited about his recent return to the Skeena where he was born. He talks about his grandfather going to petition Sir John A. and predicts roadblocks again this fall when the tourist season is over and the fishing is done. He talks about his people living and surviving off the land, something Robert seems to have done. The two do not connect on this subject, though; when it opens a crack Robert starts talking about Native tribes warring with each other and needing to have educated people to argue their case. Mel shrugs him off and starts assembling breakfast. He makes toast, puts water in the skillet, and poaches an egg while Robert carries on with his story of growing up in Texas and bush-whacking through Oregon and Louisiana. Born in Ontario, he, too, has recently come home. Neither pays much attention to Annie, who has lived at the Pioneer Rooms for seven years and carries on her own routine, ignoring everyone save the characters on television. She wears her waist-length wimple like a badge of office, keeping it tied tightly under her chin and attached with a band to her forehead as if it might float away on the slightest draft. As Robert, Mel, and I talk, we are joined by another, Ann, who has just arrived from Bella Bella and is still coping with the shock of Prince Rupert—that and having to find work and a place to live all at once. She makes her phone calls and departs for the day's circuit. Mel drifts off with her. The TV drones on. Annie sails by on her own private ocean, and Robert offers to cook me a salmon for supper.

Eventually I get to the phone and reach Freda Diesing, who gives me directions to her place. Look for a grey house and a white one, she tells me. I'll find hers set back in between. When I called from Vancouver, she had asked if I had the time to see some poles, and I had assumed she was talking about the four she's carved, which are here, in Terrace, and at Kitsumkalum. Now I realize, as we talk over iced grapefruit juice, that she means the poles she knows and has learned from, which means a trip that will take us up the river to Hazelton and the 'Ksan village built at the confluence of the Skeena and the Bulkley rivers. We make plans to meet at McDonald's in Terrace in two days, and to make our way from there to the old villages of Kitwanga, Kitwancool, Kispiox, (now known as Gitwangak, Gitanyow and Anspayaxw) and 'Ksan. I am reminded that Freda Diesing is Haida, although she has lived along the Skeena all her life. She is one of only a few women carvers of her generation, but her mother's mother also carved. Freda's grandmother grew up in Masset on Haida Gwaii and had memories of staying in the famous great house of Chief Weha. She married a much older man whom she assisted in carving various large items, including a canoe. She was a skilled basket-maker and seamstress who married a Swedish ship's carpenter after her first husband died, moved to Inverness, and worked in the cannery there. Freda has been writing about her grandmother and her mother, both of them strong Haida women widowed several times over by European husbands who succumbed to tuberculosis.

Freda, too, contracted TB, and spent three years in a sanatorium near Kamloops at the crucial ages of eighteen to twenty-two when, she jokes, she would have learned to cook. (Freda is notorious for her non-cooking and for eating the same breakfast every morning at McDonald's.) Her rehabilitation was long and difficult, she tells me. It was the mid-1940s when antibiotics were new and somewhat untried, so she opted for the old approach, which involved collapsing the lung once a week. She stopped going to the outpatient's clinic before her treatment was completed because there was a bus strike and she found it too far to walk. Even now she says she feels guilty about quitting, although the authorities never tried to find her either. We swap stories about TB clinics, I having been in one in Toronto twenty years later; I find it depressing to think about how she was left on her own while I was cared for and coddled and the clinic's head doctor kept checking in with me long after my treatment was completed.

Freda was in her thirties when she went south to the Vancouver School of Art. She recalls making a mask while she was there, and meeting Ellen Neel, the Kwakwaka'wakw artist who had a store in Vancouver at the time and was making money selling mementoes to tourists. Neel was a source of enormous encouragement for Freda because she was successfully selling her own work. At the time, the work of the older carvers like Mungo Martin was emerging from the shadows of the potlatch laws and gaining recognition in the White world, and two young men, Bill Reid and Doug Cranmer, who would spearhead a popular resurgence of West Coast art, were just starting to carve. It must have been daunting to think of becoming an artist then; not surprisingly given the disincentives, Diesing took a while getting there. "I never apprenticed, I just began," she says. In the 1960s, she took courses given at the 'Ksan Centre by people like Tony and Henry Hunt and Robert Davidson, and she worked at 'Ksan coordinating projects, designing displays, and making button blankets, some of which are on permanent display. As a child she was aware that people didn't carve much; she knew the regalia was kept hidden away and that anything new could be confiscated—and often was. You get the clear sense that the missionaries were busy enforcing the ban wherever they could, with much more informality and vigour than official history divulges. Moral suasion lent itself to intimidation, which bred deceit and destruction. Freda remembers hearing about an uncle of her mother's who converted and then took all the masks and sacred possessions he had inherited and burned them on the beach. "Other people didn't like the idea of destroying things, but sometimes when people died kids would end up playing around with them." The clerics' message, endlessly repeated, was that just the possession of such objects was sinful. With the collectors and museums prowling around, there was official permission for people to cash in their family treasures. Sometimes it was done on the sly without the knowledge of everyone concerned—kids stealing their grannies' old things to cash in for transistor radios.

I met Freda when I first saw her work at an exhibition of contemporary art by women of Native ancestry, which opened the 54th International Congress of PEN in Toronto in 1989. The show was called Changers—a Spiritual Renaissance and was curated by Shirley Bear, a Maliseet painter and writer from the East Coast. Freda, who loves to berate herself for her slow pace, produced three new pieces for the exhibition, including a self-portrait mask in alderwood, which is remarkable for the eagle crest design used to represent her hair. Diesing's work is traditional but often has a contemporary twist, and always an eye for shape and character. This one bears an arresting likeness to its creator, so that despite the sober gaze, its expression seems jocular, just like Freda. An earlier mask of an old woman carved in 1974 uses braided cedar bark as hair, incised lines to indicate the webbing of wrinkles over the smooth planes of the face, and abalone shell for the labret worn in her lower lip. Freda's mother remembered seeing women wearing labrets, which were apparently a vogue among Gitksan women. Labrets, ornaments inserted into small holes made on either the inside or on the outside of the lip, are fashioned of inlaid wood or sometimes stone. The forcefulness and naturalism of Freda's mask belies the unusualness of this feature—which might be the postmodern 1990s speaking. At the turn of the century, when Freda's mother was young, the custom was reviled by the missionaries and marvelled at by curio seekers who catalogued such fashions precisely because they violated perceived ideas of feminine beauty. It was aesthetically unintelligible to Europeans—and probably still is in spite of the rage for body piercing among North American youth. The response of White authorities was puritanical as well as biased. Native women were warned not to decorate their bodies or engage in personal display for fear of tempting the devil. What's tempting, of course, is to draw a comparison between this extreme stretching of the lip and the extreme cinching of the waist and rib cage by whalebone stays, especially as this latter custom was not only fashionable among European women, but physically hazardous to their health. The history of White colonization is rife with such contradictions. Railing against West Coast dances such as the hamatsa, which was reputed to be cannibalistic, missionaries and settlers failed to see how the rituals of the Eucharist and the Mass might appear in a similar light to non-Christians. Castigating Native marriage practices, they couldn't recognize similar customs in their own culture. For example, what is a *gwalth* if not a dowry?

Freda Diesing comes from a long line of strong-minded Haida women, and she's fond of pointing out how Native women are the keepers of the stories, the ones who train the chiefs and tend tradition. Women had to, for men went off to war and endangered their lives hunting. Thus when the anthropologists came around collecting stories, they invariably asked the wrong people, she laughs. White folks have a hard time understanding the matrilineal structure of Native society, Freda tells me, alluding to the insurmountable difficulties White women face when they marry Aboriginal men and attempt a life on the reserve. The tolerance for Native women going with White men does not work in reverse; a non-Native woman coming in cannot possibly have the knowledge to function in the traditional way. If anyone should have lost status marrying out, Freda reasons, it should have been the men.

*

Back at the Pioneer Rooms for Robert's salmon supper, I cautiously approach Mary Ellen for dispensation on her booze rule. Could we get away with a glass of wine? She responds with another French-Canadian horror story and then tells us to go ahead and bend the rules, but do it in Styrofoam cups. Robert rummages in the fridge and comes up with his arms laden. A knife and chopping board appear and while the cabbage is dissected, finely chopped ginger is fried in the electric frying pan. Rice follows the ginger, some precooked wild rice is added, then the cabbage and topped, finally, by two frozen salmon steaks. As we wait, he shows me pictures of his troller and talks about the conversation he'd had that morning over coffee with a man who'd studied Buddhism in Japan. Mel arrives, and conversation turns to the disappearing fish, which Mel puts down to the greenhouse effect. "Anything warmer than fifty-two degrees and they stay away," he informs us. I tell them about my visit to the museum and what I'd learned about the area; that before 1790 this was one of the most populated places on the coast, and that after the arrival of the Europeans, the Coast Tsimshian left for Fort Simpson. Thirty minutes have passed and the fish is done. Robert busies himself dishing it out onto plates. Mel turns to me and winks. "Prince Rupert has been a meeting place for aeons, you know; people from all over got together here on the peninsula. Still do."

At the museum I had looked over exhibits about local history, reading placards with texts explaining events. The note on missionaries declares, "Their impact was significantly different from that of the fur traders. The missionaries could not agree that their influence should be restricted to their 'legitimate business,' as the Hudson's Bay Company believed." This reminds me I am a short boat ride away from the famed village of Metlakatla where William Duncan ran his Utopia for fifteen years. Duncan was a lay missionary with the Anglican Church Missionary Society, a young Yorkshireman with no experience except in business when he decided to take up mission service and come to this outpost to work among the Tsimshian. He first appeared in the vicinity in

1857, against the advice of James Douglas, the chief H B C official in the region, who had pressured him to remain at Fort Victoria to work with the Natives there. Duncan was resolute. He was also intolerant, dictatorial, and in a hurry. In 1863, he led a band of Tsimshian followers to a new settlement, which he named Metlakatla, where he set about building a Christian community complete with a school, a jail, a church, a dog pound, a sawmill, a printing press, and a rigid set of rules that everybody had to observe. A black flag was raised in the village when anyone transgressed. The dead were buried in the churchyard according to Western custom, and headstones were commissioned from stone carvers in Victoria whose attempts at translating Tsimshian imagery into granite will probably last forever. "I was the pope of Metlakatla," the museum quotes Duncan as saying honestly, if not modestly, "so it had to be the way I wanted it or not at all." And the way he wanted it was "White" and European—clapboard houses, English dress, and manners. In his day, Duncan was a hero and his experiment at Metlakatla a miracle read about far and wide. "It was, along with Niagara Falls and the Grand Canyon, one of the things not to be missed by rich Victorian travellers on safari to the new world," writes historian Howard White in *Writing in the Rain*. White quotes the eminent anthropologist Wilson Duff on the maniacal Duncan. "[He] was the personification of the missionaries of the time; he had immense faith and courage and the gigantic audacity required to move uninvited into a large community of foreign and hostile people and single handedly assume absolute control to reshape their lives." The museum plaque continues with its twentieth-century reassessment: "As far as Duncan was concerned it was most definitely the `legitimate business' of the missionaries to interfere in all aspects of the Indians' way of life in order to rescue them from barbarism and to bring them salvation. Their aim was the complete destruction of the traditional integrated life."

Today Duncan is seen as an anti-hero; his project is judged to have been malevolent and deluded as well as doomed. His

outsized ambition is symbolized in the immense church he had his
followers build, which was a wooden replica of the mediaeval
stone cathedrals and capable of seating all 1,200 souls who lived
in the community. In a period photograph, the church belfry and
spire tower over a clutch of black-frocked men huddled on the
steps below, just as Duncan towered over their lives. There is
another side to Duncan's story, of course. It tells of his faltering
ministry at Port Simpson, and the fact that by 1859 he had won
few converts and repeatedly run up against Tsimshian custom,
which demanded that he adapt himself. This he resolutely refused
to do. Then the smallpox epidemic swept through the area;
Duncan had his trump card. Before removing himself to
Metlakatla he did the rounds, asking the people one last time to
accept redemption. When they didn't, he warned them the wrath
of God was nigh, never mentioning the disease or the concept of
contagion or advising quarantine. He left them to die and the
survivors to assume the pox was fulfilment of his prophecy. Many
did follow him to Metlakatla. For those who accepted Christianity,
there were smallpox vaccinations and a whole new way of life.
The arrangement meant Duncan acquired a dedicated workforce
as well as a congregation and, with his considerable entrepreneurial skills, he built Metlakatla into a significant trading centre.
The experiment came to an end in 1887 when he clashed with his
superiors once too often. The bishop pulled strings and had
Duncan evicted when he refused to resign, a move that sent
Duncan to court to contend that the land belonged to the Indians
and not to the federal government. Thus it was by a curious back-
hand route that land claims entered Canadian courts for the first
time. Of course, Duncan was not really interested in land claims,
and when he lost the first round, he pulled up stakes and moved
his entire community to Alaska.

A few families still live at old Metlakatla, and recently they
erected a wooden archway down by the wharf, a replica of the one
set up in Duncan's time, which reads "Welcome to Metlakatla
1865–1990." Already it has acquired a patina of green. The day I

visit with a museum tour, three dogs race down to the boat to do
the honours. We walk around for a while, but there is little to see.
The monuments to Duncan's ego have long since disappeared.
What was left after he and 820 Tsimshian departed burned in a fire
in 1901. A modest little church has been built in the meantime and
in the old cemetery the headstones lie on their backs in the long,
green grass. No one is about and some of the houses are boarded
up. It has been a cool morning, and now a rain-spiked wind blows
in with a low hollow howl. I turn back to the boat with the others
to leave, and as I do a tiny girl calls out from a house nearby and
motions me over. Would I give the plastic bag she's holding to
Benny? Benny is the young fellow piloting the boat, I gather; he
ferries the kids to and from school in Prince Rupert, and apparently obliges with extracurricular deliveries of mislaid clothing. On
the way back we pass by Hospital (Digby) Island. Benny pulls over
and slows so we can get a good view of the old sanatorium. I can't
see it at first, the old building having become so indistinguishable
from the surrounding vegetation. Built before the first World War
for TB patients, it is said to have only ever housed a single patient
before it was mysteriously abandoned to the rain. And here it still
stands, the perfect counterpart to Duncan's cathedral.

It is still dark the morning I leave Kaen Island and head out across
the Tsimpsean Peninsula for the Skeena and Terrace. The weather
lifts as the road turns eastwards into the dawn, and I gradually
become aware of the great river rising beside me. Still and flat at this
hour of the morning, her broad surface mirrors the sun's brilliant
display rising behind mountain and clouds in the distance. Only the
occasional ripple breaks her immense calm, announcing the presence of otters out sniffing the morning. For the next two hours I
follow the otter trails, watching the mountains come and go as giant
rain-clouds descend to feed the river and then retreat back up the
valleys. Much in this territory is determined by the river. Emerging
in the Gunanoot Mountains high in the province's northeast corner,

Dawn on the Skeena River, August 1991.

the Skeena runs nearly 400 miles through dense forest and implacable granite, past the Coast Range to the sea. The river defines life for the people who live beside her, just as the mountains frame it. Since the ice of the last ice age melted, she has brought the salmon, marked the seasons, and carried people—traders, travellers, hunters, and seekers—up and down her length. When Europeans arrived, they too saw the river as a highway, first for fur traders' canoes and flat-bottom sternwheelers, then as a ready-made route for the CPR's northern track into the western terminus at Prince Rupert. Mostly they regarded the river as a marine gold rush, a boundless supply of fish for the catching and the canning.

In Terrace I meet Freda at McDonald's for breakfast as planned, laughing to myself at the circumstances that have driven me to break my lifelong boycott of the establishment. I myself don't usually eat breakfast and Freda only eats breakfast at McDonald's, so here we are. I watch her dissect an Egg McMuffin, discarding parts she doesn't want, and decide to ask her what she knows about Emily Carr. The two women are rather alike, I think, at least when it comes to being loners. Freda has lived a good part of her life by herself, and travels often on her own. She has been to Scandinavia, Spain, and the Dominican Republic, places she is invited to as an artist. Her husband died some years ago and they had no children. "I guess they fried my eggs," she says when I ask, referring to the X-rays she had with the TB treatment. Freda figures Carr was drawn to the Native way of life and people accepted her. Emily wasn't your usual White person, she points out, which gives me pause to consider what your usual White person would have been in 1928 and more particularly what the usual White woman was. Unlike the majority, you could say Carr came to the Skeena with neither conversion nor coercion on her mind, and she came unattached to Church, state, or male authority. She did want something, of course, and the question, suggests Freda, is whether there was an exchange. "Because that's the key." This leaves me pondering what we know about Carr's practice. There is no evidence that she paid individuals or families like Mrs. Douse's for reproducing their poles, for instance, although the idea of paying individuals a model's fee was not foreign to her. She knew some owners expected to be asked, and reported being found once by an old man who returned from fishing to find her sketching his poles. "'Go away, you stealing my poles,' he shouted. I explained that they were beautiful and I wanted to show them to my friends. 'Why you not ask me?' 'How could I when you weren't home?'" So asking permission would seem to have been a courtesy extended only if the owner was on the spot. Emily also knew enough to realize she had crossed a boundary in appropriating Native design for her pottery. Her justification served to advance the myth of her own expertise and herself as someone whose renderings were faithful to the originals in a way others' were not. As if this were not simply rationalizing appropriation. She seems also to have differentiated between the pots and her paintings, seeing the use in the first as artificial, and the second as not. If she talked to Barbeau about such issues, she might have learned something about Aboriginal attitudes to ownership of the poles; they could have talked about the renovation project at Gitwangak, which had required lengthy negotiations with unwilling owners, some of whom flatly refused.

Even if she did not hear such stories, Carr understood you could not simply walk into a place and set up shop. It wasn't polite or safe. She had been warned off sketching people at Ucluelet (and apparently accepted the advice) and her journal attests to some attempts to solicit local people's approval by showing them her work. She talked of having painted duplicates on occasion to leave behind. Though it seems unlikely that that happened often, there are stories, Freda says, of paintings belonging to Native peoples in the area. I hear about two of these from several sources, both paintings were stolen and are now gone. Finally, I put it to Freda: would Emily Carr have seemed unusual enough as a White person to have been trusted? Could she have met carvers and learned anything from them? The answer I get is an emphatic "No," yet I find myself resisting and I am forced to question whether that resistance comes from the need to justify Carr's appropriation of Native art. I have become curious about the source of Carr's understanding of First Nations culture—whether it was entirely derived from reading books and talking with the likes of Dr. Newcombe. Most particularly I wonder about her association with the Dzunukwa in her journals and *Klee Wyck* as well as in her paintings. She recorded three encounters with her in the forest and described her as the old woman of the woods, a "supernatural being who belongs to the Indians." Her experience at Quatsino with Dzunukwa and the cats in 1930 was something special and private, as well as awe-filled. "She appeared neither wooden nor stationary, but a Singing Spirit, young and fresh, passing through the jungle. No violence coarsened her, no power domineered to wither her. It was graciously feminine. . . . She caught her breath, this D'Sonoqua, alive in the dead bole of the cedar. She summed up the depth and charm of the whole forest, driving away its menace." When a visitor to her open house exhibition in 1935 asked what meaning lay behind the painting *D'Sonoqua and the Cats*, Carr realized she was not prepared to share it and removed the picture. She is cagey about what she saw, wanting to make sure we understand that something unusual occurred without being explicit. "I am rewriting D'Sonoqua's Cats living it bit by bit—the big wooden image, the deserted village, the wet, the sea and smells and growth, the lonesomeness and mystery, and the spirit of D'Sonoqua over it all and what she did to me." In 1930, even as she was moving away from Native imagery, Carr painted several imposing pictures of the Dzunukwa, underscoring the significance the figure had for her as a metaphor and borrowed totem. Critics have picked up on this in recent years, reinterpreting the three meetings as central to Carr's self-discovery as an artist and as a woman. The Dzunukwa was Carr's way of coming to terms with the wilderness and its dark dangers, of ascribing a positive feminine character to nature. The Dzunukwa experiences are thus now being understood as ecstatic interludes, moments when she stepped outside herself and her own cultural paradigm. We are warned not to romanticize Carr's attitudes to Native peoples by imposing New Age narratives on top of her stories; narratives which are artefacts rather than facets of an integrated culture. Perhaps her perception of the connection between the totems and Native spirituality was accurate and she was envious. "Those old religious painters lived in their religion, not themselves. Our B.C. Indians lived in their totems [. . .] becoming the creature that was their ideal and guiding spirit."

Emily Carr's Dzunukwa has become a metaphor for transformation in the literature, for her coming to intuit the natural world as a cosmos. She perceived a connection between the carved images and the spiritual expression of a culture, and she experienced them as vehicles of spiritual transport. The Dzunukwa is known to many West Coast people, the Kwakwaka'wakw and Nuu-Chah-Nulth especially; she is usually female and always frightening, and Carr may well have heard some of the stories, but she does not retell them. So in her rendering, the Dzunukwa is a doubly mysterious character because she is never precisely described and because she is enfolded into Emily's romance. Freda, like the other Native women I've asked, insists that Carr could not have understood what the Dzunukwa was, that the meaning of Native spirituality was not open to her and the old carvers would not have spoken with her. Emily may have been an unusual White person, but she was still White and her connection to the Native world superficial. I have to ask why it might seem important to discover Carr had contact with Willie Seaweed or Mungo Martin, and whether this stems from the desire to legitimize her claim to special privilege. Perhaps we have to conclude, as the art historians have, that what she learned about Native art she learned by observation, by reading, and by "hanging out" with Native peoples, which is to say from the occasional conversations she had during her travels. Yet I find myself unconvinced and inclined to re-evaluate the connections she had with the few Native people she knew.

Breakfast done, Freda and I head out of Terrace in my car. The day unfolds without prompting from either of us. Freda is good company; she combines a curious mind with a generous take on the world and is evidently pleased to be going to places she hasn't visited in a while. At Gitwangak the poles are grouped on a grassy flat near the river in view of the railway. We get out and walk around glancing at the weather. It's dull midday; in the grey distance the 2,700-metre peaks of the Seven Sisters mountains sit shrouded in silence. Low-slung clouds float in the background, giving the setting an Oriental cast. These were the first poles Freda studied, I learn. They were carved in a style that no one works in anymore, she tells me, a style that is more realistic than the Haida and Kwakwaka'wakw with their ovoids and decorated U-forms. Several poles have free-standing figures on the top: an eagle about to take flight, a mountain goat leaning out over his perch looking down at the people and animals below. All of them relate to real events, she explains, adding when I look puzzled that they recount events relatively close to living memory that have not been embellished much by time. The pole stories she remembers best are those people have told her rather than those she has read. And she demonstrates this by reciting one pole, which tells of the daring getaway of a young woman with her child in a boat. Freda sprints through the ins and outs of the tale, groaning at the part where the mother sticks the tongue of her dead husband (and abductor) into the baby's mouth to quiet it; I recognize some of the details from Emily Carr's handwritten notes for her 1913 "Lecture on Totems." Freda continues with her explication, informing me that the oldest standing pole on the coast, well over a century old by her reckoning, is the "Hole in the Sky" pole at Gitanyow, though the hole is really a hole in the ice, for the story is about a boy who saves his starving family by catching a fish in a frozen lake. I watch Freda reacquainting herself with her old friends and find myself remembering Carr's horrified response to the renovation project, which had involved righting these very poles and painting them in preservative and primary colours. A.Y. Jackson, who was there in 1926 when the work was being done, found the colours absurd and complained to the CPR official who was sinking the poles in concrete and setting them upright that they should be left leaning. "I would do anything I could to please you artists," Jackson records the man as saying, "but as an engineer I cannot put up a leaning totem pole. You can make them lean any way you like in your drawings."

I ask Freda about Marius Barbeau and the other anthropologists who worked in the field here. "I sit in the middle," she tells me. A great deal was saved by people like Barbeau, so she cannot bring herself to be a hard-liner on the issue of the Whites shipping the carvings and poles out to museums. She also sits in between two cultures and is aware of belonging to both, just as she is aware of the absurdities the two bring out in each other.

For a moment I dwell on the scene with A.Y. and the engineer (actually, Edwin Holgate was there, too, advocating for leaning poles) and their collective obliviousness to the idea that the poles were not created with forever in mind, but were meant to weather and lean and fall back into the earth. The cycle has little to do with aesthetics, and cementing them in any position is a bit like soldering a boat to the wharf.

We push on for Gitanyow, a short ride over a macadam surface into the hills. Over our shoulder the Seven Sisters and Stekyawden remain hidden, picking their moment for an entrance. What was it about that mountain and Temlaham that so fired Barbeau's imagination? The idea that it was real, perhaps. According to Freda, people believe they know where the city was located—along a stretch of the river, which is bordered by a long, flat, verdant bank sloping gently up to the mountains. I ask about the city and what happened. Freda tells me some of the stories used by Barbeau in *The Downfall of Temlaham*, about a painted goat, about children who tortured animals, about people who did not bury fishbones so the animals could return to nature, about widespread disrespect. In the city below the mountain, society became unwieldy and dysfunctional. A series of wars and ecological disasters eventually caused people to abandon it. Last year, I read the story again in another celebration of the people and the place written by a White man with an enormous empathy for the Gitksan culture. In *A Death Feast in Dimlahamid*, journalist Terry Glavin alludes to the old stories, but sets them in the context of the contemporary effort of the Gitksan and Wet'suwet'en people to assert their rights. Anchored in the present, he sees the past reflected in the current situation, which includes roadblocks against logging companies, protests against the removal of resources from hereditary lands, and the court case, *Delgam Uukw vs. the Queen,* now underway in Smithers. The Gitksans' first blockade, Glavin notes, was prompted by the burning of Gitsegukla in 1872 by some White prospectors, who claimed the fire was accidental. No one was injured as the village was virtually empty when it happened, but the miners failed to offer compensation for the twelve communal houses and crest poles lost. Two gunboats were subsequently sent to the mouth of the Skeena when the river was blockaded, and Lieutenant-Governor Joseph Trutch met with the Gitsegukla chiefs, hoping to quell the trouble. Six hundred dollars was paid and the matter settled to everyone's satisfaction. Not so fifteen years later when White and Native custom collided again and people were killed. Glavin presents us with an amended version of Kitwancool Jim's story, which we encountered earlier in Marius Barbeau's book and is known as the Skeena River Rebellion in the history books. Sunbeams (Fanny Johnson), in her campaign to secure the chieftainship of Hanamuk for her son, angered an uncle who had his own ambitions for the title. Neetuh was a powerful medicine man (*haldowget*) who cursed Sunbeams' son when he succeeded. Shortly afterwards, the measles cut a swath through the valley and many blamed White people for the deaths. Sunbeams blamed Neetuh. He had uttered the curse; her son and his brother had died. The execution of Neetah and the subsequent retribution paid was done according to Gitksan law, Glavin explains. "But the whites were afraid because the Natives were afraid, and the Natives were afraid because one P. Washburn, a sometime-prospector and meddler in local affairs, had announced high and low that he was off to Victoria to ensure that British law, not Gitksan law prevailed in the circumstances of Neetuh's death." The next spring British law arrived on a gunboat. Kamalmuk, Sunbeam's husband, decided to surrender, but for some reason when the two special constables confronted him at Gitwangak, he fled. Billy Green took the opportunity to shoot him in the back. A hundred years later the Gitksan and Wet'suwet'en chiefs have turned to White man's law and taken their claims to court.

The village is quiet when we arrive. Few people are about and there is hardly a sign of tourists, although it is still officially summer. We take our time moseying about, looking at the poles, which are mainly grouped around the flats above the riverbank. I recognize several immediately from Carr's paintings and Freda's descriptions. The totem mother and her baby, and the "Hole in the Sky" pole, which is squatter and more ornate than I had imagined and stands white against the sea-blue mountains. Freda tells me parts of the story and I watch with amazement as the elaborate spirals at the mid-section turn into bear entrails and the little boy scampers to life. There is a uniqueness to these poles, a plasticity to the carving and a whimsy to the figures. There are numerous, free-standing figures perched on the pole tops, and I am drawn to one in particular, of a man holding a bow and sporting a very large bird on his head. I tease myself with the question of whether the bird is sitting on a man or a totem pole, and just how far the carver was willing to take realism. Carr, I realize, didn't paint the old pole and avoided these comic pole-top figures. Looking about, I recognize the grave houses she wrote about, and imagine that the empty and decrepit wood cabin across the way might have been new when she visited in 1928.

The poles are a link backwards and forwards in time. A community centre has been built nearby, and a low, open-sided carving shed sits in between, protecting two old poles from the ravages of inquisitive visitors and inclement weather. They look like fallen warriors lying in state, flanked by innocent uncut logs waiting for carvers and a feast. There are poles in other locations about the village, so we do a tour, noticing on the way back that someone has opened a gift shop that offers refreshments as well as gifts. We drop in and Freda chats with the woman, who is interested to hear that Freda was born into the eagle clan, which is one of the least numerous along the Skeena. We don't stay long but head for 'Ksan where we spend some time examining the displays. Set up in 1970 at the historic site of Gitanmaax, 'Ksan is both a cultural centre open to tourists and a training centre teaching traditional Gitksan arts. By the time we get to Anspayaxw (Kispiox) late in the afternoon, the weather has lifted and the Seven Sisters are visible at last. A rainbow arches over the village and a wedding is taking place at the community hall, which is bulging with guests and hilarity. Freda pokes about the edges of the crowd, asking discreet questions until she figures out who the principals are. We spend some time examining the village poles grouped in the middle of the reserve on a commons behind a railing. I try taking photographs, but am defeated by the exaggerated slant of the sun's sinking rays, which bathe everything in a golden glow and obliterate detail.

Eventually hunger drives us to Hazelton. Freda knows the Islander Hotel in Old Town from her days at 'Ksan. It was owned by Polly Sargant and her husband then. Polly, a driving force behind the training centre project, had helped secure the grants to get it started. We settle at a table in the cosy dining-room and Freda looks around. Not much has changed, she declares. A young woman comes over to fetch our order; she and Freda exchange a few pleasantries and establish their connection. We order a roast beef sandwich with fries, and one fried chicken with potato salad, which Chrystal tells me is home-made. Before our dinners arrive, Chrystal's brother breezes in, recognizes Freda, and comes straight over. Freda smiles a welcome, but I sense her stiffen. A handsome man in his thirties, Arnie leans over the table and pours on the charm, talking us both up, a notch or two too loudly. He takes a table by the door and tries to wangle a beer from his sister, who won't cooperate unless he eats a meal. "Are you a reporter?" he shoots across the room at me—a pretty good guess these days. Enough is going on in "Indian country" to bring in the southern press on a regular basis. I look at him without saying anything. "Hit on something, eh?" he needles. "She is a writer," concedes Freda, at which he strides across the room again, drapes his arm over my shoulder and whispers conspiratorially at Freda. "She's recording it all." This is the kind of man who knows exactly where the discomfort zones lie in social situations, and who likes to play the edges. "If I write about her, she'll be the first to know," I say to his cynical grin, feeling defensive all the same. He continues a one-handed conversation with the room, calling out to the cook in the back. "Hey, woman, whatcha got there for me?" but returns like a moth to a flame. I realize he's strutting his stuff only ostensibly for me; the dangerous comments are all for Freda.

"Everyone's related along the Skeena, which is why I chase White women," he informs her. Freda's not anxious for the exchange to continue. She resolutely pursues her fries around her plate. I follow suit with a piece of chicken. Arnie surveys the room, assesses the talent, and unceremoniously departs.

He was right, of course. I was recording everything. Drinking in the sheer majesty of the landscape I was passing through, attending carefully to the things Freda was showing me, to her conversation and the history it was describing for me.

Chief Justice Allan McEachern was treated to a similar experience as a White man although on a grander scale, in a courtroom in Smithers in 1987. The Gitksan and Wet'suwet'en elders, one by one, opened their sacred *ada'ox* and *kungax* and told the stories that were evidence of their ownership and jurisdiction, naming the landscape and their relationship to it. In doing so they were revealing a huge expanse of land as neither wild nor unknown, as White people often assert, taking on the theory of *terra nullius*, which Canadian courts have so often used to deny Aboriginal rights, and taking issue with the long line of government lawyers who have asserted that the Gitksan and Wet'suwet'en do not exist as a people worthy of the designation as such. However, Judge McEachern, like D.C. Scott before him, was obdurate. After 318 days of evidence and 23,500 pages of transcript evidence at trial, he concluded with stunning bathos, "The most striking thing that one notices in the territory away from the Skeena-Bulkley corridor is its emptiness. I generally accept the evidence of the [Crown] witnesses . . . and others that very few Indians are to be seen anywhere except in the large river corridors . . . the territory is indeed a vast emptiness." The judge's decision, released in March, dismisses the elders' testimony and Aboriginal title with it. His words were knife-sharp and meant to cut off debate. His judgement carries the same peremptory tone as the Special Committee Report of 1927 and reflects the same view of the nation as something unitary and White. In 1991, though, it grates on public opinion like an anachronism. Even people who oppose the land claim are offended by the judge's language and apparent ignorance. It put a lots of White liberals on the spot.

Arnie's question was likewise provocative, meant to put me on the spot, but I admired the irreverence behind it. Why shouldn't a writer be asked to declare her intentions? Why shouldn't I define my relationship to the cliché of the southern White professional who comes here to collect material or to dispense expertise to the Aboriginal population? To get her story, to make the fee, to get out? I am here collecting, too, collecting historical information about an artist who came here, to Indian country, a lifetime ago and found something to anchor her own art. As I travel I am searching for a way to understand Carr's problematic relationship with Aboriginal culture, in so many ways a metaphor for the puzzle that is Canada. I am grappling with the quirks of history, which make her the ancestor of both Terry Glavin and Allan McEachern.

There is a white cat perched on the roof of the old wooden house when I return to Gitanyow on my own. Almost invisible against the pale sky, she sits immobile like the wooden figures opposite, effecting heraldic dominion of the decaying structure beneath her. Freda has left for home and I've come back to look for Emily Carr. The village is alive with children just released from school for lunch. I am commandeered by one little pixie to drive her over to her grandpa's house, and after circling back, I park in front of the Gitanyow band office. The village has taken back its old name. The Kitwancool, which I later learn means "people of a small village" are once again the "awesome warrior people." They have always had their own take on things, most recently refusing to join the other Gitksan in the *Delgamuukw* case, and contesting some of the Nisga'a claims in the Nass Valley. The view from Gitanyow *is* unique. In Carr's time the village may have seemed inaccessible to outsiders, but to the Gitksan the trail up past Gitanyow leading to the oolican-rich fishing grounds of the Nass River has been a major thorough-fare since ancient times. "Footworn a metre deep in places from thousands of years of use, the Kitwancool Trail was just part of a network of trails in the territory, linking the Gitksan to each other and to nations far away," reads the current *Traveller's Guide to Aboriginal B.C.* Today it is paved and called Highway 37.

Entering the band office I find Bonnie Douse at the desk opening mail. Some young children mill about the reception area and are repeatedly told to go outside to play. A dog tries his luck getting in and is shooed out with a cloud of kids. I look around to see a stylish woman dressed in a jean skirt and a Guatemalan vest sitting on a couch in the corner. A fellow in a peaked cap comes in from a room at the back, gives her an admiring glance, and ducks out the front door. I introduce myself and tell Bonnie what I am curious about, and that Lillian Gogag at the gift store sent me over. She looks at the photo of Emily Carr's painting of Mrs. Douse, "the chieftainess," and calls her brother from the next room. Richard Douse is the band administrator who, like Bonnie, is large and imposing and in his thirties. He looks at the photo. Neither has ever seen the painting, though Bonnie had heard of it being at the museum in Prince Rupert. When she was there she looked all over, but didn't find it. "People hereabouts thought she was crazy," Richard begins. "She'd come up to the station at Gitwangak and get off and no one would pick her up to take her here to Gitanyow. Or want to." Whenever White people came to the village, they would always stay at his father Alfred's house, he explains. "People used to joke about Carr hanging around him so much." I tell him that people in Victoria say the same sort of thing, and relay a couple of crazy-lady stories about Carr; how she assaulted one of her tenants and gave others tongue-lashings. "Some say her pictures looked hallucinogenic," he says, suggesting the old girl may have been on some weird trip. Bonnie picks up the phone and calls Abel Campbell, one of the elders in the village. She speaks to him in their language and I catch the word "Vancouver" in the flow of sounds. She hangs up and, when there is a break in the conversation, tells me to go on over, offering directions. The woman on the sofa is on to a third cigarette by this time. When she hears that I have come looking for someone to talk to, she mockingly suggests that I come around to wash off her trailer while she talks to me. I tell her that if Mr. Campbell can't help, I'll be right over and smile sweetly.

I find Abel Campbell's place and Abel in the shed out back. He emerges from its recesses as I approach, stopping me in my tracks, for he resembles a childhood friend and teacher, long since dead. After shaking my hand he asks if I haven't been here before "a long time ago." I smile inanely and murmur something until the moment passes and then try to explain myself. Bonnie had thought I might need Mr. Campbell's niece to interpret, but I understand the old man just fine. He doesn't think he ever met Emily Carr, but he knew about her, and saw a picture of hers once. His grandfather, Albert Douse, was Mrs. Douse's husband, he tells me, but she didn't look much like the woman in Carr's portrait. (Lillian Gogag had said the painting looked like her mother-in-law.) He talks on a bit about the old days when people went by cart and team to Gitwangak for groceries and it took two days. Like most men, Abel went off to the coast to fish, and later hauled logs with a three-ton truck. No one can afford those machines now, he says, and the companies just keep coming. There are clear-cuts on his territories where he used to trap beaver, marten, weasel, and mink. In the old days the boundaries of hunting grounds were strictly kept; you would be warned twice if you went onto someone else's and then you could be killed on the spot. Abel Campbell is disapproving, saying he wouldn't have done such a thing, but he admits things have not changed for the better. The story comes around to unruly young folk who don't pay attention or give respect. "Young people now don't want to learn," he shrugs. "They can't skin a beaver." After his wife died ten years ago, he didn't want to go back to his hunting grounds, and now he supposes his traplines are gone.

Mr. Campbell invites me inside and makes me a seat on the sofa in the room he has set up in the basement. He looks at me carefully through large smoky-lensed glasses. I explain how I have come to be in his village, about Freda and my interest in Emily Carr. Did

people think Carr was crazy, I ask. Well, he painted all those paintings, Abel points out, referring to Carr in the masculine. It's a
convention I've heard before and wonder if it is prompted solely by
grammatical difference. "Those pictures are not accurate," he
continues, indicating the reproduction of *Kitwancool Totems* I have
with me. "Have you seen those poles here?" He digs out a copy of
Wilson Duff's monograph on the Gitanyow poles and we look
through it. He does not press his opinion, but it is clear nonetheless.
Carr's pictures are not accurate. Her desire to paint the poles may
have been unusual (they had, of course, been photographed before),
but her representations still violated custom. I ask then if he has
read her portrait of the village in *Klee Wyck*, and offer to send him
a copy when it appears that he hasn't. That would be fine, he says
after some consideration, but I should write my name in it. He asks
if this is all I've come for, and once again I am made aware of the
long line of individuals who have preceded me, the non-Native
journalists, academics, and writers who have come onto reserves
looking for stories to fill their notebooks and tape recorders, leaving
their business cards behind. The shoe is on the other foot now, I
realize. *We* have become stereotypes. I find myself sidestepping the
cliché, self-conscious about taking notes or photographs, and
repeatedly rehearsing my purpose to myself, training my focus on
the history I have come here to understand—that is, my own
history—the legacy of the European newcomers who created
Canada and the White Creation story that mythologizes the land
grab as rightful and colonization as a gift, the story that lives on in
judgements like Judge McEachern's, despite the cracks and gaping
holes in its logic, the story that is embodied by Emily Carr.

What does Emily Carr's success in Ottawa reveal? In the first
place, her debut was entirely fortuitous. Her life intersected with
the Group of Seven's at an auspicious moment in history when a
national identity was being consciously constructed and the visual
arts—painting in particular—were central to the enterprise. It

coincided with the rise of modernism and straddled the period between colonialisms—British and American. Carr had an unusual role to play in the move to an independent Canadian identity. She proved Fred Housser's thesis about the Group of Seven being part of a national movement. At the same time, she demonstrated what other artists have before, that new talent and major breakthroughs often come from the periphery, from places and traditions outside the Western centres of art. (Velasquez and Picasso are examples of that, as is Tom Thomson.) The emerging idea of Canada was directly associated with the images of the wilderness created by the Group of Seven. The lone pine tree by a windswept lake was evocative of the ethic of nordicity and symbolized survival in an unforgiving environment. The Canadian mythos these painters embraced imagined a national character tempered by terrain and climate. It was hardy, enduring, superior, and White like the North itself. The men in the group were not the first artists to be inspired by the Canadian landscape, though they were the first to idealize the North as something mystical and majestic, as well as masculine and quintessentially Canadian. Carr expanded on that concept and feminized it. The group conceived of basing a national art on the natural peculiarities of place and in doing so contributed significantly to the process of accommodating the terrors of nature and of assuaging the loneliness associated with wilderness. They mythologized the North in the course of trying to imaginatively possess the country, and this was the subtext of all their activity and anxiety: the old desire for belonging. If Emily Carr shared anything with the Group of Seven, this was it. Her great spiritual affinity with Harris was peculiar; with the others it was the project of capturing the land in paint. The group's agenda included improving the situation for Canadian artists and taking leadership in public debates about art and culture. Harris, Jackson, Lismer, and MacDonald all wrote prolifically on the subject of political and cultural affairs; they were more than enthusiasts, they were ideologues. Carr was not drawn to that side of their work and it was a rare moment in her life when she stepped into the public sphere. She had opened her studio to the public at various times, held Christmas sales of her crafts, and in 1913 she undertook the documentary project, but there was only one major foray into this realm otherwise, the People's Gallery of 1932. The idea was to turn the lower flats of her apartment building into a permanent exhibiting space where the work of local artists would be displayed and the objective would be to make art accessible to "all classes, all nationalities, all colours," and, incidentally, make a living for herself. Carr lacked the organizing skills and charisma to pull people behind her, but the timing in the middle of the Depression was also poor. Even with the support of other artists and the National Gallery, she failed to attract a crew of willing volunteers to carry the idea further.

Carr was no camp follower; she did not share the Group's notion of the North, and she did not use the term. Instead, she spoke of "God's tabernacle" and "Mother Earth," indicating that her eye and her emotions were centred on a particular kind of landscape that she saw as essentially female. Moreover, where the men went into the bush seeking transformation, Carr, I would argue, went into the woods seeking transcendence. She was not looking for a way to change herself so much as a way to overcome herself, to reach beyond her physical shell towards immanence. Gitanyow had symbolic significance for Carr because of the danger it exuded and the fear it inspired. It was new and strange terrain for her and it may have triggered the mystic response she associates in her journals with the Dzunukwa. When she came to Kitwancool, she had nothing to lose except the promise of her sudden and unexpected recognition. She came to find her vision as an artist and her faith as a maverick soul and the trip was as much spiritual quest as a test of her creative strength. Something happened here, I suspect. She never talked about it, but she changed subtly. At long last she was able to let things go; and at this point her spiritual journey began.

This is what I am thinking as I take my leave of Abel Campbell, standing outside by his shed looking at the mountains in the distance and inhaling the green scent of the forest all around. I imagine Emily here, rummaging about in the rain, giving Mrs. Douse a fit as she trampled through the grave houses. I take a walk over to the main stand of poles by the community centre and wander down a small embankment to the Kitwancool River rushing past the village on its way to the Skeena. Picking my way along the path, I can hear its treble sounds and smell it before I can see anything—cedar and balsam overwhelmed by the stench of decaying flesh. At first the scene is horrifying: half-dead creatures pushing their deformed bodies against the current, past rotting carcasses lying wedged between rocks or stranded on shore. A final drama is being played out to the song of the river. It almost seems fitting, this scene of carnage in the midst of beauty, for at the heart of Emily Carr's legacy is an unpleasant truth that taints the surrounding air. Here at Gitanyow there is no avoiding the brutality of her incursion into Native life. But it is here, too, that she reached beyond the totem poles, and beyond herself.

Chapter Four

Over the Horizon

New York, 1930

There is a chill to the April air despite the absence of
snow and the appearance of buds on the trees in the park.
Winter leaves the eastern seaboard with the reluctance of
a lover and spring arrives habitually late. Walking along
Madison Avenue towards Fifty-third Street, Emily Carr is
thinking about the hummingbirds and huge-blossomed
rhododendrons back home across the continent where
spring is already two months old. She shivers and stops to
look around, searching for the entrance to the building on
the corner. New York is not so claustrophobic and "cram-
jam" as she had feared. Yet she lingered with friends on
Long Island for several days before braving Manhattan,
tormented by flashbacks to the bad times in England and
France. Cities defy human scale by definition (especially
hers), and New York is full of giant buildings—skyscrapers they call them—which all require elevators. How
could anyone do that, live without a garden or even a tree
outside the window, she wonders. Georgia O'Keeffe and
Alfred Stieglitz are said to live twenty-eight storeys up in
one of the tallest. In the clouds.

An eager wind sails along the streets and Emily feels
invigorated, light-headed almost, as she fills her lungs
with sea-salted air. She is glad, suddenly, to be here. It
was Lawren Harris's doing. Harris had insisted that she
grab the chance while in the East to see the new work by
American artists, plying her with lists of places to visit

(the just-opened Museum of Modern Art down the street, for example) and letters of introduction to wealthy collectors and like-minded artists. This is her last day. The collector has not answered her note, and Emily is feeling faintly relieved. Curiosity had gotten the better of dread in the end, and she now finds that she likes the city. The streets are clean and the people courteous; only the elevators continue to terrorize her, but at the Roerich Museum, one of them had produced Arthur Lismer, who was in town to see the spring shows himself and happy to team up with her. Lismer had known what to do about elevators, how to get the operator to ascend at a snail's pace so you don't leave your stomach on the ground floor.

This afternoon Emily has actually been savouring the experience of being on her own. She finds small, private galleries like the Roerich immensely appealing, Nicholas Roerich being an artist and a modernist himself, and a theosophist friend of Harris. She is on her way now to An American Place, drawn by Harris's descriptions of the circle of landscape painters attached to the gallery and their investigations of the spiritual in art. Georgia O'Keeffe exhibited there in February, and Arthur Dove is currently showing. The elevator glides gently to the seventeenth floor where the entrance to Alfred Stieglitz's latest "cathedral and laboratory of American art" is easily found. Through a set of frosted glass doors, Emily steps into a white, light-filled room. For a moment she is stunned by the brilliance; her eyes register pain and take several minutes to adjust. She stands still taking it in. The walls are long and white, the floor a smooth, glossy grey. Three large windows engulf the space with afternoon sunlight, sifted through shades that roll up from the bottom. Dove's paintings float in this luminosity like rainbows at the end of a sun shower. His is a vision of nature in thrall to the sublime and the simple. Edging into abstraction, many of

them depict the sun, direct and resplendent, playing on
optical effects and emotional allusion, and filling the room
with sweet, airy energy. Perhaps it is her imagination, but
Emily feels she can tell the difference between this place
and the others she's visited. Stieglitz's exhibition rooms
aren't galleries, as Harris had explained. They are not
meant for spectators or browsers or even the public really,
although the public is invited. They are meant for people
who are serious about art. Visitors are invited to study the
work on display, and even to discuss it with Stieglitz
(who, Harris says, can usually be found on the premises),
and there are special "silent hours" when visitors are
asked not to talk at all. Still, The Place opened only in
December. O'Keeffe's show was its second exhibition and
it may be that things have changed.

After about ten minutes, a woman emerges from a room
at the back, breaking Emily's reverie. She is dressed in
black, slashes of white at the neck and cuffs of a slim,
pleated frock, dark hair smoothed against a broad elegant
brow. She has some colour swatches with her, and is
followed by a young woman who listens to the instructions about the pearl-grey paint the older woman wants
for the walls. A cool blue-grey with some depth to it, but
very pale, she is saying. The visage is unmistakable.
Three years ago Emily would not have been so forward,
but she is fifty-nine this year, a productive, confident
artist who doesn't let opportunity slide. She introduces
herself, mentions Harris's acquaintance with Stieglitz and
gets straight to the point. Could she see some of the work?
The New Mexico paintings perhaps?

Georgia O'Keeffe is taken aback by the approaching
figure, large, rumpled and steadfastly attired in hat,
gloves, and thick-heeled shoes. Obviously not one of the
stylish New York "ladies" who flock to her shows, whom
the critics love to ridicule. And hardly one of those "Santa

Fe" women either. Carr looks more like something a
church basement, rather than the art world, might
produce, yet her presence is compelling, and the story she
tells of travelling the coast and painting the forest is
intriguing and even sounds familiar. Somewhat to her
surprise, O'Keeffe finds herself listening. Perhaps it is the
fact that the Canadian doesn't fawn but seems strictly
interested in her work. It dawns on her, as she listens to
Carr explain herself, that she has never met an older
woman like this: a working artist, travelling on her own,
acting as a free agent, and showing with the men. She
reminds Georgia of Rosa Bonheur, the hugely successful
French painter who was granted special dispensation by
the Paris police to wear men's clothing in public so she
could paint her favourite subject, which was horses and
other large animals, from life. Rosa in matronly drag, she
thinks, for according to Stieglitz, Mme. Bonheur actually
only wore skirts when she went out on social occasions; at
home and on the job she habitually wore trousers. A smile
creeps across O'Keeffe's face, and she disappears into the
back, reappearing a few minutes later with the doe-eyed
young woman, both of them carrying canvasses.

Nothing much is said as the paintings are set up along
the wall. Emily is allowed to absorb them quietly.
O'Keeffe carries on with her tasks and after a long time
comes back in looking as if she is preparing to leave. It
was luck catching her here in the first place, Emily thinks,
and decides to speak again. "I admire them, Miss O'Keeffe,
more than I can say," she ventures, feeling foolish even as
she speaks.

"How so?" snaps O'Keeffe. Then, looking at Emily as if
suddenly remembering to be polite, she adds, "I've never
been to the Canadian West. How do you suppose it is
different from our Southwest?"

"Well, it's green, not pink, to begin with," Emily offers

with an awkward laugh. "But the scale is the same. Huge, that is. I'll bet the desert is the devil to paint, and just as hard to get. The dimensions are entirely different, though. Quite opposite."

"I have to tell you something, Miss Carr. I detest green. I've always felt smothered in green here in the East, quite closed in and deprived of the sky. I think that's why I like Taos so much. I think I belong in the Southwest."

Emily nods and gestures towards two paintings of sand hills in the high desert. "That vista seems alarmingly open to me. But then the space there runs horizontal instead of the vertical I'm used to. I'd find it impossible to gauge distance." She stands back and turns towards the opposite wall, taking in the four tall canvases that feature large black crosses set in the foreground, framing sweeping views of the desert beyond. "Or scale. I can't tell what those crosses . . . are they as large as they look?"

"They're Penitente crosses and I suppose they're large if life size is large. I didn't know what they were when I first saw them, though I knew I had to paint them. They were erected decades ago by members of a sect of Catholic mystics who perform flagellation and crucifixion rites at Easter. At one time they used nails instead of thongs to attach themselves to the cross. They say some people died. The sect was secret, but the crosses and the little Peni- tente churches—*moradas*—are everywhere." She pauses to look from one painting to the other.

"When I painted that one," she continues, pointing to *Black Cross, New Mexico,* "it was in the late light and the cross stood out dark against the evening sky. If I turned a little to the left, away from it, I saw the Taos mountain—a beautiful shape. So I painted the cross against the moun- tain, although I never saw it that way. The crosses are a way of painting the country, I suppose. Anyway, I painted it with a red sky and I painted it with a blue sky and stars."

"I've come across the giant cedar poles of the Haida and Kwakiutl in much the same way, out in the open and there to be seen like your crosses in the hills. But I've stumbled on them in the forest, too; once a giant raven, another time a monster figure known as the D'Sonoqua. I painted them in their setting, buried in the underbrush. But I was careful about altering things."

"Is that a speciality with you, the Native subjects?"

"My paintings began as a historical exercise. I decided to document the poles as precisely as I could, for posterity. The carvings were in a sorry state twenty years ago. Those that weren't decaying were disappearing, and it seemed important to make a record. The paintings I do now are quite different; more and more I have been using the pole figures as you use the crosses, as emblems, abstracted and drawn up to the picture plane to provide a way into the landscape. More and more, I paint the landscape alone."

"And do you know about these carvings? Do you know what they mean?" asks O'Keeffe.

"At first I saw them only as religious decoration, but the more time I spend with them, the more I've come to respect their power, and to see them as works of art made with an intimate understanding of nature. The she-bears and thunderbirds seemed carved by people who knew the animals by name. I don't know what they mean exactly, but they are connected to the spirit of the place."

O'Keeffe listens thoughtfully. "To me the black crosses are markers where the spirit of the land and the people touch. It is very simple. Clear like the air and the sky. At the same time, I think of them as the thin dark veil of the

Catholic Church spread over New Mexico. They represent
what the Spanish felt about Catholicism—dark and
sombre. That is how I paint them."

"Your colours are anything but sombre and the land is
full of light to my eye, but those crosses do cast a pall.
That's another difference I detect. The church is not very
visible in the British Columbia landscape. The missionaries haven't been there long enough, I suppose, and the
Native presence is still strong in the places I know. I
painted a church just recently, a pretty little white one at
Friendly Cove, which came out looking so shy and fragile
against the voracious forest."

"Well, as far as that goes, people say the Christianity
practised by the Indians in New Mexico is half Native,
that it has merely been adapted and grafted onto the old
ways. In fact, the Natives perform rituals there just as
they always have."

"Really? Where I live the authorities dislike Native
ritual, and have tried to ban it completely."

"In the Southwest, the big effort has been
to control the crush of tourists who flock to the big
ceremonials."

"Did you paint in Native villages yourself, then?"

"I was close to Taos Pueblo and went there several
times. The people do not particularly welcome the
Anglos—and who would want the invasion of men with
their noisy cars and cameras looking for spectacles, which
is what happens? When the stampede of people to watch
the Snake Dance at the Walpi Pueblo in Arizona got to be
too much with everyone running around trying to make a
fast buck, restrictions were introduced. That was before
the war, and in the meantime the Hopi have learned to
manage the greedy and the curious. There is a charge now
if you want to photograph or sketch; so much for so many
times on the same painting and so much for each new one.

I can't blame them, but I didn't like the feeling it gives me of being watched."

"You prefer being off on your own?"

"Yes. I think you understand why. I can touch the land better when there is no distraction. To me, it's like the crosses. I can't help feeling that anyone who doesn't feel those crosses doesn't get the country."

Emily turns back to the paintings, drawn by one very curious one she's spied in the corner. It looks quite abstract at first glance. A flat, overall pattern in ultramarine blue and burnt sienna. Spots of white like stars. She turns her head one way, and then tries the other. "Ahh. I see it," she finally exhales.

"I call it *The Lawrence Tree*," O'Keeffe tells her, sounding a bit triumphant at the guessing game she's provoked. "It is a very old pine tree that grows outside a house I stayed in last summer. There's a bench set beside it that I'd lie down on, and this is the view I got. The owner of the house is D.H. Lawrence, the writer. So I named it after him."

"I'm fascinated by the way it makes you feel completely surrounded, enveloped by the thick foliage of that tree."

"Which is odd because I expect you'd find it a pretty scrawny tree from any other view. Thin gruel compared to the hefty ones you're used to. Even so, it is quite symbolic."

"Yes, of the daringly obvious, I'd say. There really aren't too many ways to capture the image of the whole tree while standing up close beside it. And that's my conundrum: How to express size close-up and proximity at a distance."

The young woman reappears at this moment and asks O'Keeffe if she wants to see the clippings from her show. "That's no business of yours," O'Keeffe retorts. "I'm leaving now in any case." The girl returns O'Keeffe's

glare with a pained expression and slinks away. "In fact,
I mostly feel it's no business of the critics either,"
O'Keeffe mutters, as if to herself. She walks to the far
end of the room and calls out, "These paintings will have
to be put in the back when this lady leaves, Dorothy."
Gathering her parcels, she says a swift goodbye and is
gone.

Carr makes her way back to the Martha Washington in
a state of quiet excitement, tired and ebullient and pleased
with the day's events. She contemplates a tasty meal in
the dining-room (which is open to gentlemen at lunch
only), followed by a leisurely evening packing for her
departure tomorrow. At the front desk she is greeted with
a change of plan. It seems the collector whom Harris was
so anxious for her to meet has answered her note after all.
She had come by the hotel and dropped off a message of
her own, which the Martha staff had mislaid. The clerk is
beside himself with apologies and offers to pay for a cab
up to Mrs. Dreier's residence, assuring Emily there will be
time for a visit on the way to the train station tomorrow.
Emily is reluctant. Her first attempt to reach the woman
had been rebuffed by a servant answering the telephone
who was audibly surprised to hear an unknown person
asking to speak with Madame herself. But the Martha's
man is adamant.

Emily retires to her room, a cubby-hole located above
the lounge and reachable by a small set of stairs. She puts
down her packages, changes her shoes, and freshens up
in the tiny bathroom. She was delighted when they'd
found this room for her, cheaper than the others, in a
quiet spot away from the elevator. But then, this is a
ladies' hotel, and the whole idea is to oblige women on
their own in New York. She eats early, mulling over the
paintings she'd seen that afternoon and the cool, spare
woman she'd spoken with. O'Keeffe seemed remote,

though friendly enough when she put her mind to it. Her
work was bracing and sure-footed, the forms abstracted,
though condensed might be a better word, for they were
vital and living. Modernism is firmly attached to the
natural with O'Keeffe, Emily thinks, and wide open to the
soul. And obviously her soul burns for that faraway
landscape. Emily had watched O'Keeffe's face as she
talked about the Southwest. She sounded matter-of-fact,
but there was a wistful cast to the eyes as they swept out
over the horizon. Emily saw how those paintings spoke
for her. She wondered if her own spoke that way of her.
And she thought about *Grey*, the great tree she had tried
to paint, secreted in the primeval forest, enfolded in a
soft, supple, half-seen centre. This was where terror was
contained and mitigated. She had wrestled with it for
months. And then the shape came to her simple and coni-
cal, shimmering like a candle at dawn. It reminded her of
O'Keeffe's crosses. It reminded her of the porous wall
separating the dream from the imaginary. This is what
O'Keeffe had meant when she said making art is about
making the unknown known.

The collector's name is Katherine Dreier. She is an artist
as well as an American phenomenon, though chalk to
O'Keeffe's cheese as a painter. The author of three books,
including one on van Gogh, she has the distinction of
having been part of the infamous Armory Show of 1913,
which introduced modernism and abstract art to America
and to horrified New Yorkers. Even President Roosevelt
had something to say about it. The scandal of the show
had been Marcel Duchamp's *Nude Descending a Staircase*,
a fractured cubist image hailed by the public as "an
explosion in a shingle factory" and the epitome of modern
art's depravity and duplicity. Carr and Lismer saw the
painting along with works by Braque, Picasso, Derain,
Kandinsky, and a host of American equivalents—Marsden

Hartley, John Marin, and Charles Demuth. They took in
the big event of the season, which was the Museum of
Modern Art's one-man exhibition of Charles Burchfield's
early watercolours. Large, numinous portraits of nature,
these were evocations of childhood impressions, moody
and moving to Emily. She wasn't so enamoured with
everything on display. The cubists could be glacial, and
the expressionists so forced they reeked of phoniness.
Some abstract paintings stirred her and she found something to appreciate in the painterly passages, but a great
deal of it left her cold. While she could not fathom the
hostility such paintings inspired, she did sympathize with
the public's puzzlement.

Lismer had stood looking at the Duchamp painting for
ten minutes without blinking. Then he solemnly had
declared, "One thing is certain; the thing is very, very
feminine." Emily was surprised by that, though she
couldn't exactly disagree. There was something lyrical in
the lines of Duchamp's moving figure, its subtle coloura-
tion, its flow. But feminine? She wonders what Lismer
would say of O'Keeffe's pink contoured hills. Dreier, she
knows, is part of Duchamp's circle. Together they had
founded the Société Anonyme, an organization dedicated
to promoting modern art, which ran a gallery in mid-town
Manhattan for a time, and four years ago sponsored New
York's second major exhibition of modern art at the
Brooklyn Museum. Dreier, her money, and her family
connections were behind it and, like the Armory Show, it
assembled work by the European and American avant-
garde. So it would appear that Alfred Stieglitz is no longer
the only champion of modernism in New York; Katherine
Dreier has joined his ranks. She remained the motive force
in the Société while Duchamp returned to his own work
and the full-time job of being Duchamp. Naturally, the
"291" artists were well represented in the Brooklyn show,

but Stieglitz would not allow their work to travel to
Buffalo and Toronto with the exhibition. Emily heard the
story from Lawren Harris, who had seen the show in New
York and then orchestrated its appearance at the Art
Gallery of Toronto and arranged for Mrs. Dreier to give a
talk while it was there. In December, when Emily passed
through Toronto, the controversy was still simmering;
Harris and former Group of Seven member Franz Johnston
had faced-off in *The Canadian Forum*. "The truth is that
works of art test the spectator much more than the spectator tests them," Harris wrote in his "Appreciation."
"These people who do these things are more dangerous
than many incarcerated in asylums for the insane, many
of whom at least are cheerful in their dementia," retorted
Johnston.

On the drive to Katherine Dreier's house—"the
Mansions," as Martha's man had called it, acknowledging
the importance of the address on Central Park West even
if his guest didn't—Carr reviews what she knows about
the woman besides the fact that she is very wealthy, very
avant-garde, and an avid collector. She is about Carr's
age, a theosophist like Harris, and utterly devoted to her
philosophy of art, which is expounded in a book called
Western Art and the New Era. Carr has purchased a copy
and has it tucked in her bag. So far she has surmised that
Dreier conceives of modernism as a spiritual force, "born
of the vibrations of the new age and endowed with
profound social and moral purpose." Apparently, Dreier
has forsaken her own painting for this philosophy, which
she advances wherever and however she can—in print,
on the radio, in public lectures. In this she's a bit like
Fred Housser on the subject of the Group of Seven. With
the Brooklyn show Dreier had tried to make a statement
about contemporary European and American painting
and its spiritual content; she wanted to impress on the

American public "the social, cultural and aesthetic benefits of deep communion with this art." She was messianic
and convinced of her moral purpose, but was not particularly convincing. Harris had also explained how
Duchamp and the others had been invited into the fold at
the new Museum of Modern Art, while Dreier was pointedly excluded.

The thought of this produces a rush of compassion that
blunts Emily's usual aversion to displays of extreme
wealth. She has experienced it before in England; she is
aware of it lurking in Lawren Harris's background, yet
the sight of "the Mansions" is still awesome. Facing into a
magnificent view of the park, it is a grandiose stone
edifice with a large formal foyer that teems with liveried
doormen and attendants. A female elevator operator in
black velvet ushers Carr to the Dreier apartments. Once
again she finds herself in a private gallery up in the sky,
only this one is larger than usual and is actually someone's home. Mrs. Dreier welcomes her at the door with a
softened Brooklyn accent. She puts Carr instantly at ease.
Attendants had warned her Madame's car had already
been ordered and Madame was about to leave for an
appointment at the bank, but on seeing Emily, the trip is
postponed. "I am just back from Europe and still getting
organized," she explains. Emily is invited into the drawing-room, offered coffee, and invited to look around.
There are pictures everywhere, large and small, prints
and paintings, and sculptures on tabletops and in book-
cases. Out in the middle of the room, where it can be
viewed from both sides, stands one of Duchamp's large
glass pieces.

"It's called *Disturbed Balance*," Dreier says without
waiting for the question. "Actually, Duchamp calls it
something impossible like *To Be Looked at (from the
Other Side of the Glass) with One Eye, Close to, for Almost*

an Hour." Emily walks around the panel carefully, noting some shattered sections. "There's a story there," Dreier offers. "This was in the Brooklyn show, you see, and the damage was done when it was in transit to Buffalo. It was patched up before being sent on to Toronto, but no one in Toronto ever noticed the break." Laughing by this time in anticipation of a punch line, she adds, "because no one ever opened the case. The curators were looking for a painting, and paid no attention to this contraption in its special box with its brass catches and wheels. We thought it lost and it was sitting in the basement the whole time." Dreier is a handsome woman who speaks with the confidence of wealth yet without affectation, just as Harris does. She is naturally friendly and courts openness.

"I am glad we finally caught up," she tells Carr. "I wanted a chance to show you my collection." She squires Emily into the library and then through the drawing-room and parlour, pointing out her favourites, and making wry comments about the artists she knows. She had studied in Paris in 1907 and 1908 where she visited Gertrude and Leo Stein, met Picasso, Braque, and Matisse and bought a painting by Vincent van Gogh, which led to the book. Eagerly she shows Carr her "gems," the Kandinsky and the prized Franz Marc painting of a deer in the forest, which she has just acquired. This one entrances Emily with its expressive colour. "What news have you of Mr. Harris and Toronto?" Katherine Dreier asks when they settle in the library with coffee brought in on a silver tray. "I have great affection for the city and the artists I met there. In my opinion, Toronto's response to the Brooklyn exhibition was more tolerant than New York's. What do you make of that?" Emily digresses into an account of the Ottawa exhibition and the art scene on the West Coast, and then asks Dreier about her own work and her own views on art. Dreier picks up on the invitation and starts to bring out samples of her work, talking all the while about abstraction, about Kandinsky, and her belief in art's innate ability to convey metaphysical meaning. She ends with a large painting of her own, which she produces with a flourish and the announcement that it's a portrait of Marcel Duchamp painted about ten years ago. Carr is flummoxed. All she can decipher is a large circle, a hooked protuberance, and a long, reddish form thrust between them. She fumbles with some niceties and gives in to frustration with the jumble of forms.

"Please, Mrs. Dreier, you will just have to tell me. Otherwise, I can't think why you have a carrot stuck through his eye like that."

"Oh, my. A carrot! Here I thought I'd shown the man's benevolence so plainly," Dreier gasps. "Monsieur Duchamp is such a fine character, so keen to talk with others, and to share his ideas. Not at all like the ribald reputation he's acquired since exhibiting *Nude Descending a Staircase*. I don't suppose *R. Mutt* helped. The press thought him mad and called him an anarchist, although even he would admit that mounting a urinal on a plinth like a piece of sculpture, calling it 'ready-made' art and signing it 'R. Mutt' was a provocative act in 1917. Probably still is in most places. One thing I notice, though. The Brooklyn exhibition did demonstrate that modern art no longer sends New York into shock. People still deeply distrust it, but they accept its existence now."

"Will attitudes be changed by the Museum of Modern Art, do you think?"

"Oh, I doubt the new museum will change much of anything, Miss Carr, because I don't think the people involved see art as transformative. Not the way I do. Nor the way you do. Am I right?"

"I wonder if you see that quality in Harris's work, or in Georgia O'Keeffe's?"

"Yes, on both counts. And that makes me wonder what you saw of O'Keeffe's at The Place."

"Quite a number of paintings from New Mexico. Some with huge black crosses, some of the mission church in that low, rounded adobe style. A night view of New York. One rather eerie abstract called *Rodeo*, I think. And *The Lawrence Tree*. Do you know that one?"

"Yes, I know it, and think it's quite ingenious. I prefer *Rodeo*, which I believe is one of her best. You probably think it looks like a bloodshot eye, but I find it magnetic and full of spiritual meaning. The burst of light in the centre, the roaring reds and gold, the vibration beneath the undulating surface. Her *Lawrence Tree* struck me as decorative."

"Only when you try to see it as design. It is a very unusual view of a tree, in painting, that is. In life trees look a lot like that to animals and people who are intimate with them. It's a close-up, looking up the trunk of the tree to the sky. I loved it. I am not sure it works, but I love it because it's painting from the source."

"Well then, tell me about O'Keeffe. I gather you bumped into her, which means you were lucky. She is rarely there and never did spend time at Stieglitz's other galleries, the '291' and the Intimate Gallery."

"Well, she is driven and very accomplished. Her land-scape is so different from mine that it is hard for me to appreciate what she's doing. It took me a while to get accustomed to the sparseness. Some of her things I think beautiful, I have to say that. But she does not seem happy herself when she speaks of her painting."

Mrs. Dreier gives an impatient gesture, as if brushing something out of the way. "Georgia O'Keeffe wants to be

the greatest painter and everyone can't be that. Everyone
has something to contribute. Does the bird in the woods
care if he is the best singer, I ask you? No, he sings
because he is happy and it is the altogether-happiness
which makes one grand, great chorus."

A sore point. Emily listens anyway, learning that
O'Keeffe doesn't have much to do with other artists and
doesn't share her success. Dreier's remark that the more
famous O'Keeffe gets, the more secretive she becomes,
sounds resentful, but Emily is enthralled by the gossip,
and hazards a question about the slim young woman at
The Place.

"That no doubt was Dorothy Norman. She is an acolyte
of Stieglitz who, they say—ah, perhaps I shouldn't be
telling you this, Miss Carr, but you've probably guessed
the rest. I have heard she's his mistress, and that O'Keeffe
knows. Dorothy has money and so has her husband, and
she has plenty of time to put into The Place. Stieglitz, of
course, thrives on the attention. What man doesn't?
There, that's all I'm going to say about it, but what a spectacular fool that young woman is. All for a footnote in
history."

Emily can hardly believe her ears. She learns that
Dorothy Norman is married and has two children, one
born *after* she met Stieglitz. No *petit amour* this, is the
way Dreier puts it. Emily's not terribly used to such
frankness, certainly not in the midst of the formal
elegance of living-rooms like Mrs. Dreier's. It feels queer,
or it ought to, only Katherine Dreier herself is so informal
and welcoming. A brash New Yorker perhaps, but Emily
is charmed. She doesn't even mind that it's assumed they
share the same dedication and interest in things like Mme.
Blavatsky and Kandinsky. Eventually the conversation
returns to abstract art and Emily is pressed for an

accounting. This time she doesn't flee.

"I find I am tremendously interested in Lawren Harris's abstract ideas, but I can't quite accept them for myself," she admits, hedging still. "They seem the right and natural development for his work, though, to be honest, I don't entirely follow the principle of abstract truth. I feel unwordable depths in Harris's work that move me very much. There is a deep, calm sincerity in his forms, which radiate energy, whereas in most abstraction I feel an emptiness."

"And in some there *is* an emptiness. Not all of it is genuine. To my mind, art is only art if it helps people 'see' the spirit. Artists are among the few who have that seeing eye; they are more capable of perceiving the spiritual underpinnings of the universe and of conveying that knowledge to others." Dreier warms to her subject. "So I agree with Kandinsky that art has to surpass the simple act of recording objects in the material world. It must derive its subject from the non-material. He insists the artist must remain true to his innermost being and not take dictation from nature or the art world. I agree."

"So then is your portrait of Duchamp not influenced by the material world, by the person you were trying to capture?"

"I was not really trying to capture his likeness. I was trying to capture his character, or his essence. Nothing very complicated. The painting is meant as an equivalent, not a replacement."

Emily pauses for a moment, sets down her cup, and gets up to look at the abstracts in the room once again. "I think I'm inclined to Harris's analysis," she says. "He admits there are two sources of abstract art. Naturalistic ones where some fleeting aspect of a scene or scenes informs the whole, and those directly created from 'inner seeing.'"

"He's right. Both sorts can convey spiritual meaning, which is the main thing. When I have traced the influences that cause that inner urge to express itself in art, I always find them attaching to the great spiritual forces. So I think of modernism as a probing of those forces; that is its special purpose, and yours."

"Sometimes I feel like I have been left behind on the beach. There is something icy and unyielding in pure abstraction, often despite great beauty. I have conversations like this with Mr. Harris, you know. What I've seen—no, *experienced*—in his work has made me curious about his religious beliefs and we have talked about that, too. Incidentally, I had word from him recently in Paris . . ."

"Yes, I know he is there. Duchamp mentioned that he would be seeing him soon."

". . . and he reports he's not found abstract things there that have any deep resonance. Nothing 'stirs or answers or satisfies the soul,' is what he said. However, he is convinced he'll discover them soon."

"I think he will. He has been flirting with abstraction for a long time now, hasn't he? It seems such a natural progression to me. If the function of art is to illuminate the invisible, then plainly the pull of worldly things like familiar objects, like narrative, interferes."

"I am not sure," Emily begins. The conversation makes her uncomfortable. Makes her want to cling to the earth, to her dear shapes, her density, her herbage, her juice. "My experience of the spiritual does not take place in the abstract but in nature, you see. I have often wondered why it is I feel things clearer when I am away from people and in the woods. God seems there more, and I've asked myself why. Whatever the reason, that is where I go to probe, as you would say. To paint, as I might."

They are interrupted by the announcement that the taxi has arrived for Miss Carr. Emily gets up to go, thanking Dreier for her hospitality. "I have your book, and I will read it, Mrs. Dreier. Perhaps it will teach me about abstraction. I've enjoyed our talk very much."

"So have I, and I hope that means you will come again. As the Italians say, 'Now that you know the way here, you must return.'"

"One last thing I have to tell you. I can't help noticing that Georgia O'Keeffe says almost the same thing about painting you do. You talk about making the invisible visible, she talks about making the unknown known."

"Fresh Seeing"

When Georgia O'Keeffe met Emily Carr, she was forty-two years old, an established artist and a budding celebrity. She had been exhibiting since 1916, was taken seriously by the critics, and her paintings, which were selling for as much as $4,000, were in demand. Even today, seventy years later, such statistics would spell stunning success. Furthermore, O'Keeffe had not had to renounce love and marriage in order to accomplish it. She had managed to find love with the one man perfectly suited to the task of launching her career.

Alfred Stieglitz had made a name for himself as an apologist for modern art, and was the first person to exhibit the European avant-garde in America, Rodin, Cezanne, and Picasso among them. O'Keeffe came to know of him and his gallery at 291 Fifth Avenue when she was an art student in New York in 1908. Born and raised in the Midwest, the second eldest of seven children, she had been supported by her family in her decision to become an artist. She left home early in pursuit of training, studying first at the Art Institute of Chicago and then the Art Students League in New York until dwindling family fortunes forced her to abandon her apprenticeship. She was twenty-one by then and her family, which had moved east to Virginia in 1903 hoping to avoid the tuberculosis that had killed every other male member of Frank O'Keeffe's family, had lost its roots and was dispersing. Her father was drifting into alcohol and her mother suffering the early signs of consumption, as it would be Ida O'Keeffe who would succumb to TB in 1916. Meanwhile, O'Keeffe's siblings were growing up and moving off to fend for themselves. Her favourite brother went to war and returned in 1918 in ruined health. Georgia slid into an emotional pit; she went to stay with aunts in Chicago and renounced art. The young woman who had said she was going to give up everything for it ignored art for almost four years and lapsed into silence. Little is known about her life during this period or the exact nature of her illness, but one biographer speculates that she suffered the first of several emotional collapses then. Eventually, in 1912 she took a position teaching art in a small town called Amarillo (Spanish for yellow) and emerged into the west Texas sun with her artistic spirit intact. She began painting again. What happened next is legendary. On New Year's Day 1916, a student friend and confidante of O'Keeffe's named Anita Pollitzer walked into "291" with a roll of Georgia's charcoal drawings under her arm, determined to show them to Alfred Stieglitz. The pictures were abstracts that O'Keeffe had sent her, undulating forms depicted with an expressionist and minimalist touch that captivated Stieglitz on sight, prompting the fabled remark, "Finally, a woman's feelings on paper!" Stieglitz kept the works and included them in a group exhibition the following May, and commenced a correspondence with the artist. The two wrote back and forth for some months until ill health and dodgy circumstances (the friend O'Keeffe was living with was consumptive, and the spectre of the flu epidemic hovered) prompted her to acquiesce to Stieglitz's insistence that she move to New York. She arrived there in the summer of 1918.

In New York O'Keeffe was instantly a quantity on the scene,

part of a circle of avant-garde artists and intellectuals, which included painters John Marin, Arthur Dove, Marsden Hartley, photographer Paul Strand, and the critic Paul Rosenfeld. These men coalesced around Stieglitz, who exhibited their work, wrote articles and edited journals, and tirelessly promoted modernism. As a photographer whose own work was collected on both sides of the Atlantic, Stieglitz was also noted for his effort to advance photography as an art in its own right. And, increasingly, he was known for his advocacy of an indigenous American art, an art that did not derive from European traditions but had its own North American source of inspiration. Georgia O'Keeffe epitomized this principle more than any of the others in his circle. She hadn't even been to Europe. Alfred Stieglitz was a middle-aged man of fifty-four and O'Keeffe thirty-one when the two came together. She had been living on her own for more than ten years by that time and had had several love affairs, with women as well as men, the majority of them conducted over distance and characterized more by passionate expression in letter than physical intimacy. She was no *ingénue*, but she had avoided commitment. Her decision to move in with Stieglitz was thus a momentous one and it involved a choice in favour of heterosexuality (and the possibility of children) as well as a move away from the open country of the West to the centre of the art world in New York. Over and above the sexual attraction, though, their interest in each other's work pulled them together and formed the basis of the life they built there. There is no doubt, for instance, that Stieglitz's interest in women artists was sincere; Georgia was no exception in that regard, but she was an exception in the intellectual and artistic talents she brought to him and to their relationship. It is no coincidence, for example, that they both responded creatively to the experience, opening up in new directions. He, for instance, began to photograph her almost immediately. Elegant, three-quarter portrait shots of her cloaked in black, wearing a hat, holding a piece of sculpture; exquisite studies of her hands and face, sometimes with her paintings in the background, and close-ups of her naked body, buttocks, breasts, and belly. In 1921, he mounted a rare solo exhibition of his work, which included forty-five from this series he called simply "Portrait." Without any fanfare or secrecy, he presented views of the female body familiar before to the public only in pornography. It was a scandalous act that attracted the curious and the prurient in droves. Rumour had it the pictures displayed female genitalia and recorded O'Keeffe in postcoital rapture. The model was never identified, but she did not have to be.

If Georgia O'Keeffe had acquired some notoriety for openly living in sin with a married man, now she courted infamy. On a personal level, she was free to do as she liked, having no elder generation of relatives nearby to whom she had to give account, or immediate family who could be offended by her behaviour. Stieglitz, on the other hand, had and did, but his tactic was denial, insisting through the traumatic first months of the separation from his wife and daughter, for example, that they reconcile with Georgia and make her a friend. (In fact, the rest of the Stieglitz family did accept O'Keeffe quite readily.) Georgia was not anxious to marry actually, and she often said so. In the end, she did so only at Stieglitz's insistence when his divorce finally came through in 1924. According to the biographers, she had little use for it and saw marriage as an impediment to women's independence. She would have said that she herself had no need of it except she did need the support and reinforcement that Stieglitz supplied. And she was eluctably drawn to the grand passion she had warned Anita Pollitzer of in 1915. "You wear out most the precious things you have by letting your emotions and feelings run riot," she said. "I almost want to say—don't mention loving anyone to me. It's a curious thing; don't let it get you, Anita, if you value your peace of mind. It will eat you up and swallow you whole." So O'Keeffe was a risk taker. Ready and willing to flout convention (and her own advice), she took on Stieglitz, kept her name and her separate identity, and kept her eye on her goal, which was to paint. It was one thing to play loose with the conventions of marriage, however, and quite another to end up in the eye of a sexual scandal.

The question facing O'Keeffe in 1921 was whether the "Portrait" and her less than anonymous role as Stieglitz's muse and mistress would eclipse her reputation as an artist.

The fact is that O'Keeffe's first solo show, held at "291" in 1917, introduced her as a modernist and also broached the theme of sex. Stieglitz undoubtedly initiated the association by encouraging the idea that her emotionally charged early works were revelations of the female sexual nature. She herself called them effeminate, "essentially a woman's feeling," but he went a few steps further. Women perceive the world differently than men, he maintained. They "receive things through the womb, which is the seat of their deepest feeling." Such ideas were echoed by Marsden Hartley, who wrote in an article on women artists published in 1921: "With Georgia O'Keeffe one takes a far jump into volcanic craterial ethers, and sees the world of a woman inside out," he wrote, adding that her paintings were "as shameless private documents as exist." Paul Rosenfeld took it over the top: "The pure, now flaming, now icy colours of this painter, reveal the woman polarising herself, accepting fully the nature long denied, spiritualizing her sex. Her art is gloriously female. Her great painful and ecstatic climaxes make us at last to know something that man has always wanted to know . . . . All is ecstasy here, ecstasy of pain as well as ecstasy of fulfilment . . . " O'Keeffe recoiled from this writing and there is some evidence she veered away from abstraction after 1917 in an effort to shake the stereotyping. Certainly she took steps to find critics who would write about her work differently, and in 1925 she wrote her friend Mabel Dodge Luhan trying to interest her in the project. "A woman who has lived many things and who sees lines and colours as an expression of living—might say something that a man can't. I feel that there is something unexplored about women that only a woman can explore. Men have done all they can do about it."

But the die was cast. The alligator pears, the lilies, and even the gentle New England landscapes she depicted over the next few years while she lived in the East were invariably viewed by the art world through the prism of her gender.

Little is known about O'Keeffe's decision to participate in Stieglitz's project, yet the biographies do not present her as the victim of his gaze. She is said to have been a willing collaborator, and some have suggested that the photographs be regarded as part of her *oeuvre* as well as Stieglitz's. Certainly she is present in them; her personality is there in the face, her strength and assertiveness in the musculature of the body. Her only comment about the pictures—that they all seemed to be of different women—indicates she distanced herself from them to a degree, a useful tactic in the face of their public exhibition. If she objected to the exhibition, though, could she have voiced it without undercutting the modernist ethos she and Stieglitz espoused, and the very idea that the photos were works of art and not pictures of naked women? O'Keeffe attended the opening at the Anderson Art Galleries, said nothing, and left early. She braved out the storm with practised aloofness, rising above the gossip by removing herself from the fray. With nerves to match Madonna's she brushed aside the rules, refusing to apologize or explain, insisting on her own integrity and her identity as an artist. She was unable to control the images Stieglitz made of her, and she had little to do with his management of her public profile for that matter, but she could create her own persona and paint her own images, and she put her faith in that. Her 1923 exhibition at the Anderson Art Galleries, which was her first large solo show, was the test. Well received and well attended (jammed, actually, with 500 visitors a day over the two-week run), it demonstrated that she had indeed managed to take the most jaded coin in the realm—her sexualized female body—and turn it to advantage. Notoriety helped create an audience for her art and, thanks to Stieglitz's canny instincts, it also helped create a market for her work.

In 1930, when Emily Carr met her, Georgia O'Keeffe was heading for a life crisis of her own. She had exhausted the creative potential of her surroundings in the East, and of the living arrangement with Stieglitz. His demands as an artist and lover were beginning to cost. Since moving in with him and putting her career under his aegis, she had been able to guarantee herself the wherewithal to paint full time, but she had lost her privacy and, she had to admit, a good deal of her independence into the bargain. She had adopted his pattern of spending the winters in the city and the long summers at the Stieglitz family retreat on Lake George in upstate New York. In the city she lived in cramped quarters with Alfred (after 1925 in an apartment at the Shelton Hotel), and in the summer with the extended Steiglitz clan at Lake George. The closest thing she had to her own studio in those years was the shack behind the farmhouse there, which she converted herself. Her painting flourished, but as the decade closed it became increasingly apparent that the eastern landscape was not hers, and that the source of her creativity lay somewhere else. At the same time, she was struggling for some leeway in the relationship with Stieglitz, and latterly in a turmoil over her husband's liaison with young Mrs. Norman. There had been dalliances before, but this was a full-blown affair that began in 1928 and evolved into a serious long-term relationship that involved Dorothy Norman in the administration and promotion of The Place. She remained on the scene until Alfred's death in 1946.

Inevitably, Dorothy Norman was the catalyst for the renegotiation of the O'Keeffe-Stieglitz marriage. She provided the permission O'Keeffe needed to make the break. On April 27, 1929, O'Keeffe boarded a train for Taos, New Mexico, where she stayed for five blissful and productive months. She was accompanied by Rebecca Strand (photographer Paul Strand's wife at the time), who was planning to paint also, and together they explored the country, camped out in the desert, rode horseback through the mountains, visited nearby pueblos, and even attended Native ceremonials. New Mexico was O'Keeffe's declaration of independence. She learned to drive a car and then bought one for herself;

she met new people and, for the first time in a long time, chose her own friends, her own lifestyle, and her own sexual pleasure outside the marriage. There are several photos of Georgia from that first summer in the Southwest. One shows her sitting, tanned and smiling, her arm encircling Beck Strand with whom she was also sharing a bed, in the Pink House visible in the background. The affair lasted a few weeks, as did the fling with their host, Mabel Dodge Luhan, but the affair with New Mexico lasted the rest of O'Keeffe's life. There was a joyful reunion with Stieglitz when she returned to New York that fall, reinvigorated and content with herself after the first summer flight, but it did not last. The Norman affair continued and became general knowledge in 1932, and Georgia was left to cope with the private betrayal and the public humiliation. Divorce does not seem to have been an option—she once remarked that she didn't believe in divorce any more than she believed in marriage—but a separate existence was, which is where New Mexico came in. In 1930, she went once again to the Southwest and thereafter made seasonal migrations across the continent until Stieglitz's death when she moved to New Mexico for good. It was a landscape perfectly suited to her aesthetic temperament—the wide open skies, the lucid sunshine, and the endless space. This was the place she had been craving.

The balance of power in the O'Keeffe–Stieglitz relationship had been shifting for other reasons as well. As O'Keeffe's artistic star rose through the 1920s, her husband's had set. In the early years she had lived under his protection and with him on his family's resources. Now it was her income that sustained them. It would appear the transition was effected wordlessly, and left her in charge of their finances as well as her own professional affairs. After 1930, moreover, she would never again be unknown or anonymous. Although her stature as a painter would be eclipsed in the 1950s, a 1970 retrospective at the Whitney Museum would reinstate her as America's leading woman artist, and the public would become infatuated all over again. After 1930 she no longer needed Stieglitz to act as apologist or agent, either. She had her own profile in the art world. What held them together, then, was the same thing that had brought them together in the first place— their work and their all-abiding preoccupation with art. Still, O'Keeffe's removal from the epicentre of Stieglitz's sexual life was a prolonged and painful process for her. It required learning to live with her husband's infidelities and New Mexico was obviously part of a strategy to remove herself from them, at least part of the time. She philosophized in a letter to Mabel Dodge Luhan, whose husband was similarly a person on whom all sorts of people, male and female, laid affectionate claim. "I feel that you haven't any more right to keep Tony to yourself than I have to keep Stieglitz. If Tony happens to go out to women with his body—it is the same thing when one goes out for a spiritual debauch . . . it is a little thing." In fact, there was more to overlook in Stieglitz's behaviour than a little debauch. There were rumblings about neglect, if not abuse, in the case of his daughter Kitty, for example. Kitty had actually been her father's main argument against Georgia's plan to have children, for Kitty had descended into a severe postpartum depression after the birth of her first child in 1923, and developed dementia praecox for which she was permanently institutionalized. Then there were the intimations of paedophilia. Stieglitz's infatuation with young girls was not much talked about, of course, but recent biographers tend to be blunt. "At the age of eighty-four Alfred fell in love with his fourteen-year-old grandniece," one states laconically. Stieglitz, in other words, was not an easy package to accommodate. O'Keeffe did it by exacting her own terms. She accepted the childlessness, the reduced role as wife and caregiver, and even his untamed libido in exchange for his continued friendship and her complete freedom. It necessitated removing a part of herself emotionally, but this allowed her to recreate herself in her own image, instead of his. Once Stieglitz was gone, however, O'Keeffe let her emotions fly. She threw Dorothy Norman out of The Place and gave her the tongue-lashing of a lifetime.

The accommodation with Alfred was by no means complete at the time O'Keeffe met Emily Carr, and the situation would fester until 1933 when it produced a full-scale physical collapse. The precipitating event seems to have been the Radio City Music Hall mural, a commission for the powder-room of the new theatre building, which O'Keeffe accepted without consulting Stieglitz. Alfred loathed the whole idea and disapproved vociferously, accusing Georgia of prostituting her art and bringing ignominy on himself. He was hostile, she realized. There had been times before when new work had roused his criticism, but this was different; she'd lost his sympathy. When the time came to execute the mural, O'Keeffe was presented with damp walls and an impossible deadline. In a state of self-doubt, she backed out. The decision may well have been prudent, but she was undone by it, assaulted by a sense of failure and the realization that her emotional commitment to Stieglitz had outweighed her commitment to her art. "She had lost her sense of direction and confidence," writes biographer Roxana Robinson. The crisis, variously described as a nervous breakdown, depression, or psychoneurosis, necessitated a lengthy stay in hospital and a limit on visits from her husband for some time. Recovery took the better part of two years and she scarcely painted during the year spanning 1933 and 1934. The day she met Emily Carr, all this was yet to be faced, although the circumstances were set.

At the age of fifty-eight, Emily Carr was experiencing the first blush of public success in the spring of 1930. She, too, was being written about seriously, and her art was beginning to sell, although for much more modest prices—more like $75–$150 per painting, which meant she was a long way from making a living from her work. On the surface, O'Keeffe was far more successful. Her choice of Stieglitz as a partner had been brilliant, for he turned out to be an inspired combination of aesthete and agent. His reluctance to make a sale—whether due to his aversion to commercialism as he claimed or not—had the effect of creating a scarcity of O'Keeffe's work, which kept prices buoyant. Carr, on the other hand, had been on her own without any such support. With some family resources behind her but not enough to allow her to paint full time, with some interest from other artists yet no way for her to find an audience for her work, she had almost ground to a halt. She had struck a deal for art and independence, as O'Keeffe had, but Carr's involved isolation from the beginning, something O'Keeffe did not seek out until middle age. Like O'Keeffe, too, it was men who opened the doors to the art world for her, although they arrived almost too late in her life to matter after years of neglect. (They were Marius Barbeau, Eric Brown, Lawren Harris, and, latterly, teacher and broadcaster Ira Dilworth.) There the similarity ends, though. O'Keeffe's lifestyle may have been the very model of determined protofeminist self-reliance, but her career was carefully shepherded. Her experiences at art school had shown her, no doubt, how difficult it could be for women, and such considerations underlay the quick decision to give up painting in 1908. She was a woman of conviction and extremes. Before she settled on Stieglitz, though, she had had a heavy dose of the life of the lone female artist. From that vantage point, throwing in her lot with him was as much a practical as a romantic choice, and though unconventional, it was not exactly radical, particularly as it involved renouncing her bisexuality.

By comparison and on the surface, Emily Carr's life choices seem utterly conventional for a spinster of the time. Her decision to remain single involved celibacy (which was never on Georgia's mind) and she stuck resolutely to it so far as the historians know. Spinsterhood was not in itself remarkable; the death toll in the First World War made it common enough. However, celibacy, its silent companion, was not much discussed, merely accepted. The idea of embracing it as a positive choice may be difficult for our postmodern generation to grasp, but this did happen. Carr chose to be on her own, a choice that we no longer need to equate with frigidity. In actual fact, we can recognize it as a bid for independence and, furthermore, see within her celibacy an erotic sensibility that is visible in her paintings, traceable in her writings, and obvious in her several friendships of the heart. Passages in her journals, written in her sixties, give some insight to the impetus behind the act. She had loved passionately, had even been prepared to express it sexually and been rebuffed. "In the passionate love of the lover . . . willing to give every bit of your body and soul and love in a floodtide ocean fairly drown the beloved and to find it was not wanted . . . to find that the caresses and kisses were only sport, selfish amusement, your heart used as a shuttlecock, good for one game." Thirty-five years later, facing a mid-life accounting, she wrote: "This being cast alone must be to teach me something. Sometimes I wonder if it was that ungovernable love that possessed me for so many years, pouring out, pouring out, wasted and unwanted 'til ill and worn with the canker of it I wrenched it out of my being . . . threw it from me and grew cold and hard and dead. By and by the roots sprouted again and wanted to grow but there wasn't any good earth . . . it was all built over in brick and stone and pavement." Carr had done more than renounce marriage for her art. She had exorcised love and done so, at least in her own mind, to free herself from the pain of it, the pain of her father's brutality and of her true love's indifference. She saw her animals as nature's love returning a little of what was lost. "The poor little roots tried to get a hold but couldn't and strong winds blew a little dust among them and kept them just alive, and the dust is the love of the blessed creatures."

This is what Emily Carr had to come to terms with: her own complicity in her loneliness. She had wrestled with depression, what she called her "long illness," and resurfaced with a burst of energy. She had overcome failure and come back from death to full blossom. She had found love in the desert. Perhaps she could recognize the evidence of a similar breakthrough in O'Keeffe's New Mexico paintings. Her one recorded comment about the encounter notes the disjuncture between what she saw in them and what she sensed in O'Keeffe. "Some of her paintings I think beautiful, but she herself does not seem happy when she speaks of her work," she said. It was a remarkably perceptive comment and truer than she knew.

This is all history gives us of the meeting of Georgia O'Keeffe and Emily Carr. It was not momentous for either of them, apparently, and it is not known if Georgia was even aware of who she was conversing with. However, because Carr sought out O'Keeffe, we know there was awareness on her part, which has led one American art historian to claim that O'Keeffe's influence on Carr was significant. The argument is largely based on stylistic associations—identifying the simplification of form that occurred in the 1930s, and the close focus on parts of trees in paintings, like *The Red Cedar,* as composition devices inspired by O'Keeffe. Much is also made of *The Lawrence Tree,* the painting O'Keeffe did of the aged pine tree that grew just outside D.H. Lawrence's house in Taos where she stayed for a couple of weeks in 1929. Lawrence describes the tree in his book, *St. Mawr,* a passage of which shows up in Carr's journals in November 1930. It's probable that O'Keeffe was the source of the connection and spoke to Carr about it when they viewed the painting. Its unusual perspective (looking straight up the gnarled red trunk of the tree to the night sky, winking through its canopy above), together with the unusual subject, at least in O'Keeffe's repertoire, must have attracted Carr's attention. Some point out the echo in her own *Above the Trees,* painted nine years later. Nonetheless, Carr is not reminded of O'Keeffe's painting when she brings up Lawrence on the subject of pine trees. She quotes a long passage from the novel, describing the old tree as "a passionless, non-phallic column, rising in the shadows of the pre-sexual world," a world, presumably, where male and female are implicit and indistinguishable. Carr is not beguiled. "It's clever but it's not my sentiments nor my idea of pines, not our north ones anyway," she writes. Not that she has yet succeeded herself in putting the feel into words. Fascinated by Lawrence and deeply disgusted at once, she turns on him. "Lawrence's book is so sexy. Everything, these days, is people talking of sex and psychology. I hate both," she gripes. "It's so impertinent, digging around inside people and saying why they did things, by what law of mind they came to such and such, and making hideous false statements and yanking up all the sex problems." O'Keeffe could have written those lines, although that doesn't mean she shared Carr's askance views of sex. O'Keeffe was a libertine who despised any intrusion into her private realm, especially on the back of artistic interpretations. So did Carr, but this was because she felt sex itself was something sullied and despoiled by dirty-minded human beings.

Is it likely that Emily and Georgia made a connection with each other, or is it pure fantasy? Many poets and artists have imagined it; historians have remained sceptical, though willing to contemplate the one-way influence of the American on the naive, north country Canadian. From what we know, Carr would have disapproved of O'Keeffe's marital and sexual arrangements, and O'Keeffe would have disparaged Carr's small-town aura. Culturally they belonged to different generations, artistically they spoke different languages, and both of them were reticent about reaching out to others, so the chances of friendship were slim. The intriguing question, really, is what did they have in common that would have allowed them to bridge their difference. In the end, all we have is the tantalizing image of two natural forces briefly occupying the same space; two women who touched the spirit of the land, who painted images of the North American landscape that ordinary people recognized as theirs, whose lives have been idolized, and whose personae have been fictionalized by everyone including themselves. Georgia O'Keeffe, the high priestess of American modernism, and Emily Carr, bag lady of Canadian nationalism.

Some time in the summer of 1889, a lively, dark-haired two year old made her way to the driveway beside her parents' house in Sun Prairie, Wisconsin, and buried her hands deep in the bright, dusty earth. Fifteen years earlier, in Victoria, British Columbia, another sturdy, dark-haired little girl had wandered out into a lily field behind her parents' home where she sat entranced by the sights and sounds and smells, swimming in a white haze of sensation. As old women, these two wrote about these first ecstatic experiences with the natural world, and it is easy to see the imprint on the lives that followed. Both Georgia O'Keeffe and Emily Carr were daughters of the West, attached by a psychic umbilical cord to the landscape they lived in and painted. Different though their visual vocabulary was, they shared a passion for the outdoors, for tramping through the woods and the high desert mountains. They drew sustenance from the environment and allowed it to shape their lives emotionally and aesthetically. In Carr's hands, the opulent cedar forest was refashioned into a green evocation of the thrust and throb of nature: the baleful presence of death animating life. In O'Keeffe's hands, the sparse elegance of desert plain and adobe architecture was translated into abstracted images of Zen-like simplicity. Her eye saw voluptuous form in the red hills of New Mexico and vitality in the bleached bones of cattle, which she suspended in the foreground of her landscapes as she had the black crosses, life peering through death. The geography of the Southwest entranced O'Keeffe. She had gravitated to the calm of west Texas in 1912, and she gravitated to the desert in the 1930s. There she remade herself. The bouts of depression and illness, which had inscribed her life with Stieglitz, disappeared and in middle age she emerged into a second phase of her life as an artist, much as Emily Carr did in 1927 at fifty-six; only instead of fifteen years, Georgia O'Keeffe's second life would last almost four decades. Her new life was characterized by a simple, rather Spartan existence that stressed self-sufficiency and harmony with the environment. She bought an old abandoned house from the Catholic church in a little town called Abiquiu and, at long last, had her own space, her own sky, and, as she often said, her own mountain. This was her beloved Padernal, which, she joked, God promised to give her if she painted it often enough.

The move to New Mexico was layered with meaning. It was not just about escaping her husband or finding herself through new artistic inspiration. It involved distancing herself from the concerns that dominated Stieglitz's milieu; it meant retiring from life at the centre of the avant-garde in New York. "I am moving it seems—more and more toward a kind of aloneness—not because I wish it but because there seems no other way," she wrote in 1934 in a letter to Jean Toomer, the Harlem Renaissance writer with whom she had a poignant "brief encounter" just as she was pulling out of her illness. Toomer brought her out of herself, and helped ease her into the solitary life she had before her. As biographer Roxana Robinson writes, "What was permanent was a sense of deep and necessary commitment to her own needs as an artist, which must take precedence over her other roles, as wife, lover, friend." To O'Keeffe, the desert represented a rededication to art and the discipline it demanded. It offered her an opportunity to design her life around her work, and the income she was making from sales made it feasible. Less obviously, perhaps, her desire for focus and clarity made it inevitable that she leave the heat and clamour of New York. It was not just the West she needed, it was solitude.

The same might be said of Emily Carr, who had taken refuge in the margins of society, identifying with people whose culture or circumstance placed them outside the Anglo-Canadian norm. She admired Native peoples for their difference, and saw in their society qualities her own lacked. However, in the summer of 1930, she took her last journey north to visit Native sites on Vancouver Island. Save for visits to see Sophie Frank and her family at Squamish Mission in North Vancouver, her direct connection with Native culture vanished. However, her visits to the forest did not. In the 1930s she established a ritual of withdrawing to the woods for several weeks at a time during the summer to paint alone. Her approach to these retreats was much like O'Keeffe's attitude in her early visits to Taos, which was to see them as both liberating and demanding; demanding of serious discipline and some physical hardship, and liberating spiritually as well as literally from the oppressive domestic routine back home. Carr chose isolation early when she retreated to Victoria in 1913, removing herself from contact with other professional artists in Vancouver. That move had had the tenor of self-imposed exile about it. Her decision to remain in British Columbia, on the other hand, had been an essentially positive choice, though it always meant accepting separation from the art world of Toronto and Montreal, never mind New York and London. The isolation she experienced in B.C., however, was categorically different from O'Keeffe's whose New Mexican sojourns brought her into the midst of a community of marginals, a frontier Bohemia of artists and writers, homosexuals, mystics, and rich people looking for space and privacy just as she was. (The roster included Ansel Adams, John Marin, Willa Cather, D.H. Lawrence and his wife Frieda, and the flamboyant Mabel Dodge Luhan.)

In no sense did O'Keeffe disappear off the art map when she went to Taos, not even when she left the East permanently. She was successful enough to dictate her own terms, which were that she be kept at arm's length from the art world and its concerns. She shared this aversion with Carr, who disparaged critics and their "drivel," and was suspicious of art theory in general. Unlike the men in their respective circles, neither artist wrote about her art or ideas, which may explain why their contemporaries tended to view them as non-intellectuals. The fact is, both women felt fundamentally at odds with the male art scene, though neither would have said so. O'Keeffe, who was central to the functioning of Stieglitz's group, was described as hovering around the edges of his gatherings, speaking monosyllabically when she spoke at all. She kept herself apart, from women as well as men, as Katherine Dreier noticed. Carr was also an outsider—never mind what Lawren Harris had to say about it. She did speak of prejudice in relation to A.Y. Jackson who, she felt, disapproved of women artists, but mostly her sense of difference was expressed in the grievances she had with various men in bureaucratic positions for lack of attention to her concerns. Her snippy behaviour with various officials of the National Gallery became notorious, and there was much chattering behind her back by curators and artists who judged her behaviour as untoward and ungrateful. Today her demands would be seen as perfectly professional, but the men who were holding her work, exhibiting and selling it, responded to her request for information and the return of her unsold paintings with the hauteur of petty aristocrats dispensing charity. Her role did not include questioning their behaviour. To many of her peers, though, Carr's attitude broke all the unwritten rules about proper deference to patrons. O'Keeffe, on the other hand, would have sympathized. She was not beyond the same sort of brusqueness herself, which she used as a way to resist public attention.

In fact, Georgia O'Keeffe rarely talked about herself or her art, and almost never rose to defend it when attacked. There was one occasion, though, a few weeks before she encountered Carr at The Place, when she took part in a public debate with the outspoken editor of the populist magazine *The New Masses*. Michael Gold had criticized her for not adopting a political stance in her work, and not reflecting the struggle of the oppressed masses in her art. O'Keeffe responded by pointing out that women are themselves an oppressed class. She used her own experience as an example and talked about her struggle as a painter to free herself of male influences and to assert her independent status. "I am trying with all my skill to do painting that is all of a woman as well as all of me." She had written about this earlier in the catalogue to her 1923 show at the Anderson Galleries:

> . . . one day seven years ago I found myself saying to
> myself—I can't live where I want to—I can't go where I
> want to—I can't do what I want to—I can't even say
> what I want to—School and things that painters have
> taught me even keep me from painting as I want to. I
> decided I was a very stupid fool not at least to paint as I
> wanted to and say what I wanted to when I painted, as
> that seemed to be the only thing I could do that didn't
> concern anybody but myself.

O'Keeffe never wavered from this defiant belief. It centred on her sense of separation as an artist, and her dedication to finding her own way in an alien world. Surrounded by men of wit and influence, she remained a shadowy figure at the centre of vivid action. Roxana Robinson alludes to this paradox in her character when she describes the encounter between O'Keeffe and Michael Gold, which left him fussed and angry while she remained self-possessed and smiling, emanating "a glowing but impersonal warmth." Like Carr, her isolation was something that gender difference imposed and her artistic temperament demanded. It was both a blessing and a curse.

The descriptions of Carr and O'Keeffe as non-intellectuals have tended to obscure the fact that both artists were seriously engaged with ideas about art and with thinking through their own approach to it. This was a philosophic engagement as much as an aesthetic one. It involved reading—particularly true of O'Keeffe, who was interested in Eastern art, mysticism, and abstraction in art school and had read Kandinsky's *Concerning the Spiritual in Art* twice before she met Alfred Stieglitz—and it involved arguing ideas out on paper. O'Keeffe did it in letters, and Carr in her journals and in correspondence with Lawren Harris. The search took them beyond books and talk, though, and tapped into a very personal part of themselves, for it was most profoundly a spiritual undertaking. Curiously, the opening quip of Henry McBride's review in the *New York Sun* of O'Keeffe's show in 1930 got it right: "Georgia O'Keeffe went to Taos, New Mexico, to visit Mabel Dodge . . . Georgia O'Keeffe got religion. What Mabel Dodge got I have not yet heard." By religion McBride meant the artist's adoption of "the Spanish idea that where life manifests itself in greatest ebullience there too is death most formidable." He was correct in registering a change in tone in O'Keeffe's paintings, of course. They were brighter in colour, bolder in form, larger of vision, and they possessed a quality of transcendence. As her biographer Roxana Robinson writes, "O'Keeffe grew up with great spaces and the long sweep of horizon was what she craved. The sense of limitlessness offered liberation. It allowed her sense of self to expand indefinitely, independent yet attached to something larger than the self. For a strong woman, the plains signified transcendence, not obliteration."

This dimension of O'Keeffe's work has been downplayed by the critics and historians over the years, partly because she herself discounted it and partly because her paintings themselves seem so forthright in their reference to the real world. O'Keeffe was interested in the world beyond the material and from 1915 she was aware of speculations among the avant-garde with regard to symbolism, the occult, and the spiritual in art. In an essay called "Beholding the Epiphanies," art historian Sharyn Udall makes the argument: "With the waning of religious faith as an impetus for artistic vision, artists like Georgia O'Keeffe sought aspects of the spiritual in the topography of the Southwest and in its storied light. Her vision, even when grounded in the material, yearned for the redemptive unity of mind and matter, of West and East, of Male and Female, of Self and Other, of the conscious and the unconscious." Udall links the artist's "periods of geographic isolation" to her "affinity for mysticism which required a degree of interiority." And she points to the tension this set up in O'Keeffe, who deplored having to speak about her work or explain it to anyone, who was very often ill when she had a show, and yet who cared deeply about the way her work was viewed. "O'Keeffe vacillated between her twin desires for public understanding and her need for private expression . . . [and] over the years became extraordinarily skilled in disguising the strong subjective content in her work." The play of these different forces in Georgia's character produced the obstinate icon of her later years, the elderly woman who refused to see feminist Gloria Steinem when she turned up at the Abiquiu house bearing roses; the rugged individualist who declined to be interviewed for an article on women artists in the 1970s, stating categorically (and contrary to her earlier opinion), "Write about women. Or write about artists. I don't see how the two are connected. Personally, the only people who ever helped me were men."

*

O'Keeffe was one in a long line of artists, seekers, and thinkers drawn to the New Mexican landscape and the old cultures rooted in its bony mesas, who revelled in the chromatic brilliance of the light, the climactic extremes, and the ethereal effects of the desert environment. There she was surrounded by people who were intensely interested in the metaphysical, who believed in the primacy of the intuitive in art and life, and in the idea that the outward physical form of things reflect a discoverable inner essence. In New York she was also connected to a network of artists seriously interested in the spiritual dimensions of creativity. There were many like Marsden Hartley and Arthur Dove, who were confirmed theosophists. Jean Toomer was a follower of Georgi Ivanovitch Gurdjieff, and Marcel Duchamp, who saw a good deal of O'Keeffe and Steiglitz in the 1920s, was seriously interested in mysticism and alchemy. Theosophy, with its anti-material philosophy, its search for the one eternal truth, and its belief in the "necessary interdependence of all that is," had great attraction for people who were looking beyond the orthodoxy of modern science and traditional religion, and for artists looking for a way past the reductionism and fatalism of the dawning atomic age. Wassily Kandinsky, the Russian painter and writer, was perhaps the most influential figure in this diffused movement amongst the artistic avant-garde in Europe. Central to his thinking was the notion that art represented the search for inner spirituality, and that it, like music, should be freed from its ties to the physical world. Stieglitz, who published excerpts of *Concerning the Spiritual in Art* before it was generally available in English, was responsible for introducing Kandinsky and his ideas to America, and for embracing abstraction as the expression of the future. The point is that the 1930s was the decade when this strain of modernism was at its height, when Theosophy was a galvanizing force among artists and intellectuals in Europe, the United States, and Canada. These early modernists turned inward towards the unconscious, away from the world, convinced that this was the way to save art's creative integrity. Artists assumed the role of keepers of spiritual values in a disenchanted world, and there were many others besides Emily Carr and Georgia O'Keeffe who longed to merge with the "unknown," who saw their art as a function of spiritual connection. This sensibility and interest was eclipsed by the ideology of "art for art's sake," which emerged in the 1940s in the guise of formalism. This was the moment when art was cut loose from its social moorings and elevated to the status of supreme autonomy, divorced from all ulterior and interior motive.

O'Keeffe may not have been an artist who followed trends, but she was definitely in touch with the zeitgeist of the 1930s. She also sprang from the American naturalist tradition of Thoreau and Emerson, and the ardent animism of Walt Whitman. New Mexico simply added to the mix. There she was in the territory of mystics, part of a colony of artists that had a long association with the ritual life of the Aboriginal inhabitants on the one hand (Mabel Dodge's fourth husband, Tony Lujan, was a Pueblo Indian who introduced O'Keeffe and many others to the Native culture of the Southwest), and with the spirituality of landscape on the other. It was an ambience that suited O'Keeffe partly because she did not have to account for the influences she was absorbing. She was free to immerse herself in the immensity and mystery of the country, watching it, walking it, breathing it, painting it. From a trip to Las Vegas, New Mexico, with Beck Strand and Tony Lujan, came *At the Rodeo—New Mexico*, an enigmatic abstract painted in a state of "unusual mental clarity," which she described in a letter to Mabel Dodge. O'Keeffe associated her vision with the consumption of bootleg whiskey the evening before, but the fact is she was coming to rely on such subconscious resources more frequently. "That memory or dream thing I do that for me comes nearer reality than my objective kind of work" is how she described it to her friend Dorothy Brett in 1932. *Rodeo* brings to mind the mystical diagrams of Theosophy and Buddhism, and (to a late-twentieth century eye) the cosmic mandalas of abbess Hildegard of Bingen. Swirling lines enclose a great light-filled vortex which pulsates with energy. Like the iris of an eye or the view through a telescope to the sky (or the sight up a tree trunk stretching to heaven), it draws in and enfolds the viewer. The picture implies the infinite in both the infinitesimal and the astronomic. O'Keeffe would return to abstraction like this every so often, but she never strayed far from physical reality. Her touchstone was the natural environment as surely as it was Emily Carr's, and similarly her work was a meditation and her purpose epiphanic.

"I am groping, horribly lost. Trying to search for that thing. It is right here and yet I do not know how to find it; it is in me and yet so far away I cannot reach it. I don't know where to look and I want it so badly I'm sick." The pages of Carr's journal are thick with anguish. Time and again she returned to the subject of her frustrated search, documenting her despair, but also revealing her intense desire to find the elusive understanding that will open her vision to the sacred. In Lawren Harris she found someone whose "religion, whatever it is, and his painting are one and the same," which was enough to compel her to explore his spiritual sources. She studied P.D. Ouspensky and H.P. Blavatsky with some diligence; she read writers on art like Clive Bell and Kandinsky, and marked up her copy of Katherine Dreier's *Western Art* with commentary and emphasis. "The recognized *function of art* is to *free the spirit* and to invigorate and enlarge our vision," Emily underlined. She corresponded with Harris and the Houssers, and from her journals we know she considered the dialogue intensely interesting and vital to her own inquiry. She referred to them as her "beloveds in the east." For Carr, the appeal of Theosophy was the credence it gave to the prophetic side of art, and the permission it gave to seek God outside the church proper and within herself. She appreciated the philosophic approach, and was drawn by the mysticism. But, in the end, she could not abandon herself to it. In early 1933, she admitted defeat. "Theosophy . . . goes round in circles and makes you giddy and doesn't land you. A sort of endless voyage with god always way, way beyond catching up distance." She hurled Mme. Blavatsky across the room and returned to Jesus Christ, the Bible, and old-fashioned prayer, which is how she characterized the rejection of Theosophy a couple of years later. At the time she was consumed with the apprehension that her Eastern friends would lose interest in her once she had lost interest in Theosophy. It was not a question of anyone trying to convert her (this was, in any case, not Theosophy's way), but of the communality of interest and her awareness of the depth of their commitment.

Although she was close to Harris during these years (1927–30), he was not her only source of wisdom. Introduced to the poetry of Walt Whitman, she immediately took the American's poetry and his panegyric to nature to heart. Whitman's pleas for intense personal expression, his concepts of the divinity of the individual and of nature, and the centrality of the here and now connected profoundly with something in Emily Carr. She returned to him again and again, lacing her journal with quotes emphasizing the solitary nature of the human journey—*"Not one can acquire for another, not one/ Not one can grow for another, not one"*—and the cosmic awareness of art. "All real art is the eternal seeking to express God," she wrote in November 1932 in a passage leading up to several lines of Whitman. Succinctly she summarized her hard-won personal philosophy: "Search for the reality of each object, that is its real and only beauty; recognize our relationship with all life; say to every animate and inanimate thing 'brother'; be at one with all things, finding the divine in all; when one can do all this, maybe then one can paint." Art historians have often noted Carr's natural affinity for the mystic elements in American transcendentalism, which the Group of Seven painters as a rule did not share (the two exceptions being Harris and Fred Varley). Carr, I imagine, was reassured by Whitman's earthiness, his uncomplicated love of life, love, and creation. He spoke to the unacknowledged raunchiness in her own make-up, the part of her that was capable of skinny-dipping in the river with only her creatures about watching, that loved roughing it outdoors. There was something in the "gay bard's" eroticism that resonated rather than repelled her, while Theosophy was too cool, too passionately unemotional, as abstract painting was, to hold her. She was bound to cast her line in deeper rivers. So the "return" to Christianity did not involve re-entering the old fold any more than it implied the resolution of her turmoil. Throughout the 1930s her struggle to match her sense of immanence in nature with her beliefs about God, and the quest for her vision as an artist were the overarching subjects of her journals. There she railed at the slowness of her progress, the resistance of the material to her desire, the elusiveness of atonement. There she also documented her exploration of the unorthodox fringes of the Protestant Church, and the teachings of evangelical preachers like Clem Davies, Garland Anderson, and Raja Singh. She avoided her sisters' church as well as their opinion of her religious rovings, refusing even to attend the memorial service for Lizzie when she died in 1936. Carr may not have been much of an intellectual or very adept at theory, but she was independent of mind and no thin-on-the-ground sentimentalist looking for pretty answers. Harris, she noted, had also "come to where he now is by diligent, intelligent grinding and wrestling and digging things out." He encouraged her to trust her own instincts and have patience with herself. Meeting Katherine Dreier was Harris's idea. Possibly he thought Emily would find something in Dreier's theories about spirituality and the potential of art to develop the soul. Perhaps he imagined the two women would strike a chord, that Dreier might be interested in Carr's work, and Carr might find herself interested in Dreier's ideas. None of that transpired, though the exchange between the two women was more substantial than the meeting between Carr and O'Keeffe. Dreier seems to have been a genuinely likeable character and Carr was obviously sympathetically disposed towards her. Some writers have assumed that Carr was awed by the display of wealth and power, and her American biographer reads her as playing the role of colonial hick, the "carrot in the eye" question being deliberately inane. Perhaps Carr was surreptitiously taking the mickey out of Dreier, being a non-believer when it came to abstraction; she could easily have been responding to Dreier's zealotry. Carr had encountered extreme wealth when she was ill in England and stayed for six weeks with the family of Mildred Crompton-Roberts in Belgravia, where straw was strewn on the pavement outside to dull the sound of carriages in the street. She had encountered it also in Harris, the scion of the Massey-Harris fortune, who was able to study in Europe and spend as much time as he wished in New York where he met Stieglitz in the 1920s and forged opportunities for exhibiting his own work and that of other Canadians.

Katherine Dreier had a similar background to Harris' but she did not remain a painter. Instead, she committed all her strengths to promoting her vision of modern art as a tonic for American society. This branded her as slightly off-balance to the emerging cool modernist mainstream. Her ideas were distinctly internationalist at a time when people were more interested in advancing the cause of American art. Her didactic approach went against the grain, and her concept of art as serving a spiritual purpose was completely contrary to the views held by the majority of American collectors, curators, dealers, critics and the like who talked about art. Although a good many of the Europeans included in the Société Anonyme's Brooklyn show were in the Armory Show as well, the Brooklyn selection stressed artists and movements outside Paris, in particular German expressionism (the Blaue Reiter and painters like Franz Marc), Dadaism, and the Berlin avant-garde. There were no new paintings by Picasso or Braque. While the slant corresponded with the sensibilities of the Stieglitz group at the time, it did not represent the direction American modern art would follow. The cue for this came instead from the Parisian avant-garde, from cubism, Picasso, and, more directly, the work of Piet Mondrian and Marcel Duchamp, who both spent several years in New York. (Duchamp is considered part of Dada and surrealism; his American legacy would include the pop artists of the 1960s, conceptual art of the 1970s and 1980s, and postmodernism generally.) To the extent that North American modernism grew from an array of cross-continental influences, the Brooklyn show opted for the wrong combination. Clement Greenberg, who would become the chief spokesman for the right one, argued that modernist art could be objectively analysed according to a set of formalist principles. In his view, the early modernists like O'Keeffe had misunderstood cubism and misused it as a vehicle for "a new kind of hermetic literature with mystical overtones and a message—pantheism and pan-love and the repudiation of technique and rationalism." He savaged O'Keeffe in a 1946 article in *The Nation,* opining that her work had technique, but otherwise no inherent value. "[It] has less to do with art than with private worship and the embellishment of private fetishes with secret and arbitrary meanings," he wrote. Formalism (and Greenberg) articulated an aesthetic that judged Georgia O'Keeffe a failed modernist and sidelined Dreier's ilk as irrelevant if not slightly nuts. Although the Société Anonyme is sometimes cited as a forerunner to the Museum of Modern Art, it was not in any significant way connected.

The Brooklyn show did not, therefore, become the cultural landmark Dreier had hoped it would. It did not touch a current of thought or connect with public sentiment as the Canadian West Coast Art show did; it did not present an image of contemporary art that Americans could identify with, much less a creation story of the sort that would absolve the American élites of their assault on nature and Native land.

Harris and Barbeau were far more successful with their countrymen. Harris, like Dreier, put tremendous energy into promoting the work of his contemporaries; he was the main organizing force behind the Group of Seven in the 1920s and did similar work for the Group of Canadian Painters in the 1940s. He built the Studio Building for other artists in Toronto, was active in the Arts & Letters Club, in the Theosophical Society, and other organizations. He made things happen, and at times he was transparent in his wielding of influence. After viewing the Brooklyn exhibition, he wrote to the Exhibition Committee at the Art Gallery of Toronto to urge them to reconsider their decision not to host it: "I have written Miss Dreier informing her that should the gallery here find it necessary to refuse the exhibition . . . that I will endeavour to have . . . [it] come here and hold it somewhere else. Needless to say I don't want to do that." Sensitive though we might be today to the self-interest involved, not to mention the sense of *noblesse oblige*, Harris was generous with his time and influence. There was a public-spiritedness to his work akin to Katherine Dreier's. Carr, who admired their *élan,* may well have had the two of them in mind when she tried to float the idea of a public gallery in Victoria in 1932. She seemed to understand the connection they made between collective action and community building, and her plan for the People's Gallery was astonishingly contemporary, both for its egalitarian appeal and the inclusion of work by the Chinese artist Lee Nam and two young artists in her first exhibit. Her actions indicate that she recognized the need for leadership, though her own bid to assume it was rebuffed. At the time, Carr was actually looking for teachers herself. Over and above the need for artistic companionship, there was her aching desire for someone to mark a spiritual path for her.

Emily Carr walked into Lawren Harris's studio in 1927 and her world changed. The man, his art, and his ideals were an inspiration that dispelled self-doubt and propelled her into action. He offered something priceless: faith in her work and confidence in her and the struggle that she had engaged. They commenced a correspondence in which he counselled her like a teacher and cared for her like an old friend. He talked about his own convictions and artistic philosophy, and occasionally mentioned personal troubles; she talked about her work and confided her worries. More than this no one knows, for Carr's side of the correspondence was not kept and her voice is there only in Harris's responses. In her autobiography she mentioned writing to him about her friendship with Sophie Frank and it may be, given that he wrote of his own spiritual sources, that she wrote to him about hers and the connection with

Native art. Perhaps, as curator Megan Bice suggests, her admiration for Native culture, plus long association with Native art, had an effect on Harris. "So-called primitive people," he remarked in one letter, "are closer to the source of things." The treatment of the Carr-Harris relationship by the biographers and art historians has pegged it as a lopsided affair in which Emily is the recipient of Harris's ideas and assistance and he of her unrequited love. More recently scholars like Alish Farrell and Ann Davis have proposed that she may not have been so passive or dependent. That she was more emotionally needy is certain, and Harris's main objective in writing her may have been to encourage her artistic career, but the admiration went both ways and he evidently appreciated the confluence of attitudes. He discussed aspects of his artistic development, which others in the Group of Seven did not sympathize with or follow, and, as his biographer Peter Larisey noticed, conversed with Carr as an artistic equal. Although Harris published several articles in the late 1920s explicating his thoughts about art, Larisey contends that his letters to Carr are crucial to grasping his development in the early 1930s, a time when Harris was in transition and under great personal stress. The letters are unique because he is "at times completely open with her," and he is relieved of the burden of having to talk down to people about art. By 1930, "Dear Miss Carr" had become "Dear T'Other Emily." Once again Carr adopted a name and an alter ego, in this case as a way of presenting herself in endearing terms that were non-threatening and maternal. Various writers have commented on Carr's propensity for relationships where she mothers or is mothered herself. Blanchard talks about her childish side, "[t]he more her imagination ripened with age, the more tenderly she would cherish the child in herself," and theorizes this as an active ingredient in her character, one that surfaces in her writing where the narrator is perpetually young and naive, the *puella aeterna* who clings to innocence. Carr undoubtedly loved the role and the attention. And she loved Harris for his friendship.

In 1930, she wrote Harris in despair over some new work. In

August she had gone back to the west coast of Vancouver Island, to the old settlements of the Koskimo people at Quatsino at the north end of the island where she spent time sketching on her own. There she had seen the Dzunukua for the third time, had come upon her unexpectedly, and this time did not take fright. That same trip landed her in a colony of feral cats, who greeted her like visiting royalty; she had felt at home there in the forest. Her painting had entered a new phase in 1928 and now she pushed it further. The shift can be seen in two large works, *Indian Church* and the evocative *Grey*, the first resulting from her visit to Friendly Cove on Nootka Sound the previous year, the second, a highly stylized tree completed around the time of her trip to New York. In both canvases the forest is reduced to simple, sculpted forms that crowd in on the picture plane with primeval insistence. The dark green chaos almost overwhelms the little white church, which sits up against the landscape like one of Georgia O'Keeffe's black crosses, framing it. In *Grey* all reference to human form is removed, and everything focuses on the tree, which lies enfolded and hidden in the "secret inner heart of the timeless, placeless forest," as Doris Shadbolt has written. *Grey* is one of the most obviously metaphysical works Carr ever produced. This tree has little in common with the lone pine made famous by the Group of Seven, the scrappy little conifer that typically stands alone, exposed, and clinging to a rock beside a storm-crossed lake. Here there are no heroics save for the artist's willingness to confront the frightful in nature, the haunted spirit of the forest. *Grey* moves, glows in iconic silence, and Emily writes in her journal: "What do these forests make you feel? Their weight and density, their crowded orderliness. There is scarcely room for another tree yet there is space around each. They are profoundly solemn yet upliftingly joyous . . . How absolutely full of truth they are, how full of reality." *Grey* depicts that experience, that ecstatic communion, and the revelation that the forest was her church, the place she went to feel God and think clearly. Trees, she said, are "like the Bible, you can find strength in them." *Grey* can also be seen as the

"Grey," Carr's most metaphysical painting and one of her most abstract.

completion of a cycle in Carr's painting as Aboriginal images fade from her canvases and are absorbed by the forest. Shadbolt makes the point that the supernatural eye prevalent in Native carvings, which lends that sense of the "watching presence," is replicated in the mythic eye of *Grey*. "The sightless, staring eyes that are so prominent a feature in Native art project a sense of silent inner watching which finds its metaphoric equivalent in the dark depths of silent forests. We might say that Carr has gone through the eye of the Indian and come out into the forest, into nature." And, finally, *Grey* carries with it overtones of her encounter with Georgia O'Keeffe. Stylistically it has something in common with O'Keeffe's work, most particularly her paintings of the inside of flowers like poppies and lilies. The mood of expectant serenity is familiar, as is the sleek simplicity of design. Carr approaches abstraction in this painting, but her mind's eye never closes on physical reality. *Grey* ushered in a new phase in which Carr's work became part of her spiritual practice. Not that her painting became subservient to her quest—it *was* her quest. The act of painting took on the form of a meditation as Carr courted intuition and allowed herself to let go. Artists are makers of connections, writes Matthew Fox in *The Coming of the Cosmic Christ*, connections between oil paint and landscape, between human beings and nature, between the past and the future. "All of these connection-making events are mystical events as well." In Fox's terms certainly, Carr was a mystic. Her use of tobacco, her periodic fasts and ritual routines described in her journals suggest this was so. And it is visible in the shimmering space and numinous colour of paintings like *Red Cedar* and *Wood Interior*.

The effort of distilling this inner view of the forest was agony. She turned to Harris and he responded, "Now that's too bad—that you are in despair—well let's be as philosophic as we can. Despair is periodic and part and parcel of the life of every creative individual . . . It cannot be conquered—one rises out of it." He carried on for five pages, offering her advice and encouragement, talking about the need to accept despair as a function of the intensity of creative work but to detach herself from it all the same, to take a new canvas and start afresh. "Let's put it differently. Any creative work is an excitation to all kinds of things within us that ordinarily are at rest. The creative individual starts something . . . stirs up devils, gods and strange entities within himself or herself and he or she must find something deeper and beyond . . . For every man jack of us is an entire cosmos with every old potentiality in us." You can hear the voice of Harris the theosophist and Harris the fellow artist in these words. But there is also Harris the man who had had a nervous breakdown in 1918 brought on, his biographer concludes, by his military experience, coupled with the deaths of two important people in his life. (One was the artist Tom Thomson, whose mysterious drowning Harris always thought a murder, and the other his brother, who was killed at the front.) The crisis had artistic dimensions. His painting languished. Confused and disheartened, he moved out of Toronto for a year and suffered through it alone, finding his way through mysticism, which gave him, among other things, a way to understand creativity. He began working out his own approach to art then, too, defining an ambition that was to embrace both the expression of the Canadian reality and the intimation of the universal. The rugged landscapes of the next decade might be seen as the embodiment of the first, and the move into abstraction after 1934 the triumph of the second.

Although abstraction was the corollary of the spiritual work Harris had done in the 1920s, he had resisted it. By 1930 the Group of Seven was reaching its peak (it would have its last joint exhibit in 1931) and he was gearing up to a major break with the past. He was painting less and less, straddling the contradictions in his work and life with increasing difficulty. In his distress he wondered aloud to Carr in December 1930 if his painting days might be over, and whether his "usefulness may take another direction." The correspondence carried on and so did Harris's malaise. In the spring of 1934 he hinted that drastic changes were in the wings. Eventually the letter came with the news—*"How should I write it? How explain the jolt?"* cried Emily in her journal—Harris was leaving his wife to marry Bess Housser, whom Fred Housser had left for Yvonne McKaque. Larisey pieces the story together thus: Bess and Lawren had met in 1920 and become close friends, Fred Housser being an old schoolmate of Lawren and a fellow theosophist, an art critic by avocation, and the financial editor of the *Toronto Star* by day. The friendship between Lawren and Bess was long-standing and intense and eventually it caused resentment. Fred left the marriage in protest. Lawren left his marriage to preserve it, claiming *it* was a strictly spiritual, non-sexual relationship. Originally, they had no thought of marrying, but friends, including Lawren's mother, convinced them it was prudent. Meanwhile, the openness with which these domestic rearrangements were undertaken shocked Toronto society of which Lawren and his first wife Trixie were conspicuous members. Harris actually feared his wife's well-connected family might have him charged with bigamy, so he and Bess remained in the States after getting their divorces. First they lived in New Hampshire and later in New Mexico where they would have stayed had the war restrictions on currency not forced them back to Canada. As Harris said, he and Bess reached Santa Fe one spring day and settled there the next. They felt at home, and found a congenial circle of artists who were engrossed in the same ideas and eager for him to join the group being formed to exhibit their work and promote their ideas. By summer the Transcendental Group of Painters was established, Harris was made president of the group's foundation, and he and Bess had bought a house.

Harris sensed his remarriage would come as a shock to Emily Carr and he was right. She was profoundly upset by it. Her journal was full of it for months. At first it was the grotesque business of wife-swapping that appalled her. She remonstrated against the indecency of "falling about into other arms" while admonishing herself that it was none of her business. Then she focused on Bess with mounting anger at what she felt was Bess's betrayal. They were supposed to be friends, yet Bess had said nothing about what was happening and Emily was bothered by the dissembling involved. At first she suspected Bess's explanation about "higher love and non-sex," and was curt with her. Mutual friends intervened and she was brought round, yet the friendship with Bess never recovered. The friendship with Lawren, on the other hand, continued—somewhat altered but intact. The expectations of him were altogether different, a discrepancy that many attribute to Carr's unacknowledged love for Harris and concomitant jealousy of Bess. Carr would have seen Bess as a rival for Lawren's attention in a way his first wife was not. Bess may have been easier to blame as there was so much more at stake with Harris. Besides the emotional support and artistic advice, he had offered a sense of community, and an access to the art world she had never had before. The trip to New York was a case in point. The introductions were all Harris's. Most significantly, though, it was through knowing him that she came to accept herself as an artist. None of this alters the fact that Carr and Harris were headed in different directions, he towards full-blown abstraction and she towards symbolic expressionism, and they were temperamentally at odds. He was a theoretical painter, which she was not, and he was a man still seeking transformation. For Carr, that had already occurred. She had pulled out of the gloom and found a sky-bright clearing. Her journey took her into the depths of the forest and to the dark side of her dreams, and then she came into light. She learned to dance. Movement coursed through the canvases, whisked the long arms of the cedar trees into arabesques, rippled the fir trunks with bands of sunlight, and tossed the salal undergrowth into a frenzy. Wind crashed through the silence, charging the air with laughter, turning density into rhythm. Emily pushed towards the sky. Form evaporated, the forest began to fade. Eventually she emerged by the seashore where the sun no longer blinded her as it did when she was young, where she could stand looking out over the horizon to infinity.

Nineteen-thirty was a watershed for M. Emily Carr. She came into her own in the years that followed; she invented a technique for sketching in the woods using house paint and gasoline, which dried quickly; she bought a caravan, which permitted her to work on her own in the woods for weeks at a time, and she found her artistic voice. In March of that year, the same month Georgia O'Keeffe debated Michael Gold in New York, Emily Carr gave a speech to the Victoria Women's Canadian Club at the Crystal Garden in Victoria on the occasion of the first retrospective of her work, which was mounted in the adjacent hall. She spoke about her recent work, which strayed a long way from the literal renderings of her early paintings. "Here I [have] wanted something more—something deeper—not so concerned with what [things] looked like as what they felt like. Here I was really sweeping away the unnecessary and adding something more, something bigger," she told her audience. Like other modern artists and like the Native carvers, she looked beneath surfaces for "the informing spirit" pervading all of nature, for the essence that cameras and machines could never capture and which can only be seized by the soul. To her, great art was a "fresh seeing" of the inner world And now, finally, it was within her grasp.

Haida Gwaii, 1994

I can't remember when I first heard of the Queen Charlottes, but they have always seemed slightly otherworldly to me. It is one of those rare parts of Canada you have to cross open ocean to get to, and the only part missed by the last ice age, or so some biologists say, because animals like the marten and weasel are too peculiar not to have been isolated for more than 10,000 years from the rest of the continent. Here you find black bears the size of grizzlies, and nesting peregrine falcons in abundance not known anywhere else. Here people live in close proximity to eagles, ravens, and whales; in the spring they collect eagle feathers in the woods, and share the love of herring roe and sea kelp with young grey whales, which come into Skidegate Inlet to graze.

What the Queen Charlottes are exactly is a coccyx-shaped archipelago of islands formed by a half-submerged mountain chain that arches up from California to Alaska. It is a lush North Pacific

paradise surrounded by the most unruly waters in the world, full
of geological and botanical wonders like the giant sandbar, which
arcs eight miles out into the tides at the northeast tip of Graham
Island, forming a disappearing dividing line between Dixon

View down Cumshewa Inlet, Haida Gwaii, August 1994.

Entrance and Hecate Strait. It is a place that takes courage and ingenuity to live in, for the terrain and the climate are formidable even
by West Coast standards. To those who learn their ways, these are
islands of immense richness. On the maps they are called the Queen
Charlotte Islands, but everyone on the coast knows it as Haida
territory, and more and more call it by the old name of Haida
Gwaii. Everyone also knows the Haida as master mariners who
built high-shouldered, ocean-going canoes and navigated great
distances by the stars, and as magnificent carvers of argillite and
cedar. Their poles, mortuary posts, bent boxes, and canoes so
amazed the French scholar Claude Lévi-Strauss that he took to
comparing their achievements to the monuments of ancient Egypt.
That was in the 1970s when Lévi-Strauss was about as famous an

anthropologist as Jacques Cousteau was as a marine biologist. In retrospect, the attention obviously had something to do with the early fame of Bill Reid among collectors and the press, whom art critics raved about, claiming he was single-handedly bringing

Rock formation at Tow Hill on North Beach near Rose Spit, Haida Gwaii, August 1994.

West Coast art back to life. In any case, and probably for a multiplicity of reasons, contemporary Native art, particularly the Haida's, was becoming visible in mainstream Canada.

One reason for this was *Loo Taas*, The "Wave Eater," a canoe built on Haida Gwaii by Reid and others for Expo '86. It made the news when it was paddled down to Vancouver, and again in 1989 when it was paddled down the Seine as part of France's bicentennial celebrations. The crew had alarmed French immigration when they turned up at the Paris airport *sans passports*. The national press loved it, and so did the French: Natives in dispute with their government over the logging of Lyell Island had issued their own passports snubbing Canadian sovereignty and Canadian identity. As a political tactic it was brilliant, and as an event it was packed with symbolism—including the disappointment of some Parisians who didn't think the Haida men looked much like Indians.

There are new poles now in the old villages on Haida Gwaii. One by Reid from the 1980s is at Skidegate and another by Robert Davidson at Masset was raised in 1968. Old and new shift in meaning. Skidegate and Masset are old compared to New Masset and Queen Charlotte City (the two White towns) and ancient when they are considered as sites of continuous settlement going back further in history than most other places in the world. They are communities with an uninterrupted consciousness as old as 100,000 years, some calculate, a consciousness that is anchored in the present by names, titles, and stories handed down seamlessly over the generations. However, they are simultaneously new villages because they are the ones that survived, that lived to be renewed. Those that didn't are the old ones—T'anuu, Hlkenul (Cumshewa), K'una (Skedans), Chataal, Sgangwaii (Ninstints), and the others—the ones abandoned just before the turn of the century in the wake of the epidemics, which plunged the population from 8,000 to less that 500 within a generation. Such a catastrophe stuns the imagination, but I find myself trying to imagine it anyway—the slow disappearance of people and the dawning awareness, then the trauma and terror at the thought, and eventually the crushing reality of what was happening. Then the grief. Emily Carr visited the old villages, I realize, just fifteen years after the final evacuation had occurred. The old people and the stragglers had finally all departed, the museums and collectors had had their way, and the skylines were levelled and handed back to nature. A few buildings and the odd pole still stood, while back at Skidegate the people who remembered grew old.

The morning we leave for Hlkenul and K'una the sun rises in a heavy-lidded fog. Half an hour before the boat is due at the wharf opposite Gracie's Place, a van pulls up and in no time we are heading for the ferry dock instead. The weather's too dense for a water taxi without radar, so we're going across Skidegate Inlet and over to Moresby Camp to take another boat. Hereabouts people are used to being outfoxed by the weather and three days of clarified sunshine at the end of August mean nothing. By eight o'clock the day is waxing hazy, and by mid-morning it has reverted to midsummer again. We arrive at Hlkenul on a flat sea, the inlet masquerading as a lake with islands, and the surrounding shoreline held fast on its glassy surface. The site is on the northern side of the inlet by a steep, scalloped beach attached to an islet by a sandbar that is traversible at low tide. This tufted hillock is a burial place called Grave Island, our Dene guide tells us as he drops us on shore. He'd anchored the boat and taken us in in a Zodiac. His name is Allan and he leaves us to ourselves with instructions to head into the forest about 200 metres ahead if we want to see the remains of the village.

The woods are sparsely treed with a little stream running through them, which tickles the ear with its burble. Underfoot the ground is thick and springy with moss and soft grass. Approaching from the beach, the view was of a curtain of trees enveloping an emerald-lit box. Inside, the sun illuminates the enclosure with patches of shivering light; the ceiling is as high as the heavens, but the effect is of intimacy. It is cool in the gathering heat, fragrant with balsam and late summer grasses. The wind lies down and the blue sea dozes. Time stretches out as I walk around breathing the calm, listening, closing my eyes, and inhaling the spicy earth. When I open them, I see the remains appear right in front of me, as moss-covered forms reconfigure into the planks and posts of longhouses in the last stages of disintegration. I blink, but the ghost images do not disappear. In 1912, when Carr first visited, there was one house left, large and low and dreadfully dilapidated. This could have been it and this idyllic view hers as she sat sketching. It could have been, but wasn't because it dribbled with rain the whole day she was here, and although she completed several sketches, including the fabulous giant raven, she left with the memory of Cumshewa as one "great lonesomeness smothered in a blur of rain."

The tide has begun its ascent back up the beach by now, so we head for Grave Island with Allan, who points to the bones lying about and the Indian crab-apple trees, which were planted male and female in order to bear fruit. "What is the protocol?" I ask him, knowing burial places are usually sacred. "Take away only what you can remember," he answers. I stand still for several moments, looking around and listening to a breeze rustling through the trees. Turning to regard the silver smooth sea, I return back over the large stone boulders girding the islet to the beach, leaving Grave Island to its private thoughts.

Skedans is different. For one thing, it is bigger. Five hundred or more people lived here once in twenty-seven houses visible in the earliest photographs taken in 1878. Fifty-six poles caught the camera's eye, spiking the skyline and crowding the shore. Carr was taken there by two friends from Skidegate whom she renamed Jimmie and Louisa in *Klee Wyck*. They anchored offshore and paddled in with a little canoe, just as we do. The wide-open beach is broader than Hlkenul's, and the village is built on a bay carved out on both sides so the light comes through the trees from behind. "Memories came out of this place to meet the Indians; you saw remembering in the brightening eyes and heard it in the quick hushed words they said to each other in Haida," Carr wrote in *Klee Wyck*.

There are two boats in the bay and other visitors on shore when we arrive, tourists like us who want to explore the site and meet the Watchman, who is living in a cabin perched over the back bay. Times have changed on Haida Gwaii. The elders have come back to live in the old villages in the summer as part of a program that started as a defensive measure to contain the damage and theft still happening at these remote sites. The part-time residency developed into a golden opportunity to educate outsiders. We land and withdraw to a shady place to wait, taking the chance to eat some lunch. Charlie Wesley, the hereditary chef of Hlkenul, is here with his wife and granddaughters. He is of the eagle clan, and Skedans, which is really K'una, was a raven village.

A group of visitors departs for the other side of the site with one of the granddaughters. Mr. Wesley motions us to gather around a large log that he is leaning against. He has a bad hip and has not been giving many talks lately. At the moment he's feeling spry, so we get to hear him tell of the sea otter trade and how the pelts used to be measured in piles the height of a rifle; of how, during the epidemic, one sick sailor was left in a village and found dead by his companions when they returned for him, along with every single other person there. "The people were in a daze. They couldn't function here, so they all came together at Skidegate." The narrative continues with the government designating certain places for villages and other areas Crown land, creating reserves and dictating who would live there. Recently the Department of Indian Affairs tried to evict a White person living on the reserve, which the Haida took exception to. "We are not kicking people out after such a long time. So one chief adopted them into his family, and the thing was solved," he tells us. This chief enjoys telling tales of his ancestors, the legendary warriors who terrorized the coast. He points out that while the mountains of the mainland are visible from Haida Gwaii, you can see nothing from the mainland, so the Haida appeared as if from nowhere. He also explains that while it was the young men who travelled the coast from Alaska to California in those canoes, it was the older men who knew the weather and could read the skies. Those who had the experience advised the young men how to navigate. Chief Wesley ends up on the subject of Parks Canada and the surreptitious plan to bring guides and interpreters into the newly established national park. He weaves a story of government obstinance in accepting joint management with the Haida, and of one trainee who sidled up to him and asked if she could tape his talk. The old villages may yet survive, I think, as I look around at the people clambering over modern K'una, and contemplate the two not insignificant forces

333

squaring off over its control—the Council of the Haida Nation and the Canadian government. Chief Wesley winds up his presentation, answers a few questions, and takes his leave, reminding us to come by the cabin to get our passes stamped. We are left with plenty of time to explore K'una and follow the ghosts, which are more numerous and not so reticent here. A handful sit in plain sight, more or less upright—nurse logs to thick moss and flowering shrubs. Several are camouflaged by trees encasing them as they stand, or are encrusted with small trees growing from their backs as they lie on the ground. A crouching wolf is almost invisible beneath two strapping young hemlocks. In the green sunshine, the tableau is not sinister; the trees could be two straight-backed aunties containing a fractious child. I am aware of the sound of people moving about the site as I do and find it comforting. It is as if the commotion fits in, as if the place remembers. The past is closer, more visible than at Cumshewa, and so is the present. A couple of hours go by and Allan announces that it is time to leave. We make our way to the cabin to retrieve our passes. Chief Wesley has a guest book for us to sign. We meet Mrs. Wesley and the granddaughters and, as if on cue from an off-stage director, a helicopter reels around the corner of the island, circles overhead, and hovers noisily to a landing on a grassy patch behind the cabin. A White couple and their two kids disgorge, apparently expected. The kids fall in with the Haida youngsters and melt into the landscape. The adults are offered tea. The scene freeze-frames in my memory even as it is happening. It has such an air of suprarealism to it, of life imitating a *Newsworld* documentary, that I am not sure for a moment how to react. As symbolism goes, it seems overworked, yet this is how you get around in the global village. The disjuncture, I conclude, belongs to those of us who came a long way from home into an imaginary wilderness.

Emily Carr came twice to Haida Gwaii, the second time staying with friends in the Native community at Skidegate. The Russes were the couple who had taken her to K'una, T'anuu, and Hlkenul in 1912, but in 1928 William was busy with his boat. Others were engaged to take her to the old villages, but the weather did not cooperate and threw them a bad storm off Skedans, which ended the trip before it began. Apart from a few anxious hours on the beach watching her Haida escort trying to save his boat in the rain, and a few more in the early morning on the fish scows off Hlkenul where a Norwegian seiner had deposited her to hitch a ride back, Carr spent no time in those distant villages. She got $50 worth of experiences, she said later, in lieu of four days' sketching. That year she managed nothing further afield than Haina on Maude Island near Skidegate, not even a trip to Masset at the north end of Graham Island, which she had visited the first time when she was ferried across the narrow inlet to Yan by a young mother with her baby and a twelve-year-old girl. The highlight of that trip was the visit to the abandoned communities, and sixteen years later memories of those places were still strong. During the second trip, besides the near shipwreck, it was the experience of staying on the reserve that lived in her memory and emerged in *Klee Wyck*. She was well looked after by Clara Russ and her family and she preferred their accommodations to those of the mission. The Russ household included a diminutive, pipe smoking grandmother renowned for having given birth to a live set of triplets who didn't survive but were photographed, and Clara's thirteen-year-old niece, named Mildred, whom she was raising at the time. It was here in Clara's house in and around Skidegate that Emily Carr spent the better part of her 1928 visit.

Contemporary writers have often questioned the romance about Carr's travels in the wilderness. In the first instance they have challenged the claim, rarely made now, that she lived among Native people. In the second, they have argued that conditions were not as arduous as Carr let on; boat service was well established and the routes well travelled by the 1920s, and Emily herself commented on the modernized living conditions at the Russes' and elsewhere. True enough, Carr was not breaking trails, much less travelling into the unknown. She had guides and even a few guardians. She did spend time in Native communities, though, and sought out Aboriginal society, but her visits were never for longer than a few weeks at a stretch. None of these observations diminish or alter Emily's experience of them, though, only our vicarious understanding of it. We do know she was close to what she imagined as wilderness and that she ventured into it cautiously and with deliberation, testing her mettle. Even today, Haida Gwaii is a long trek, geographically and psychologically, from the Lower Mainland; it is still a terrain outsiders do well to approach with trepidation. But in facing her fears as she did in the storm off K'una, Carr was reaching beyond her physical limits. Others looking at her life have thus compared her coastal travels to a rite of passage because of the element of physical ordeal. Judging from *Klee Wyck*, however, the main event of her visit to Haida Gwaii was this encounter with nature *in extremis*. It was a life-confronting experience just as Gitanyow had been. Both situations required fortitude and called on her psychic resources.

If Carr's letters and journals do not give us the full story about her spiritual journey through the late 1920s and early 1930s, the paintings do, and they speak of an artist obsessed with the forest, who buried herself in the darkness at the bottom of its thick green space. Eschewing the long vistas and majestic views favoured by the Group of Seven, she delved into enclosed, penumbric places close to the ground, next to the seethe and stink and close-up ugliness of nature's grandeur. She abstracted the image, as Lawren Harris did, blunting the edges into soft, malleable forms that lift up and fold back, revealing and concealing. She discovered movement, looked at Vincent van Gogh with new eyes, and settled into an earth-swelling rhythm that mimicked the vital force she perceived in the pull and prod of nature, the theosophists' vibrations, Ouspensky's fourth dimension. She met the young American modernist Mark Tobey and absorbed from him a cubist sense of design and the incipient unity of colour, line, and form. She took stock, integrated, paused to interrogate herself, and pushed on. This is the moment she chose to return to the Dzunukwa whose spirit had shadowed her all along. Native motifs remained in these pictures but Carr treated them differently now, rendering them either as topographical elements in a larger scene (such as the poles in *Vanquished*) or as close-up "portraits" of totem figures (as in *Nirvana, The Raven, Totem Mother*). At this point they ceased to be the subject of Carr's paintings and became channels of emotion. Like the forest interiors that dominated her work after 1927, the vision was dark and close, elemental and expressive, the mood melancholic. The effect for some people is claustrophobic and lugubrious; they read the images as the mark of a depressed person. For others, the same work, though sombre, is, on the contrary, brimming with energy and sexual innuendo. They recognize female imagery in these forest enclosures and see the paintings as metaphysical statements couched in an awareness of the cosmic unity of nature—exactly as Carr came to perceive them herself.

The romance continued; in her mid-sixties and against all the odds, Emily Carr had an artistic breakthrough of radical proportions. She took flight with this new work, heading towards the light shedding density as she went. The paintings poured forth. The vision was elemental and ethereal. She invoked the universal by dematerializing *terra firma* until, as poet George Stanley has said, she was painting air. This was where the journey led. She did not approach the woods as a rugged individualist or wilderness explorer as did the men back east, but rather as a regionalist and a Native, rooted in the place she was depicting. There is a profound difference there: Carr did not seek a landscape other than the one she knew and identified with and thought of as expressly Western, nor did she see her forest as a metaphor for the entire country as the Group of Seven did. She preserved a degree of separation from the centrist perspective. She admired their public spirit, though she engaged with the public in a much more reserved fashion and not as an apologist or debater. Carr was a storyteller. She brought her private self to the public in her art, insofar as her painting coincided with her spiritual quest. Her personal self she kept hidden.

Carr's mystical relationship to the landscape she painted was obviously closer to Harris's than to any other members of the

Group of Seven. With Harris, though, the spiritual led inexorably inward and into formula; for the latter part of his life he produced work that art history and most collectors have chosen to ignore, the spiritual in his case having absorbed the art. By contrast, Carr kept faith with the country, expounding a geographic loyalty foreign to Harris whose nationalism assumed an internationalism that contradicted personal commitment to a particular community. In the end, he abandoned landscape altogether. Carr was at the point of coming to terms with both the land and Canada at the time Harris left both behind. Although he and Bess kept in touch and resumed a friendship with Carr after they settled in Vancouver, Carr was on her own again without confidants as she headed into the last efflorescent phase of her life. She was in a better position than before, for she now had some recognition and support from her peers, but the intellectual intimacy—some have said dependence—of the early friendship with Harris was no more. On her own, Emily pushed beyond his apolitical spirituality to a place in which she was, as critic Robert Linsley says, painting for the future rather than against it. To Linsley, these later paintings are a verdant counterpoint to Harris's arctic imagery and style, which he irreverently describes as "the great freeze out" of Canadian landscape. Far from passively receiving Harris's teaching as the biographers had it, Carr recognized what Harris was doing, absorbed what she needed from him, and headed off on her own.

When she broke through into the clearing, Carr took note of where she was and what she was looking at, that is to say, the devastation in the forest, which she evoked in paintings with titles such as *"Scorned as Timber, Beloved of the Sky," "Loggers' Culls,"* and *"Odds and Ends."* As Linsley remarks, Carr struck a different balance between the subjective and the universal in such paintings. This is no empty landscape, no ideological dream of humankind reconciled with nature. The country the Group of Seven depicted lies pristine and clean, free of human encumbrance, at the feet of the explorer-artist. It lay there awaiting exploitation and transformation by social forces that are kept out of sight but

338

which nevertheless helped construct the image and provided a bourgeois audience with an imaginative landscape for its delectation. Carr acknowledged this hidden story by permitting the signs of industrialization to be seen, and in doing so repudiated the Group's narrative. According to Linsley, "she rejects the authoritarianism implicit in the view from the height as she rejects the heroism of the mythic North." Her role as an artist was not to be as a spokeswoman for the nation; she would be instead an "open medium for history." In Linsley's view, Carr undercut the antimodernism implicit in the Group of Seven's position, positing her own cosmopolitan regionalism against their provincial nationalism. Insofar as the group's romantic attachment to rural Canada can be read as a denial of the urban thrust of modernism, and the racialist underpinnings of their ideas understood as an expression of "deep anxiety about racial and ethnic mixing," Linsley maintains that their image of the Canadian landscape was ethnocentric and reactionary. Carr may have been no less a product of her time and her background than Harris when it came to racial attitudes, but she did not share this closed view of the world. She was no more willing to accept the group's fuzzy notion of the Great White North than she was willing to submit to the dictates of Theosophy.

What, then, was her touchstone? What was her conception of the land—and what was so different about it? With the language and analysis of contemporary feminism, scholars now talk of how Carr came to terms with the wilderness by ascribing positive feminine values to it. Rereading *Klee Wyck,* they have lingered over the imagery and the themes that play on the power of subversive womanhood. They notice when Emily was questioned by the R.C.M.P. following her trip to Gitanyow that she answered their warnings about the danger to Whites, particularly women, with "Perhaps it is because I am a woman that they were so good to me." Feminist scholars observe how the forest itself and the Native carvings in particular became memorable characters in the book; how keenly Carr cloaked everything in female garb. "As the canoe glided on, her human cargo was as silent as the cedar-life that once had filled her. She had done with the forest now; when they shoved her into the sea they had dug out her heart. Submissively she accepted the new element, going with the tide . . . [Yet] some still element of the forest clung yet to the cedar's hollow rind which resented the restless push of the waves." However, in lieu of the Freudian interpretations, which presented Carr's attachment to nature as a sign of sublimated sexuality and repression, these writers tend to see it as a technique for sidestepping the paradigm of patriarchy and racial privilege. Some, such as Roxanne Rimstead, argue that Carr's stories are an unwitting attempt to empower Native women, to give presence and voice to individuals from an eclipsed minority. Perhaps even more significantly, they draw a connection between the totem figures, Carr's sense of female connection, and the spiritual dimension she detected in nature. Today we have access to the theory that Carr's choice of celibacy was made so she could devote herself to her painting, more specifically to painting nature and, more specifically still, to painting a landscape with which she was imaginatively and emotionally connected. Carr gave herself permission to express a physicality about the forest that was loving and sensuous. Rimstead's point is that her motivation was not romantic. She was reaching for immanence, not transcendence, so her landscapes, her *paysage imaginaire,* convey the sense of welcoming space, of cyclical pattern, of blurred limits between consciousness and cosmic connection and of erotic pleasure. In the vibrant, throbbing, green-growing world Carr inhabited, a kind of "animistic reciprocity" took place between herself and the place, between her being and the being in the animals, trees and rocks surrounding her:

> One night I had a dream of greenery. . . . I saw a wooded
> hillside, an ordinary slope such as one might see along
> any Western roadside, tree-covered, normal, no particular
> pattern or design to catch an artist's eye were he seeking
> subject matter. But in my dream that hillside suddenly
> lived—weighted with sap, burning green in every leaf,

every scrap of it vital . . . I never attacked the painting of growing foliage quite the same after that.

The green Carr saw was the life force of nature, the sensuous part of nature which she readily embraced, for when she closed down on human sexual expression, she opened up her senses in other directions. Her descriptions of the land in *Klee Wyck* are evidence of that. They are also evidence of her mystic connection—one might also say obsession—with the forest and the trees. She was seduced by them, enticed by them, and, metaphorically speaking, green nature became her lover. The name of Hildegard of Bingen often crops up in these discussions of Carr's relationship to nature. Both women have attracted the admiration of contemporary women artists and scholars as well as the wider public interested in women's history, perhaps because of the confluence of art, mysticism, and verdant nature in their lives. Hildegard, the twelfth-century sage who wrote theological texts based on her visions, composed music and hymns and the first recorded morality play, was an abbess and prophet who became known for her knowledge of plants and medicines as well as her visions. Her cosmic vision of Christ, and her intimate connection with the natural world, mark her as exceptional for her time. She broke the codes of gender behaviour by writing in Latin and preaching in public, yet she rationalized what she did by describing herself as a passive instrument of God's design, remaining conventional in other attitudes. Like Carr, a psychological crisis precipitated her creative breakthrough. At forty-two, after a severe illness, Hildegard began recording her visions. These she had had since childhood, but had rarely acknowledged. Now they became the springboard for the creativity of her middle age. She acquired a following and her convent became famous for its music and ritual. Most improbably, her teachings attracted the support of the pope (Eugenius III) and the influential reformer, Bernard of Clairvaux. Theologians and scholars like Matthew Fox and Barbara Newman have reinterpreted Hildegard's writings, considering her life in the context of her time—the twelfth-century renaissance and the

Marian cult—as well as in the context of Church history. Newman claims Hildegard as "the first Christian thinker to deal seriously with the feminine as such," and Fox eulogizes her for what he calls the deeply ecological quality of her spirituality. To both, Hildegard represents the lost side of Christianity, the side that was in tune with the elements, rooted in mysticism, and still connected to the female past. In Fox's mind, this was the lingering influence of ancient goddess religions in the culture.

My own first encounter with Hildegard was in the mid-1980s when Toronto artist Joyce Wieland enthused to me about her vision of nature. I was writing about Wieland at the time of her retrospective at the Art Gallery of Ontario, inevitably an occasion for reflection. She had returned to landscape herself as a subject and recently produced a series of lyrical colour drawings, which the critics were pooh-poohing. Her sensual appreciation of the natural world was roused by Hildegard's luminous, juicy, green vision. To Hildegard everything depended on *viriditas,* which the translators have dubbed greening power and which Joyce saw as the libidinous female force. The Holy Spirit was greening power in motion; spiritual salvation was the result of the return of *viriditas* after a drying up period of sickness, and God was "the breeze that nurtures all things *green.*" Joyce fancied this moist and musky Mother Nature, and pegged Hildegard as an erotic as well as a mystic. We sat together having tea in the front room of her house on Queen Street East, talking and looking at books while a tape of the abbess's incandescent "Feather on the Breath of God" keened in the background. Joyce spoke about Emily Carr in the same terms, saying that she felt Carr was female and earthy and ethereal in the same way Hildegard was. "So would she have known about making love immersed in water, then?" I blurted out, tongue-in-cheek. I was thinking of the sex scene in *The Far Shore,* Wieland's feature film based on the story of Tom Thomson. It happens when the heroine, Eulalie, flees her brutish Anglo husband and goes off with Thomson. The film caught many people off guard with its unconventional and painterly approach to film making as well as its political over-

tones. There, in quasi-mainstream language, Wieland unmasked the
violence embedded in the Group of Seven's myth, underscoring the
connection between their endeavour and the work of industrialists
like Eulalie's husband, who had silver mining interests in the bush.
The connection, of course, is not simple or direct. Harris was critical of the growing materialism of middle-class culture, a perspective
that owed a lot to Theosophy and which was not without irony
given his own privilege. At the same time, the vision of the North
that the Group of Seven championed was deliberately devoid of
people or any hint of human habitation. Harris may have been a
conservationist but he was no reformer. Carr had her contradictions, too, not the least being her hard-to-pin down sexuality. Given
Carr's virginal status and prudish reputation, my question about
underwater sex sounded odd, but Joyce figured there was an erotic
side to Carr's physicality too. The elemental love of nature ran deep
and passionate in Emily, as it did in Hildegard of Bingen, who likewise admired the purpose and even the pleasure of sex in nature,
but despised it in human beings. Matthew Fox speaks of Hildegard
as a mystic and prophet who struggled against the suppression of
her talents and was driven to her sickbed before she could break
convention and begin writing. To him her life was a celebration of
creative expression, and indeed Hildegard believed that the sin of
drying up connoted the loss of the ability to create. This seems to
me to be the point of connection between Hildegard and Emily Carr,
this belief in the power of green.

I heard about Gracie's Place in Queen Charlotte City from a friend
who makes nature films for the CBC and has visited Haida Gwaii
often. It was a simple B&B sort of place that won't cost half your
savings for a week's stay, he said. Besides, you'll love Gracie. A
gravelly voiced single Mom with attitude was the description.
Gracie's Place began as a couple of sleeping units in the downstairs
of her small home, which has been expanded several times and
now comprises six suites tucked in and around the original house,

each with a mini kitchen and separate entrance. Gracie and her teenage daughter live upstairs in nifty renovated quarters, with Gracie's combination office and kitchen occupying the main space in front. There's usually a hubbub going on as she orchestrates her various enterprises (which now include the car rental agency and a long-distance telephone franchise for the islands), chats with visitors, and cooks up a heap of lasagne for the party she's hosting tonight. Gracie's Place, like Gracie herself, is right in the thick of things, situated on the main drag (3rd Avenue), in full view of the inlet and the comings and goings of boats, tourists, and tides.

The community, which spreads out behind Gracie's in both directions, is the oldest White settlement on Haida Gwaii, but it is no longer the largest since the armed forces set up a station outside Masset in 1971, swelling the population there to 1,600. Queen Charlotte City is named for Captain George Dixon's ship, which put in here in 1787, and who knows whose Queen Charlotte. The Queen part tends to get dropped in local parlance anyway, and this Charlotte is so far removed and long gone that I can discover no one on this trip who remembers she was the wife of George III, though everyone knows a ship is involved somewhere.

A few short kilometres down the road, past the ferry dock and the Q.C.I. Museum, is the village of Skidegate, which is more like a town and currently bustling with the influx of people returning in the wake of the repeal of 12(1)(b), the clause in the Indian Act that stripped Native women of their Indian status when they married out. A mission was set up here by the Methodists in the 1890s, while the Anglicans claimed Masset at the top end of Graham Island for Canterbury. Over the century, other outsiders have come looking for adventure, escape, and opportunity and stayed on Haida Gwaii because of logging, fishing, and government jobs. They settled around Sandspit where the airport is now, at Queen Charlotte City, and in pockets along the main highway— Tlell, Port Clements, and the new town of Masset situated close to the reserve from which it takes its name. By now I recognize this arrangement as common—White and Native communities living next to each other, together and separately at the same time, the proverbial two solitudes. On Haida Gwaii they've been doing this for four or five generations, not always amicably, as recent tensions over the logging of Lyell Island and South Morseby illustrate. These tensions reverberate through the non-Native community and my conversations with two local tour operators are indicative. The first one didn't mind when I asked about people accompanying the tours to the old villages and their connection with the Haida, but launched into a lecture on her company's philosophy, which is to pay as strict attention to the ecology as to the weather. She told me about Allan and talked about the Watchman Program. The second tour operator took immediate umbrage at the question, turned my query into a political position, and berated me for idealizing the Haida as conservationists. The barbed exchange these two would have were they ever to meet at a microphone would probably produce more sound than light. The original contention between the Haida and White people was over logging, but the debate can never be separated from land claims for long, and the defensiveness on the Whites' side usually descends into allegations of Native wrongdoing before long.

How would Emily Carr have talked about Native-White relations and the history of White aggression? I notice that while her response to environmental issues is often evoked, her stand on things like the Nisga'a treaty or Oka, where the political rubber meets the road in our time, are never imagined. Like many Canadians, Carr despaired for Native peoples and their situation. She was cutting about White attitudes towards them. The intolerant behaviour of the missionaries at Ucluelet, which she described in *Klee Wyck*, irked her and the abuse of Native designs by other artists did too. But she did not express opinions on political issues that mattered to Native people, and she did not turn her critique of White artists on herself. She could write the following in her journal about a man with a summer house on a beautiful 175-acre cedar lot: "Everything in it done up Indian. Much nicer if he had left things raw, but his soul rolls around Indian design, Indian colour,

Indian robes. There's falseness about a white man using those symbols to ornament himself. The Indian believed in them. They *expressed* him. The white is not expressing himself, he's faking." But her social conscience only went so far. Even as I pose the question I am forced to wonder why, if I can put someone dead on the spot, she cannot demand an accounting back from me. I scroll through the history I have studied since being on the coast, and consider what I've seen on my travels and learned from listening to people, especially Native people. Glimpsing your own world through someone else's culture forces you to notice things like the subjects you avoid and the experiences you dread. As I've followed Emily Carr around British Columbia, I have tiptoed around the matter of the White women who came to these parts attached to churches or husbands. They had a role in the schooling and nursing of the sick and the young, and in the administration of assimilationist policies of the time. It is easy to villainize Halliday, Hall, and Scott, who left large imprints behind on the public record. Not so easy is the lost history of White women, which would have to include their contribution to colonization. And I still wonder what I will make of oolichan grease when I finally encounter it, having read so often of Whites' aversion to its strong taste and smell. To many, the oil is delectable, and I recall my friend Viola drooling at the thought she might come into some when an aunt was visiting Vancouver from the Interior. Rendered from the little candlefish, which are left to rot in the summer sun, this is the commodity that made the Nisga'a rich and influential, for everyone in the coastal region wanted to trade for it. For Whites, though, oolichan grease is a metaphor for fetishized difference and a symbol of the unsettled questions associated with unsettled stomachs.

For me, the big unsettled question is how we square what is happening now over Aboriginal title and forest lands with what we know about history. "We" in this equation are the White non-Native newcomers like myself. I am not sure if this is a political question, an ethical one, or a spiritual one. I have thought about it, asked other people their views, and here on Haida Gwaii decide to

get in touch with a man who lives in Masset and who undoubtedly
has thought about it too. At least he won't balk at the question from
a near stranger. I met Peter Hamel while researching a magazine
piece about bird-watching. He is a magnetic individual, passionate,
talkative, and as committed an environmental activist as you'll meet
this side of Greenpeace. He is also one of Canada's top "listers,"
those bird-watching pros who keep count, and inevitably ends up
searching for the rarest birds in remote pockets of the globe. When
he isn't birding, Hamel is an Anglican minister who was working as
an adviser to the Anglican Church of Canada on environmental and
Native affairs when I interviewed him in 1990. He had just set the
all-time Canadian bird-watching record, sighting 432 of Canada's
578 species of birds in a single year (1988), a feat made possible by
the travelling his work for the Church entailed, and which, his
friends joked, put his immortal soul in danger. I remember him
speaking quite seriously about subversive bird-watching, claiming
that birding was a natural introduction to conservation. "Because it
flows from personal experience it generates a sense of ownership,"
he explained. "You see one tufted puffin and you want to see
another." Peter Hamel is a man of conviction, and I was not
surprised to find that he resigned his position with the Church hierarchy in Toronto and returned to his parish in Masset. When I tele-
phoned, he invited me with alacrity to stop by.

The road into Masset crosses a causeway at the south end of the
Delkatla Wildlife Sanctuary, a 1,370-acre preserve of wetlands
that serve as a stopover for migratory birds on the Pacific flyway.
This being Haida Gwaii and the first major landfall on several
north-south routes, many birds come by design and quite a few
come by accident, blown off course by storms. For Peter Hamel, in
or out of favour with the bishops, this must be like living in
paradise. I pull up at the appointed hour just as he swooshes into
the drive in his Jeep. He ushers me into the house, a neat bunga-
low with an astonishing collection of Aboriginal art on the walls.
He asks if I mind removing my shoes, makes coffee, and rounds up
some cookies in the kitchen. Then he heads onto the deck outside

where he can smoke. Lithe and wiry, he moves with purpose, looks at you squarely with clear blue eyes, and engages in conversation at once. From the deck we look back over the causeway and he fills me in on the story behind the big sign at the crossroads. The causeway is slowly draining the sanctuary, so an effort is being mounted to raise the money to build a bridge to replace it. He inquires about Emily Carr and I reverse the question, asking him what his connection with her is. He leaps into an animated conversation about the power of her work and her expression of the sanctity of the earth. Before I know it, he is on to the Book of Job, poor long suffering, lying-on-the-dung-heap Job who, when he finally gets his day in court with God, doesn't talk about suffering but alienation from the land. It's the same in the Song of Solomon, which is replete with examples of the powerful connection to nature—rarely mentioned now. "Even Matthew Fox missed this," Peter is telling me." It is part of a tradition of Christian spirituality which is very old and has been lost." He talks about the connection between language and the land, how in the Native cultures he knows the words for birds are not descriptive—as in our roseate spoonbill and indigo bunting—but behavioural, so a bird is named for the way it dives, or the sound of air rushing through its wings. Eventually he returns to the subject of Carr whom he knows only from her paintings, not her books. These he has looked at closely, concluding that she knew something first hand about the sacred in nature. "It was not just empathetic projection on her part. There *are* sacred places here after all," Hamel says. I press him, wondering if he is going to tell me stories about the Golden Spruce tree, the genetic wonder even foresters can't explain. "Well, you know Rose Spit, the sandbar that runs off Rose Point like a needle nose—which incidentally, is what the Haida call it, Nai-kun? I'm convinced it is the most sacred spot on the planet. I've been up there with the tide coming in from both sides and can tell you, you get spooked. It is an extraordinary, huge, and powerful experience."

I can imagine it, having spent the morning walking on the beach, gazing at the spit in the far-off, faded distance. As someone raised a long way away from the sea and the concept of tides, I am amazed by this perpetual motion and the force behind it. Back and forth between the gulf islands at home I watch the tide drive the sea through narrow channels. Even at high tide when the push hesitates in the transition to pull and the agitation lulls, the surface of the water boils with pent-up energy. I am struck by two things traversing Gabriola Passage, the visual beauty of swirls and whorls and whirlpools, which, I remember, Leonardo da Vinci sketched with endless fascination, and the eerie sound of the water, idling at the bidding of an unseen force. Standing on Rose Spit, suspended between two huge bodies of water moving at opposite purposes, off shore where the wind blows unimpeded save for your upright body, the sound must reverberate through your bones. Finally, I ask Hamel the question about the history of the Church on the coast and how to square it with what we know now. "You don't." The answer snaps back, firm, clear, and delivered as if he'd been asked before. "I eventually made a personal apology, which is something we can all do—speak out our truth." I ask him about his work with the Church. "I always knew I was skating on thin ice with the bishops, and was prepared to lose my job. In fact, I finally left on a point of principle. You ask about history—well, how do we finally deal with the fact that the Israelites seeking their own freedom pushed other people living in Mesopotamia out and took their lands?"

We retreat into the house, down to the basement where Peter has his books and documents and a small office. Native studies are lined on shelves against one wall; religion, spirituality, and birds on another. He shows me binders full of notes and documents from various activities; he points out memorabilia on the walls (the telex he sent on behalf of the Haida Nation to the stockholders' meeting of a logging company in New York), and pictures from a session he chaired for the Gitksan and Wet'suwet'en when they were deciding about their court case. Hamel's question is rhetorical, of course, and it relocates guilt by supplying a broader context, suggesting the behaviour is a chain reaction. He may be right. History cannot be squared or made right; it can only be named and learned. "Have I answered your question?" he finally asks.

Skidegate, 1998

Happenstance brings me back to Haida Gwaii, following in the steps of my friend, Shirley Bear, who works as First Nations coordinator for the art college in Vancouver. Another friend, visiting B.C. from New Brunswick, wants to make the trip to talk to people about patriation, the return of the bones of Native ancestors from museums around the world where they were kept as anthropological specimens. The return of the ancestors' remains to their communities raises issues of procedure and protocol for those receiving the remains. Shirley tells me about Karen Perley, who works as an archaeological adviser to the province, adding that she has also heard of a young student on Haida Gwaii whose grandmother was a friend of Emily Carr. "We three could go," she proposes. Karen and I would do our research while she painted and talked to students. The trip takes shape from there.

Skidegate is booming. A new Elder Centre has been built since I was here last, as well as a new co-op supermarket and a wonderful deli that beats anything in Charlotte for lunches and cheesecake. Once here, we quickly find out that Dorothy Russ, who works at the health centre, is in union negotiations but free over the noon hour. She meets us at the deli for a carrot-curry soup and pasta salad lunch. Her husband Fred's family knew Emily Carr, she tells me. There aren't family stories to speak of, except about the book. "What Emily wrote was full of lies," she says. "Frankly, there's not much interest in Carr." Dorothy's daughter Sara arrives with her two-year-old niece in tow. Sara is the one interested in art school, who talks about her grandmother and the stories of Emily Carr.

After we've eaten, the four of us head back to the house to see Fred. On our way out, Dorothy spies a relative whom she beckons over and introduces to me, putting the question about Emily Carr to her. Grace repeats the story about Emily's lies.

Fred is working outside when we arrive, but follows us into the big family living-room to talk. He has been a fisher and has logged for MacMillan Bloedel for over twenty years now. His raven dark hair is tinged with grey, but his features are youthful, and he smiles with evident pleasure when he talks about Clara, the grand-mother who raised him in the old ways. He even remembers his great-grandmother, Mrs. Greene. At the mention of her, Sara dives into a box behind the sofa and comes up with the old photo of the three dead "triples" Emily Carr wrote about. Fred explains that they were born alive, but their mother was so weak after the birth that she was unable to nurse them. Someone else tried, but the little ones died. He remembers hearing of Emily Carr and of Clara's going down to Victoria to visit her. Emily's house was full of monkeys, cats, birds, and dogs. I laugh at that, knowing how many Native people I know dislike the idea of dogs in the house. Clara probably thought Emily unclean. "The break came with the book," Fred informs me. "It angered Clara. It was full of lies and bullshit. But you should visit Mildred Pollard. She'll have more to say."

Millie Pollard was Clara's adopted daughter who was living with her in Skidegate when Emily visited in 1928. Now in her eighties and in hospital, Mrs. Pollard is nevertheless well enough for a visi-tor. She has just washed her hair and is blow-drying it when I discover her in the solarium at the end of the hall. I sit beside her wheelchair and she invites me to talk. Her voice is strong, and she has the air of the inquisitive young woman she once was. She was thirteen when Emily Carr came to stay, and remembers Carr didn't have much to say to her. To Millie's young eyes, Emily was some-one short and round who was always in the kitchen cooking with Clara. (Clara was a wonderful cook, which also meant the house was always full of people at mealtimes.) Millie does not remember Clara's reaction to Emily's book, only the parts in it describing the house as large and elastic. I ask about carvers in the village and she offers nothing except the fact that she herself carved argillite and has a couple of pieces in the museum. Willie Russ made cedar trays, which sold well, and she loved them, but they were too fiddly to make. "I made small things: pendants, earrings, souvenir spoons. Things that were too small to put your name on . . . and what I liked best was signing my name to the bottom!" She goes on to explain that she had to sell cheap and therefore didn't want to put any more time into something than need be. I ask if Clara made baskets. "Making baskets is a privilege," she states. She then talks on about the stone she carved, how the men who quarried it knew which was soft and which would be good to carve, and how she liked to make her tools herself. Her voice follows her memories back to those teenage summers when Willie and Clara would go to their fishing place on the west coast of Haida Gwaii and she would go with them.

As I leave, one of the White nurses approaches, saying she couldn't help overhearing us talking about Emily Carr. I tell her about my project and Mrs. Pollard's connection to it and she chats on enthusiastically about the artist whose paintings she loves. A statuesque and handsome woman, she is wearing a small fortune in gold and silver Haida jewellery. I find it arresting and rather perplexing for I've noticed hardly any First Nations women wearing jewellery. Is her interest to be read as appreciation of Native design, or solidarity with Native culture? And how does it look to her Haida charges? What does it symbolize in the larger picture of cultural politics? Questions I have to answer for myself.

I join up with Karen and Shirley at the Elder Centre just as some gifts are being presented, and everyone is enjoying tea. Songs have been sung and special coffee mugs given in return. Some warm knitted toques are being passed around by a dapper old man with a jaunty air about him and beautiful snowy white hair. I notice the Haida old folks are being cared for by a flock of White women, highly paid health care professionals who smile a lot and use the geriatric "we." This is the reverse of the situation in my mother's retirement home in Toronto where the largely White residents are looked after by Black and Philippino women working for working-class wages.

Out on the highway, on our way north to Masset, Karen and Shirley explain that the dapper old guy with the toques knits them himself on a little machine. He is Millie Pollard's husband Jack, and we have reason to bless him for the hats during the next few nights we spend sleeping by the sea on North Beach. The first two nights are spent in a driftwood summer cabin built right on the sandy beach and owned by a young couple in Charlotte who welcomed us to use it. The front is fitted with large windows that give us a view of the sea and the dunes with their grassy toupees and the deer passing through, all visible from our sleeping platform inside. The last night we set up a tent in a sheltered spot on the Agate Beach campground. It is early May, and summer is clearly in a hurry, for the snow is off the mountains and the ocean warm enough (just) to swim in, but at night it is cold and the wind blows with a steady roar.

Searching for Emily Carr on Haida Gwaii in the company of two First Nations women allows me a perspective I didn't have on my last trip. In the first place, I can now sense a narrative to the friendship between Carr and Clara Russ. Clara reciprocated Emily's visit, the two women kept in touch for several years, and then *Klee Wyck* was published and the relationship shattered. Clara did not figure in Emily's private writings, though she was there as Louisa in *Klee Wyck* in the story called "Friends." Louisa lives in a two-storey house and is obviously prosperous. There's a player piano in the outer parlour and people drop around to make music in the evenings. They show up at dinner time, too, for everyone knows about Louisa's good cooking. What happened to the friendship, and why did Carr not make it to the villages she so badly wanted to see again in 1928? I find myself remembering Barbeau's report that Carr was disappointed with her trip because people had changed and were preoccupied. Knowing how unlikely it is that White outsiders get to see things the Haida don't want seen, it makes me suspect that more than weather kept her from the old villages. It prompts me to ask why Carr used a pseudonym for Clara in *Klee Wyck*, when she did not for Sophie Frank. The name change could be read as an indication that the piece was fictionalized to some degree, the source perhaps of the "lies" that hurt Clara. It is also true that Clara was still alive when the book was published, whereas Sophie had died two years before so her privacy could not be invaded by being mentioned by name, and her name could not be libelled.

The true nature of Carr's personal connection with Native women like Clara is not easily ascertained with one half of the testimony missing. Unlike Carr or Georgia O'Keeffe, whose lives can be reconstructed from the public record, the Aboriginal record is hard to come by. We do know that Emily Carr's spiritual search took her to Native art and to what is currently called Native spirituality, an orientation towards nature and a oneness with it. If she had glimpses into the spiritual practice of Native peoples it would have been happenstance, but it could, just possibly, have been with some guidance.

Chapter Five

The Old Woman and the Elephant

Victoria, 1939

Sophie is dead. The news hit me like a fist in the stomach.
I should have expected it, I suppose—she's been in such a
bad way for so long—but I didn't. Frank wrote to say she
slipped into a coma and went quickly. Death was easier
for her than life and I am glad of that, but bereft at the
thought of no more visits, no more toothless smiles of
welcome. *"I have watched all day yesterday and tomorrow
for you, My Emily,"* she would say. Usually I would arrive
unannounced, and sometimes it almost seemed she was
expecting me. Her house faced the sea and we would sit
outside on the porch listening to the waves. Inside we
drank tea and ate biscuits cooked on the wood stove.

They will bury her in the cemetery in North Vancouver, I think, and there will be no money for a marker.
Frank could carve something in wood, except the priests
always insist on stone. Sophie traded baskets for her
tombstones and it cost her dozens and dozens to "buy"
stones for all those children. I bought one for the twin she
named after me and it was nearly forty dollars.

Sophie was the best, and it breaks my heart that her
grave will go unmarked because she deserves the finest.
She was upright and generous and her trust was absolute.
I knew that the first day I met her. There was a knock at
the studio door one morning and I opened it to find a little

Indian mother standing there with a fat baby on her back.
She had on a full skirt of loud plaid, a bright yellow silk
handkerchief about her head and a gay shawl securing the
baby. A little girl clutched at her skirt and a heavy boy
dawdled behind.

"Baskets?" she said, looking at me.

She undid a large cloth bundle tied at the four corners
and displayed a beautiful selection, all of her own making.

Portrait of Sophie Frank painted by Emily Carr in 1907 or 1908.

"Haho chuckimen," I said, meaning no money.

"Warm skirt just same," she replied.

"Haho warm skirt. Next month maybe. Catch um Victoria," I told her.

The basket I wanted was about eighteen inches wide and twenty-four inches long, stoutly woven from cedar root and inlaid with designs in cherry bark and split cedar. It was square-cornered with handles and a firm, fitted cover.

"Come into the studio and rest a bit," I suggested. She was happy to stop a while, and the children were thirsty. I made a cup of tea and we all ate some bread and jam. After a while the little boy crept over to watch the squirrels cavorting in their cage; the girl never left her mother's side. The mother was tiny and strong featured. She wore her ink-black hair in two thick braids joined at the ends and smiled at me with deep brown eyes and heart-shaped lips. She passed me the little one to cuddle and then took her back to nurse her discreetly under the shawl so you hardly knew anything was happening. When it was time, she packed up the smaller baskets with her baby onto her back and got up to go.

"Take the basket. I will come to North Vancouver to get it when I come back from Victoria with my clothes," I said, handing her back the beauty I'd selected.

"Just the same, bymeby," she said.

"How can I find you in the village, then?"

"Me Sophie Frank. Everybody know me."

It's hard to fill the hole somebody creates in your life when they go. I have known Sophie longer and closer than anyone besides Alice and Lizzie. She is the only friend I have who has seen me through life, through three decades and more of it, anyway. When I left Vancouver, she wept and told me she loved me like her own sister—

357

more because her sister sometimes forgets her. "You will
not forget," she said. I told her I felt just the same, that
she was to me the sister I longed for. I told her if she ever
wanted me, she should send word and I would come.

We didn't see each other terribly often after I moved
back to Victoria. We neither of us had the money or occasion to make the trip and we both detest sea voyages, but
we never lost touch. Whenever I went to Vancouver, I'd
slip over to see her. And she sent for me once when the
last child died. After that she turned to drink. It was the
grief that did it. How can you love children as much as
Sophie did, lose so many, and not crack open somewhere?
I saw it brutally one day when I arrived to find her sitting
on the floor by the stove, semiconscious and semiclothed.
The place smelt vile with liquor and neglect. She was startled to see me and to have me see her like that, and the
shock of it sobered her, but then shock melted to shame
and released the floodgates. It was devastating to behold,
and I felt all the worse for being the cause of her torment,
so I didn't stay. I made tea and helped her to bed and
vowed never to surprise her again. That was the worst I
ever saw her, though it wasn't the worst she got. The last
few years, she and Frank lived on the reserve and kept to
themselves, drinking to the rhythm of Sophie's deteriorat-
ing health.

*Squamish Mission, March, 1915—My dear Emily, With
great pleasure I write you these few lines in answer to your
letter. I am well and Frank too but he is just as bad in
drinking. I just begin to feel alright and good of heart and
then he drinks and makes me down-hearted again. I
cannot get cheerful for I can't make him good. I am very
tired of selling baskets. I have lots though no one cares
much for them. All say that they have no money I
love the warm weather that is coming. I have not been*

working in my garden for I am in Vancouver every day
selling baskets . . . Your ever loving friend, Sophie Frank

I can't help regretting seeing so little of her in the last few
years. Old age has slowed me down or I'd have gone on
my own. There were several opportunities to visit with an
escort: Edythe and Nan offered on different occasions but
I didn't want to go, not with them. I suppose I feared
we'd find Sophie in a drunken state and they would have
an eyeful to talk about. I suppose I didn't want observers,
or other artists sitting about while I was with Sophie and
her kin. To me the friendship was private. I should laugh
at that, for well I remember the time I asked her to introduce me to Chief Joe Capilano's wife and she refused.
"You are my first," she said fiercely. I was hers, and she
was mine, and that was that.

Sophie and I were always happy when we were together.
There was something very tight between us. We didn't
talk much, but what we said was important, and some of
it beyond words. I painted her portrait and keep it with
me still. Once she presented me with a tiny exquisite
basket. I didn't like accepting it knowing how hard up
she always was. "Someday Sophie die, then I like Emily
have my basket and see me," she insisted. So now I have
it and the memory of her folded together with the little
handful of things I think of as peculiarly mine.

I had trouble finding her house the first time. Everybody I
asked smiled and was helpful, but they all gave different
directions. It was summer and the gardens were full of
vegetables and flowers. Sophie greeted me at the door and
took me inside. I gave her the parcel of old clothes, which
she set aside, leading me by the hand to a single chair by
the window. As I sat, she held onto my hand, turning it

over and examining it, tracing her fingers over the lines as
if reading my palm. I took in the clean, spare house with
its iron bedstead and the piles of newly minted baskets by
the door. The air was warm, scented with fresh baking,
and I was aware of feeling immensely, physically comfortable. Sophie set about making tea and produced the
biscuits I had nosed, and showed me her baskets. Her
small private collective included some of her great-grandmother's. She talked about how you collect and cure the
roots, a laborious process taught to her by her grandmother and an uncle, and how these are combined with
various barks and wood strips to produce serviceable (and
sometimes airtight) shapes and designs. I told her about
my painting and my ambitions for the totem poles.

Later we went to see her graves and stopped in at the
little Roman Catholic church where I obliged her faith by
dipping my fingers in holy water and crossing myself. She
told me she had been distressed to learn I'm not a
Catholic, but that the priest had reassured her whatever
church I attended it was pretty much the same thing. I
could see how bizarre that sounded to her, knowing how
the priests usually say it is a sin to darken the doorstep of
another church. So I quickly and cheerfully agreed. In the
larger scheme of things, the churches *are* all the same.
When I left that time, she told me she thought I had loyal
and capable hands. Hers, I noticed were soft, thin, and
uncommonly warm. I held them together in my own for a
moment, and thanked her for inviting me to tea.

The worst I only heard about. In September 1930, on
my way back from the trip east to Toronto and New York,
I had gone straight over to the North Vancouver to see
Sophie as I usually did. I walked through the village
aware of the usual dilapidation, and arrived at Sophie's to
find the gate nailed up and the house forsaken. My heart
stood still; I thought she might be dead, but the Indian

next door who came to my rap told me she was away with Frank. I went to the church and prayed earnestly for help with my work and for Sophie. Then I went to find Sara. The news was bad. Sara said she had nothing to do with Sophie any more, even though she is her aunt. I wondered how much was true and went next to the priest's house to ask him. I had never talked to him before and found him a dirty little man who ambled downstairs at my knock in his shirtsleeves. He lisps unpleasantly and was all too willing to relay the horrid details. Sophie was a prostitute and drinking hard. She was always in town and was a terrible example to all the young girls. "She hath given hersthelf to the sthreet and become the chattel of the lowest waterfront derelicths," he hissed. Frank would take her to them and wait while she earned, he added; then they would go drinking together.

I was aghast, shocked especially by the last part. It made me feel Sophie lied hideously about herself or she could never have allowed herself to be used that way. Yet, I told myself, she's had so much trouble in her life. Twenty-one children all dead. I couldn't see where I had call to judge.

August 6th, 1915—My dear Emily. I would be only too glad to go if I could go, but I am not feeling well. The waves make me sick. So you must not be sorry about it. I would bring the mat or send it but the lady is not sure to buy it. The Indians are not like white people, The lady is not allowed to go alone anywhere . . . Sara is well and Mary Annie too. She is gone to her home in Sechelt to get dried herring. Granny is well and at Squamish River. I'm still selling baskets for a living. Frank tries to get odd jobs . . . I will close now with my best love, Your dear friend, Sophie Frank

My memory of the years in Vancouver are punctuated by
my visits to Sophie. Whenever life hit me hard I would
take the ferry across the bay and sit a spell with her. There
was calm inside her house even when the children were
ailing, even after they were gone and sadness had settled
in her face like sediment. In those days, there was an open
invitation to tea at my studio on Granville Street, and
every so often Sophie would appear with Susan or another
friend and several children in tow. Sophie had three more
after I met her, and by the end of the decade, they, too,
had perished. I suppose the trouble was tubercular. Like
Sophie, Susan buried child after child until it became a
regular cycle. A new papoose is woven for a new child in
the spring, and before many months pass a small coffin is
ordered and the relatives summoned. All the while, the
flow of new baskets from their hands never stops, and,
whenever they can, they disappear to Vancouver to sell
their wares door to door. During their visits with me I
spent my time trying to lure the kids out of their shyness,
opening the animals' cages, drawing cartoons, and plying
them with sweets. Eventually it worked. At Sophie's they
would loll about the floor as she squatted making baskets.
Perhaps they preferred having adults at their level instead
of sitting high up on chairs.

I loved Sophie's house, too. It was always changing. I
noticed that about Indian houses. They never seemed to
get finished, but they were always being renovated
anyway. Sara hacked off her entire porch once, and when
I came 'round looking for her, I walked up and down the
street several times before recognizing it. When I first
knew Sophie, hers had three rooms; later it became one
when she decided that one room would mean only one
stove, which was better than three. Thereafter Frank
kept moving that old stove around as the single room

reconfigured, poking its chimney out whatever opening was available or carving out a new one in the wall when there was none.

I remember arriving one day in early November when it was a two-roomer. Sophie hugged me close and took me into the tiny front room Frank grandly referred to as Sophie's office. She kept her clothes and special belongings there, her shrine to the virgin on a little table, and photographs of the sons and daughters who made it past infancy set in elaborate velvet frames on the wall. We sat together on cushions. Sophie brought tea and we talked our ritual talk about her babies and my sisters.

"I have something to tell you, Emily," she said after a while. "Yesterday, I met a woman in town who showed me an Indian pot made by Emily Carr. I was so excited. `Emily is my friend,' I told her. I thought the woman would buy a basket if she know that." Sophie sipped some tea and chewed on the cherries I'd brought.

"Go on," I urged her. "Please tell."

"The woman got angry. She stared at me, curled her lips and walked away. That's what happened." She shook her head. "I do not say more." I could tell she was upset. I also knew exactly how the woman had reacted. I felt her scorn ripple through my body and I shivered with angry thoughts. I also knew Sophie well enough to know something else was troubling her.

"What about the pots, Sophie?" I prodded her, curious about her opinion. "You know why I do them. I need money so I sell things just like you do. I've tried selling small fruit, hens, rabbits, dogs, and now I'm trying pottery, which I decorate with Indian designs because tourists will buy them." I stopped and waited for her to say something.

"I hate myself for prostituting Indian art, you know. I

am aware our Indians did not 'pot.' Their designs were
not intended to ornament clay. But I do keep the Indian
design pure. Tell me what you think."

"You know Mary Annie, Emily? The old one who lives
with Ernie and Mae and sang you that song? She is afraid
the White man will disturb the spirit of the clan symbols
and hurt the people."

"She may be right to be," I said, assailed momentarily
with the awful thought Sophie might not understand.
"There is something wrong when people distort and
cheapen things. There's a group of potters in Victoria who
specialize in 'brown' pottery like mine—simple, unglazed
pieces. They copy my stuff because mine sell. They follow
my lead and knowing nothing about Indian art, they
falsify it, which makes me angry. I loath seeing those
designs being thrown around by people who do not
understand or care as long as their pots sell. But you tell
me, Sophie."

"I think of the dream I told you about, Emily, the one
that said the White man will become rich using our
designs. Do you remember we talked about that the night
you stayed here and we described our dreams." She was
looking at me intently as she said this. I couldn't hold her
gaze for thinking about what she said. More and more
artists *are* making use of Indian designs and subjects.
There's the work of this Mildred Thornton, who does
dreadful portraits of the old chiefs in their ceremonial
robes. Her work is stiff and decorative. I don't think she
sells much; certainly civilization wouldn't lose much if all
her paintings sank in a storm. Still, it shows you there's
growing interest; maybe enough to make Indian things
popular some day.

"This is strange, Sophie. I dreamt about you just the
other night. Maybe a couple of weeks ago now. You had
an expensive motor car and were dressed in flowing

chiffon and you were radiant. What I remember, though, was looking up at you and seeing you were unchanged, knowing you were still the same old Sophie."

Sara came just then, and threw her hands up. "Ah! Sophie's Emily's come," she exclaimed with delight and called out to Elizabeth across the way that a tea party was on. I don't know if it was that day or another soon after, but the subject resurfaced. I asked Sophie about my pots again. She answered with another question.

"Well, you say that art should be made for the spirit, not for money, Emily. What if you are hungry?"

"Oh, goodness. I didn't mean you, Sophie." I was overcome with remorse at the thought of her misunderstanding. "I didn't mean me either. I would much prefer not to have to sell my work at all, actually. I hate assigning prices, and I loathe extracting the money from buyers. They so often act as if they are doing you an enormous favour by purchasing your work; it makes me want to give it away." Sophie said nothing and I saw she was deeply perturbed.

"That is not the point, though, is it?"

"My baskets are my art so I am glad when people buy them. I am glad, too, for the money because I always need to buy food for the babies. What would happen if I could not do that? Not everyone can make baskets and I think there are worse things than selling your body."

I gave up making pots soon after that. It was far too laborious a process, stoking up the kiln in the basement and keeping it going all night. The only way to make more money at it was to spend more time sweating it through the night. I don't know if Sophie liked the pottery or not; she never asked to see any.

March 9th, 1929—My dear Emily, I received your letter of the 4th and we was sure glad to hear from you once

*again. Sorry to hear you was sick with the flu. Yes, I am
selling and making baskets for my living. Frank can't
work now. My father is old and his house burned about a
month ago. I feel bad for I can not get to see him up
Squamish Valley. I hope you'll be alright soon. Your
friend, Sophie Frank.*

My friendship with Sophie was based on honesty and
trust. We never had to pretend to each other. Perhaps that
was because we were so different, because so many veils
fell between us. Veils of religion, of civilization and
language. Sophie's English was awkward to my ears at
first, but I quickly learned its idiom and never thought
about it again. We reached around the gaps in vocabulary
just as we reached over customary prejudice. The woman
in us met on common ground, and I could hug her, and

*Photograph of Emily Carr in her studio in 1933, her portrait of Sophie Frank on the
wall behind her.*

hold her, and kiss her affectionately when I said goodbye. She made me feel protective, being so diminutive in size, so weighted with misfortune. Or so I always thought. Yet when I think of her now it is not an image of sadness I recall, but of lightness.

She was wiser than I, and in many things, my teacher. Motherhood, for example. Sophie was the mother of twenty-one and I of none. I have sometimes wondered if elsewhere things will be arranged so we have to go through maternity before we become complete. I only wish that I had felt it in this life, the stupendous wholeness of it. Fatherhood seems such a paltry little thing by comparison. To me, Sophie was all mother and maternal, and I envied her her patience and ingenuity with children, and with her lot in life. Women so often seem to turn into stupid cows when they become mothers, running after their calves, pushing and prodding them instead of gently leading them, and impressing them with maternal care. Sophie was quiet like that. You hardly knew when she was guiding you as she never instructed and rarely answered a question. Mostly she told stories. Stories about her family, the people in her village, and legends from the old days. I called them ghost stories.

One thing we shared was the woods. I loved them and she knew them as if they were an extension of her body. She planted her feet on the ground and when she could, dispensed with shoes so she could feel the earth with her toes. A few times I went with her collecting roots and plants. She always pointed out something that Granny had said was good for this or that. It included the stinging nettle, which, amazing to say, can be eaten as a vegetable and drunk as tea to cure arthritis, and the burdock leaf, which draws off nettle stings when applied directly to the skin. Sophie showed me some of her customs; I didn't have to show her mine as they are all around her, but we talked about it and she asked me questions occasionally, like how White people make love in beds. "Those things move every which way when you are in them. They don't ever stay still and they cause my old bones to ache." When Sophie is sick, she takes to the floor, and Frank often takes the opportunity to haul the bedstead out into the yard and repaint it a brilliant blue or red.

When Sophie and I met I was just beginning to paint the totem poles, and was researching their meaning by reading what ethnologists had written and by talking with Dr. Newcombe, who knew as much as anybody. I wasn't sure how we could really know what the poles had meant to the Indians. I surmised they were religious objects, but not worshiped as idols. Sophie was nearby, so I asked her. This was a revelation. I had thought of them as ancient and half-forgotten, but when Sophie talked about them and the ceremonies, they were as vivid as yesterday.

"Are the carvings spiritual?" I asked. I had brought along some sketches to show her that day, but first she wanted to know what I meant by spiritual, so I told her that to me it means seeing beyond form to the life essence of things, it means being determined to stick to the ideal at all costs, to an ideal undiluted by vagueness or exaggerated emotion. Listening to myself, I was suddenly self-conscious, and stopped talking while I spread my pictures out for her to look at. I settled into my usual chair by the window, and she sat on the floor among my trees, regarding them curiously. She nodded at me to continue. "I think you can see it. I have wanted to capture the spirit of the totems in my paintings."

"Many things have spirit-power, Emily. Places can have it. People. Animals. That's why it is a good thing to ask permission of the tree before you chop it down, or the salmon before you catch him. Maybe the poles have spirit

Photograph of Emily Carr with her animals at the door of the Elephant in 1994.

because they keep the trees alive they were made from, and the artists who carved them, too."

"Is that why people revered them? I think then there was more than symbolism involved. Something akin to magic."

"When carvings talk, they talk through the dancers and storytellers at the ceremonies. That is why it is bad the feasting stopped. It gets harder and harder to hear."

I have sometimes felt closest to Sophie when off in the woods on my own. Out under the trees in the Elephant, just me and the creatures and the elements, I often found myself thinking of her as I went about my routines, fetching water, making fires, cooking. I'd watched her execute the same chores over and over again and learned from her how to fan a fire into flame, chop wood with a small axe, and warm rocks on the wood stove. The caravan arrangement allowed me to live outside most of the time, preparing meals under a canvas flap that extended from the roof on one side and was secured to a couple of posts. I slept in the cosy cabin created inside with Willie Newcombe's help. The upper portion of the other side would rise up on hinges to form an awning open to the sky and the stars. It was heaven living with the Elephant even though it was little more than a lopsided box on wheels. I gave her the name in honour of her grey bulk and lumbering gait, but in camp she transformed, opening up and spreading her sides with the heraldic grace of a cormorant sunning its wings.

Inside everything was very like Sophie's small house on the reserve. Mine was festooned with boxes, bags, and Sophie's baskets, lanterns hanging off nails, and a row of makeshift shelves and dog boxes. When the rains came, I'd retreat inside with dogs, rat, and monkey, let down the awning and hibernate. It was an ideal situation for writing and thinking. In good weather I could paint all day, with pauses for lunch and tea, and produce as many as four sketches. In bad weather, depending on the light and the temperature, I could paint indoors equally well, warming my feet on the biscuit tin containing a brick cooked to a turn on the little gasoline stove I kept going outside. After experimenting with cottages and (once) the houseboat moored above the Gorge, I decided I preferred the rustic existence. The beauty of the Elephant is she gives you an infinite choice of sites and neighbours. If things don't suit, you can leave. And once, when unseasonable rain turned the grassy field I was camping on in Esquimalt Lagoon into bog, I did. If things do go well, you can return to your favourite places. But being a trailer and barely ambulatory, the Elephant required a truck to get anywhere. It was always a production packing up and stowing all the gear inside, with the overflow plus animals plus myself bundled into the cab. Once deposited at a chosen spot, I'd stay until the appointed date when the truck would return. I lived on my own, more or less, sharing my daily tasks with the creatures and occasionally entertaining visitors from Victoria. I shared the creatures' tasks, too, come to think of Maybbe's puppies born in the Elephant one June. That was an experience I lived through with trepidation. The puppies got sick and I had to steel myself to drown two of them in a bucket of water outside in the early dawn. Watching Maybbe with her babies made me wonder how she could put up with the constant pull and tug of their appetite for life. It's as if she stood aside and became a sieve for life to pass through. Her whole being was handed over to those pups who lapped it up voraciously. Mothers are life spreaders, I decided. They take keen joy from this instinct to help things go, to push and grow, an instinct that seems stronger than life itself.

I saw that same quality in Sophie. Now that she is gone, I recall the conversations about the carvings, and appreciate how my understanding has expanded over the years. Now my aim is to capture that being-ness of nature in which everything is in the act of becoming and nothing ever is quite become. That is the secret of the totem figures, I believe. The carvers weren't trying to describe anything, they were reaching out to touch it.

Why is it that I feel things are clearer when I am away from people in the woods? God seems to be there among the silent things more than with his so-called higher species. Man answers back, and is irreverent while dumb nature obeys and quietly follows the seasons. Is nature

then the purer instrument? Whatever the reason, it
explains my affection for the wild. If one's place of
worship is that place which allows you to draw nearest to
the universal spirit, then the forest is that for me. It is my
church, my tabernacle, my refuge. And whatever leads a
person towards grace, be it music or art or gardening or
singing or the stories you heard as a child, whatever
brings you in tune with God and yourself, is religion.
This is something no man can judge for another because it
isn't just a matter of doctrine. Bodies themselves are aware
of being in harmony with their surroundings. They get
cranky and ill when they are not. As Sophie would say,
you have to listen to what the body thinks as well as what
the heart says. And mine thinks difference is deceptive.
My sisters and I are fundamentally different, though we
come from the same stock and were raised by the same
people. We can go only so far into each other because we
don't know one another's song. Sophie and I come from
different worlds and different races but we sing the same
tune. I always marvel at our friendship. I am touched that
she would accept me as she did. Occasionally I have
spoken of Sophie to others, but not often. I wrote to
Lawren Harris about her once, and he replied that it
proves race, colour, class, and caste mean nothing in reality. "Quality of soul alone counts and deep love tran-
scends even quality of soul," he wrote. She and I never
quarrelled and nothing came between us. When she fell
into disgrace, my love for her was not affected; never once
did I feel betrayed by her as I have been by so many
others. Lawren understood how her love for me was real
as mine was for her.

Sophie made me notice things and think twice about
myself. "Why did you paint the carvings?" she asked me
not long ago. I wasn't sure I could tell her. There was that
time a few years ago when I opened the downstairs suite

to the public and put my paintings on display, some
Indian paintings along with new ones. I watched people's
reactions and saw that they talked more and more superfi-
cially about the Indian paintings. They pontificated about
Indian ways and the value of Indian things once the
people and culture have ceased to exist. Around the new
sketches the attitude was quieter and more inquisitive.
They ignored the chairs and benches and stayed on their
feet, moving back and forth, studying the pictures. Value
was not discussed, but something seemed to wake up
inside them which had slept gently through the Indian
exhibit. I can only think what I know. The old Indian
pictures expressed the Indian and there was only an
insignificant splatter of me. They made the cake and I
only had to cut it and hand it around. Any fool can do
that.

Most of all Sophie made me think of friendship, and my
luck in having hers.

Squamish, B.C. December, 1939. My dear friend, I guess
you thought I forgot you but I still think of you so I just
thought I would drop you a line and let you know how I'm
getting along. I am quite well at present and I am still stay-
ing at Squamish as I left North Vancouver after my wife
died. I am keeping away from drink and better off here. I'm
having a hard time but I get along. I cannot forget my wife,
it's pretty hard and sure is lonesome without her. I hope you
are well and please answer. Jimmy Frank.

I don't think it was a man who first noticed women are
fickle. I'll bet money it was a woman. Time and again, I've
seen Man's queer effect on Woman. And I have deduced
that a woman may love another woman, but let a man
come into her life and *phizz*, out goes the other woman.

You are just an incident and the man is all supreme. I
don't think that would ever be the way with me if the
other woman were close. But it is with many, enough to
convince me that women friends are not "stickers."
Maybe married ones who have families in common are.
But then married women always act so superior to spinsters, and you know anything you say to them is passed
on to their men. So it is best to say goodbye forever when
a woman gets a man. As for men, I do not know of one
that I'd trust, and don't imagine I'd feel different even if I
had married one.

I thought Bess was an exception to all that, but men got
the better of her, too. Even before news came about the
divorces, I felt something had gone wrong. She and I had
somehow dropped out of touch and out of sympathy. The
details came in the letter from Lawren telling me that the
Housser marriage had bust up, and that he had decided to
leave Trixie and wanted to be with Bess. He had been
hinting for some while that there were changes coming,
and I knew his life was in turmoil. Certainly his art was.
Bess, on the other hand, confided nothing, and kept her
troubles to herself. So I didn't quite know what to make
of it when word came she was coming west and wanted to
see me. I was looking forward to having her at my house
and letting her see my sketches. I had several things I
wanted to show her, but at the last minute she wired
asking me to meet her in Vancouver instead. I caught the
2:15 boat and worked on my stories the whole way over,
feeling disappointed and put-upon. It didn't help to
discover Bess at the dock waiting to meet me in the
company of a male cousin of Fred's. The man was slender
and smarmy. She was all in grey and seemed very pleased
with herself, eyeing the cousin while chattering away to
me and steering the three of us off to a downtown hotel.
There she proceeded to send wires off to half the country

while I waited and wilted, cursing my sore feet and the July heat wave. The cousin scuttled off somewhere, leaving me to smoulder. When Bess finally finished, I did not hold much back. Why, when she knew our time together was so short, had she not done all this business beforehand? Well, she snapped back, would I rather not hear the truth about things?

We took a cab to the Stanley Park Pavillion in polite silence, and sat on a glorious veranda under the great trees until we eased up enough to talk. She told me the long story and it was sad to hear how lives were being messed up by it all. Still, I think they ought to have done it sooner because they were living terribly falsely. I didn't feel hurt by Lawren as much because he'd been as frank as he could with me, but Bess and Fred made me feel I couldn't ever trust them again, and I figured the special friendship I had with her was gone.

I tried to be absolutely honest with her, and I don't suppose she liked it. I began by saying that for many months I'd felt she had no interest or part in my life, nor had she let me into hers. I watched her eyes go cold and sparkey like Woo's when she's angry. The voice thinned out and turned brittle. She cleared her throat several times and talked vaguely about her beliefs (always sincere) and desires (always selfless).

"Why did you ask Lawren in that letter if I was sincere, Emily?" I had to think for a moment. I had been watching her more closely than listening to what she was saying.

"I suppose it's because underneath I felt you have been living one life and acting another, Bess. Forgive me for saying it so bluntly."

"Well, there were people I was protecting. And I made a pact with myself a long time ago, never to say anything to anyone I wouldn't say to Fred about our marriage and my feelings towards him—and I didn't, not even for the

longest time to Lawren. Misplaced loyalty in the circumstances, you might think."

They hadn't cheated on anyone and hadn't lied, she
maintained. "Fred slowly came to resent our friendship. It
took him years, but finally he issued an ultimatum and
when I refused, he left. And that pushed over the house
of cards. The irony is that the gossip—and there is plenty
of that in Toronto—has Lawren and me leaving our
spouses for each other, shucking respectability for the
rough and tumble of *la vie bohème*. Imagine, the idiots!

"The truth is we never committed adultery and we
aren't sure we want to be married. I'll admit we are
intensely close and we love each other, but not as man
and wife. This is love, not lust."

"What will it do for Lawren's work," I asked. "Will he
go back to it? Will the life come back into his paintings?"
I had to tell her I feel his work has grown dead and inert.
"The images are still beautiful, filled with colour and
light, but they don't live," I said. Bess wasn't pleased to
hear that, but didn't refute any of it. She was convinced
that everything would be blissful, that Theosophy had
been their salvation, that there was truth in purity and so
forth. She prattled on about non-sex and the higher love
until I felt quite sick.

Tea done, we made our way back to the hotel where we
said a rather stiff goodbye. I wished her well (for I do).
She said she'd write and I fled to the boat, feeling
wrought up and exhausted from the emotional effort.
Why can't people be decent? Why this business of
tumbling in and out of marriage? I'm not for squabbling
couples. If there's a reason to, I say, divorce. Drinking,
women, cruelty, or beastliness I would not stand, but just
to flop out of one pair of arms into another without even a
good fight to warrant it like Bess and Fred disgusts me.
Our paths have definitely diverged. We are apart on the

two great subjects, religion and art, and the truth is, she doesn't care.

I continue to, though. I have dreams. Sometimes happy ones with Lawren and Bess together and married and nothing changed between us. Bess chatting and Lawren saying nothing as is always the way. He never speaks in my dreams. This time, though, he put his two hands on my shoulders and smiled. Poor Lawren, I love his work and his soul, but his body . . . I don't know how to put it; it shivered and I was repelled.

I realized something the night I spent at Sophie's talking about dreams as we waited for the winter storm to ease, and that is that I dream more than most people do. Not everyone likes dreaming, and some would rather avoid it altogether. I love it. Things happen to me in those other-conscious places, which I sometimes reach in wakeful states. So I welcome sleep each night, curious about what it will toss up.

Dreams don't frighten me, but they do grip my emotions. Sometimes I wake anxious and spent, other times I float into consciousness, filled with sweet-smelling joy, like the languid vision I had not long ago of being young, in tune with a sleek and beautiful body, and in possession of an equally marvellous singing voice. It was heavenly.

And sometimes dreams make demands. They speak to me and often make me think of Sophie's stories about the ancestors. They can hurt, and they can bring you down hard, as one about Bess did. I had gone to the station to meet her and she had brushed me aside, flashing off and up a set of stairs to meet someone else. I followed her to a hotel and once there wandered around aimlessly. Eventually, I spied her on a balcony off a room in which I could see a wicker chair with Lawren's coat slung over the back. She had Tantrum there with her and as I watched, she began grooming him. I was dumbfounded, for she knew how much I'd want to see and touch that little dog. She had not even mentioned him, and Lawren had not come to speak to me either. I turned away sore, and woke up in a lather, tears wet on my face.

Friendship—what does it mean? none of us know another, not truly. It sickens me sometimes, those close hugs and those kisses and confidences, which don't mean a thing except for a heartbeat or two. The connection was never fast grown. It broke so easily.

"Wording the Picture"

Friendships did not come easily to Emily Carr. Her journals, particularly the unpublished sections, record the misery they provoked, the self-reproach, the disaffection, the acid tongue. Individuals come and go in those pages, their character and exploits are often commented on, celebrated, and castigated with equal vigour, for Carr is not without generosity or joy in her recitations. However, her preoccupations put her on the defensive with many people, especially her own kin and kind, even while she remained unusually open to others. This aspect of her temperament, the identification with outsiders and marginals, is a side of Carr the public knows well; the prickly egoist who fought with her tenants, took no guff from curators, and yearned to have been born Indian. She once exclaimed in her journal that she could count among her friends a lunatic, a prostitute, and a Chinese artist. She was referring to a Harold Cook, a young man from Kispiox whom she visited in the provincial mental home on the outskirts of Victoria, to Sophie Frank, and to Lee Nam, a painter whose work she admired and supported. All three pop up repeatedly in her journals, and all three have been described as people Carr could lavish attention on without fear of judgement or repost. These were safe, one-sided relationships that have been pathologized by Blanchard and Tippett, among others, as manifestations of Carr's need to dominate. Less well known is the side of her that formed attachments to strong people who would be considered her peers. Although she is often depicted as inept in this department, unable to put aside her need for centre stage and to calibrate her moodiness, she did forge several significant friendships during the 1927–41 period, which her journals span. Her association with Lawren Harris is routinely mentioned, as is her friendship with Ira Dilworth. Both men were influential in the mainstream world and took an active interest in her work and her career. The others, most of them women, are given short shrift in the Carr literature and have evidently been dismissed as influences in her life. Carr herself was effusive about the men in public and some of her younger friends were put out by the preference (and deference) she showed them. However, she had little to say about these others in her journals. The fact remains that the two people besides her sisters who troubled her most as she wrote, who haunted her conscience and visited her in dreams, were neither Harris nor Dilworth but Bess Housser and Sophie Frank.

Bess was a friend from the East, a devotee of Theosophy and part of the Toronto cabal that emerged around the Group of Seven in the 1920s. Her husband, Fred Housser, made his name in the art world with his book on the Group of Seven, *A Canadian Art Movement*. As a couple, the Houssers had befriended Carr. They talked quite openly to her about their beliefs and counselled her endlessly. Bess was the one who usually wrote, addressing Emily in her letters as "Dear Mom," relaying news and carrying on a conversation about spiritual matters. Carr wrote back and eventually in the winter of 1934 sent them some of her literary sketches, inviting their critiques. The first batch elicited an honest response from Fred, who thought the material was good, but the approach and construction poor. Bess gave them a passing mention and hived off into theosophical topics. Emily was dejected and pleased at once. Fred's exposition was not very illuminating—"He says there's too much *me*, too much *originality*—I suppose he means *striving for effect*"—but it was serious and he was a writer. A few weeks later she sent "Cow Yard," an early attempt to write about her childhood and the piece in which her alter ego, Small, makes her debut. She then waited anxiously for an answer. What came back some long time later was "meagre and foolish" so far as Carr was concerned. The story was very good, according to Fred, but the grammar and spelling were awful. No comment from Bess. This time Emily was miffed, reading their offhandedness as a sign of waning interest in her, something she had predicted might happen when she abandoned Theosophy a few months earlier. She wasn't much mollified by the news that Fred and Bess had separated, although it ostensibly explained their distraction.

Carr's relationship with Toronto and Theosophy seemed to focus on Bess and, if her journals are to be believed, she was deeply troubled by the break with her. Very little is said about Lawren Harris by comparison; Carr evidently separated the two in her mind, although history is no longer able to. The rupture she decried did not seem to implicate him. Nonetheless, the usual interpretation of the falling out between Carr and Bess chalks it up to conventional jealousy aggravated by Carr's introverted sexuality. The first Mrs. Harris was no competition for attention, certainly not on aesthetic matters; Bess was. She was part of Lawren's artistic life and Carr felt upstaged by the rearrangement, yet was unable to admit to herself what she was feeling. The hostility Emily directed at Bess could have derived from sexual rivalry, a case of misplaced anger as, in this senario, the real object of her affection was the person guilty of jilting her—or, at least, the romantic image she had of their relationship. This interpretation suggests that Carr balked at the idea of sharing Lawren with the second Mrs. Harris, but in actuality she already was sharing him with her. While this doesn't rule out shock and annoyance at the new arrangement, it does imply that there was more to Carr's continuing resentment of Bess than meets the eye and has been written about. It is possible to write another scenario; one for instance, that credits the attachment to Bess as something genuine and inspired by Bess herself. For one thing, the relationship allowed for a personal frankness, which the friendship with Lawren did not, perhaps for no other reason than the natural barriers of wealth, gender, and social position. With Harris and Dilworth, as Blanchard writes, Carr came closest to recreating the early relationship she had with her father. In correspondence with both of them she adopted a childlike persona—Dilworth called her "Small," and Harris wrote to her as "T'Other Emily." Although fourteen years younger than Carr, Harris played mentor to her. Though class and gender would have been factors in the authority he assumed—and she accorded him—the transaction mainly had to do with his professional experience and the confidence that he lent to her. Dilworth was twenty-three years her junior and the regional director of the CBC in British Columbia at the time he met her in the winter of 1939. He quickly became her editor and *de facto* literary agent. There was a similar protective note in his relationship with Carr. For her part, Bess treated Carr like an ageing parent, deferring to her and stroking her ego. Emily must have seen her as an ally, someone like Mrs. Gibb in Paris, who had explained things for her when she arrived on the continent, ignorant and uninitiated in the ways of the art world. Bess was a guide, an insider in the men's club, and her sympathy was elemental. She touched an emotional chord somewhere in Emily. The dreams and the angst are the evidence.

Meanwhile, Harris was exceptionally unavailable, a heterosexual in the process of forming a celibate marriage. Emily confessed that she was physically repelled by him, so obviously the sexual infatuation was operating on an unconscious level, if at all. Saying that does not rule out the possibility of an unconscious emotional dimension in Carr's relationships. However, there is no reason to assume this didn't also occur in relation to women as well as men, for Carr did have strong female attachments. There was a lesbian side to her nature that she expressed in her identification with female values, "womanliness," as she called it, and in her preference for female company. Jealousy can be just as easily hypothesized in connection with Bess as with Lawren, though the nature of the underlying friendship was different. Bess was not a mentor, nor a professional associate; she was someone Carr thought of as a soul sister more than a teacher. Emily's rant about Bess was not unlike her remonstrations over her sisters, a seesaw of love and rancour, petty and principled by turns. With Bess, too, she sensed she was not being seen, that she was being handled. The rupture was never repaired, only papered over, which is another indication that the passion ran deep despite the platonic gloss. Almost the same thing might be said of Harris who she cared for deeply and called a friend. And indeed, accepting Carr's sexuality as unpractised (and probably never consummated), she might be labelled bisexual, or for that matter polysexual, considering that the forest, her green lover, lived with equal vibrancy in her mind. Carr had different expectations of Bess because she was a woman, because she had offered spiritual support, and because their friendship was built on confidences rather than aesthetics. However, Bess's way of addressing Emily in their correspondence put a distance between them, a formality that precluded the intimacy Emily was looking for. Bess could well have been sending signals Emily refused to read, indicating she did not imagine a peer relationship the same way, but a mother-daughter friendship. The betrayal Emily felt was in the discovery that they were not on the same wavelength at all, that Bess did not recipro-cate her feelings or think of her as a personal friend. In retaliation she rejected Bess, some would say cruelly, others would say with a vehemence that matched the hurt. The story buried in the journals may only be half of it, of course, but, at the very least, it does indi-cate that Carr's jealousy didn't involve only Lawren.

The relationship with Bess and Lawren Harris continued, now reconfigured as a threesome, with Bess writing for the two Harrises. Carr occasionally mentioned Bess in her journals after 1934, typically taking the opportunity to remark on her superfi-ciality. "October, 1940: I did write Bess I'd had a stroke. She wrote back a long dissertation on her magnificent petunias. Everyone on earth is self absorbed these days." And when both Harrises came to visit her after settling in Vancouver, she was unimpressed. Bess had not done Lawren much good, she observed. "His second marriage has seemed to me to weaken him. He refers to Bess's crits all the time and I have never felt them much worth while. She uses theosophical jargon."

Carr, as we know and as she repeatedly stated in her journals, was not enamoured of marriage. In her somewhat jaundiced view, the wifely role was usually a constraining one. "It is the lifelong building up and tying down to another's will, not being free that bothered me," she said when thinking about her own reasons for rejecting it. Though she had seen evidence of real affection between spouses, married life in her estimation was far from blissful. "They say cruel things to each other, then they are sorry. When away from the other they are very loyal and tender; when together they twang each other's nerves to breaking. Familiarity breeds contempt, all right." She suspected that marriage functions mostly, and perhaps at best, as a convenience. "Looking at marrieds I often wonder how much is love and how much the ordinary needs of life, like when one is in danger of losing [one's] job and being afraid of being without it." Save for her childhood years when she lived with her parents and experienced their dour union, Carr lived her life outside the realm of familied couples. She keenly observed them as a landlady, a neighbour, and occasionally as a visitor, and on the whole she viewed the institution as seriously flawed, one that operated like an exclusive social club. Spinsters like herself were admitted on sufferance and treated as extras. If she didn't resent the contempt, she at least called it. Naturally enough, many of her friends were single, and most of them were women. With the resurgence of her career in the 1930s, a raft of new acquaintances appeared in her life—professional people and intellectuals, as well as art lovers. She was increasingly in demand and when she suffered a stroke in 1937, a circle of admirers and supporters from all over Canada rallied with cheques and purchases to help her over her difficulties. Besides these professional connections, though, Carr had a string of staunch women friends in Victoria. Through the 1920s and 1930s there was Margaret Clay, a librarian at the Victoria Public Library; Ruth Humphrey, an English professor at Victoria College; Flora Hamilton Burns, the daughter of one of Carr's earliest supporters who inherited the friendship with Emily from her mother; and Kate Mather, who met Carr when she rented a flat in Hill House. All of them were allies in Carr's various schemes to earn a living to support herself and her painting. Kate Mather was a buyer for the CPR gift shops and purchased Carr's pottery in quantity. She didn't stay long in Victoria, but she remained in touch and Emily visited her in Toronto in 1927. The other three took particular interest in Carr's early efforts at writing, Flora Hamilton Burns' having agreed to enrol with her in a correspondence course on short-story writing in 1926. Emily called them her "Listening Ladies," and the epithet stuck, though the fact is that Flora (and later Ruth) worked endlessly on the stories, editing and typing manuscripts, and encouraging Carr's tentative attempts. They were the ones who first tried to interest publishers in her work.

In the 1930s a crew of much younger women artists began appearing in Carr's life, notably Nan Cheney and Edythe Hembroff-Schleicher. When she met Carr, Cheney was a medical artist living in Ottawa. Later she relocated to Vancouver with her husband when he took an appointment at the Vancouver General Hospital. Hembroff-Schleicher lived in Victoria with her new husband, after having spent some years studying art in San Francisco and Paris. Carr, who read about her in the newspaper, was struck by the similarity in their backgrounds and contacted her. She found Hembroff-Schleicher amenable and a congenial sketching companion to boot. No doubt she appreciated Edythe's energy, and Edythe responded to Carr's mothering nature. In due course the roles reversed, and Hembroff-Schleicher began keeping an eye out for the elder Emily. Cheney did the same thing, assuming the role of Carr's chief promoter in Vancouver and arranging the all-important first solo exhibition at the Vancouver Art Gallery in 1938, as well as facilitating other shows and sales. Like Hembroff-Schleicher, Cheney saw herself as a cohort of Carr, not as a protegé. She painted Emily's portrait and then campaigned to have it hung with Carr's Toronto exhibition in 1943, for example, until Carr finally put her foot down. Portraiture was Cheney's *métier*, but this painting, realistically rendered, was a flaccid example that robbed Carr of her brusque physicality while subtly and strangely prettifying her. Cheney worked from a set of photographs of Carr similar to the photograph taken by Harold Mortimer-Lamb in 1936 which has been frequently published. It shows Carr sitting in her studio in a smock and cloth cap, her strong arms folded in front of her, looking squarely into the camera. Behind her *Sunshine and Tumult* swirls, some out-of-focus arts supplies lie on a table in the foreground, and in the middle sits Carr, her outline (shoulders and head) strangely imitating the thick fir tree in the painting. Dark eyebrows wing over steady eyes, hair wisps over her ears, framing a handsome face that grabs and holds the viewer's stare in hers. Unvarnished and butch. Cheney recoiled from the woman Carr actually was.

Both Edythe and Nan took on Emily Carr as a project, much as Bess Harris had done. They were sympathetic fellow artists, but their behind-the-scenes machinations (interceding with National Gallery officials, for example) seems to define them more as facilitators than friends. Both were busy pursuing artistic careers, and saw the Carr association as helpful, but they did not regard her as a mentor. One of the leitmotifs of the surviving Cheney-Carr correspondence is Emily's gentle attempt to support Nan's struggles as an artist. In her letters to others (but not to Emily), Cheney fretted about the burdens of housewifery, which interfered with her efforts to paint. In 1940, she suffered a nervous breakdown, and Carr, who knew something about depression, wrote offering encouragement: don't fight the healing process or begrudge it time. Drawing on her own experience with long illness and unwelcome confinement, she offered sage advice. Neither woman would have characterized the gesture as sharing wisdom, or seen it as an older artist helping a younger one cope with the doubts of being an artist, woman, and wife, and the dilemma of how to order those roles. Cheney may not even have wanted Carr's understanding, and it may never have crossed her mind that Emily, ageing spinster that she was, could tell her anything she needed to know. Rather it was for her, the big city artist, the married woman, to school and protect the old lady.

Cheney's troubles did not bring the two together as artists or as women. In fact, they hardly engaged on artistic matters at all. That was a pattern with Hembroff-Schleicher, too. Both were willing to take it upon themselves to explain Carr and even represent her to others, yet they had very different attitudes to the art world than she did. To them, Carr's remonstrance against National Gallery officials seemed rude and untoward. They saw themselves as more knowledgeable than Carr when it came to art matters, though their approach assumed none of her agency or independence. From a distance, moreover, their attitude seems sycophantic. By their account, Emily was headstrong and self-absorbed, and as such, she was not someone either of them took sustenance from or saw as an inspiration; rather there was an unspoken rivalry between them. They were the first of Carr's acquaintances to accuse her of making up her own story and trading on it. Hembroff-Schleicher had a lot to say on this score later when the public's fascination with Carr produced the first wave of histories and documentaries in the 1960s. She began writing articles correcting the misconceptions and falsehoods (as she saw them) sprouting all over the Emily Carr myth. She was the first Carr expert recognized by the provincial government before art historians, biographers, and curators took over the field. Her work culminated in 1978 with *Emily Carr: The Untold Story*, an apologia that took them all on—the academics, the critics, and curators—in detail and at length. Edythe's portrayal of Emily is large and forceful like the portrait she painted of Carr in which Emily fills the frame with a strong and calculating presence, not unlike the Mortimer-Lamb photograph. Edythe did not bevel the edges or shrink from the nasty side of Emily's character in her book or the painting. And she was no shrinking violet herself when it came to taking hold of the Carr legacy.

Nan Cheney, though not as determined a keeper of the flame as Edythe, also tended to be critical of Emily. In letters to others (notably fellow artist Humphrey Toms) she complained about Emily's manipulative behaviour, passing on gossip to the effect that Emily had "thrown a heart-attack" at a dinner party to get attention. "She doesn't like her friends to be ill when she is," was Nan's take on Emily's egocentricity. The leitmotif here may be Carr's unconscious rebellion, her refusal to take on the maternal role being assigned her, and her inchoate sense that she was being trivialized.

Carr's other contemporaries left traces of their opinion in memoirs, correspondence, and interviews, too. These women emerge as much more confident and dynamic than Cheney or Hembroff-Schleicher, and certainly more than willing to take on Carr's irascibility. To someone like Margaret Clay, Carr's habit of plain speaking was a gift, an honesty of opinion that she saw reflected in Carr's painting. The picture of Carr that Ruth Humphrey and Flora Hamilton Burns paint is of a talkative and entertaining person, an earthy, genuine friend. The competition and envy that laces the letters and texts of Hembroff-Schleicher and Cheney is absent, and even if their solidarity and affection for Emily marks them as partisan in the eyes of historians, their loyalty was affective. Particularly poignant is Carr's correspondence with Ruth Humphrey during the year Humphrey spent travelling around the world. All the same, Carr was a demanding friend, short-tempered and quixotic—and they understood this as a function of being self-absorbed and single-tracked. The point is, they did understand it. She was no victim or charity case to them.

Oddly absent from the contemporary accounts is much mention of Sophie Frank. Carr wrote about Sophie more extensively and publicly than about any of her other friends in *Klee Wyck* and *Growing Pains* and in the journals (both published and unpublished versions), yet no one else seemed to know much about Sophie in real life. Emily repeatedly expressed boundless affection for her. Almost as often she declared a sense of privilege in being accepted and, reading over her shoulder, you can feel the pleasure she derived from Sophie's caring.

> *December, 1927: Sophie was terribly glad to see me. She'd*
> *fretted. . . . there'd been a train wreck and she thought I*
> *might be hurt and couldn't sleep. Her love for me is real and*
> *mine for her. Somewhere we meet. Where? Out in the*
> *spaces? There is a bond between us where colour, creed,*
> *environment don't count.*

Carr's friends knew about Sophie and of Carr's fondness for her, but few of them ever met her. It appears Emily did not speak of her in any detail to them; she kept Sophie in a separate compartment of her life. Lawren Harris and Ira Dilworth were the exceptions; when she wrote to them about Sophie, she spoke as if confiding something deeply personal. They confirmed the unusualness of the connection, thereby reinforcing Carr's belief in the specialness of the relationship. She held Sophie to her like a talisman, she prided herself that Sophie saw something in her others did not. Theirs was a thirty-year friendship, anchored deep in the past and the present, and it outlived all of Emily's friendships with other women. Sophie was unique, but Emily didn't talk about it when Edythe Hembroff-Schleicher tried asking about the strange affinity between them. "She is good. I love her," was the terse reply, which struck Edythe as being "as artless as the friendship itself." In Edythe's experience, relationships with Carr always erupted in fireworks. What saved this one, she concluded, was the fact of Sophie and Emily's inequality. "Perhaps it was a relief to have an uncomplicated person like Sophie for a friend, with whom she could not quarrel. Sophie asked nothing in return for her affection. She was a model of submission—as a wife, as a friend, as an Indian." This was the only explanation Hembroff-Scheleicher could credit. How else was

Emily, with her conservative Protestant background, able to develop deep spiritual ties with "a semi-literate, primitive woman whose only interest in life aside from her Catholic church seemed to be her twenty-one dead children and their equal number of tombstones." According to Hembroff-Schleicher, Sophie wove beautiful baskets and there her talents stopped.

Carr wrote about Sophie, yet she told us almost nothing about the real person—where she was raised, who her mother and her siblings were, and how well known she was as a basket-maker. Carr did not seem to have regarded Sophie's work as anything more significant or important than her own backyard craft-making, and significantly (although true to the prejudices of the time) she did not present her as an artist. Her representation of the interactions between the two of them are stylized and two-dimensional: Sophie disappears behind a haze of platitudes and invented jargon, jargon that gets so mannered that Emily herself ends up speaking fractured Chinook to Sophie's English in an early version of "Sophie." Carr's Sophie is quiet, unassuming, and unschooled, and thus conformed nicely to contemporary White prejudices about Native women. Some might argue that Carr had her bigoted audience in mind and was merely inventing a Sophie she thought would be more palatable to the public—more "Indian," in any case—but the fiction was accepted as truth. The assumptions about Sophie were passed on to friends and reiterated by biographers, and the story of Sophie's "funny" English led many to assume the friendship with Emily was romantic projection, more symbol and surface than real exchange. As a result, Sophie has not been considered a significant figure in Carr's life except, latterly, by other artists who, like Jovette Marchessault in her play, *The Magnificent Voyage of Emily Carr*, have seen her as a mythic figure. The biographers have tended to agree with Hembroff-Schleicher, who saw Sophie as a submissive creature, easily dominated by Emily. They understand the friendship primarily as an expression of Carr's stunted personality, a case of her childish self seeking a motherly other and another manifestation of her manipulative nature. Marchessault, who is herself a visual artist and Métis, has imagined Sophie differently. She sees her as Emily's companion, a wise woman who could see the invisible world around them, who gave Emily lessons about life and was her one great soul friend.

Carr never divulged what inspired her love for Sophie, much less the content of their conversations. In her hands, Sophie is an enigma dressed as a stereotype. The jolt comes when reading Sophie's letters and realizing the degree to which her voice has been muted, her presence disguised. Hembroff-Schleicher may be right in saying that Emily deliberately "downgraded her friend to make a better story." According to Ruth Humphrey, Carr's critical estimate of her own writing was that "her places [were] more successful than her people, and [she] felt definitely unhappy over the pidgin English which her Indians were made to speak." Beneath the illiterate exterior and the tale of personal woe was Sophie, a woman of skill and strength who gave Emily many things besides a silent shoulder to cry on. On the face of it, and assuming a modicum of intimacy between them, it would have been odd had Emily not talked to Sophie about Native art, had she not thought to ask her about its connection to spirituality. Who else did she have access to with direct knowledge of Aboriginal ways? For Sophie, the association with Emily, a White woman, carried a certain prestige in her community and brought with it resources she would not normally have had access to. She was being more than trusting when she left the basket with Carr on their first meeting, she was being canny. Perhaps she simply figured Emily was good for more than warm clothes, and that this arrangement would bring her to the reserve. Having seen her at work in her studio, Sophie also knew Carr was not one of those squeamish Whites who would recoil at the sights and sounds of an Indian village. On the contrary, Emily was eager and curious. Sophie may have been chary about introducing her around, but that reticence did not extend to her own family whom Emily came to know quite well over the years—Aunt Sara Denny, for example, and Frank, Sophie's husband, whom everyone seems to have called by his English surname, ignoring his first name, Jimmy. Letters from Sophie to Emily indicate that she talked with Emily about her relatives and about her travails with Frank. Possibly she spoke about her childhood in Squamish River where her mother's people were and her father was living out his days; probably Emily talked about her family, too.

A few months after Sophie's death, a letter from Jimmy Frank reached Emily. One wonders what Emily thought of the news that he'd left North Vancouver and was staying off the bottle, and whether she blamed him for not taking such steps earlier and for not helping Sophie avoid her early death. There is nothing Carr left in her writings to tell us what she thought of Frank, or what sort of man he was. From Sophie we know he had trouble finding jobs and making money. With contemporary eyes we wonder why Sophie would fall silent when he was around, as Emily reported, and whether it was only because her English was poor compared to his. By 1915 he was drinking badly, and though it would be a while before Sophie joined him, the vicious cycle that would consume them both had begun. In 1930, the year Emily discovered Sophie had taken to prostitution, Sophie would have been in her forties. Emily must have recognized it as desperate behaviour even as she was appalled by the notion. Likely as not, the subject was never raised between them, Emily out of *politesse* mixed with embarrassment and Sophie out of self-esteem. If it was spoken of, Sophie might have challenged Emily's assumption that it was an immoral choice, or a "choice" at all when baskets don't sell and your husband can't find work.

Jimmy Frank, among other things, was a carpenter. Carr described a little boat he built, which she saw at Brackendale in 1933 when she was visiting her niece Lillian Rae who lived with her husband and small children on a farm nearby. There were several old communities still in existence at the confluence of the salmon-rich Cheakamus and Squamish rivers, attached to the larger Native community a few kilometres away in the town of Squamish. This was the territory of the Squamish people, which stretched back from Burrard Inlet up Howe Sound and the Squamish Valley into the mountains: Garibaldi, Whistler, and Blackcomb. It is terrain where eagles nest and the mountains reach down and kiss the ocean. This was Sophie's home, the landscape she knew by sound and touch as well as by sight. Here she had been raised in the old ways, despite the onslaught of the Oblates, the early Catholic missionaries, and the slow seep of English and alcohol into Native communities. Emily had not realized how close Lillian lived to Sophie's ancestral home and was delighted for the chance to show off her favourite niece and her favourite special friend to each other. Sophie and Frank had duly been invited to lunch at the Raes, and they arrived along with Sophie's sister and her little girl, turning it into a wonderful family occasion. There was much talk of Frank's boat with the result that Larson Rae went to see it, bought it on the spot, and brought it back up river from Squamish where everyone tried it out and Emily christened her the *Waterlily*. This was a memorable day for Emily, one that demonstrated Sophie was in recovery and tweaked her fantasy about friends and her family coming together. Perhaps that is why Frank's effort to keep in touch with Emily after Sophie's death is so moving; it shows a desire not only to keep up the connection but to honour the bond that lay between the two women. *The Woman in us meets on common ground and we love each other. By and by, out in the spaces, Who knows? What will be.*

To characterize the Carr-Frank friendship as one-dimensional and one-sided, as many historians do, seems gratuitous. Admittedly, Carr's rendition of the relationship strives for superficiality, too, but she leaves lots of evidence to the contrary. Obviously Sophie had a use for a White patron (and friend) like Emily Carr, and equally obviously Emily had a desire, a need even, for an Indian friend (and patron) like Sophie. It validated her endeavour and fit the narrative she had constructed about her life as Klee Wyck and a painter of Aboriginal themes. They were useful to each other. To Emily, though, Sophie was more than myth-dressing. She was a source of personal support, possibly insight, and, it is true, someone who also offered unsullied affection. Further-more, Carr was deeply gratified by the experience of loving across the chasm of difference. She may not have expressed it well, but she felt changed by Sophie's love, and this (or the idea of it) became an emotional touchstone for her.

The elliptical story of their devotion leaves burning questions: What would Sophie have said of her friendship with Emily? And, why did Carr not tell us more about her? Why did she disguise her? Edythe Hembroff-Schleicher contends that Carr was never a real friend to Sophie because she did not—could not—regard her as an equal. The barrier wasn't language, in her estimation, it was class and race. Without doubt these barriers were there. Sophie would have recognized them and viewed Emily through them. Whatever she may have felt for her White friend, she would have understood what Emily was doing in helping herself to Native art as, indeed, Emily did. A literary analysis of "Sophie" in *Klee Wyck* reveals that if Emily reduced Sophie's character to a childish simplicity, she did roughly the same thing to herself. She infantilized the persona she adopted, (mis)representing her age (fifteen when she visited Ucluelet rather than the twenty-seven she actually was, for exam-ple) and rendered herself the feckless innocent. She used this liter-ary device as a mask and as a way of suspending the hard-nosed present in favour of a vague, elegiac past in which she need take no responsibility. She and Sophie drank tea in a never-never land of possibility. Behind the simple style, the pared-down syntax, and plain words of *Klee Wyck* lies another story, and a relationship Emily did not want to share with the world, or even with her good friends, so she fictionalized things. She gave Sophie the part of long-suffering victim, emblem of the collision between the old and the new, between White and Native ways—just like Kamalmuk in Marius Barbeau's story of Kitwancool Jim—and for herself like Barbeau, she chose the part of interlocutor. In Emily's story, Sophie embodies the tension between the races: history is written on her body and buried in tiny pieces in the earth. It echoes in Emily's words in her "Lecture on Totems" and in the article she wrote in

1930 called "Fresh Seeing," where she assumed the part of someone who made contact with Native culture and with the poles she pictured, the raw experience of which gave her authority to speak for the people and explain the art they produced. In that same vein, her literary effort owes its initial fame to the Native subject matter and the appeal of the "primitive" to British and Canadian readers. In Sophie's story, Carr was a White woman who built her reputation on Native culture and used it as a central feature in her painting. She used Sophie too, appropriating her person, and in fictionalizing her character, she hides her from the record. This is not how Carr would have perceived it, obviously, but it is, in fact, what she did.

Emily Carr was very probably sick in hospital at the time she heard of Sophie's death. A mild stroke set her on her back for several weeks in March and April 1939. It was not as grievous as the heart attack she'd had two years previously, but ill health was beginning to dog her. There was less and less time for journal writing. A whole year had passed and she hadn't written a single entry; there was nothing about Sophie's passing. Not too long afterward, however, Emily began drafting sections of her story about Sophie. When *Klee Wyck* eventually appeared, it was dedicated to her and the treasured 1914 portrait reproduced as a frontispiece. Carr had considered dedicating her first book to Eric Brown and had written his widow about it, but this may have been before she knew the travel stories were to be published first. It is significant that the publisher and Dilworth selected these stories as the ones most likely to find an audience, and it is equally significant that Carr chose to introduce herself to the reading public using Sophie as a symbol. Her second book, *The Book of Small*, published in 1942, was dedicated to Ira Dilworth, who in the meantime had become a close friend and adviser. Happenstance produced Dilworth in the winter of 1939, the result of Ruth Humphrey's refusal to give up on the book project. Macmillan and

Ryerson Press in Toronto had both turned down the manuscript, and Ryerson had managed to mislay it during a move. There was no reason to anticipate that interest would materialize anywhere else without some pull. Humphrey's and Margaret Clay's opinion obviously cut no ice with eastern publishers, but they thought Dilworth's might, so Humphrey approached him. It was not unlike Anita Pollitzer's visit to Alfred Stieglitz in 1916 and it had a similar outcome. Carr's work was brought to the public and she became famous.

Ira Dilworth's immediate response to Ruth Humphrey's approach was to put two of Carr's stories on air as part of a radio series he'd pioneered on the CBC called "Spoken Word." He agreed to work on the manuscript, and within the year he had a collection ready. Then he took it off to Toronto where he called on Oxford University Press and talked its editor, William Clarke, into publishing it. Once convinced, Clarke became an ardent fan. Furthermore, despite the war, the book was a huge success when it came out in 1941 in England and Canada. Dilworth, who had been an English professor at UBC when he was recruited to run the CBC, did more than find a home for Carr's stories. He edited the material for publication, a task that aroused suggestions at one time that he did more than clean up her prose. Ira Dilworth was very quickly absorbed into Emily's life as a trusted friend and literary collaborator. He replaced Nan Cheney as her main promoter in Vancouver, and displaced other artist friends like Edythe Hembroff-Schleicher, partly because his arrival coincided with the advance of ill health which impeded Carr's painting, pushed her towards writing. He soon assumed the role of confident as well as adviser. The relationship was sustained by letters, which was the key to its candour and ardour. "The absence of the flesh in writing brings souls nearer," Carr once noted in her journal, and certainly that was true of Ira and herself. She wrote to "Eye" at a furious rate that he was, of course, incapable of reciprocating. At the beginning this elicited a reprimand from her, swiftly followed by an apology from "Small," the character she invented in the *Cow Yard* and who now stood in as an alter ego. Small became a device for explaining (and excusing) her behaviour and eventually for permitting the expression of emotion. "There is a side to friendship that develops better and stronger by correspondence than contact, especially with some people who can get their thoughts clearer when they see them written," she wrote in 1935. "Another thing—that beastliness self-consciousness is left out, shyness, shamedness in exposing one's inner self there face to face before another, getting rattled and mislaying words."

Dilworth was able to respond to Carr's caring and playfulness. He entered into the ruse of Small, and accepted Carr's overweening behaviour because he, too, was hungry for friendly intimacy. He was also a lifelong bachelor, possibly celibate, singularly alone, although he had family about him, just as she did. When he died in 1962, radio colleagues remembered him as distant and almost European in his cultivated affect. He was the personification of the old spirit of the CBC, a public servant by day and a practising humanist and patron of the arts by night. (Dilworth was passionately interested in music and was the first to put live orchestral and chamber music on the air.) To the writer Eric Koch, who worked for Dilworth when he headed Radio Canada International in the 1950s, he seemed pathetically alone, rarely mixing—"he never attempted to be one of the boys, carrying on with his lonely pursuit of knowledge and understanding." This was the side of his character Emily Carr related to and the reason they could be soul mates. He was a loner as was she, a master of displaced desire as was she, and he no doubt recognized in her someone who accepted his sexuality, whatever that was. The same questions about homosexuality arise in connection with Dilworth as they do with Carr. In her case, though, she lived an explicitly woman-centred existence and in no way eschewed women's company or the social stigma attached to spinsterhood. She talked about womanliness as a fundamental value, she celebrated motherhood, and she disliked men. This conviction took an Ira Dilworth to shake—and she admitted having to rethink her opinion of men after meeting him. He was much younger than she, but willing to engage with her world. He respected her and accepted her affection. Actually, Dilworth can be described as the last great love of Emily Carr's life. This is not to suggest that the love was even subconsciously carnal. The attraction of a man like him may have been, in fact, his asexuality and gentlemanliness, and the same might have been true of Lawren Harris. It allowed Emily latitude to express herself because it would not be misconstrued. Moreover, in those days there was a code of courtly behaviour, complete with language and rituals, which fit this situation very well. This was the role of the gentleman and lady, which Carr knew by heart and which provided a framework for her attentions. Given Emily's distaste for sex—"Oh how splendid it will be when there is no more sex. It should be beautiful but we've spoilt it, made it loathsome"—one can speculate that its absence was an ingredient in her relationship with Dilworth. It may have been what made love possible for her. Distance and the mail helped because together they permitted an intensity on Carr's part that might not have survived proximity. She opened her heart to him.

People who do not marry and create their own families, often find love in other ways and in other places. Dilworth's situation was somewhat unusual in that regard. He lived with his mother, and was also the adoptive father of two daughters, one of them a niece, children whom he took and raised as his own. He began his professional life as a high school principal in Victoria and was known as a charismatic teacher who tutored after hours and read out loud to his class on Friday afternoons. His fatherly side is evident in his relationship with Emily Carr, too. And to her he was the last and best re-creation of the father-brother she remembered from her childhood. Dilworth offered her sympathetic understanding along with permission to be herself in her writing, so it is not surprising that she speaks to dear "Eye" about her father and the "brutal telling." Eye would seem to have been a catalyst for her to come to terms with that legacy. He became the repository of her dearest feelings and she was prompted to write on the back of her portrait of Sophie ". . . at my death the property of Ira Dilworth of the CBC from his love Emily, because the life of Sophie meant so much to him. He understood her womanliness & my love for her. To him she was more than an Indian, she was a symbol."

Sketching in the big woods is wonderful. You go, find a space to sit in and clear enough so that the undergrowth is not drowning you. Then being elderly you spread your campstool and sit and look around. "Don't see much here." "Wait." Out comes a cigarette. The mosquitoes back away from the smoke. Everything is green. Everything is waiting and still. Slowly things begin to move, to slip into their places. Groups and masses and line tie themselves together. Colours you had not noticed come out, timidly or boldly. In and out, in and out your eye passes. Nothing is crowded; there is living space for all. Air moves between each leaf. Sunlight plays and dances. Nothing is still now. Life is sweeping through the spaces. Everything is alive. The air is alive. The silence is full of sound. The green is full of colour. Light and dark chase each other. Here is a picture, a complete thought, and there another and there . . .

Out in the woods waiting for the picture to come to her, Emily Carr often took out a little notebook and wrote in it, trying to capture her perceptions. She called this "wording the picture." Such comments about her creative process are few and far between in her writings, and the testimony of others is slight and contradictory. One says she hated people seeing her work in progress, another claims Carr happily showed her sketches. Trying to plumb her depth, critic Judith Mastai has referred again to dreams. "In my view . . . Carr sought to create a visual

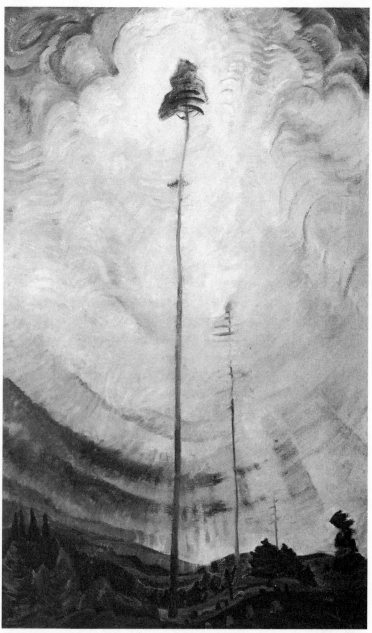

"Scorned as Timber, Beloved of the Sky" painted by Carr in 1935.

language which did not heretofore exist; a language devised out of her deep emotional ties with the land. . . . To me this dilemma is analogous with the experience of waking from a dream and languishing in the dream-like state, almost conscious. In this state, awake and asleep at the same time, a multiplicity of images converge." Of course, in giving these visions physical form, some of the subtlety is lost and the magic disappears. Mastai is also of the opinion that Carr's work displays a longing for a state that constantly eluded her in a psychoanalytic sense. She has theorized a connection between the moody depressive climate of Vancouver Island, the story of sadness and loss implied in the depiction of Native culture in Carr's early canvases, and the artist's melancholic frame of mind. She uses the theories of Julia Kristeva, who ties the state of depression to the creation of art, contradicting those who say there can be no poetry after Hiroshima and Auschwitz with the view that there *has* to be poetry. Mastai suggests that Carr's work provided a means of rebirth and survival. "The psychoanalytic paradigm would appear to hold as self-evident that the human condition is a metaphor for depression and melancholia. Traumatic events such as the Holocaust, side by side with the creation of intellectual new orders and works of art, would all seem to be manifestations of the denial of loss." In Carr's case the denial of loss involved accepting or in some way turning a blind eye to the logging companies' invasion of the forests. Similarly, it meant tacitly supporting the government's policies of negating Aboriginal rights while building a nation and a national culture using Native land and art. Quebec critic Nicole Jolicoeur adds to this train of thought the notion that the hysteria Carr suffered in England in 1902 allowed her to push through the crisis that had rendered her mute. Jolicoeur points out that the hysteria afflicting Carr was neither the dramatic malady of Charcot nor the deeply disturbing sickness of Freud "whose patients demanded he avert his eyes when they spoke of their troubles, things of the sort one can neither speak of nor speak." Hers was a Victorian hysteria, depression accompanied by nausea and aphasia. And Jolicoeur believes that Carr used it to cure herself. While hospitalized Carr drew cartoons and wrote ditties making fun of herself, regarding the world with an ironic slant. Eventually she found her way back home to British Columbia and to herself, not a self she was entirely comfortable with, but a self she now believed in. The melancholia and self-doubt returned after 1913 and dug in deep. However, not all her energies were siphoned off into bleakness. She was functional and, despite her complaints, enjoyed aspects of the life she had made for herself. This was something she expressed in her journal in 1936 when she moved from Hill House and dismantled the home she had made for more than two decades. Her painting takes form against, or in opposition to, this experience of depression; it was a way past the annihilation she feared for herself, particularly the destruction she observed in the woods and Native villages. The fictions she created, the paintings she made, and then the books she wrote were driven by her desire to break—and break with—the order of things. According to Jolicoeur, hysteria gave her permission to create.

The relationship between madness and creativity is a subject of endless fascination, copious theory, and few absolute truths. The torment of van Gogh, the suicides of Virginia Woolf and Sylvia Plath, the alcoholism and self-destructiveness of long lists of writers and artists, have entered the popular culture as myth, embellishing the stereotype of the creative genius as social misfit and misunderstood genius. The life story of Emily Carr can be read as a variation on the theme in which psychic stress played a role in accessing creative expression. It was part of Georgia O'Keeffe's story as well, and in both their cases physical breakdown and depression functioned as a prelude to artistic breakthrough. There are many other woman artists of whom this can be said, some we know about like Hildegard of Bingen, and many we don't or have yet to hear about—for the phenomenon has followed us into the twenty-first century. What is intriguing are the conundrums these women's lives describe, beginning with the misogynist culture they have had to negotiate before reaching the starting line. At times the conditions they have faced or been forced to live with have been crazy-making. Sometimes they have prevailed by being willing to live beyond the pale, to be a bit crazy in order to stay sane. (Perhaps the most affecting example of this was the French sculptor, Camille Claudel, whose extreme disregard for social convention in choosing to live by her art led her family to commit her to an insane asylum where she was kept for the last thirty years of her life.) In other words, the diagnosis of madness and the condition of mental disorder can be two very different things, and the debate about depression and the production of art encompasses situations where mental illness precedes (or accompanies) artistic expression, as well as those where the business of reinventing oneself as a woman, as an artist, and as an independent agent produces coping strategies that others might find bizarre and label crazy. Emily Carr has been handed down to us by biographers and historians flaws first. She has been bequeathed to us in a state of delusion, accused of fixing her story, of being her own worst enemy—and yet some of that delusion led her to mysticism, and to a lyric, loving relationship with nature.

Love is the most tangled of topics when it comes to Emily Carr. Did she, could she, was she? Did she ever have a lover, could she love, was she lesbian? Taking the published and unpublished evidence together, the answers remain stubbornly ambiguous, the possibilities perhaps more numerous than we thought, but the probabilities no greater. After her traumatic rejections (of her father and by the young man with the strong arms) no other men who stirred her passions turn up on the record until Lawren Harris and Ira Dilworth, who were both sexually unavailable. Moreover, her love for Bess Harris and for Sophie Frank has to be taken into account. She was more intimate and more demonstrative with them, and, in Sophie's case, she clearly expressed a spiritual connection defining their love as something special. To her, Sophie's was the love that made her feel she belonged; it may not have been unalloyed, free of sentimentality or opportunism, but it was real. Mastai sees Carr's spirituality as either an obtuse means of legitimization or as "yet another building block in the wall she built to separate herself from those around her, to remain distinct and to substantiate her own version of the world." The investigations seem endless and inveterate; Carr's life (and love life) is a portable enigma like the Mona Lisa's smile. More and more people believe the evidence of their eyes and see Carr's sexuality in the liquid and libidinal forest imagery of the early 1930s. They reject the frigid label and entertain instead a notion of love and loving quite as pantheistic as Carr's notion of worship. Her love of nature was visceral and fulsome, and had far more in common with Walt Whitman's than Pauline Johnson's. But in the effort to buttonhole Carr, to name and frame her, you discover she never sits still. She keeps moving. Her fame means that no one can own her, and there can be no standard version of her life. Too many people have researched it and come back with their own interpretations of her character and their own theories of her evolution. Too many have taken the ambiguous record, with its oblique references and half-told stories, to heart.

Naturally the picture of her has shifted over the years. We can now understand her as less lonely than previously imagined, more tuned in to the subconscious. Her decisions about love were less tortured, but her affairs of the heart were more so. And friendship, however mixed a blessing, did bring her love as well as aggravation. She was resilient, and though she suffered deep depression, found the strength to remake herself in middle age, hitting her stride as an unrepentant, postmenopausal crone. Her life is a testament to perseverance and patience, it tests the clichés about creativity (that it belongs to the young, for example) and puts paid to the notion that people—or artists—living on the periphery of society are condemned to the margins. Emily Carr came from the edge of nowhere in 1927 and marched straight into the national consciousness. Her quest for self-knowledge and reconciliation with Aboriginal culture tapped into the mainstream desire for national emblems. Since her death Carr has had several lives, both as a national monument and as a feminist mystic. She has been judged as a modernist, but in fact she makes more sense from a postmodern perspective, which takes a dim view of the old standards, those that classified some art as fine art (and everything else as craft), and treated subjective opinion about excellence as an absolute and measurable phenomenon. Carr herself conformed to the prevailing views about such things, and would not have recognized Sophie Frank's basket-making as art, for example, nor would she have differentiated with any degree of knowledge or sophistication between the Native cultures in the area. Postmodern theory favours the de-centred and the pluralistic, and has sanctioned the irreverent mixing and matching of cultures and genres that is the hallmark of contemporary art. It has questioned the authority of the author in the light of new ideas about language and psychology in the construction both of human culture and individual identity. It could be said that it has given appropriation an intellectual justification and a political critique at the same time. But it has left us, as has Emily Carr, with the problem of appropriation unresolved all the same.

Gabriola Island, 1999

There is an eye-splitting sunset the evening of the big meeting at the Surf Lodge. Driving across the island, I slap on my sunglasses and draw down the truck's visor, anticipating temporary blindness when the orange blaze hits straight on. It is mid-September and summer is giving no hint of retreat. School has started, the holidays are over, and the weather carries on with day after day of stunning sunshine. We used to call it Indian Summer. Was that because the extra weeks of growing warmth were taken as a gift and associated with Native culture? Or because the Protestant ethic saw such beneficence as an enticement to sloth and uneconomic behaviour—the sort of thing said of the Native peoples in connection with the potlatch in Emily Carr's time? My attention flits over these notions, overlaying them on the event about to unfold. Like everyone else gathering in the Surf Lodge lounge, I'm oblivious to the symbolism

View from Gabriola Island down the Strait of Georgia, April 1997.

provided by the sunset; I've come because the meeting has been called by the Snuneymuxw (Nanaimo) First Nation, and the rumour is that the elders will be here.

Two years ago when the local museum unveiled its petroglyph exhibit, the elders did not attend. A representative from the Treaty Office came on her own, and assured the small crowd of Gabriolans assembled for the ceremony that she felt they were there in spirit. The rock carvings, she went on to say, were Salish, markings and images that her people knew about and recognized. And have stories about, I added in parenthesis to myself. Gabriola is one of the largest of the southern Gulf Islands, with a very present Aboriginal past. No Native communities are left, though obviously they flourished here at one time because they show up as tiny parcels of reserve land on maps. Mostly the Native presence is archaeological and thus a comment on this absence. It is also a window onto the past visible in the middens and shell debris common in several sites indicating long-term habitation, in the stone objects unearthed from time to time, and in the rich assortment of petroglyphs carved onto rock faces all over the island. Sacred places are known to exist here, too. One man discovered recently when he started digging out a basement that he had been planning to build his house on top of an ancient burial ground. For the most part, the petroglyphs are found in out-of-the-way places, carefully chosen (as Gabriola obviously was) for its buttery sandstone. For a long time, their existence was largely unknown to local Whites. A few discoveries were made and then people began searching for more. The inevitable book was published with maps and drawings and clues to the location of the largest site. Today the petroglyphs remain sequestered, but the images are everywhere, having been well and truly discovered by non-Natives. Marius Barbeau would be delirious at their popularity and with the creative ways with which artists and craftspeople have incorporated them into their work. The figures have appeared on T-shirts, decorative plaques, glassware, wall hangings and in books and all manner of jewellery, paintings, and prints. Festival Gabriola uses the "dancing man" figure as its logo; the museum uses them in promotional material and on its web site, as do dozens of individuals who incorporate them on business cards and signs. In short, the petroglyphs have been taken over and commercialized just as they have been taken to heart by the people living on the island. Visitors love them too, snapping up the earrings and watercolours and returning each summer for more.

All this attention—and human traffic—invited damage at the site. The main grouping, a field of flat rocks in a clearing ringed by Garry oak and broom, is particularly vulnerable to the pressure of people in numbers, well-meaning tourists and vandals alike, the ones who can't resist scratching their initials onto the rock when no one's looking, and the atavistic ones on dirt bikes. People were becoming alarmed when the museum stepped in with a protection plan involving posted warnings at the entrance to the site and concrete replicas of several petroglyphs mounted outside the museum itself. The theory was that people could be persuaded to do rubbings and drawings from the models provided, and not to disturb the originals. The museum went through proper channels and followed all the rules it could find. It secured special government funding and museological approval, and contacted the band to solicit its support, which seemed to be forthcoming. One elder agreed to give the process his blessing, so the project proceeded. Now, quite unexpectedly, the museum has been informed that the band has registered a number of the petroglyph images as trade marks. Tonight's meeting is about the land claim of the Snuneymuxw First Nation, a tricky one because of the dearth of Crown land in the area, but everyone has actually come to talk about the petroglyphs. Intellectual property may be an unfamiliar term, but everyone understands the news to mean that the familiar images can no longer be used with impunity. Several display boards have been set up around the lounge with documentation and background about trade marks as well as photos of the dig in the El Verano basement.

The place is packed an hour before the meeting is due to start. When it does, the visitors and the four local people at head table (representing the Chamber of Commerce, the Ratepayers Association, and the Regional District Council) are introduced and a procedure is outlined emphasizing the discussion will be controlled and civil. The delegation from Nanaimo includes four elders and three younger experts. We are told the meeting has been called to inform us about the land claim and the trade mark registration, and that the elders want to answer questions. Everyone waits impatiently through the presentation on the claim, probably the only such gathering a Native community could arrange with its White neighbours where questions of art would upstage the disposition of land. Leading up to the meeting, the band had contacted several Gabriolans who are major users of petroglyph images to alert them to the new situation and to ask if they would like to seek permission. Most refused. Some deny the band's right to claim any kind of ownership and promise to continue using them. Others have voluntarily stopped, but they have not been the vocal ones on the issue. There is good reason to expect an acrimonious discussion. A CBC Radio reporter arrives with a bomb mike.

Eventually, the meeting turns to the petroglyphs. The band's lawyer, Murray Browne, explains how he was given the task of finding a way for the Snuneymuxw First Nation to protect the petroglyphs. Trade mark registration was one option he explored and the one pursued by the band, which then applied to the federal trade mark office as a public authority rather than as a private corporation as is usually the case. The applications were successful and so, as of 1998, the band has owned the legal rights to the petroglyphs, rights that will not expire as patents and copyright do after a set term, but which can continue so long as the owning authority exists and renews them. The presentation takes a while and when the questions finally come, Browne is concise: any use made of the images after the registration date is a violation unless authorization has been expressly given. The new ground rules mean business, but Browne is careful to point out that if people object, there is a procedure for them to do so officially. Then the elders speak and it becomes evident that they are not spoiling for a court battle. We are not read the riot act or told what to do, but it seems the elders' permission is not going to be easy to come by either. They do not speak with a single voice on the matter, and some of them, we learn, are offended by the display of the petroglyphs in front of the museum. One message is clear—the petroglyphs are powerful and perhaps dangerous and non-Natives are meddling with things they don't know about when they use them. The Snuneymuxw have turned the tables and it is now up to White people who want to use the images to figure out what is permissible as they wait for a licensing system to be set up—if indeed one ever will be. It is not a foregone conclusion that the elders will find a compromise. They may take the images out of general circulation entirely.

The first comment from the audience takes up the defence of the concrete petroglyphs outside the museum, suggesting that the Native people had not done much of a job protecting the originals on their own. Another man reminds us that the petroglyphs were buried under moss until recently and wonders how they could belong to anyone if no one knew about them. Browne answers with the example of an uncle leaving you a house you didn't know existed, which would not be any the less yours for not knowing about it. Several people press for specifics. A local folk-singer wants to see the trade mark documents. Others offer stories, and one artist attests to the fact that she has made art with the petroglyph images in the past but has ceased doing so. Another woman speaks passionately about her attachment to the spirit places on the island, and to a particular set of earrings bearing one of the petroglyph images. She tells us of travelling in West Africa and being in a village where there were petroglyphs, and her pride in describing the existence of similar stone carvings back home in her community. Not carved by her ancestors, she cautioned the villagers, but the ancestors of those who came first. Her plea is to know if she can still wear her special earrings. Finally, a man stands up to talk about his experience seventeen years ago when he stencilled petroglyphs on T-shirts and tried to sell them. He met with little success, he says, an edge of resentment in his voice at the current fad he missed. Then he lays down his opinion. Had someone or some people come to him and said they were offended by what he was doing, he would have willingly stopped, he tells us. But when someone approaches him waving property rights, he does not feel so disposed. Quite the opposite. This declaration wins a round of applause from the audience, the first of the evening. Earlier on, Murray Browne had pointed out that the legalistic route was not the Snuneymuxw Nation's first choice, but that they had found it necessary to have that kind of backing to win people's attention and respect. The purist position that art and ethics are perverted by legalities (and that all Native peoples have to do is ask and White people will respect their claims) doesn't pass the reality test, of course, but it does save face in the moment and the crowd seems released by the act of bravado.

This is a story with several scripts, of course. The Native peoples have responded to the proliferating misuse of their heritage by availing themselves of White European property law. White people feel affronted, and they are correct in sensing that something changed when they weren't looking. The Snuneymuxw people's move puts the entire question of use onto a contractual basis where there is no room for charity or assumed authority. It shifts the ground, it puts talk of respect to the test, and sidesteps issues of intent and justifications like "I am not making any money from this, but I am bringing attention to Native art." A second story concerns the legal ingenuity and political daring behind the move, the élan with which it confronts mainstream culture in its own language. Various First Nations groups have tussled with copyright laws over the years, attempting to find ways to access protection for traditional art and designs. From the Aboriginal point of view, Sophie's friend Mae was right. The Northwest Coast heritage has been plundered by non-Natives who have exploited it for their own purposes, and made money while Native creators have not. No doubt the non-Natives in question would argue that artefacts like the petroglyphs belong in the public domain, which is to say they ought to be freely available to everyone and anyone. In this one instance, the Snuneymuxw First Nation has intervened and rearranged things definitively so that the small slice of the public described by the band and its ever-changing membership have become the custodians of the images. All other users must now be accountable to them, and must seek permission. Were this a cautionary tale, the story might also be a lesson about misappropriation not being inevitable; one Native community, finding itself in possession of something the White community determined to take, has found a way to keep it.

Another story, much harder to decipher, is the one behind the current popularity of Native imagery among non-Native artists. While there is great diversity of media and styles among Gabriola artists and artisans, what is most striking is the prevalence of

Aboriginal motifs in their work. I became aware of this phenome-non one Thanksgiving Saturday when I joined a group of friends on an "art crawl," visiting studios around the island, which were opened to the public over the long weekend. The effect was cumu-lative. Everyone seemed to be dealing in pastiche but after a while the borrowing seemed obsessive and exploitative in a way it did not on an individual basis. Most common were the petroglyph images, but the bead-makers were into feathers and dream-catch-ers, and the New Age painters filled their panels with the signs and symbols of Native spirituality. As most of the artists are of European heritage, it prompts the question of how we are to read this preoccupation. Is it a rejection of the artists' own ethnic back-ground and heritage as an artistic source? Or should we under-stand it as an identification with some "other" believed to possess special aesthetic power? Is it a fad, perhaps, or a search for authen-ticity? In our age, Native imagery not only demands attention, it commands respect and connotes an aura of indigenous connected-ness, which the user accesses by association. It may well ground their work, but the point is that it also renders it commercially visible because it deals in a common cultural coin.

That coin is Western art's century-long infatuation with primi-tivism, which is at once a romanticized view of difference—in this case an association of the ambiguous naturalism of Native images with a supernaturalism—and an implied critique of the frag-mented and individualistic world of industrial modernity. Some have argued that primitivism, although rationalized as something entirely foreign, is actually integral to modernism's conception of itself because it counterposes the non-rational, integrated, and intuitive with the linear, dualistic, and reasoned approach of Western art and thought. Primitivism is therefore a means by which society constructs itself as a self-conscious, self-defining entity through a process of projection and introjection, of identi-fication and differentiation. As British artist and critic Susan Hiller writes in her anthology, *The Myth of Primitivism*, the practice of drawing on ethnographic models as exotic subjects has been part of the modernist tradition since before the turn of the last century and this has functioned as "a kind of charter of possibilities." She cites the mythic moment when Picasso discovered African art, and "bound the imperialist conditions of possibility with the appropriative strategies of modernism." She describes the expansion of Europe's aesthetic horizons brought on by the importation of new visual ideas from distant countries, and the assumption of European artists at the time that the artistic riches of those far-off lands were just as available as the mineral resources were. Prized out of its context and community, primitive art becomes an empty vessel set adrift in the midst of an art movement that was itself severing ties with social and physical reality and withdrawing into a century-long contemplation of its formal component parts. Primitive art is a sacrificial object into which new meaning can be poured. But even as it floats about, it is an anomaly, an abstract construct, mere fantasy really. For outside of the imaginary circle all objects labelled "primitive"—like Fred Alexee's paintings, for example—cease to be considered primitive or necessarily even art.

Emily Carr's paintings of totem poles belong to this tradition of aesthetic adoption—the first most obvious feature being the fact that while the subject matter may have been foreign to European aesthetics, the paint and painting style were not. Carr also detached objects from their context, recording their visual demeanour but not their names, their owners or makers, some of which information was available to her. She, too, poured her own meaning into these found and borrowed images, absorbing them into a Canadian narrative and ascribing to them a historical purpose. Carr's paintings and Carr herself also belong to a culture possessed of an unfettered curiosity about foreign people and places, and an appetite for foreign culture. A walk through the exhibition halls of the British Museum in London is one way to review the evidence not only of this fascination and desire to possess things, but of the British Empire's fabulous lack of prejudice in looting the world of its human-made treasures. The Elgin Marbles and the Madonna of the Rocks are only the most famous examples. The Louvre in Paris groans under the weight of imperial excess and acquisitiveness as do the National museums in Berlin, Madrid, and Rome. The list is monotonous, the post-modern irony being the cost of housing and keeping all that high-maintenance plunder—an example, you could say, of the sins of the Empire being visited on the grand-generation. However, this acquisitiveness, this "appropriative strategy," as Hiller calls it, is one strand of the trope of late twenti-eth-century culture as we know it in North America. The West celebrates difference and has been able to incorporate it into its own agendas by commodifying it. So the lessons and needs arising from difference have never actually been taken into account; it has not altered the functioning of the colonial machine, or the opera-tion of racial hierarchies within society. This, in brief, is the thesis that critic Deborah Root presents in a book provocatively entitled *Cannibal Culture*. Root's study, as the subtitle suggests, focuses on "art, appropriation and the commodification of difference." She traces things back to the traumatic encounter of the invading Span-ish with the Aztec culture of sixteenth-century México, which explicitly and ritualistically organized violence and mass death. Public sacrifices rendered the consequences of the hierarchical and imperial social order visible in a way that was an anathema to Euro-peans who, by contrast, rationalized the violence and mass death sanctioned by their own societies as accidental or divinely inspired. The idea that Western atrocities are part of the function-ing system, part of the nature of our public culture, is rarely even entertained as an idea. "Historically, Europeans' tendency to attribute cannibalism to people they sought to colonize (as well as internal 'deviants' such as Jews and witches, both of whom were subject to blood libels) seems to have been a way of displacing and drawing attention away from the extent to which European elites were prepared to consume bodies." Not just the bodies of young men going to war, but the bodies of everyone absorbed in the capi-talist machine.

Root sees cannibalism as the key activity and the key character-istic of our commercially driven culture of capitalism, the denial of which is the source of psychosis. "Cannibal psychosis involves the consumption of real bodies. But it is also useful to extend the definition of cannibalism to forms of consumption that occur beyond the physical body of the individual or even the community. It is possible to consume somebody's spirit, somebody's past or history or somebody's arts and do so in such a way that the act of consumption appears beautiful and heroic." Art is not disinterested, in other words, and aesthetics are not value free; they are related to a set of power relations. Furthermore, art can be deployed in the service of political goals (*vide* Roman statuary all over the Mediterranean world and Leni Riefenstahl's films for the Third Reich), and it can function as an alibi for power. That is, it acts as a testimonial or advertisement for the imperial story, and it can be used to launder images. There is the example of the landscape exhibition mounted at the Art Gallery of Ontario in the mid-1970s when the Anishnabe of northern Ontario were fighting the effects of mercury poisoning in the English and Wabigoon river systems caused by the local paper-mills. These paper-mills were owned by the Reed Paper Company, which was the main sponsor of the exhibition, titled (in what must be one of the PR boners of the century) Changing Visions: The Canadian Landscape. A number of artists protested the use of their work in this connection, and denounced the hypocrisy of corporate image managers bent on whitewashing their actions by association with the pristine purpose of landscape art. As most of the work had been borrowed from public and private collections, the artists stood on their moral rights as creators under the Copyright Act and forced the gallery to accept a disclaimer, which was prominently displayed at the entrance to the exhibit. They argued that their work had been recruited to support a message they did not endorse by a corporation whose activities they didn't approve of, and suggested that their reputations had been damaged. Whether for good or ill, their work had been appropriated and their reputations traded on without their permission. This, when you get

down to it, is the argument of the Snuneymuxw First Nation about
their petroglyphs.

The practice of sharing and exchanging ideas and images across
generations and cultures is not at issue here, although that is
often what critics hear when the subject of appropriation comes
up. The Writers' Union of Canada resorted to speaking of "misappropriation" in order to distinguish between the stock-in-trade
activity of all cultures and cultural production, and conditions of
imbalance or dependence and theft. Those are situations where
borrowing displaces original production, sometimes by the
borrowers themselves (as is often the case with colonies), where
creations are stolen or simply taken and the originating community and artists are left the poorer for the experience. Admitting
power relations into the account reveals that White artists' use of
Native imagery is not a neutral act, nor can it be excerpted from
outside the history of White/Native relations, where Aboriginal
voices have habitually been silenced or, worse, dubbed. The set-
up leaves Whites in a position of exploitation almost by definition. Furthermore, given the commercial rationale of the art
market and the mass media generally, personal intention and
integrity won't count for much once something leaves the studio
and enters the marketplace. Emily Carr's protestations about the
purity of her pottery carried no weight, and not just because they
obviously were not true to Native designs (although it would be
hard to know what truth would look like in such circumstances).
The claim is specious because it is in the order of a mantra, a statement of desire rather than fact, for who is to say her imitators
didn't burn with the same desire she did? Her position is a bid for
special dispensation.

Emily's work naturally invites judgement in the light of
contemporary debates about race and identity politics, not to
mention the preoccupation with naming practices such as appropriation. While some might deem the exercise anachronistic, Carr
did speak about Whites' handling of Aboriginal material, and she

did understand that there were ethics involved. "You have to be careful that you do not write or paint anything that is not your own, that you don't know in your own soul. You will have to experiment and try things out for yourself, and you will not be sure what you are doing . . . But don't take what someone else has made sure of and pretend it's you yourself that have . . . it's stealing to take it . . . if you're going to lick the icing off somebody else's cake you won't be nourished and it won't do you any good and you might find the cake has caraway seeds which you hate, but if you make your own cake and know the recipe and stir the thing with your own hand, it's *your* cake." Carr was aware of her debt to Native art, and thought about her use of it. What is galling is that she didn't always practise what she preached, she borrowed and took and it is hard not to think that to her, Sophie's friendship was a justification for her.

Aboriginal tradition in Canada tends to treat cultural artefacts— such as stories, dances, and songs—as family, clan, or community possessions passed down according to the rule of custom. Use is strictly defined and ritualized with privileges and obligations attached. But because it is an oral culture, and ownership is something that has to be demonstrated in public, there is no way to privatize these cultural materials or to remove them from the collective memory—the only way to do so being to remove a critical mass of the population, which is usually called genocide. In Euro-Canadian tradition, possession is conceived of as an individual right over his/her own creation, which lasts for a period of time (the life of the author plus fifty years in the case of copyright) and is exclusive. When the term expires the work passes into the public domain where no one owns it and everyone is free to use it—Shakespeare's plays, for example. To the European mind, the Aboriginal concept of common ownership makes no sense; it has been as difficult to fathom as the European concept of land ownership has been for Aboriginal peoples. Furthermore, copyright and intellectual property came into being because there was friction between creators and people who wanted to reproduce their work without sharing the profits. Charles Dickens made a speaking tour of the United States in the 1880s to plead with the American public and American publishers to stop stealing his work and to respect intellectual property rights by asking permission and paying royalties.

There is a tendency in our culture, still very evident, which sanctions the theft of intellectual material—frowns on it perhaps, but forgives it. People aren't turned into pariahs for keeping library books, or reproducing magazine articles and photographs without permission, or bootlegging computer programs. These are not thought of as crimes in the same category as stealing stereo equipment or, for that matter, computer equipment, although the courts are beginning to treat infringement just as seriously. At the same time, there is general awareness that there are certain things you can't mess with, such as corporate trade marks. It is one thing to make an illegal tape of a CD, but it is quite another to fool around with someone's corporate imagery. Many artists have found this out the morning after exhibiting an art work that included, say, a large replica of a famous brand of cigarettes, or after publishing a take-off of *Life* magazine called *File*, when the heavily embossed lawyer's letter arrives from New York, threatening suits and claiming damages. The point is that some owners of intellectual property are in a much better position to enforce their rights, while others seem to have no means at all to protect their creations. All cultures have ways of regulating imagery and assigning value to it. When two cultures collide, as Native and newcomer societies have and still are in Canada, these systems are interrupted and someone usually gets hurt. While lamenting the demise of indigenous races, people like Eric Brown, Marius Barbeau, and Emily Carr encouraged the preservation of the Aboriginal past and, in doing so, promoted the collection, analysis, and use of Native culture by non-Natives for their own purposes. The trade mark registration of the Snuneymuxw petroglyphs is the first instance of a Native group reacquiring control over its heritage imagery in a way that gives it the means to manage its disposition absolutely and the right to decide who can use it. It is significant that once armed with this legal means, the Snuneymuxw Nation held public meetings and explored various compromises before deciding to restrict the petroglyphs' general circulation. The elders spoke and this time everyone had to listen.

It isn't always easy to negotiate these issues, even when you think you are awake and watching. Six years ago I was asked to lead a workshop at a women's writing retreat in Vancouver, and as part of the two-week session, the three other instructors and I gave a public reading, which was taped and broadcast on Co-op Radio. I decided to read from some notes for an article on Emily Carr and I remember wrestling with the way I depicted Lawren Harris's asexuality, worrying that what I was alleging publicly was based more on art world hearsay than any documentary evidence. (This was just before Peter Larisey's biography was published.) My piece also included a section about Carr and the Dzunukwa, which went into some detail about her reputation, quoting incidents from stories of her exploits. This was done by way of describing the character being introduced for readers. I gave not a thought to how it would be heard by owners of those stories. Following me, Lee Maracle, the Stó:lo writer, spoke and read from her book, *Ravensong*. Afterward she delivered a stinging rebuke of my appropriation of her people's stories, commingled with an elegiac prayer for her ancestors. I was numbed, transfixed as much by the flash of recognition as by mortification. It was tantamount to being called a racist. It took me most of the night to absorb the incident and find some sort of balance. Two thoughts finally surfaced. First I had to recognize the inevitability of making mistakes like this. To write or work cross-culturally and cross-racially these days means bumping into things, sometimes your own prejudice. Mistakes are part of the process of establishing new protocol and, most important, new understanding. Secondly, as scathing attacks go, this was one was dignified. Lee's legendary public encounter on the subject occurred at the International Feminist Book Fair in Montreal in 1987 when she told Anne Cameron, author of the best-selling *Daughters of Copperwoman,* to "move over" and stop using Native stories. I was present at another public event in Vancouver, the Writers' Festival in 1989, when Montreal novelist Neil Bissoondath cautioned the audience against using the word "racism" in a country like Canada where it doesn't really exist as a matter of state policy as it did, say, in South Africa. Lee came to the mike and, with searing eloquence, asked us all what the reserve system was if not apartheid. "You can call it what you like, but we know what it is," she said.

After breakfast the following day, I sought her out. She wasn't angry or unfriendly and I wondered why. I even asked her why, given history, Native peoples tolerate the company of Whites. I feel rage myself at the rank injustice of the White justice system and the absurdity of allowing someone as inept and unsophisticated as Allan McEachern to make pronouncements on Native land claims. She shrugged and told me that my *faux pas* didn't change the fact that we were friends. As for Emily Carr, she guessed it was my choice if I wanted to rehabilitate a racist. That spring a controversy had erupted over this very question when a trenchant analysis of the portrayal of Native peoples by White settler society was published by Haida/Tsimsian art historian Marcia Crosby. Crosby had taken issue with the shibboleth that Carr had a profound understanding of Native peoples. A special emotional attachment might be conceded, but Carr's knowledge of Native culture was fragmentary and minimal otherwise, she wrote. Crosby rehearsed Carr's attitude to the work she sketched, which was to assume that she had the "right to use Native figures, myths and visual arts for various purposes—including the colonization of Native culture— and in a search for [her] own 'roots.'" She pinpoints Carr's assumption of the salvage paradigm, which was widely exploited by artists, academics, politicians, and settlers. This activity or cultural approach is "predicated on the concept of a dead or dying people whose culture needs to be 'saved.' [T]hose doing the saving choose what fragments of a culture they will salvage. Having done this, they become both the owners and interpreters of the artefacts or goods that have survived." Crosby writes about Carr's role in the construction of the Imaginary Indian and the introduction of First Nations history and culture into Canadian institutions as a lost Canadian heritage. Most poignantly she speaks about Emily Carr's slights. In the Aboriginal world, the refusal to eat when food is offered is almost as bad basic etiquette as failing to offer food to a guest in the first place. The disregard for the ownership of the poles was another serious affront not lightly taken. Now we have to add the treatment of Sophie Frank in *Klee Wyck*. This is perhaps the most devastating of Carr's insults to Native custom because it involves personal betrayal. Her literary device was the appropriation of Sophie's authenticity.

The response to Crosby's opinions was extreme. Crosby was invited onto one radio panel after another to defend her views; Toronto critic Robert Fulford was detailed to write an article in *Canadian Art*, nipping them in the bud. Fulford's take was that Crosby's recitation of the Carr legacy from a Native point of view represented the triumph of postmodern theory and its preoccupation with context over art. He describes appropriation not as a problem of imbalance between people and interests in a particular time and place, but as a doctrine of cultural conduct he denounces as "ethnic possession." "According to this doctrine I hold a form of ownership in the culture produced by members of my race, even if I myself actively produced none of that culture. More than that, I am, by virtue of my race, inherently more knowledgeable about 'my' heritage than people of other races can ever be." Presented this way, it does sound absurd, especially if you understand that things like race and culture are indiscreet and incapable of being hermetically sealed. But Fulford speaks from within the canon of modernism where it is deemed desirable and possible to rope off art from the rest of life, to consider it exclusively in formal and aesthetic terms. Despite the presence of postmodernist and feminist critiques, the institutions of art, the galleries and arts schools in Canada and elsewhere in the Western world remain overwhelmingly modernist in ethic and approach. Moreover, while postmodern theory questions the very idea of excellence by revealing the artificiality of a single universalist point of view, it has not welcomed a general audience itself. The new criticism is no different than the modernist mode of art criticism in that it too privileges the abstruse and abstract in a way that seems calculated to keep art and people apart.

As always, interesting ideas crop up around the edges of monumental ideologies. Writers like Suzy Gablik and Lucy Lippard in the U.S., and Scott Watson and Robert Linsley as well as Marcia Crosby in B.C., have consciously attempted to write from without their cultural centres. Gablik, in her moving book *Has Modernism Failed?*, speaks of art as it has come to be in the American mainstream—i.e., a billion-dollar market attended by dealers, collectors, curators, and critics. What was once an amorphous series of relationships has shifted over the century into a clear-cut power structure irradiated with corporate values, celebrating an individualist, bureaucratic, secular world view that has turned art into a commodity. "[Art] was a living thing . . . a means of coming into contact with the life-force of nature . . . not something external to the artist to be sold at a profit" and, having lost connection with place and community, "art must now proceed in a world that is neither structured by authority nor held together by tradition." In Gablik's estimation, art has consequently lost its magic, which is to say its capacity to bring either personal transformation or spiritual cohesion into play. She links the modernist refusal of the sacred to this loss of symbolic resonance between art and the public. "In a society where faith has no currency can myth be anything but banal and dysfunctional?" she asks.

Gablik describes an art world that has lost its centre, where the artist stands alone in relation to society, and is left to invent art and its destiny without direction. "He has lost his shadow," she remarks. Moreover, because postmodernism has encouraged eclecticism while questioning the primacy of the author and the value of "the original" in art, it seemingly legitimizes the rifling of art history (and everything else, including other art forms like text) for visual content.

Lucy Lippard, on the other hand, looks at the connections between certain strands of contemporary art and the art of prehistory. In a book called *Overlay*, she examines the confluence of images found in ancient artefacts, petroglyphs, mounds, henges, and so forth, with the work of modern artists, some of whom have followed the lead of the ancients and created earth art works of their own. In a section on feminism and prehistory, she alludes to the double affinity with nature and with "primitive" cultures paramount in the work of Mexican Frida Kahlo, American Georgia O'Keeffe, and Canadian Emily Carr. The latter two artists painted landscapes that reinforce "an almost sculptural view of place, nature concretized, that appears particularly female." Carr's 1931 painting *Grey* is reproduced and Lippard writes, "The oval spaces of her rain forests seem to wrap themselves around the viewer like enormous cocoons. The individual trees disappear and the place is epitomized as a swooping, dipping parabolic curtain of organic matter, fearsome in its height, age and claustrophobic stillness. She makes us understand why during the rise of Christianity the northern forest was considered the pagan stronghold; to enter it was to risk one's soul." From these two maverick American critics come a picture of Carr as connected to a much longer and older tradition that has nothing to do with concepts of cultural production and everything to do with the primeval, feminine, and spiritual. The modernist *manqué* turns out to have anticipated her posthumous audience and the sentiments of this *fin de siècle*.

The fallout from Marcia Crosby's intervention made one other thing clear. There is a western Canadian view of Carr that rejects the eastern establishment's idea of her, which considers both Carr's and the Group of Seven's landscape drained of its strength. This view is intent on preventing Carr from being stuffed and mounted as an icon. It requires getting into murky depths of her legacy, which is what is happening as a third generation joins in the discussion. The dialogue between contemporary West Coast artists and Emily Carr is irreverent, probing, and critical. "Out here on the Edge of the Continent, Emily is kind of like our grandmother, a figure who nurtures our rebelliousness and our suspicions of poseurs, especially those emanating from Ontario," wrote Scott Watson in a letter to *Canadian Art* in reply to Fulford's article. "Emily Carr is not on trial, nor are her achievements in doubt. But Canada doesn't just celebrate Carr as a painter and a writer but as myth about reconciliation between two cultures." In the end, says Watson, he does fault her for not knowing where she lived, for accepting the demise of Native peoples without acknowledging the role of "government policy and unbridled entrepreneurial greed" in their decline. Carr's work he insists, has been seen differently by different generations, and his has tuned in to "her morbidity—a love of decay and upturned roots—[which] was a necessary condition that allowed her to portray the coast forest in an anti-pastoral (i.e., non-European, truly Canadian) idiom." Robert Linsley likewise has taken a picture of Carr that goes against the grain of received wisdom, and most particularly the eastern, nationalist concept of her landscapes. Linsley makes the argument that the tradition in B.C. comes out of a unique set of circumstances, the typical hinterland-metropolis relationship being reversed, so it is the city that has become dependent on the region for the creation of wealth. "For the urban dweller whose very existence depends directly or indirectly on the resource hinterland, images of nature are a necessity yet socio-economic realities demand that these images hide rather than reveal the nature of the divided relationship," he writes in an article on painting and social history. Part of that divide is the historical irony created by land-tenure policy, which has allowed Crown land, theoretically belonging to the public, to be managed and exploited by foreign-owned forestry companies. "The colonists and immigrants who displaced the indigenes from their land are themselves the dispossessed." He goes on to discuss Carr's work in the light of its essential contradiction: the attempt to achieve the unity of subject and object through expressionism by an artist who is herself "rooted in a society founded on alienation from nature as the precondition for its exploitation." Thus he recognizes the tension in Carr's work, which sometimes allows enough distance between subject and nature for social protest. For him, Carr redeems her expressionism with canvases such as *Scorned as Timber, Beloved of the Sky,* painted in 1935, which depicts two spindly fir trees standing lonely and vulnerable amid the tumult of a clear-cut. The pathos is not romanticized, and the traumatic shock to the land by the violent intervention of man and machines is not mitigated either. Her intervention is conscious.

In the same article, Linsley writes of Carr and Jack Shadbolt, a senior artist of the next generation, who was greatly affected by Emily's work and who, like her, associated Aboriginal culture with the land. Linsley points out that both the environment and Native society have been victims of the same rapacious exploitation, "but the native as symbol of the land is purely a white projection. As long as native people continue to walk and talk and make their claim to the land they will be, for whites, at once a witness to their guilt and a hope for redemption." These two artists, Shadbolt and Carr, giants of their respective generations on the coast, associate Native motifs with a generalized spirit of place, which can be read either as melancholy witness to the destruction or to utopian hope. However, Linsley notes, such affirmative interpretations "break up on the silence of the native."

When you listen to silence, as Emily Carr noted, it is full of sound. In the silence of Native peoples can be heard the hum of people waiting with fraying patience until their story can be heard by non-Native ears. More and more frequently, the hum is interrupted with voices like Marcia Crosby's and Lee Maracle's. And now the elders of the Snuneymuxw First Nation.

.

It was like this from the beginning—people arguing. Even before Emily Carr died, people fought about her, criticized her behaviour and her stories, not just the ones she published about her family but the ones she told of herself. Emily Carr was quite exceptional among artists, though, because the stories she told about herself were published to a loving public who took them to heart. Emily therefore had the first word and the critics and biographers have been running to catch up ever since. Her manipulation of her own public image, though, probably not consciously contrived as such, outclasses Georgia O'Keeffe's attempts to control hers for sheer audacity, and effectiveness. O'Keeffe tried to do it by absenting herself and frowning down the world when it showed up at her doorstep. Carr, who did it by occupying centre stage and refusing to leave, has been laughing merrily since 1941.

When she first came on the art scene, people were amazed by the strength in her work. Max Stern, a Montreal art dealer, said he was speechless when he saw the first canvases. "I'd never seen anything of this kind in Canada; they were much more modern, and powerful and emotional than any I'd seen on this continent." Paul Duval was bowled over by the "strangely unfeminine power of attack" in her canvases. At the same time, they and others reacted to her appearance as if it were an unnatural phenomenon. The fact that she worked alone on her remote island, associated with no school or style, was part of the mystique. Like Frances Hodgkins when she "arrived" in London art circles in the 1930s, Carr was also regarded as some sort of unexplained artistic event. In 1941, Robertson Davies reviewed *Klee Wyck* for *Saturday Night* with unreserved praise, ascribing to Carr an understanding and sympathy for Native life "far beyond the ordinary," along with an ability to present it to readers without sentimentality or conde-scension but with "great love and great art." He concludes by noting that Carr "writes like a woman who has led a lonely life, free from the pretences and flatulent enthusiasms which bedevil literary folk." He was rationalizing her, then, as an outsider, some-one who came from the margins and owed little or nothing to the artistic milieu that was now welcoming her and she was the purer for it. There are elements in this narrative that parallel that of the primitive's encounter with civilized life. In the eyes of the men who knew her in the last fifteen years of her life, Emily was a *naïf*; she had a way with animals, communed with nature, and lived a simple if disordered life. It was easy to cast her in the role of an idiot savante, a woman of little education and poor letters, and inevitable that people would claim her as theirs.

And so from the beginning there were several Emilies. In addition to Small and Klee Wyck, there was the amusing friend the Listening Ladies knew; Harris's and Dilworth's needy protégée; the pugnacious, ill-mannered, and self-assured Millie known to the Carr family; M. Emily Carr, the professional artist; and "Indian Sophie's" nosy White companion. From 1927 on Carr was written about in terms of the Native peoples whose culture she painted, and preposterous claims were made for her. The catalogue claim about Carr's reviving Native arts perhaps was the start of the "St. Emily Among the Indians" narrative. The success of *Klee Wyck* sealed its popular fate, but the unfolding of history right up to and including the 1998 *Delgamuukw* decision by the Supreme Court of Canada has kept Native rights close to the surface of mainstream Canadian consciousness. In the last decade, this timeliness has brought a critique of the narrative and of the perception that Carr represents any sort of reconciliation with Native history or the treatment of the land by Europeans. On the contrary, she represents the consumption of Native culture by White society and our eternal uncertainty about place and our place here. The "our" is the settler society of newcomer, non-Native colonials who stocked British Columbia and made themselves dependent on the resource-extracting industries, who elected provincial governments, that perpetuated the fiction for four generations that the people originally living here did not own their land and did not constitute proper candidates for land ownership. They include those who have been here long enough to be affected by the geography and the spirit of the place to feel themselves rooted, and others who still fashion themselves as removed and isolated, apart from some other centre somewhere else, be it Toronto, New York, New Delhi,

Hong Kong, or the distant past. These attitudes are part of the consciousness and the economic reality of the region.

The second Emily of public acclaim is the Emily who did time in the desert, the solitary soul who believed in herself and persevered in art-starved Victoria as a social misfit and artistic loner. The biographers, Maria Tippett in particular, took issue with aspects of this narrative, arguing that Carr was not rejected by her own as she said, that the story of struggle and neglect was fabricated. What seems to have irked Tippett was the allegation that the West in its myopia rejected Carr while the East embraced her, saw and celebrated her genius. Still, several people close to Carr (Ira Dilworth, Margaret Clay, and Flora Hamilton Burns) were aware of the lack of local support and spoke of it after Carr's death. When questions were asked about Carr's leaving her paintings to Vancouver rather than Victoria at her death, Dilworth's answer was acerbic. "Perhaps Miss Carr felt Vancouver had been a little kinder to her than Victoria." On the other hand, Arthur Lismer spoke of Carr's neglect as her saving grace. (She had given him a dressing down for mentioning her in a talk he gave on art in Victoria in 1932. She preferred to be in the background, he concluded, so she would be able to get on with her work.) Flora Hamilton Burns also figured that Carr's isolation in Victoria was not a bad thing, but, unlike Tippett and Lismer, she did not see it as self-imposed, nor did she equate Carr's temperament with her treatment (real and/or perceived) by the public and Victorian society as they do, but she did feel Carr's "fifteen years in the wilderness" was necessary to her process and part of her maturing.

A subset of both these Emilies is Emily the Enigma, the patient subject of so much posthumous analysis, psychological and sociological as well as literary. Here is where the riddle of her various personae, particularly her association with Small, is most discussed; where her deliberate cultivation of the child in herself, and her sense of innocence in nature is revealed. Said Ira Dilworth of Emily ten years after her death, "This strange genius was a twofold character. [There was] Emily Carr, the person who became the great painter who had all the assurance of a genius. Something came between this person and her friends because she [would] sacrifice them to protect her work. Then there was this other person, a winsome, imaginative child. [Miss Carr] was very conventional at times, and at times the great adventurer."

The third and most recent manifestation of Emily's public persona is Emily the feminist heroine. Like St. Emily and Emily the Reluctant Recluse, Emily the Goddess attracts debate. In this narrative, she appears as the rediscovered woman artist, her achievement reclaimed from his-story and redefined in terms of her struggle as a woman against the grain of socialized gender. Her life, her art, and her declared sensibilities are sometimes claimed as an affirmation of lesbianism. Other times, her animism, her erotic approach to nature, and her connection to Native spirituality give her crossover status as a New Age original. Perhaps this explains why painters like Emily Carr and Georgia O'Keeffe strike the chord they do with the public today. They represent the distaff branch of modern art, the side that championed the spiritual connection in art on the one hand, and the appreciation of land and the environment on the other, the largely discredited branch that represents the missing element in contemporary art, one that meets up with the popular desire for the re-enchantment of art.

"Spiritual yearnings have been part and parcel of some of the worst, most pretentious art of the past century and a half. And they have been particularly prevalent in provincial situations . . . In the provinces artists are more isolated and, literally, more lonely. In that situation, spiritual and literary art theories may help justify an activity . . . otherwise . . . virtually pointless."

"[H]er art has less to do with technique than with the then-popular idea that art should be the servant of the 'dynamic forces' of 'nature' (or, worse, the 'spirit'), and should be uplifting. This is a pernicious idea, but particularly so when the mind in question is as full of barmy opinions as that of Emily Carr." So sayeth the gatekeepers of excellence, the art critics who compare Emily Carr with international heavyweights and declare her short, dumpy,

The Old Woman and the Elephant

and provincial. In this narrative Carr is the modernist *manqué*, the target of formalists like curator Terry Fenton writing in a history of modern painting in Canada, and John Bentley Mays sniping in *The Globe and Mail*. The extreme version of this would exclude her from the front ranks of modernism as a serious artist, as O'Keeffe is, for that matter. And for her non-secular leanings, it relegates Carr to the status of a minor miracle, notable only because she lived so far from the centre of art and had so much in common with the Group of Seven. She has settled into art history as a major figure, but a long way from the cutting edge of contemporary art, a trail-blazer in her own time and place, but not an innovator. Postmodern writers have come to roughly the same position from another direction, allowing us to draw a line from Hildegard of Bingen to Emily Carr through the ideas of French theorist Julia Kristeva. Judith Mastai, for example, postulates that Carr's "genius" does not lie in her artistic production so much as in the "contemporary viewer's narcissistic recognition of themselves in it." And indeed, every step of the way Carr's life can be viewed as an expression of her sociocultural milieu and a product of historical circumstance. Few artists, in fact, have run their artistic careers so close to history as she. At the same time, few have sowed so many doubts about their own veracity. In Emily's case, both Whites and Native people accuse her of lying, specifically for concocting stories in *Klee Wyck*, which were not factual. They say she cooked her books. People like Clara Russ felt misrepresented. In Clara's case, it may have been the vignette describing her laboured attempt to read, perhaps it was the description of Clara's and William's return to Skedans when they took Emily there in 1912, perhaps the description of Sophie. Literary critics and historians have tended to talk at cross purposes, the one seeing her literary efforts as flawed because of their documentary inaccuracy, the later using them as primary source material.

Along with Emily the Failed Modernist comes Emily the storyteller, not unrelated to Emily the Witch. This narrative may be the most convoluted. It takes in the crazy-lady behaviour, the anti-

429

social attitude, the chairs strung up to the ceiling in her studio, and the depression; it encompasses the traumatic, undisclosed legacy of the brutal telling, of her three crushed loves, and her sublimated sexuality. It highlights her failure at love and friendship, and demonizes the relationships with Lawren Harris and Ira Dilworth. In defiance of the popular Emily-as-survivor story, this narrative asserts that if she is the victim of anything, it is her own bad habits. This is Emily the Hysteric, who of all the Emilies, is responsible for the plethora of psychoanalytic theories attaching to the Carr *corpus* like seedlings to a nurse log. Some of the recent thinking has been done under the rubric of literary criticism, some as feminist art theory, both of which focus less on Carr's credibility as an artist and author and more on an investigation of how she constructed her identity and visual language, and was constructed by it.

And finally, there is Emily the Sinner, the Wild Woman of the Woods who steals things, including, some would say, her spiritual experiences. This Emily is not often seen, but she exists nonetheless. She is the persona who is a continuing affront to First Nations people who do not celebrate her, who see her instead as an example of White arrogance. Declaring Carr was ahead of her time in her attitudes to race is of no use in the contemporary world because she has been adopted in our time by so many without reference to her exploitation of Native art, and in a way that allows her to be mistaken for a Native person herself. This Emily stands as an embarrassing reminder, her popularity demanding acknowledgement and a response to her ideas and acts, and to the concept of Canada she has come to symbolize, which also deserves deconstruction and reconfiguring. And this Emily is the one who tells anyone who wants to listen that until Canada, as a nation and a community of newcomers, deals honourably with the land claims and faces her racist history, there will be no honourable way to claim Emily Carr.

The Emily I have come to admire is the ageless Emily who defies all the others. Emily the Elephant, the Ganesh, the old crone whom artists turn to, to study and divine. In this last decade Carr has become increasingly a source of revelation and imaginative grist to poets, choreographers, singer-songwriters, painters, and playwrights. Her influence, felt particularly by visual artists, has travelled in all directions, beyond B.C. and, through her books, beyond Canada. Toronto artist Winsom, who works in fabric, mime, and fable, read Carr's *House of All Sorts* and *The Book of Small* as a young woman in Jamaica; they influenced her decision to come to Canada. In 1994, when she came west for the first time to a writers' conference in Vancouver, she boarded a ferry before registering and made her way directly to Victoria and Hill House where she smiled her way in to see the famous painted eagles on the inside roof of the attic where they had kept middle-aged Emily company at night. In Vancouver choreographer Jennifer Mascall has created a dance called the "Brutal Telling," drawing on Carr's life and, more specifically, the parts of it that she felt had "had an impact, had left an epitaph on our brain and psyche." A maverick artist with an interest in Ouspensky, Mascall commissioned a musician of similar reputation, Veda Hille, to compose a suite for the piece. For Hille, Carr's paintings were stale, but the writings proved a rich resource for lyrics. Mascall was mesmerised by the prose, too. "She feels all the time when she writes. That is how dancers work, it is exactly the same." She sees Carr as a body artist, someone who worked out from the centre, and in conjunction with auras and organs and her physical sensors. The idea of creating the dance came to Mascall when she was on an arts jury and reading proposals from older women artists—"the forty year old dancers in need of a one woman show. I was thinking about Emily Carr as an older woman willing to persevere, of dancers having to leave at fifty, giving up and becoming choreographers, which is therefore about understanding the necessity of constantly reinventing and reassuring oneself as artist." Mascall was attracted to Carr because of what she calls the split between her visionary life and her foibles—Carr's sense of herself as not being a good painter even while she plods on. "She wanted to do things her way, and she developed all sorts of inventiveness around that." This is the spirit that drew the dancer's feeling eye to the internal physicality of the Carr landscapes, to the movements that echo the same conventions on canvas that her own body knows as a dancer. "As a dancer alone what I create is a duet with space. And as a dancer creating dance I find places that have more power than others—and ask why. I find powerlines and find movements and run them together, searching for forms that exist, that can tell us things." She calls her work creative non-fiction, and says she avoids narrative but not the telling of things. "Narrative doesn't work in dance. I'm interested in how something is done, not *that* it is done." And she finds a parallel in Carr.

There are many others in Winsom's and Mascall's company, playwrights Eileen Whitfield, Joy Coghill, and Jovette Marchessault; poets John Barton, Florence McNeil, and Kate Braid; and composers Jean Cloutland, Henry Freedman and Anne Mortifee; choreographer Anna Wyman, among others. These are artists who find connection, instruction, and subjects for their own work in Emily Carr's; who see an uncommon human being who claimed herself and then her own space. The struggle she endured in order to make her art was exceptional, which is why someone like Jennifer Mascall, upon hearing Lawren Harris's quote, "You are one of us," reacts with self-confessed rage. "Carr wasn't one of them, she was one of a kind," she says.

The Elephant sidles up to us puffing gently. The message of contemporary artists and writers Native and non-Native is that they refute the picture of Emily Carr in the biographies and art galleries. They have gone back to the woman in the icon and demanded not only a reckoning but a prophecy. Like all icons, Emily is amenable. She allows us to use her, blame and excuse her, to see through her foibles to ourselves. This is the essence of an icon. Her life story unfolds as a palimpsest of our fables.

She was a child of colonial society and Victorian principle and a reflection of both. Her pursuit of art took her to the centre of the Empire and patriarchy and into conflict with both, and out of that she forged an accommodation with convention and expectation, her social and sexual deal. She took fame by the hand when it appeared, amazed that she would still be asked to dance. She was a nationalist, and she appreciated the story of the Group of Seven's cultural ambitions, but she did not share their endeavour. She did share in the creation of the White Creation myth of British Columbia, and at the same time she fashioned her own brand of place-ness, a cosmopolitan regionalism that tapped into a defunct vein of modernism. Her painting did not come out of a consciously female tradition in Canadian art, but she helped create one. And so other women have followed in her footsteps, myself included.

Other readers and art lovers of all genders and spiritual persuasions have followed Carr into the woods, and into the greening spirit. Her fame continues to spread, propagating interest and controversy until it is hard to tell where she leaves off and we begin, where the past turns into the present. Her neurosis about land and belonging is every immigrant's; about family and creativity, every artist's; her ambiguity about identity echoes my family's, and perhaps yours, her travails and her triumphs are everywoman's. An albatross, a touchstone, a latterday crone, an uninvited guest, a moveable feast. She is all of that and more. The icon becomes us.

Photograph of Emily Carr with her griffon dog and black cat in 1930.

Chronology

1863　Carr family emigrates to Victoria, British Columbia.

1869　Frances Hodgkins born in Dunedin, New Zealand.

1871　British Columbia joins Confederation. Emily Carr is born in Victoria, British Columbia, on December 12, the fifth daughter and eighth child of Richard Carr and Emily Saunders Carr.

1883　Marius Barbeau born at Ste-Anne-de-Beauce.

1886　Emily Saunders Carr dies of tuberculosis. Her youngest daughter is fourteen at the time. Emily Carr begins taking art lessons at age seven in 1879 and continues painting and drawing through her teens.

1887　Georgia O'Keeffe born in Sun Prairie, Wisconsin.

1888　Richard Carr dies, leaving a trust fund for his six surviving children. The eldest, Edith ("Dede") is left in charge of the four children still living at home. Emily is sixteen and Richard, the youngest, is twelve. Emily leaves high school to concentrate on her painting.

1889　Hodgkins joins the Otago Art Society as a working member.

1890　Carr enrolls in the California School of Design in San Francisco where she studies drawing, portraiture, still life, and landscape. She meets other women artists including, in all probability, Alice Chittenden (1859–1944). She remains in California three years and returns to Victoria in 1893, her studies incomplete. She spends the next five years at home giving art classes to children in the converted loft of the barn, while continuing to paint and to show her work. She wins drawing prizes at the local agricultural fair in 1894 and 1895.

Frances Hodgkins exhibits for the first time with the New Zealand Art Society. Studies at the Dunedin School of Art 1895–96.

1899 In April Carr accompanies her sister Lizzie on a visit to the Presbyterian mission at Ucluelet where she acquires the name "Klee Wyck," the Laughing One. She meets William Locke (Mayo) Paddon on board the *Willapa*, the steamship which makes a stop at the post there. Having finally saved the money to study abroad, she leaves for England in August. The first letter she receives from home brings news that her brother, Dick, has died of tuberculosis.

1900 Paddon visits Carr in London and proposes marriage. Carr rejects his suit and returns to her studies. After some months in London suffering from a variety of ailments, she leaves the Westminster School of Art and makes for the countryside where her health improves. She studies with Julius Olsen and Algernon Talmage at St. Ives in Cornwall, and then with watercolourist John Whiteley in Bushey, Hertsfordshire. Her health deteriorates and in January 1903 she enters the East Anglia Sanatorium where she is diagnosed with hysteria and set on a regimen of enforced lassitude.

1901 Frances Hodgkins sails for Europe. She travels and paints in England, France, Italy, Morocco, Belgium, and the Netherlands over the next three years, exhibiting in three London galleries. She is the first New Zealander to be "hung on the line" at the Royal Academy.

1903 Hodgkins returns to Wellington, where her widowed mother and sister now live, to teach and paint. Shares a studio with Dorothy Richmond, and the two hold a joint exhibition in 1904. Engagement to T.W.B.Wilby announced that year and broken off soon after.

1904 Carr leaves the sanatorium after an eighteen-month stay, and returns to Canada. She remains in Victoria for a year contributing political cartoons to *The Week*.

1906 Moves to Vancouver where she rents a studio on Granville Street and begins to teach, first to adults at the Vancouver Studio Club and the School of Art, and later on to children. She exhibits in the Club's first annual show and forms a friendship with Sophie Frank, a basket-maker who lives across the inlet at Squamish Mission.

Hodgkins returns to Europe; paints and teaches in England, France, Italy, and Holland.

1907 Carr travels with her older sister Alice to Alaska where she sees large-scale Native carvings for the first time and conceives the idea of documenting the Natives' disappearing heritage. Wins one of four purchase prizes at the Studio Club exhibition.

Marius Barbeau graduates from Laval and is granted a Rhodes Scholarship. Studies at Oxford for three years, and attends the Sorbonne.

1908 Carr becomes a charter member of the British Columbia Society of Fine Arts (BCSFA) and exhibits regularly with the BCSFA for the next few years. Travels to Kwakwaka'wakw villages at Alert Bay and Campbell River, and sketches at nearby Native communities in Sechelt and North Vancouver.

Hodgkins settles in Paris.

O'Keeffe visits the Rodin exhibition at Alfred Stieglitz's gallery with classmates from the Art Students' League. Late in the year, she announces her determination to give up art.

1909 Hodgkins wins 500-franc first prize in the American-Women Artists' Association exhibition and becomes the first woman on the staff of the Académie Colarossi.

1910　Carr holds a studio show and auctions her work to
raise funds for her sojourn in France. She and sister
Alice leave in August for Paris. She is introduced to
modern art by Harry Phelan Gibb and Duncan
Fergusson.

Barbeau becomes Assistant Ethnologist at the
Geological Survey of Canada, joining Edward Sapir
who is Senior Anthropologist.

1911　Carr joins Gibb in northern Brittany at Crécy-en-brie
and St. Efflam. For six weeks in the early fall she studies with Frances Hodgkins at Concarneau. Two paintings of her landscapes are hung in the Salon
d'Automne in Paris, which Carr attends just prior to
her departure for Canada.

Hodgkins conducts her own school in Paris and
Concarneau.

Barbeau commences fieldwork with the Huron-
Wyandot in southern Canada and the United States.

1912　Carr resumes her career in Vancouver, holding studio
exhibitions of her French work and engaging in
public debate about modern art. She sets off on a six-
week sketching expedition to northern Native sites in
the regions around the Skeena River valley, Haida
Gwaii, and Alert Bay. Spends the winter painting
large-scale oil paintings based on material gathered in
the field.

Hodgkins returns to Wellington via Australia. Holds
exhibitions of her work in Melbourne, Sidney, and
Adelaide as well as Wellington and Dunedin in New
Zealand.

O'Keeffe surfaces in the summer, takes a course with
Alon Bement at the University of Virginia and in the
fall takes a job teaching art at the public high school in
Amarillo, Texas.

1913   Carr stages a solo exhibition of her "Indian Paintings"
in Vancouver and delivers two public lectures
explaining the totem images in her work and describing her journeys to "Indian country." Her hopes that
the collection will bring her acclaim, and will be
bought by the provincial government, are disappointed. She returns to Victoria where she builds a
small apartment house on Simcoe Street.

Hodgkins leaves New Zealand for the last time.
Paints and teaches in Italy and France.

Duncan Campbell Scott is promoted to the position
of deputy superintendent general of the Department of
Indian Affairs.

The International Exhibition of Modern Art, the
Armory Show, takes place in New York City.

1914   Carr's apartment project is a financial failure and she
spends the next fifteen years trying to make ends meet
in a variety of ways: raising sheepdogs, selling fruit,
making pottery and hooked rugs decorated with
Native designs for the tourist trade. She spends eight
months in San Francisco painting ballroom decorations
for the Hotel St. Francis. Depression overtakes her and
she paints rarely.

Marius Barbeau's first field trip to the Northwest
coast. C.F. Newcombe travels to Ba'a's (Blunden
Harbour) and purchases artifacts from Willie
Seaweed. Carr's work attracts the attention of both
men during these years.

The First World War breaks out and Hodgkins
resettles in St. Ives, Cornwall.

O'Keeffe enrolls in teachers' college in New York.
Visits 291 and sees Alfred Stieglitz.

1915   O'Keeffe takes a job teaching in South Carolina.
Completes a series of lyrical drawings, which she
sends to her friend Anita Politzer in New York who in

turn takes them to Stieglitz at 291. Stieglitz keeps the drawings and includes them in a show of gallery artists. O'Keeffe begins a correspondence with Stieglitz.

1916 O'Keeffe's first one-woman show is also the closing show of the 291 gallery which is succeeded by the Intimate Gallery and then An American Place.

1918 O'Keeffe arrives in New York and moves with Alfred into his sister's studio. O'Keeffe is welcomed by the Stieglitz family at the family summer home at Lake George.

1919 Hodgkins attempts to establish a studio in London, and returns to St. Ives after a few months.

Barbeau organizes the first of the Montreal folk concerts that become the *Veillées bon vieux temps*.

1920 Stieglitz exhibits *The Portrait* series of O'Keeffe at the Anderson Galleries on Park Avenue.

1923 Barbeau publishes *Indian Days in the Canadian Rockies* which wins the first English Language Prix David.

O'Keeffe shows 100 paintings at the Anderson Galleries.

1924 Carr slowly resumes artistic activities, showing in Seattle and making contact with several American artists including Mark Tobey. She enrolls in a correspondence course in fiction writing.

Georgia O'Keeffe and Alfred Stieglitz marry.

1925 Hodgkins abandons her European career although she continues to winter in France. Books a passage to New Zealand which is cancelled when she is appointed designer to the Calico Printer Association in Manchester. Loses the position in December.

Barbeau publishes *Folk Songs of French Canada*. Sapir resigns as chief of the Ethnology Division and is replaced by Diamond Jenness. Barbeau is passed over for the job but remains a full Ethnologist at what is now called the Victoria Memorial Museum until he takes formal retirement in 1949.

O'Keeffe and Stieglitz move to the Shelton Hotel. O'Keeffe addresses the National Women's Party convention in Washington.

1926   Death of Hodgkins' mother.

Dorothy Norman starts visiting The Place.

1927   The *Canada West Coast Art–Native and Modern* exhibition, organized by Marius Barbeau, opens at the National Gallery of Canada. Barbeau and Eric Brown visit Carr in Victoria in the fall and invite her to participate. She travels east for the opening in Ottawa in December and meets members of the Group of Seven. She becomes friends with Lawren Harris and begins an active correspondence with him that lasts into the 1930s. Through him and Barbeau she establishes a connection to the art world in eastern Canada. She resumes painting and begins keeping a journal.

Joint Commons Senate Committee on aboriginal land rights declares them non-existent. The Victoria Museum is renamed the National Museum of Canada. The first of the two Canadian Folk Song and Handicraft Festivals organized by Marius Barbeau takes place in Quebec City.

O'Keeffe has surgery for a benign cyst just before her annual show at the Anderson Gallery opens.

1928   Carr makes second major expedition to Native communities up the coast, visiting and sketching at sites along the Nass River, the Skeena River, on Haida Gwaii, and around Alert Bay. American artist Mark Tobey gives a class in Carr's studio. The National Gallery purchases three watercolours.

Hodgkins has solo exhibition at Claridge Gallery.

Barbeau publishes *The Downfall of Temlaham*, and *Three Songs of the West Coast* in collaboration with

Duncan Campbell Scott and Ernest MacMillan. The former wins a second Prix David.

1929 Carr begins the next stage of her search into the spiritual in art. Inspired by Harris she explores Theosophy, and reads Walt Whitman. She continues to exhibit in the local societies, and is now included in important national and international exhibitions as well. She makes sketching trips to the west coast of Vancouver Island (Koskimo villages around Quatsino Sound) and Port Renfrew.

 Hodgkins joins the Seven & Five Society (with Ben Nicholson, Winifred Nicholson, Cedric Morris, Ivon Hitchens and Henry Moore among others.)

 O'Keeffe and Rebecca Salsbury Strand visit Mabel Dodge Luhan ranch in Taos, New Mexico.

1930 Carr visits Toronto, Ottawa, and New York where she meets Georgia O'Keeffe and Katherine Dreier. Sees the work of other Americans such as Marsden Hartley, Arthur Dove, and Marcel Duchamp. Makes last trip to Native sites on Vancouver Island. Paints the Dzunukwa but otherwise moves away from Native motifs towards nature as subject matter. Starts the pattern of spring and summer sketching trips to locations near Victoria.

 Hodgkins concludes an agreement with St. George's Gallery in London and receives a stipend to paint. Exhibits once at St. George's before it is closed.

 O'Keeffe returns to Taos.

1931 O'Keeffe wins the Museum of Modern Art's competition for the Radio City Music Hall mural. Travels to the Gaspé peninsula with Stieglitz's niece Georgia Englehard.

1932 Carr travels east for the last time. Visits Toronto and goes to the Chicago World's Fair. She misses the art exhibit but sees work by William Blake at the Art Institute and in Toronto visits with Harris, Bess Housser. Travels to the B.C. interior to paint mountainous scenery. Purchases a trailer which serves as a mobile cabin for four summers. Becomes a member of the Canadian Group of Painters.

Hodgkins concludes a new agreement with the Lefevre Galleries and has first solo exhibition there. Has three shows at Lefevre or at the Leicester Galleries over the next four years. Lives in various parts of Britain—London, Somerset, Dorset, Cornwall. Travels abroad to France and Spain.

1933   O'Keeffe has a breakdown, is hospitalized, and does not paint for a year. Continues her annual migration to the Southwest in the winter and accompanies Stieglitz to Lake George in the summers.

1936   Carr gives up Hill House and moves to Beckley Street.

1937   Carr suffers an angina attack. Turns to writing when her painting activities are restricted. Visited in hospital by British critic Eric Newton.

1938   First annual solo exhibition at the Vancouver Art Gallery. Several works shown at the Tate Gallery in London which attract critical attention.

1939   Carr has a serious heart attack. Ruth Humphrey introduces her to Ira Dilworth who agrees to edit her stories for publication. Sophie Frank dies.

Hodgkins settles at Corfe Castle, Cornwall, for the duration of the war. Invited to show in the British Pavilion at the New York World's Fair. Contract with dealers cancelled.

1940   Carr moves in with Alice at 218 St. Andrew Street, behind the old family house.

Hodgkins shows at the Venice Biennale. Moves to Bradford-on-Tone and lives either here or in Corfe Castle for the last seven years of her life.

1941   *Klee Wyck* is published and wins the Governor
        General's Award the next year.
1942   *Book of Small* published. Last sketching trip. Major
        exhibition at the Art Gallery of Toronto.
            Hodgkins granted a Civil List pension.
1945   *House of All Sorts* published. Exhibition at Dominion
        Gallery in Montreal. Emily Carr dies on March 2.
            O'Keeffe buys house in Abiquiu, New Mexico.
1946   Hodgkins retrospective at the Lefevre Galleries.
            O'Keeffe has a one-woman show at the Museum of
        Modern Art. Alfred Stieglitz dies in October.
1947   Frances Hodgkins dies in Dorset on May 17.
1969   Marius Barbeau dies in Ottawa.
1986   Georgia O'Keeffe dies in Santa Fe on March 6.

Notes

Chapter One
THE LONG BEGINNING

Ucluelet, 1899

This recreation of Emily Carr's trip to Ucluelet is based on Carr's own accounts contained in "Ucluelet" in *Klee Wyck*, and "Home Again" in *Growing Pains*. Two incidents included draw on sections published in the original 1941 Oxford University Press edition of *Klee Wyck* and thereafter deleted. These are Carr's first night at the mission house with her sister Lizzie and Miss May Armstrong— the Greater Missionary and the Lesser Missionary, in Carr's parlance—and the visit to the "Place of the Dead." I am indebted to professor Gerta Moray for alerting me to the existence of these passages.

The description of Carr's relationship with Martyn Paddon is also drawn largely from Carr's published account in her autobiography, *Growing Pains*. The biographical detail about Paddon comes from the two main Carr biographies: Maria Tippett, *Emily Carr: A Biography* (1979) and Paula Blanchard, *The Life of Emily Carr* (1987). The story about "Jamie" comes from unpublished sections of Carr's journals. The name is my invention, but the chronology is as Carr suggests. Emily Carr did not keep a journal at this time in her life so far as we know. Paddon's diary is completely imagined.

Details about the Ucluelet mission, Reverend Swartout and his family, and Mr. McKenzie at the Ucluelet post come from four main sources: John Telford Ross, *Reminiscences* (an unpublished memoir in the British Columbia Archives); *On the West Coast*, a memoir of Reverend Swartout's stay in Ucluelet written under a pseudonym (Charles Hiacks), also in the British Columbia Archives; Father Brabant, *Mission to Nootka, 1874–1900: Reminiscences of the West Coast of Vancouver Island* (1977); and Women's Missionary Society of the Presbyterian Church of Canada, *The Story of Our Mission* (ca.1915). John R. Jewitt, *White Slaves of the Nootka* (1815), and Gilbert Sproat, *The Nootka: Scenes and Studies of Savage Life* (1987) were also useful. Reverend Swartout died at sea in May 1904 while making his way across Barkley Sound in his sealing boat. His body washed up on the beach at Wreck Bay several days later. For general history about the Christian mission in British Columbia, see Robin Fisher, "Mission to the Indians of British Columbia" in W. Peter Ward & Robert A.J. McDonald, *British Columbia Historical Readings* (1981), and John Webster Grant, *Moon of Wintertime* (1984).

Fred Bodsworth, *The Pacific Coast: The Illustrated Natural History of Canada* (1970); Don Watmough, *West Coast Vancouver Island Cape Scott to Sooke including Barkley Sound* (1984); local histories and memoirs, as well as maps and weather reports, were invaluable references. William and Frances Barkley's story is found in several histories. Beth Hill, in "If Such a Frightful Appendage Can Be Called Ornamental" (1980), notes that according to the Barkley family story, the Native peoples worshipped Frances as a goddess when they saw the shower of red gold that fell to her feet when she unpinned her hair.

Nota bene: My main sources for basic British Columbia history have been: Hugh J.M. Johnston, ed., *Pacific Province: A History of British Columbia* (1996); Jean Barman, *The West Beyond the West: A History of British Columbia* (1996); and Margaret Ormsby, *British Columbia: A History* (1976). Unless otherwise noted, the history I detail can be found in these standard references. Similarly, my main factual sources for the life of Emily Carr come from Maria Tippett and Paula Blanchard, cited above.

The Making of Klee Wyck

P. 52   "fabled city of wickedness . . ." San Francisco was described by Mark Twain as a "wild, free, disorderly and grotesque society." H.D. Thoreau, in 1862, the last year of his life, wrote of the California Gold Rush as a disgrace to mankind. "That so many are ready to live by luck and so get the means of commanding the labour of others less lucky without contributing any value to society—that's called enterprise," he wrote. The American West was more than the frontier of civilization at the time, it was a rebuke of the eastern establishment's puritan roots.

P. 52   "Chittenden participated . . ." See Susan Landauer, "Searching for Selfhood: Women Artists of Northern California" in Patricia Trenton, *Independent Spirits: Women Painters of the American West, 1890–1945* (1995).

P. 53   "woman of mature years . . ." See "Difference between Nude and Naked" in Emily Carr, *Growing Pains* (1971).

P. 53   "'Child, don't let false ideas . . .'" Ibid., p. 31.

P. 54   "Mrs. Tucket, a single mother . . ." See "Mrs. Tucket" in ibid.

P. 56   "She couldn't imagine herself in Alice Chittenden's situation . . ." Alice Chittenden (1859–1944) was the exception among San Francisco women artists in this regard. The Canadian situation is described in Maria Tippett, *By a Lady: Celebrating Three Centuries of Art by Canadian Women* (1992), and Maria Tippett and Douglas Cole, *From Desolation to Splendour: Changing Perceptions of B.C. Landscape* (1977).

Notes

P. 56 "The town was full of single men . . ." The male/female ratio among the adult, non-Native population of British Columbia remained roughly at 3:1 through the last thirty years of the nineteenth century.

P. 57 "The ships were called brideships . . ." See Barman, *The West Beyond the West*, p. 90, and Joan Weir, *Catalysts and Watchdogs: B.C.'s Men of God, 1836–1871* (1995); Jackie Lay, "To Columbia on the Tynemouth: The Emigration of Single Women and Girls in 1862," (1980). A third ship carrying women arrived in Victoria in 1863 with thirty-six women on board.

P. 59 "I can feel the awful relief . . ." Unpublished journals, Phyllis Inglis Collection, B.C Archives. The identity of the young man with the strong arms is carefully kept secret.

P. 60 "As a young Hudson's Bay trader . . ." Douglas's story and that of fur trade society can be found in Sylvia Van Kirk, *Many Tender Ties: Women in Fur-Trade Society 1670–1870* (1980), and Jennifer Brown, *Strangers in Blood: Fur Trade Company Families in Indian Country (*1980).

P. 61 "Angry about the brutal slaying . . ." This incident is often mentioned. See Barman, *The West Beyond the West*, p. 44; Van Kirk, *Many Tender Ties*, p.113; Jan Gould, *Women of British Columbia* (1975), p. 48; and Kate Pullinger, *The Last Time I Saw Jane* (1997), p. 64.

P. 62 "At Fort Vancouver, Amelie encountered . . ." For details about Amelie Douglas, Reverend Herbert Beaver, Chief Factor John McLoughlin, and Fort Vancouver in the 1830s, see van Kirk, *Many Tender Ties*, p.159; N. de Bertrand Lugrin, *The Pioneer Women of Vancouver Island 1843–1866* (c.1928); *McLoughlin's Fort Vancouver Letters 1825–1838*, (1941) p. 161.

P. 64 "After William Connolly died . . ." See Van Kirk, *Many Tender Ties*, p. 240–241.

P. 65 "'I have no objection . . .'" Quoted in Barman, *The West Beyond the West*, p. 46.

P. 65 "Lady Douglas was part of the world . . ." See Elizabeth Forbes, *Wild Roses at their Feet: Pioneer Women of Vancouver Island* (1971); Helen Meilleur, *A Pour of Rain: Stories from a West Coast Fort* (1980); Barbara K. Latham and Roberta J. Pazdro, eds., *Not Just Pin Money* (1984).

P. 67 "'I had not dreamt social obligation . . .'" Carr, *Growing Pains*, p. 161.

P. 67 "Life at the mission house . . ." Ibid., p. 77.

P. 68 "More English than the English . . ." See Barman, *The West Beyond the West*, p.111; Harry Gregson, *A History of Victoria, 1842–1970* (1970); Charles Lillard, *Seven Shillings a Year: The History of Vancouver Island* (1986); W. Peter Ward & Robert A.J. McDonald, *British Columbia Historical Readings*; Barry Gough, *Gunboat Frontier: British Marine Authority and Northwest Coast Indians 1846–1890* (1984).

P. 69 "There was also a substantial Chinese population . . ." The Asian population grew through the last three decades of the nineteenth century from 4.3 per cent to 10.9 per cent of the total population of B.C. In 1880 there were 3,000

Chinese and 7,000 non-Native non-Asian adults living in Victoria.

P. 70   "The Songhees' situation . . ." See Jeannie L. Kanakos "The Negotiations to Relocate the Songhees Indians, 1843–1911" (1982); Wilson Duff, "The Fort Victoria Treaties" *B.C. Studies* (1969); Wayne Suttles, *Coast Salish Essays* (1977); Wayne Suttles, "Affinal Ties, Subsistence and Prestige among Coast Salish" (1960), p. 296–305; Wayne Suttles, "*Central Coast Salish* (1990), p. 453–450; Esquimalt Silver Threads Writers Group, *Seafarers, Saints and Sinners* (c. 1994).

P. 70   "She relates a story . . ." *The Book of Small*, p. 88.

P. 70   "'the Indians love raisins . . .'" *The Book of Small*, p. 96.

P. 70   "At home Wash Mary . . ." See "Wash Mary" in *Klee Wyck* (1971) and "Servants" in *The Book of Small*.

P. 71   "the Cherokee in Alabama . . ." The Trail of Tears saw 10,000 people set out for Oklahoma in 1838, 2,000 of whom perished on the way.

P. 71   "'I have always found [Indians] . . .'" Quoted in Blanchard, *The Life of Emily Carr*, p. 15.

P. 71   "The history went like this . . ." See Kanakos, *The Negotiations to Relocate the Songhees Indians*, for a detailed history of the Songhees' community.

P. 72   "The popular story concerning Douglas . . ." See Chris Arnott, *The Terror of the Coast: Land Alienation and Colonial War on Vancouver and the Gulf Islands, 1849–1863* (1999), particularly Chapter Five, "Pay the Indians for the Land or We'll Have an Indian War," p. 98.

P. 73   "In 1885, the Songhees had had to go to court . . ." See Kanakos, "*The Negotiations to Relocate the Songhees Indians*, p. 97–98.

Tofino, 1997

P. 76   "Gilbert Sproat was the man . . ." See Sproat, *The Nootka* (1987), p. 184–187.

P. 76   "'Habitual contact with a superior people . . .'" Ibid., p. 191.

P. 80   "'There's a torn and splintered ridge . . .'" Emily Carr, *Hundreds and Thousands* (1966), p. 132.

P. 80   "This forest, these trees . . ." For the place of the forestry industry in the B.C. economy, see Patricia Marchak, *Green Gold* (1983). Also see Elizabeth May, *At the Cutting Edge: The Crisis in Canada's Forests* (1998), and Daniel Gawthrop, *Vanishing Halo: Saving the Boreal Forest* (1999).

P. 87   "and in the spring of 1993, another government . . ." The 1993 decision declared that one-third of the sound would be protected; however, as nearly one-half was already a provincial or natural park and the rest largely bog and mountaintop scrublands, it meant that seventy-four of every 100 trees could be chopped down. The Tla-o-qui-aht injunction remained in effect for over ten years. MacMillan Bloedel was bought by U.S.-based Weyerhaeuser Co., which turned over its Clayoquot forestry tenure to an ecoforestry venture called Iisaak Forestry Resources, which has said it will not log the pristine valley, and will log only on a small scale. Interfor continues to log in the area, but clear-cut logging has stopped. In May 2000, the sound was designated a United Nations biosphere reserve.

P. 88 "all through the fall of 1994 . . ." See Jean McLaren, *It's Worth a Try* (1999), and Howard Breen-Needham et al., *Witness to Wilderness: The Clayoquot Sound Anthology* (1994).

P. 88 "It concerns the land . . ." This section is largely based on the work of Alexander Wilson, *The Culture of Nature* (1991), and Carolyn Merchant, *The Death of Nature* (1976). See also Susan Griffin, *Woman and Nature*, 1978, Paula Gunn Allen, *The Sacred Hoop: Recovering the Feminine in American Indian Traditions* (1986).

P. 90 "the relocation of the rock temple of Abu Simbel . . ." The temple was built by Ramses II, pharaoh of the New Kingdom, Nineteenth Dynasty, 1301–1235 B.C.

P. 90 ". . . man's for the taking . . ." This use of the universal "he" was common then. Museums were conventionally called the musée de l'homme or Museum of Man, and Expo '67 in Montreal was called Man and his World.

P. 91 "The savages of the new lands . . ." Merchant, *The Death of Nature*, p. 131.

P. 94 "'It would not be accurate . . .'" from Chief Justice Allan McEachern's decision in the Gitksan-Wet'suwet'en case, quoted in Dara Culhane, *The Pleasure of the Crown: Anthropology, Law and First Nations* (1997), p. 236.

P. 95 "Meanwhile the project of staking out reserves . . ." In 1875 a three-person Commission for the Settlement of Indian Reserves was appointed by the province and the federal government, which proceeded to allot considerably smaller reserves than in the rest of Canada. (The provincial standard was less than a third the standard size adopted by the federal government.) In 1878 the province withdrew from the process, leaving Gilbert Sproat as sole commissioner. By 1900 the reserves had all been staked out and in 1913 a royal commission was set up to make a final determination. Known as the McKenna-McBride Commission, it reported in 1916. All this was undertaken and decided without the consent of the First Nations.

P. 96 "The service was over, . . ." *Klee Wyck*, p. 10.

P. 97 "'To us it was tame . . .'" Mo-chu-no-zhi quoted in Breen-Needham et al., *Witness to Wilderness*, p. 53.

Chapter Two

CASTING OFF

Paris, 1991

This imagined meeting between Frances Hodgkins and Emily Carr in Paris in October 1911 could have happened, and there is some possibility that it did—or something like it. Betty Rhind was probably not in the scene as described here, but she was part of Hodgkins's life as depicted. Her recorded memories of Hodgkins include the story of Frances weeping at the easel.

Carr's recollections of France are culled from her published memoirs in *Growing Pains*; the biographic detail concerning her art comes from Doris Shadbolt, *The Art of Emily Carr* (1979), and Doris Shadbolt, *Emily Carr* (1990), as well as the Tippett and Blanchard biographies. The individuals Carr studied with and was impressed by in England were Algernon Talmage and John Whiteley. In Paris she studied with Harry Phelan Gibb and John Duncan Fergusson. Theodore J. Richardson was a Minneapolis artist whom Emily Carr encountered in Alaska in 1907.

The story of Frances Hodgkins's life and background comes mainly from the following sources: Arthur Howell, *Frances Hodgkins, Four Vital Years* (1951); E.H. McCormick, *The Expatriate* (1954); E.H. McCormick, *Portrait of Frances Hodgkins* (1981); *Ascent: A Journal of the Arts in New Zealand*, Frances Hodgkins Commemorative Issue (1969); Ian Buchanan et al., *Frances Hodgkins: Paintings and Drawings* (1995); *Art in New Zealand* 16, Frances Hodgkins issue (1980); Avenal McKinnon, *Frances Hodgkins 1869–1947* exhibition catalogue (1990); Myfanwy Evans, *Frances Hodgkins* (1948); Linda Gill, *The Letters of Frances Hodgkins* (1993). I am indebted to professor Andrée Lévesque for the information about the catastrophic floods in France in 1910 and 1911, and for her biography of Communist organizer Jeanne Corbin: Andrée Lévesque, *Scènes de la vie en rouge: L'époque de Jeanne Corbin, 1906–1944* (1999).

"M. Emily Carr"

P. 119 "Change of medium . . ." *Growing Pains*, p. 226.

P. 120 "Following Carr's death . . . National Gallery officials . . ." See documents in the archives of the National Gallery of Canada, including a letter from K. Fenwick to Duncan MacDonald of the Alex Reid & Lefevre Ltd. Gallery, 21 January 1947, and a letter from H.O. McCurry, director of the National Gallery, to Sylvia Brull, 16 May 1947.

P. 121 "'Hers is twilight colour...'" Eric Newton quoted in Linda Gill, Editorial Note in *Letters of Frances Hodgkins* (1993), p. 9.

P. 121 "'She had without question . . .'" Graham Sutherland quoted in June Opie, "The Quest for Frances Hodgkins," *Ascent* (1969), p. 61.

P. 121 "'It is one of the tragedies of leaving home . . .'" Hodgkins quoted in E.H. McCormick, "Frances Hodgkins, a Pictorial Biography," (1969), p. 8.

P. 122 "As New Zealand art critic Linda Gill . . ." See Linda Gill, *The Letters of Frances Hodgkins*, (1993).

P. 124 "'What are the qualities . . .'" Hodgkins quoted in E.H. McCormick, "The Path to Impressionism: 1892–1912" (1980), p. 34.

P. 124 "'My chief aim . . .'" Hodgkins quoted in E.H. McCormick, *Portrait of Frances Hodgkins* (1981), p. 78.

P. 124 "'Where original talent . . .'" Ibid.

P. 125 "'I will not tag on to Colonial life . . .'" See Gill, *The Letters of Frances Hodgkins*, p. 259.

P. 125 "His name was Thomas Wilby . . ." Thomas Wilby was a talented journalist, linguist, and traveller who was on his way to New York when he met Frances Hodgkins. He married an American woman shortly after and went on to write books about his North American travels, including his journey across Canada by car in 1913. He cut quite a memorable figure, according to his editor at the *Christian Science Monitor*, who described him as an eccentric in spats and monocle with a capable and retiring wife by his side. What Wilby was looking for, apparently, was an assistant, not an artist following her own star.

P. 125 "'slowly settling down . . .'" Hodgkins in 1895 quoted in E.H. McCormick, "The Path to Impressionism," p. 29.

P. 125 "'It must be alone. . . .'" See Gill, *The Letters of Frances Hodgkins*, p. 218.

P. 125 "'my art is everything . . .'" See ibid., p. 104.

P. 127 "'Maybe if I had not killed love . . .'" Carr, *Hundreds and Thousands*, p. 163.

P. 127 "'make myself into an envelope . . .'" *Growing Pains*, p. 139.

P. 127 "This was Paris in the twilight of the Belle Époque . . ." See Sheri Benstock, *Women of the Left Bank* (1986).

P. 131 "Germaine Greer's . . . *The Obstacle Race* . . ." Emily Carr does not appear in this history either, which says something about the ideological obstacles that colonial artists, especially women, have had to overcome in finding a place in the art historical record.

P. 133 "In March 1913 . . ." The sum of $11,500 is said to have been offered each family in 1913. The Squamish claim to the site was finally settled in 2000 as part of a larger $92.5 million settlement, including 1,220 acres covering most of the town of Squamish at the head of Howe Sound, and seventy-four acres in North Vancouver (*The Globe and Mail*, 28 July 2000).

P. 134 "The City Beautiful movement's moment of glory . . ." See Robert A.J. McDonald, *Making Vancouver: 1863–1913* (1996).

P. 134 "The first effort to establish a civic art gallery . . ." See ibid, and William Wylie Thom, "The Fine Arts in Vancouver" (1969).

P. 135 "A partial exception to that rule . . . Pauline Johnson . . ." See Betty Kellor, *Pauline: A Biography of Pauline Johnson* (1981); Veronica Strong-Boag and Carole Gerson, *Paddling Her Own Canoe: The Times and Texts of E. Pauline Johnson* (2000); Peter Unwin, "The Mohawk Princess" (1999); Marlene LeGates, *Making Waves: A History of Women in Western Society* (1996).

P. 137 "In retrospect . . ." For a discussion of Pauline Johnson's complex personality and a re-evaluation of her work—her "resistance to demeaning narratives" and her "public championship of a more inclusive and tolerant nationality"—see Strong-Boag and Gerson, *Paddling Her Own Canoe* (2000).

P. 137 "'the voice of the nations that once . . .'" quoted in Betty Kellor, *Pauline*, p. 60.

P. 140 "by 1911, Pemberton was long gone . . ." Sophie Pemberton (1869–1959) married in 1905 and moved with her husband, Canon Beanlands, to India and later to England. Widowed, she remarried and remained there until 1947. She did continue to paint for pleasure, but she abandoned her career and her métier after she married. In April 1899 she was awarded the Prix Julien in Paris.

P. 140 "Meanwhile . . . the old job . . ." Paula Blanchard maintains that Crofton House School refused to rehire Carr. See Blanchard, *The Life of Emily Carr*, p. 126.

P. 140 "According to her biographer Maria Tippett, Carr also ran afoul . . ." See Tippett, *Emily Carr*, p. 102, and Gerta Moray, "Northwest Coast Native Culture and the Early Indian Paintings of Emily Carr, 1899–1913" (1993). Moray disagrees with Tippett's interpretation of Carr's reaction, and makes the point that Carr had professional stakes in breaking with the British Columbia Society for Fine Arts.

P. 141 "people 'whose ideals and views have been stationary . . .'" Quoted in Tippitt, *Emily Carr*.

P. 142 "Newcombe's opinion of the paintings . . ." See "Miss Carr's Collection of Paintings of Indian Totem Poles," a report to Francis Kermode, curator of the Provincial Museum, by C.F. Newcombe, 17 January 1918, Newcombe Papers, British Columbia Archives. The original inquiry was made to H.E. Young, the provincial secretary and minister of education.

P. 145 "'Your silent Indian will teach you . . .'" Carr, *Growing Pains*, p. 220.

P. 145 "Carr's notes for the 'Lecture on Totems' . . ." Unpublished manuscript, Phyllis Inglis Collection, British Columbia Archives. This text was not intended for publication. It is a script from which Carr presumably read her public lecture and it is written by hand.

P. 148 "the prevailing concept of Aboriginal societies as 'primitive' . . ." This section owes much to the essays in Susan Hiller, ed., *The Myth of Primitivism* (1991), in particular essays by Kenneth Coutts-Smith, David Maclagan, Daniel Miller, Guy Brett, Rasheed Araeen, Annie E. Coombes, and Jimmie Durham.

P. 148 "Carr's 1913 exhibition . . ." See Moray, "Northwest Coast Native Culture."

P. 149 "In the face of what she managed to do . . ." See Gerta Moray, "Northwest Coast Native Culture and the Early Indian Paintings of Emily Carr—1899–1913," p. 377.

Alert Bay, 1991

The main history texts informing this section are: Paul Tennant, *Aboriginal People and Politics: The Indian Land Question in British Columbia 1849–1989* (1990); Robin Fisher, *Contact and Conflict: Indian-European Relations in British Columbia, 1774–1890* (1977); Bruce G. Trigger, *Natives and Newcomers: Canada's "Heroic Age" Reconsidered* (1985); Ronald Wright, *Stolen Continents: The "New World" Through Indian Eyes Since 1492* (1992); Olive Patricia Dickason, *Canada's First Nations: A History of Founding Peoples from Earliest Times* (1992); W. Peter Ward & Robert A.J. McDonald, *British Columbia Historical Readings* (1991); Daniel Raunet, *Without Surrender, Without Consent* (1984); Brian Shein, "Playing, Pretending, Being Real," (1987).

P. 154 "'All their ideas centre on the potlatch . . .'" William Halliday, *Potlatch and Totem and the Recollections of an Indian Agent* (1934).

P. 155 "Meanwhile, the Indian agent, William Halliday, took a scow . . ." Accounts of this story can be found in Douglas Cole and Ira Chaikin, *An Iron Hand Upon the People: The Law Against the Potlatch on the Northwest Coast* (1990).

P. 155 "A token $1,495 was then paid . . ." The price did not begin to include the value of the coppers seized with the potlatch carvings. See Cole and Chaikin, *An Iron Hand Upon the People*, p. 123.

P. 157 "the bighouse erected here in 1963 . . ." This building burned down two years later, was rebuilt, and the new ceremonial bighouse was inaugurated in May 1999.

P. 158 "the German-American ethnologist Franz Boas . . ." See Ralph Maud, *Transmission Difficulties: Franz Boas and Tsimshian Mythology* (2000), and Douglas Cole, *Franz Boas: The Early Years, 1858–1906* (1999).

P. 158 "a document called *Prosecution or Persecution?* . . ." See Daisy Sewid-Smith, *Prosecution or Persecution?* (1979).

P. 159 "'She developed a nervous disorder . . .'" Quoted in ibid., p. 54–55.

P. 160 "'The system nearly approaches socialism . . .'" Quoted in ibid., p. 17.

P. 160 "'As you may be aware . . .'" Quoted in ibid., p. 17.

P. 160 "'The law against the potlatch . . .'" Quoted in ibid., p. 16.

P. 167 "'We want to know whether you have come to stop our dances . . .'" Quoted in many books and prominently displayed on the wall in the U'mista Cultural Centre.

P. 167 "'Will the reverend gentleman . . .'" Letter from William Dwyer published in the *Vancouver Province*, 1896, quoted in Cole and Chaikin, *An Iron Hand*, p. 51.

P. 168 "The potlatch's most ardent defence . . ." The Sapir testimony can be found in the Potlatch documents file in the Barbeau Archive at the Canadian Museum of Civilization.

P. 168 "'could mean the complete . . ." Letter from Sapir to D.C. Scott, 11 February 1915, ibid.

P. 169 "The Sapir testimony . . ." Ibid.

P. 169 "According to historians, . . ." See E. Brian Titley, *A Narrow Vision: Duncan Campbell Scott and the Administration of Indian Affairs in Canada* (1986); Stan Dragland, *Floating Voice: Duncan Campbell Scott and the Literature of Treaty 9* (1994); K.P. Stitch, ed., *The D.C. Scott Symposium* (1979); Stan Dragland, ed., *Duncan Campbell Scott: A Book of Criticism* (1974); D.C. Scott, "The Last of the Indian Treaties" (1947); D.C. Scott, "The Administration of Indian Affairs in Canada" (1931).

P. 170 "'Against the determined opinion . . ." Quoted in Cole and Chaikin, *An Iron Hand*, p. 136.

P. 170 "'In an area where few cared . . .'" Ibid., p. 137.

P. 170 "'The efforts of the Department . . ." Scott to Kwawkewlth Agency, 1919. Quoted in Tennant, *Aboriginal People and Politics* (1990).

P. 172 "Coincidentally, a market for the old poles . . ." See Douglas Cole, *Captured Heritage—the Scramble for Northwest Coast Artifacts* (1985).

P. 173 "'She wasn't the type . . .'" Interview with Emma Cook Kenmuir by Gerta Moray, July 1998.

P. 173 "Jane Cook married another mixed-race convert . . ." It is interesting to note that Jane Cook, along with several other leading anti-potlatch campaigners, changed her position by 1935. At that time she wrote, "We gave up the potlatch and in return you gave us nothing. You lied and cheated and stole from us." I am indebted to Dara Culhane for bringing this to my attention.

P. 175 "'Hers was an art . . ." Doris Shadbolt, *The Art of Emily Carr* (1979), p. 95.

P. 176 "'Indian art broadened my seeing . . ." Carr, *Growing Pains*, p. 211.

P. 177 "While her writings may be used as primary source material . . ." For example, see Barman, *The West Beyond the West*.

Chapter Three

RIVER OF CLOUDS

Kitwancool, 1928

The story of Emily Carr's visit to Kitwancool is largely based on her own accounts in "Kitwancool" and "D' Sonoqua" in *Klee Wyck*; her comments and attitudes derive from *Hundreds and Thousands* and the unpublished sections of the journals in the Phyllis Inglis Collection in the British Columbia Archives. I have consulted many books about the Skeena and its history, but here relied especially on Marius Barbeau, *The Downfall of Temlaham* ([1928] 1973); Laurence Nowry, *Marius Barbeau: Man of Mana* (1995); Terry Glavin, *Death Feast in Dimlahmid* (1990); Joan Skogan, *Skeena: A River Remembered* (1983); Doreen Jensen and Polly Sargent, *Robes of Power* (1986). I have also used Doreen Walker, ed., *Dear Nan: Letters of Emily Carr, Nan Cheney, and Humphrey Toms* (1990); Edythe Hembroff-Schleicher, *Emily Carr: The Untold Story* (1978), and a 1990 interview with Marius Barbeau's son-in-law Marcel Rioux in Montreal, May, 1990.

There has been some controversy about the date of Carr's first meeting with Marius Barbeau, and the identity of the person who "discovered" her. The other contenders are Eric Brown, first director of the National Gallery, and Harold Mortimer-Lamb, who wrote Brown about Carr in 1921. Unfortunately, the documentary evidence is contradictory. Nowry's research indicates that Barbeau first went to the West Coast to do fieldwork in 1914 and did not return again until 1920. He went back in 1923, 1924, 1926, and 1927, so it would seem that Barbeau was wrong when he stated that he first met Carr in 1916. However, there is no reason to doubt his recollection that it was early. He may have heard of her in 1914 and visited her in 1920 when he went to see if she could provide illustrations for his fieldwork. He recalled that his first visit with her was abortive, and his second visit found her making pottery. This could have been in 1923. See Edythe Hembroff-Schleicher, "The Carr-Barbeau Mystery" in *Emily Carr: The Untold Story* (1978), and Maria Tippett, "Who Discovered Emily Carr?" (1974).

See also Carr's letter to Barbeau, 1942, quoted in Nowry (1995) p. 281–2; Barbeau's letter to Grace Pincoe, August 1945; and Barbeau's letter to Eric Brown, 5 October 1927, in the Library of the National Gallery of Canada, and correspondence in the Barbeau Archive in the Canadian Museum of Civilization. It is unlikely that Carr read *The Downfall of Temlaham* as early as the spring of 1928 as the book was published that fall.

The short sections in italics are imagined revelations.

"You Are One of Us"

P. 202 "'Have the carps, and frets and worries . . .'" Carr, *Hundreds and Thousands,* p. 8.

P. 202 "The paintings would seem to confirm . . ." See the two reproduced together in Shadbolt, *The Art of Emily Carr,* p. 80–81.

P. 203 "When Eric and Maud Brown . . ." See F. Maud Brown, *Breaking Barriers: Eric Brown and the National Gallery* (1964), p. 103.

P. 203 "the travails of running Hill House." These are recounted in Carr's memoir, *The House of All Sorts.*

P. 203 "chance encounter with Mayo Paddon." Paddon had married on the rebound a few months after returning to Victoria from England and his visit with Carr. The marriage failed and he was separated at the time he met her again in San Francisco where he was then living. He lived twenty-seven years alone before finally remarrying.

P. 206 "'cross gouty sexy old man . . .'" Unpublished journals, Phyllis Inglis Collection, British Columbia Archives.

P. 206 "'I resented his omnipotence his selfishness . . .'" Ibid. See also *Growing Pains.*

P. 207 "'My love had those three deadly blows . . ." Carr, *Hundreds and Thousands,* p. 299.

P. 207 "'I have loved three souls . . .'" Ibid., p. 300. Only the first six words of this sentence are to be found in the published journals. The last six are quoted from the unpublished journals in the British Columbia Archives.

P. 207 "The second 'relative' . . ." See the relaxed photo of nineteen-year-old Emily with her sixteen-year-old brother published in Tippett, *Emily Carr,* p. 19, a companion piece of the formal Hall and Lowe photo in the British Columbia Archives and reproduced on p. 534. Both indicate a closeness between brother and sister.

P. 207 "the brutal telling." Emily Carr to Ira Dilworth, 17 November 1942, Phyllis Inglis Collection, British Columbia Archives.

P. 208 "'I can see he must have been a fine young man . . .'" Unpublished journals, Phyllis Inglis Collection, British Columbia Archives.

P. 209 "'I must get back to it . . .'" Carr, *Hundreds and Thousands.* p. 5.

P. 212 "'in its inherited Europeanness or its developing North Americanness." Ramsay Cook, "Cultural Nationalism in Canada: An Historical Perspective" (1977), p. 17.

P. 218 "'Lamenting the fact that Confederation . . .'" Carl Berger, "The True North Strong and Free" (1966), p. 5.

P. 218 "added to the Canada First spirit . . ." The Canada First Movement founded in 1868 by Haliburton, Charles Mair, George Denison and others was inspired by D'Arcy McGee. It "sought to promote a sense of national purpose and lay the foundation for Canadian nationality," according to the *Canadian Encyclopedia* p. 264. The group also provoked reaction against the Métis, the French and the First Nations, among Orange Ontarians especially, during the Red River uprising of 1869/70.

P. 218 "Voltaire's famous dismissal" is the description of Canada as "quelques arpents de neige"—a few acres of snow.

P. 219 "'We know that it is only through deep and vital experience . . ." A.Y. Jackson to Harris, quoted in Peter Larisey, *Light for a Cold Land.*

P. 219 "You are one of us." Carr, *Hundreds and Thousands,* p. 8.

P. 219 "At the centre of this story is . . . Marius Barbeau." See Nowry, *Marius Barbeau;* Heather Robertson, "Totem Poles and Tall Tales" (1996); Pascale Galipeau, *Les Paradis du Monde: Quebec Folk Art* (1995); A.Y. Jackson, *A Painter's*

Notes

Country (1958); Sandra Dyck, "These Things Are Our Totems: Marius Barbeau and the Indigenization of Canadian Art and Culture in the 1920s" (1995); Douglas Cole, "The origins of Canadian Anthropology, 1850–1910," *Journal of Canadian Studies* (February 1973); Richard Preston, C. *Marius Barbeau and the History of Canadian Anthropology,"* (1976); Wilson Duff, "Contributions of Marius Barbeau to West Coast Ethnology," (1964), and the Barbeau Archive in the Canadian Museum of Civilization.

P. 221 "'We have to deal here with puritans . . .'" Quoted in Nowry, *Marius Barbeau*, p. 281.

P. 223 "'Perhaps all good Canadians . . ." Editorial in *Canadian Forum* (1928).

P. 224 "'Should we be so bold as to disclose . . ." See "French and Indian Motifs in Our Music" in Bertram Brooker, *Yearbook of Arts in Canada 1928/1929*.

P. 224 "'There is little left now . . ." Barbeau, "Our Indians: Their Disapearance" (1931), p. 692.

P. 224 "'false promises and rank injustice . . ." Ibid., p.705.

P. 224 "'the most painful experience . . .'" Ibid., p. 706.

P. 224 "'the nearest thing to an inquiry.'" Cole and Chaikin, *An Iron Hand*, p. 133–134.

P. 225 "'I also object to having an Indian agent . . .'" Quoted in Nowry, *Marius Barbeau*, p.199.

P. 227 "In 1924, . . . to oversee restoration of the totem poles . . ." See David Darling and Douglas Cole, "Totem Pole Restoration on the Skeena, 1925–1930: An Early Exercise in Heritage Conservation" (1980).

P. 228 "'I considered Monsieur Barbeau . . .'" Interview with Marcel Rioux, Montreal, 15 May 1992.

P. 231 "'They were a link between herself and nature . . .'" Interview with Barbeau on "A Portrait in Memory," *CBC Wednesday Night* by Elsbeth Chisolm, CBC Radio, April 1958.

P. 231 "he was not repelled as other men were." See Harry Adaskin, *Sunday Supplement*, CBC Radio, April 1973.

P. 232 "'I feel as if I have met the 'worthwhiles' on this trip . . .'" Carr, *Hundreds and Thousands*, p. 11.

P. 232 "In February 1927, while the Canadian West Coast Art show . . ." The story of the Joint Committee and the history of native-White relations on the coast can be found in Tennant, *Aboriginal Peoples and Politics*, p. 107–108. Other sources begin with the famous document called the *Papers Relating to Indian Land Question*, which is now easily accessed in the Municipal section of the British Columbia Archives [33.2 pap 1875] and include recent works by Whites highly critical of the legal history of Aboriginal rights such as Thomas R. Berger, *A Long and Terrible Shadow: White Values, Native Rights in the Americas 1492–1992* (1991), Dara Culhane, *The Pleasure of the Crown* (1997).

P. 233 "D.C. Scott would likely have received one . . ." Scott did have many friends in the art community and was involved with the National Gallery. A photo in Maud Brown's reminiscences of her husband's years with the gallery shows Scott at a tea party in the director's office "celebrating arrangements for the Tate Gallery exhibition in 1938" along with Bess and Lawren Harris, A.Y. Jackson, H.S. Southam, and others.

P. 234 "aboard the *Komagata Maru* . . ." The *Komagata Maru* arrived from India with 376 individuals aboard, all British subjects who were seeking to enter Canada, and testing Canadian laws which then excluded non-White citizens of the British Empire. See Philip Jensen, "A Passage from India" (2000).

P. 237 "'The Committee notes with regret . . .'" Quoted in Tennant, *Aboriginal People and Politics*, p. 111.

P. 238 "Scott's not-so-double double life . . ." See Dragland, *Floating Voice* (1994).

P. 238 "'They were to make certain promises . . .'" Ibid., p. 43.

P. 240 "She was treated as an adventurer . . ." See Muriel Brewster, "Some Ladies Prefer Indians" *Toronto Star Weekly*, 21 January 1928; N. de Bertrand Lugrin, "Emily Carr as I Knew Her," *Victoria Sunday Times Magazine*, 22 September 1951; and N. de Bertrand Lugrin, "Women Potters and Indian Themes," *Maclean's*, 15 March 1927.

Skeena River, 1991

P. 249 "I met Freda . . . the 54th International Congress of PEN." PEN is a worldwide association of writers, founded in England in 1921 to defend freedom of opinion and the right to express such opinion. It works on behalf of writers persecuted for expressing their thoughts.

P. 249 "Freda's mother remembered seeing . . . labrets . . ." See Glavin, *Death Feast in Dimlahmid*, p. 120, and Hill, "If Such a Frightful Appendage."

P. 250 "Railing against West Coast dances such as the *hamatsa* . . ." The curiosity about the forbidden side of First Nations' culture is a source of continuing fascination to White historians. See Jim McDowell, *Hamatsa: The Enigma of Cannibalism on the Pacific Northwest Coast* (1997).

P. 251 "famed village of Metlakatla where William Duncan . . ." See Howard White, "William Duncan and the Miracle of Metlakatla" (1990), and Peter Murray, *The Devil and Mr. Duncan* (1985).

P. 252 "'It was, along with Niagara Falls . . .'" White, "William Duncan," p. 86.

P. 252 "'the personification of the missionaries of the time . . .'" Wilson Duff quoted in ibid., p. 93.

P. 256 "'Go away, you stealing my poles' . . ." *Lecture on Totems*, Phyllis Inglis Collection, British Columbia Archives.

P. 257 "'She appeared neither wooden nor stationary . . .'" Carr, *Klee Wyck*, p. 39.

P. 258 "'I am rewriting D'Sonoqua's Cats . . ." Carr, *Hundreds and Thousands*, p.155. In fact, the section in *Klee Wyck* is simply called "D'Sonoqua." Her painting *D'Sonoqua and the Cats*, however, links the two incidents as they are in Carr's journal—that is, the visit to the cat village near Quatsino where she also sees the Dzunukwa for the third time.

P. 258 "Critics have picked up on this in recent years . . ." See Roxanne Rimstead, "Klee Wyck: Redefining Region through Marginal Realities" (1991); Hilda Thomas, "Klee Wyck: The Eye of the Other" (1993); Nancy Pagh, "Passing Through the Jungle: Emily Carr and Theories of Women's Autobiography (1992).

P. 258 "'Those old religious painters lived in their religion, not themselves . . .'" Carr, *Hundreds and Thousands*, p. 95.

P. 260 "A.Y. Jackson, who was there in 1926 . . ." See Jackson, *A Painters Country*, p. 89. Jackson credits Mortimer-Lamb as the first to "realize the potentiality of Emily Carr's work" (p. 91).

P. 261 "In *A Death Feast in Dimlahamid* . . ." See Glavin's update of the story of Kitwancool Jim in Glavin, *Death Feast*, p.162–166, and Maureen Cassidy, *From Mountain to Mountain: A History of the Gitksan Village of Ans'payaxw* (1984).

P. 265 "'The most striking thing that one notices . . .' Quoted in Culhane, *The Pleasure of the Crown*, p. 237.

P. 266 "'Footworn a metre deep . . .'" Cheryl Coull, *Traveller's Guide to Aboriginal B.C.* (1996), p. 187.

P. 269 "He digs out a copy of Wilson Duff's monograph . . ." See Wilson Duff, "Histories, Territories and Laws of the Kitwancool" (1959).

Chapter Four

OVER THE HORIZON

New York, 1930

The story of Emily Carr's trip to New York is recorded in *Growing Pains* and *Hundreds and Thousands*. Carr mentions the meeting with Georgia O'Keeffe; however, the O'Keeffe record, which is voluminous, does not. The conversation constructed between them here is imagined, but the sentiments expressed are taken from the published record. In O'Keeffe's case, this includes: Laurie Lisle, *Portrait of an Artist: A Biography of Georgia O'Keeffe* (1980); Jeffrey Hogrefe, *O'Keeffe: The Life of an American Legend* (1992); Roxanne Robinson, *Georgia O'Keeffe* (1989); Sue Davidson Lowe, *Stieglitz: A Memoir/Biography* (1983); Benita Eisler, *O'Keeffe & Stieglitz: An American Romance* (1991), Barbara Buhler Lynes, *O'Keeffe, Stieglitz and the Critics, 1916–1929* (1989); Sarah Whitaker Peters, *Becoming O'Keeffe: The Early Years* (1991); Georgia O'Keeffe, *Georgia O'Keeffe* (1976); Christopher Merrill and Ellen Bradbury, eds., *From the Faraway Nearby: Georgia O'Keeffe as Icon* (1992); Sharyn R. Udall, *Contested Terrain: Myth and Meanings in Southwest Art* (1996). Rosa Bonheur had a huge following in the

United States that reached as far as the midwestern states. See Susy Loeb, ed., *Feminist Collage* (1979), p. 6; Rozsika Parker and Griselda Pollock, *Old Mistresses, Women, Art and Ideology* (1981); Germaine Greer, *Obstacle Race: The Fortunes of Women Painters and their Work* (1979). There is no evidence that Emily Carr actually saw the Burchfield exhibit, although she could have.

Katherine Dreier's ideas are taken from her own writings, Ruth Bohan, *The Société Anonym's Brooklyn Exhibition: Katherine Dreier and Modernism in America* (1982), and L.R. Pfaff, "Lawren Harris and the International Exhibition of Modern Art: Rectification to the Toronto Catalogue (1927) and Some Critical Comments" (1984). The story of the "lost" Duchamp and the Art Gallery of Toronto comes from Dennis Reid, "Marcel Duchamp in Canada" (1987).

O'Keeffe's comment about Roman Catholicism was made in 1932 just after a summer trip to the Gaspé and just before her breakdown. "In New Mexico the crosses interest me because they represent what the Spanish felt about Catholicism—dark, somber, and I painted them that way. On the Gaspé, the cross was Catholicism as the French saw it—gay and witty." Robinson, *Georgia O'Keeffe*, p. 376.

"Fresh Seeing"

P. 293 "'Finally, a woman's feelings on paper!'" Quoted in Hogrefe, *O'Keeffe*, p. 59.

P. 295 "'You wear out the most precious things you have . . .'" O'Keeffe quoted in Robinson, *Georgia O'Keeffe*, p. 200.

P. 296 "'essentially a woman's feeling . . .'" O'Keeffe quoted in Udall, *Contested Terrain*, p. 89.

P. 296 "They 'receive things through the womb,'" quoted in Lynes, *O'Keeffe, Stieglitz and the Critics, 1916–1929*, p. 33.

P. 296 "'With Georgia O'Keeffe one takes a far jump . . .'" Marsden Hartley, 1921, quoted in Robinson, *Georgia O'Keeffe*, p. 240.

P. 296 "'The pure, now flaming . . .'" Paul Rosenfeld, 1921, quoted in ibid., p. 240.

P. 296 "'A woman who has lived many things . . .'" Mabel Dodge, quoted in ibid., p. 292.

P. 300 "'I feel that you haven't any more right . . .'" Quoted in ibid., p. 339.

P. 300 "'At the age of eighty-four Alfred . . .'" Benita Eisler, *O'Keeffe & Stieglitz*, p. 465. In old age, O'Keeffe noted on a folder containing drafts of letters from Stieglitz to his daughter Kitty at the time he left her mother: "Art is a wicked thing. It is what we are."

P. 301 "'She had lost her sense of direction . . .'" Ibid., p. 385.

P. 303 "'In the passionate love of the lover . . .'" Emily Carr, unpublished journals, British Columbia Archives.

P. 304 "However, because Carr sought out O'Keeffe . . ." Ruth Stevens

Applehof, *The Expressionist Landscape: North American Modernist Painting 1920–1947* (1988).

P. 304 "'Lawrence's book is so sexy.'" Carr, *Hundreds and Thousands*, p. 22.

P. 305 "Many poets and artists have imagined it . . ." See, for example, Kate Braid, *To This Cedar Fountain* (1998); John Barton, *West of Darkness* (1987); Elizabeth Hay, *Captivity Tales* (1993).

P. 306 "'I am moving it seems . . .'" O'Keeffe to Jean Toomer, quoted in Robinson, *Georgia O'Keeffe*, p. 404.

P. 307 "What was permanent was a sense of deep . . . commitment . . ." Ibid., p. 404.

P. 308 "She did speak of prejudice in relation to A.Y. Jackson . . " See Carr, *Hundreds and Thousands*.

P. 309 "'I am trying with all my skill . . .'" O'Keeffe quoted in Robinson, *Georgia O'Keeffe*, p. 351. The New Masses was founded in 1926 with John Dos Passos as its first editor. It grew out of *The Masses*, an illustrated socialist magazine that the Ash Can school of artists—Robert Henri George Luks, John Sloan—contributed to. See Haftmann, *Painting in the Twentieth Century* (1965) p.155–158, and p. 293.

P. 309 "'one day seven years ago . . .'" Quoted in Robinson, *Georgia O'Keeffe*, p. 257.

P. 310 "'Georgia O'Keeffe went to Taos, New Mexico . . .'" Henry McBride, *New York Sun*, 1930, quoted in ibid., p. 351.

P. 310 "'the Spanish idea . . .'" Ibid., p. 351.

P. 310 "'O'Keeffe grew up with great spaces . . .'" Ibid., p. 356.

P. 311 "'With the waning of religious faith . . .'" Sharyn Udall, *Contested Terrain*, p. 6–7.

P. 311 "'periods of geographic isolation . . .'" Ibid., p. 85.

P. 311 "'O'Keeffe vacillated between her twin desires . . .'" Ibid., p. 91.

P. 311 "'Write about women. . . .'" quoted in Robinson, *Georgia O'Keeffe*, p. 485.

P. 313 "'That memory or dream thing I do . . .'" O'Keeffe to Dorothy Brett, 1932, in Udall, *Contested Terrain*, p. 93.

P. 313 "*Rodeo* brings to mind the mystical diagrams of . . . Hildegarde of Bingen." See Udall, *Contested Terrain*.

P. 314 "'I am groping, horribly lost.'" Unpublished journals, Phyllis Inglis Collection, British Columbia Archives.

P. 314 "'religion, whatever it is, and his painting are one . . .'" Carr, *Hundreds and Thousands*, p. 17.

P. 314 "'The recognized *function of art* is to *free the spirit* . . .'" Katherine Dreier, *Western Art and the New Era*, (1923)

P. 314 "'Theosophy . . . goes round in circles . . .'" Unpublished journals, Phyllis Inglis Collection, British Columbia Archives.

P. 315 "'All real art is the eternal seeking . . .'" Carr, *Hundreds and Thousands*, p. 29.

P. 315 "Art historians have often noted Carr's natural affinity . . ." See Ann Davis, *The Logic of Ecstasy: Canadian Mystical Painting, 1920–1940* (1992); Ann Davis, Megan Bice and Sharyn Udall, *The Informing Spirit*, 1993.

P. 315 "'Search for the reality of each object . . .'" Carr, *Hundreds and Thousands*, p. 180.

P. 316 "'come to where he is now . . .'" Unpublished journals, Phyllis Inglis Collection, British Columbia Archives.

P. 317 "The cue for this came instead from the Parisian avant-garde . . ." Duchamp lived in New York in the late 1910s and early 1920s and thereafter returned frequently; Mondrian lived there from 1940 until he died in 1944.

P. 318 "'new kind of hermetic literature . . .'" Quoted in Robinson, *Georgia O'Keeffe*, p. 178.

P. 318 "'[It] has less to do with art than with private worship . . .'" Ibid., p.177.

P. 318 "'I have written Miss Dreier . . .'" Letter from Lawren Harris to the Art Gallery of Toronto, December 1926, Art Gallery of Ontario archives.

P. 320 "Perhaps, as curator Megan Bice suggests, . . .'" Megan Bice, "Time, Place, & People," and Ann Davis, "Missing Links" in *The Informing Spirit*, 1993; Alish Farrell, "Emily Carr's Vision of the Real"; Joyce Zemans, "First Fruits: The World and Spirit Paintings" (1989); Ann Davis, "Emily Carr's Mystic Soul" (1993).

P. 320 "'So-called primitive people . . .'" Harris to Carr, ca. 1931, Phyllis Inglis Collection, British Columbia Archives.

P. 320 "Larisey contends that his letters to Carr . . ." Peter Larisey, *Light for a Cold Land* (1993).

P. 320 "'Dear T'Other Emily . . .'" The exact origin of the nickname is not known, but it is generally taken at face value as an alter-ego or persona assumed by Carr in her relationship with Harris.

P. 321 "'secret inner heart . . .'" Shadbolt, *Emily Carr* (1990) p. 143.

P. 321 "'What do these forests make you feel?'" Unpublished journals, Phyllis Inglis Collection, British Columbia Archives.

P. 323 "The sightless sharing eyes . . ." Shadbolt, Emily Carr (1990) p.143.

P. 323 "All of these connection-making events . . ." Matthew Fox, *The Coming of the Cosmic Christ* (1980) p. 51.

P. 323 "'Now that's too bad . . .'" Lawren Harris to Carr ca. 1930, National Gallery of Art archives.

P. 324 "'Let's put it differently.'" Ibid.

P. 324 "But there is also Harris the man . . ." See Larisey, *Light for a Cold Land*, p. 34.

P. 324 "'usefulness may take another direction.'" Harris to Carr, December 1930, quoted in ibid., p. 108.

P. 324 "'*How should I write it?*'" Unpublished journals, Phyllis Inglis Collection, British Columbia Archives.

P. 325 "By summer the Transcendental Group of Painters . . ." See Dennis Reid, *Atma Buddhi Manas: The Later Work of Lawren S. Harris* (1985); Davis, *The Logic of Ecstasy*; Alfred Morang, *Transcendental Painting* (1940); Roald Nasgaard, *The Mystic North: The Northern Symbolist Landscape in Northern Europe and North America 1890–1940* (1984).

Haida Gwaii, 1994

P. 329 "In retrospect, the attention . . ." The so-called renaissance of Northwest Coast art is better understood now as a resurgence, and not the creation of one man. However, Reid was the one, because of his White connections, to bring Haida art to the attention of the art world. Mungo Martin died in 1962 and his last pole was raised in Thunderbird Park, Victoria, in 1961. Willie Seaweed died in 1967.

P. 332 "'Memories came out of this place . . .'" Carr, *Klee Wyck*, p.18.

P. 333 "The old villages may yet survive . . ." See John and Carolyn Smyly, *Those Born at Koona* (1973).

P. 336 "She met the young American modernist Mark Tobey . . ." See Mark Tobey, "Reminiscence and Reverie" (1951), p. 228.

P. 337 "as poet George Stanley has said . . ." George Stanley in conversation, Terrace, B.C., May 1992.

P. 339 "'she rejects the authoritarianism . . ." Robert Linsley, "Landscapes in Motion: Lawren Harris, Emily Carr and the Heterogenous Modern Nation" (1996), p. 91. See also Allan J. Fletcher, "Industrial Algoma and the Myth of Wilderness: Algoma Landscape and the Emergence of the Group of Seven" (1989).

P. 339 "'Perhaps it is because I am a woman . . ." Carr, *Klee Wyck*, p. 107.

P. 339 "'As the canoe glided on, . . .'" Unpublished papers, Phyllis Inglis Collection, British Columbia Archives.

P. 340 "Some, such as Roxanne Rimstead, argue . . ." See Rimstead, "Klee Wyck: Redefining Region through Marginal Realities" (1991) in which she makes the argument that Carr bonded with her West almost as if it were a lover. She chose celibacy in the same moment that she chose the forest. "But the psycho-sexual implications of the wilderness passages in *Klee Wyck* seem more to point beyond romantic, which is fundamentally transcendent, to a more earthy and holistic attachment to the particularity of place," Rimstead writes, quoting the notion of critic Annis Pratt, who postulates the green-world lover: "Through the 'green-world lover, who appears as an alternative to societally acceptable suitors, husbands and lovers,' female heroes may reclaim the erotic potential which patrilineal society has made an object of shame, fear and taboo" (p. 37). See Annis Pratt, "Affairs with Bears: Some Notes Towards Feminist Archetypal Hypotheses for Canadian Literature" (1987).

P. 340 "'One night I had a dream of greenery . . .'" Carr, *Growing Pains*, p. 262.

P. 341 "The name of Hildegard of Bingen . . ." This section is based on the following sources: Matthew Fox, *The Coming of the Cosmic Christ* (1980); Tamara Bernstein, "Hildegard of Bingen" *Ideas*, CBC Radio, 1992; Sabina Flanagan, *Hildegard of Bingen 1098–1179: A Visionary Life* (1989); Barbara Newman, *Sister of Wisdom: St. Hildegard's Theology of the Feminine* (1987); Matthew Fox, *Illuminations of Hildegard of Bingen* (1985).

P. 342 "My own first encounter with Hildegard . . ." Interview with Joyce Wieland, April 1987. See Susan Crean, "Notes From the Language of Emotion" (1987), and "Standing Up for Canada" (1987).

Chapter Five

THE OLD WOMAN AND THE ELEPHANT

Victoria, 1939

This monologue is based on "Sophie" in *Klee Wyck*, the brief mentions of Sophie Frank in *Hundreds and Thousands*, several unpublished sections of the journals, and the letters from Sophie, and from Jimmy Frank to Carr in the British Columbia Archives. It is informed by researches into the life of Sophie Frank carried out in collaboration with artist Shirley Bear. Bear and I created a piece, performed on 23 May 1999 at the Vancouver Art Gallery, called "Dear Sophie/Dear Emily—a dialogue about art, appropriation, and friendship." The exchange about Carr's pottery and Sophie's remark about prostitution derive from that script. Although Sophie's exact age has yet to be established, Bear estimates that she was younger than Carr by ten years or so and died when she was about sixty. This would mean that she was still making a living as a prostitute in her late forties or early fifties. (Were she the same age as Carr, as has been assumed, she would have been having babies into her late forties, and hooking in her fifties.) Art historian Gerta Moray pointed out that, since several letters from Sophie to Carr appear to be written in different hands, some or all may have been written for her at her dictation. Bear rejects the assumption that Sophie Frank was illiterate. Indeed, Sophie was living on a reserve surrounded by the English language, a place where it would have been difficult to avoid schooling. Even if the early letters were dictated to someone with a better hand than hers, the voice in the letters is unmistakable.

I have taken some liberties with chronology. Emily Carr, who knew of Mildred Valley Thornton and disliked her work, did not know of her in the early 1920s when she was making pottery. Thornton moved to Vancouver in 1934 and in the 1920s was painting people from plains cultures on the Prairies. See Mildred Valley Thornton, 1890–1967: an exhibition of Paintings and Watercolours, Butler Galleries, Vancouver: November–December 1985; Reg Ashwell,

"Tribute to a Lady who Painted Indians" *Vancouver Sun*, 8 April 1971. Willie Newcombe, son of C.F. Newcombe, was a good friend of Carr's who helped with many tasks such as framing and crating paintings.

The first four italicized passages are excerpts from the Sophie Frank and Jimmy Frank correspondence in the British Columbia Archives. The last one is from the unpublished journals in the British Columbia Archives.

Wording the Picture

P. 379 "Carr herself was effusive . . . younger friends were put out . . ." See Edythe Hembroff-Schleicher, "A Cluster of Sunburst: Our Emily" (1977).

P. 380 "'He says there's too much *me* . . .'" Fred Housser, Unpublished papers, Phyllis Inglis Collection, British Columbia Archives.

P. 380 "Carr's relationship with Toronto and Theosophy . . ." See Carr correspondence with Bess Harris, Lawren Harris, and Ira Dilworth in the Phyllis Inglis Collection in the British Columbia Archives.

P. 382 "'October, 1940: I did write Bess . . .'" Unpublished journals, Phyllis Inglis Collection, British Columbia Archives.

P. 383 "'His second marriage has seemed to me . . .'" Ibid.

P. 383 "'It is the lifelong building up . . .'" Ibid.

P. 383 "'They say cruel things to each other . . .'" Carr, *Hundreds and Thousands*, p. 190.

P. 383 "'Looking at marrieds I often wonder . . .'" Unpublished journals, Phyllis Inglis Collection, British Columbia Archives.

P. 384 "In the 1930s a crew of much younger women artists . . ." See Walker, ed., *Dear Nan*, and Hembroff-Schleicher, *Emily Carr: The Untold Story*.

P. 387 "Carr's other contemporaries left traces . . ." See taped interviews in the British Columbia Archives with Ruth Humphries, Flora Burns, Kate Mather, and Margaret Clay, "A Portrait in Memory," *Wednesday Night*, CBC Radio, 9 April 1958, and *Between Ourselves*, CBC Radio, December 1969.

P. 388 "'December, 1927: Sophie was terribly glad to see me . . .'" Extract from unpublished journals, Phyllis Inglis Collection, British Columbia Archives.

P. 388 "'She is good, I love her . . .'" Quoted in Hembroff-Schleicher, *Emily Carr*, p. 288.

P. 388 "'Perhaps it was a relief to have an uncomplicated person . . .'" Ibid., p. 289.

P. 389 "'a semi-literate, primitive woman . . .'" Hembroff-Schleicher, *Emily Carr*, p. 288. Gerta Moray notes, "I agree Edythe Hembroff-Schleicher was not interested in Sophie because she was an Indian and from a completely different social class and world. The picture she gave me in several long talks about this was that no relationship with Sophie was at all in evidence during the 1930s when EHS and Carr were seeing each other frequently. That is why she was so sceptical about it later." (Note to author, August 2000.)

P. 389 "by other artists who, like Jovette Marchessault . . ." See Jovette Marchessault, *Le Voyage Magnifique d'Emily Carr* (1990). Marchessault won a Governor General's Award for this play, which was originally written for radio and subsequently performed across the country in English and French.

P. 390 "'her places [were] more successful . . .'" Ruth Humphrey, taped interview, British Columbia Archives.

P. 390 "On the contrary, Emily was eager and curious." Carr's descriptions of the reserve in her unpublished journals make it clear that she saw the poverty and the clutter and judged it in her culture's terms as squalor. It did not put her off visiting Sophie, however, nor did she spare the Catholic Church or the priest her disapproval. And she developed connections with several of Sophie's relatives.

P. 392 "'*The Woman in us meets* . . .'" Unpublished journals, Phyllis Inglis Collection, British Columbia Archives.

P. 393 "It echoes in Emily's words . . ." See Emily Carr, "Modern and Indian Art of the West Coast (1929), p. 18–22, and *Fresh Seeing: Two Addresses by Emily Carr* (1972).

P. 395 "a task that roused suggestions . . ." See Dilworth, "A Portrait in Memory," *Wednesday Night*, CBC Radio, 9 April 1958.

P. 395 "'The absence of the flesh in writing . . .'" Carr, *Hundreds and Thousands*, p. 206.

P. 396 "'There is a side to friendship . . .'" Carr, *Hundreds and Thousands*, p. 206.

P. 396 "'he never attempted to be one of the boys . . '" See "Portrait of a Public Servant," *Wednesday Night*, CBC Radio, April 1963.

P. 397 "'Oh how splendid it will be . . .'" Unpublished journals, Phyllis Inglis Collection, British Columbia Archives.

P. 398 "'at my death the property of Ira Dilworth . . .'" Text of inscription courtesy of Gerta Moray.

P. 398 "'*Sketching in the big woods* . . .'" Carr, *Hundreds and Thousands*, p. 193.

P. 398 "'In my view . . . Carr sought to create a visual language . . .'" See Judith Mastai, "Abjection and Politics: The Work of Canadian Modernist Emily Carr" (1992).

P. 400 "'The psychoanalytic paradigm . . .'" Ibid.

P. 400 "'whose patients demanded . . .'" [author's translation]. See Nicole Jolicoeur, "La Riposte d' Emily Carr" (1991). See also Judith Mastai, "Hysterical Histories: Emily Carr and the Canadian West" (1996), and "Excerpts from an Invitation Seminar on the Life and Work of Emily Carr" (1991).

P. 402 "(Perhaps the most affecting example of this . . . Camille Claudel . . ." See Anne Delbee, *Camille Claudel, une Femme* (1992), and Reine-Marie Paris, *Camille: The Life of Camille Claudel, Rodin's Muse and Mistress* (1984). Claudel (1864–1943) was a prodigy, an extraordinarily gifted artist who was eighteen when her father took her to study in Paris, where she met Rodin. She lived and worked with Rodin into the 1890s. After she broke with him, she tried to continue sculpting on her own but failed to get commissions. Her father protected her by keeping her from destitution, but within days of his death, her mother and brother had Claudel forcibly removed from her studio and committed to an asylum. She never saw her mother again. Her brother, the poet/diplomat Paul Claudel, continued to pay for her institutionalization until her death. Although the records show that the director of the hospital advised Mme Claudel early on that there was no reason why her daughter could not return home, the family chose to keep her there. Reine-Marie Paris, a grand-niece of Camille Claudel, maintains the family story that Camille was mad, but this has been contested by others. See the film *Camille Claudel,* which was a project of actor Isabelle Adjani, who plays Claudel to Gerard Depardieu's Rodin. See also Elaine Showalter, *The Female Malady* (1985).

P. 403 "'yet another building block in the wall . . .'" See Judith Mastai, "Some Notes on the Narcissism of the Viewers with Respect to the Work of Emily Carr, Hildegard of Bingen and Julia Kristeva" (1991). See also Julia Kristeva, *Black Sun: Depression and Melancholia* (1989).

P. 403 "'Since her death Carr has had several lives . . .'" See Barry Lord, *Towards a People's Art* (1974), and Catherine Sheldrick Ross, "A Singing Spirit: Female Rites of Passage in *Klee Wyck, Surfacing* and *The Diviners,*" *Atlantis* 4, no. 1 (Fall 1978).

P. 403 "She has been judged as a modernist . . ." See Daniel Francis, "Who's Afraid of the Group of Seven?" *Geist* 5, no. 21 (Spring 1996). Karen Wilken, "Maple-leaf Modernist: The Case of Emily Carr" (1993), and Terry Fenton and Karen Wilkin, "Two Isolated Modernists" (1978).

Gabriola Island, 1999

P. 413 "'Historically, Europeans' tendency to attribute cannibalism . . .'" Deborah Root, *Cannibal Culture: Art Appropriation and the Commodification of Difference* (1998), p. 15.

P. 414 "There is the example of the landscape exhibition mounted at the Art Gallery of Ontario . . ." See Susan Crean, *Who's Afraid of Canadian Culture?* (1976), p. 266.

P. 416 "'You have to be careful that you do not write or paint . . .'" Unpublished journals, Phyllis Inglis Collection, British Columbia Archives.

P. 417 "Many artists have found this out . . .'" Both these examples are true. *File* magazine was the brainchild of General Idea, the Toronto collective consisting of Jorge Zontal, A.A. Bronson, and Felix Partz.

P. 419 "That spring a controversy had erupted over this very question . . ." See Marcia Crosby, "Construction of the Imaginary Indian" (1991). See also Robert Fulford, "The Trouble with Emily" (1993), p. 33–39.

P. 421 "As always, interesting ideas crop up . . ." See Suzy Gablik, *Has Modernism Failed?* (1984) and *The Re-enchantment of Art* (1991); Robert Linsley,

"Painting and Social History of British Columbia" (1991); Scott Watson, "Race, Wilderness, Territory and the Origins of Modern Canadian Landscape Painting" (1994) and "Disfigured Nature: The Origins of the Modern Canadian Landscape" in *Eye of Nature*, Banff: Walter Phillips Gallery (1991).

P. 421 "'[Art] was a living thing . . .'" See Gablik, *Has Modernism Failed?*, p. 90.

P. 422 "'The oval spaces of her rain forests . . .'" Lucy Lippard, *Overlay: Contemporary Art and the Art of Prehistory* (1983), p. 50.

P. 423 "Out here on the Edge of the Continent . . .'" Scott Watson, letter to *Canadian Art* (Spring 1993), p. 31.

P. 423 "'For the urban dweller whose very existence . . .'" Robert Linsley, "Painting and Social History of British Columbia," (1991).

P. 425 "'I'd never seen anything of this kind in Canada . . .'" See "Portrait in Memory," *Wednesday Night*, CBC Radio, April 1958.

P. 425 "'strangely unfeminine power of attack . . .'" See "Emily Carr Was a Growing Art," *Saturday Night*, 3 November 1945.

P. 425 "In 1941, Robertson Davies reviewed *Klee Wyck* . . ." "The Revelation of Emily Carr," *Saturday Night*, 8 November 1941.

P. 426 "inevitable that people would claim her as theirs." The question is does it really matter who "recognized" Carr first? The phenomenon is indicative of the proprietary response to Carr and the need people have felt to account for her lack of support. Harris said on CBC's "Portrait in Memory": "We each encouraged her to start painting again. She'd stopped a few years before. Here was one of Canada's greatest artists, apparently at the end of her career. She was, indeed, too far advanced, too modern, too vital for B.C., and was almost completely ignored." He implies that the public's apathy had something to do with Carr's inactivity, and that she was really "discovered" in 1927 when she travelled east and met the Toronto artists who respected her. The pattern here is familiar and to be found in Frances Hodgkins's biography, too. Hodgkins's London dealer, Arthur Howell (who later wrote about her), assumed that she came out of nowhere when she arrived on the art scene. If he hadn't heard of her and couldn't account for her among his own contacts, she didn't exist.

P. 426 "the 1998 *Delgamuukw* decision . . ." See Culhane, *The Pleasure of the Crown* (1997). The 1997 Supreme Court decision ruled that Judge McEachern had erred in dismissing the oral evidence of the Gitksan and Wet'suwet'en chiefs and elders and ordered a new trial. Culhane quotes Ray Jones on the day the decision was announced: "I have mixed emotions today. I am filled with joy and also with remembrance of people who have worked so hard. I remember our Elders who passed on with broken hearts and the words of Chief Justice McEachern in their ears. Today's decision begins to heal the wounds."

P. 427 "'Perhaps Miss Carr felt Vancouver had . . .'" See "Portrait in Memory," *Wednesday Night*, CBC Radio, April 1958.

P. 428 "'Spiritual yearnings have been part and parcel . . .'" See Fenton and Wilkin, "Two Isolated Modernists," (1978).

Notes

P. 428 "[H]er art has less to do . . .'" John Bentley Mays, "Signs of Struggle" *The Globe and Mail*, Saturday, 7 July 1990. Mays goes on to say: "I am completely at a loss to understand what serious people find attractive about Carr's opinions, those hackneyed Wordsworthian warblings about nature, the pious twaddle on the subject of God or 'nature.'"

P. 429 "They say she cooked her books . . ." First Nations people who have made that charge are speaking of Carr's misrepresentation of their lives or communities. The White critics who make the claim are saying that Carr was not truthful about herself.

P. 430 "In this last decade Carr has become . . ." Conversations with Jennifer Mascall, Winsom, and Kate Braid, among others. See/hear Veda Hille, *Here is a Picture* (visit: noplace.com/Veda). See also Braid, *To This Cedar Fountain* (1995); Kate Braid, *Inward to the Bones: Georgia O'Keeffe's Journey with Emily Carr* (1998); Barton, *West of Darkness* (1987); Florence McNeil, *Emily* (1975).

Bibliography

This is a listing of the main books and articles consulted in the writing of this book. The Carr literature is vast, and this list does not include the large archive of newspaper articles.

Abbott, Donald N. *The World Is as Sharp as a Knife: An Anthology in Honour of Wilson Duff*. Victoria: B.C. Provincial Museum, 1981.

Adams, Howard. *Prison of Grass*. Saskatoon: Fifth House, 1989.

———. *A Tortured People*. Penticton: Theytus, 1995.

Adams, Timothy Dow. "Painting Above Paint: Telling Li(v)es in Emily Carr's Literary Self-Portraits." *Journal of Canadian Studies* 27, no. 2 (Summer 1992).

Adamson, Jeremy. *Lawren S. Harris: Urban Scenes & Wilderness Landscapes*. Toronto: Art Gallery of Ontario, 1978.

Alfred, Taiaike. *Peace, Power, Righteousness: An Indigenous Manifesto*. Toronto: Oxford University Press, 1999.

Allen, Lillian. *First Steps on the Road to Cultural and Racial Equity*. Toronto: Ontario Ministry of Culture and Communications, 1992.

Allen, Paula Gunn. *The Sacred Hoop: Recovering the Feminine in American Indian Traditions*. Boston: Beacon Press, 1986.

Amsden, Philip. "Memories of Emily Carr." *Canadian Forum* (December 1947).

Appelhof, Ruth Stevens. *The Expressionist Landscape: North American Modernist Painting 1920–1947*. Birmingham: Birmingham Museum of Art, 1988.

Armstrong, Jeanette. *Looking at the Words of Our People*. Penticton: Theytus Books, 1993.

Arnott, Chris. *The Terror of the Coast: Land Alienation and Colonial War on Vancouver and the Gulf Islands, 1849–1863*. Vancouver: Talonbooks, 1999.

Art in New Zealand 16, Frances Hodgkins issue (1980).

Ascent: A Journal of the Arts in New Zealand, Frances Hodgkins Commemorative Issue (December 1969).

Asch, Michael, ed. *Aboriginal and Treaty Rights in Canada: Essays on Law, Equality, and Respect for Difference*. Vancouver: University of British Columbia, 1997.

Barbeau, Marius. *Downfall of Temlaham*. Edmonton: Hurtig, [1928] 1973.

———. "The Indian of the Prairies and the Rockies: A Theme for Modern Painters." *The University of Toronto Quarterly* 1, no. 2 (January 1932): 197–206.

———. "Canada and the Red Man." Manuscript, Barbeau Archive, Canadian Museum of Civilization, 1931.

———. "Native Indian Art of the Northwest Coast." Manuscript, Barbeau Archive, Canadian Museum of Civilization.

———. "Our Indians: Their Disappearance." *Queen's Quarterly* 38 (Autumn 1931): 691–707.

———. *Indian Days in the Rockies*. Toronto: Macmillan, 1923.

Barman, Jean. *The West Beyond the West*. Toronto: University of Toronto Press, 1996.

Barton, John. *West of Darkness*. Kapuskasing: Penumbra Press, 1987.

Bear, Shirley, et al. *Enough is Enough: Aboriginal Women Speak Out*. Toronto: Women's Press, 1987.

Bell, Leonard. *The Maori in European Art*. Wellington: Reed, 1980.

———. "The Representation of the Maori by European Artists in New Zealand, ca. 1890–1914." In *Art Journal* (Summer 1990): 142–149.

Benstock, Shari. *Women of the Left Bank 1900–1940*. Austin: University of Texas Press, 1986.

Berger, Carl. "The True North Strong and Free." In *Nationalism in Canada*, edited by Peter Russell. Toronto: McGraw-Hill Ryerson, 1966.

Berger, Thomas R. *A Long and Terrible Shadow: White Values, Native Rights in the Americas 1492–1992*. Vancouver: Douglas & McIntyre, 1991.

Bernier, Leon, et al., *Homage à Marcel Rioux: sociologie critique, création artistique, et societé contemporaine*. Montreal: Editions Saint-Martin, 1992.

Bernstein, Tamara. "Hildegard of Bingen." CBC Ideas, CBC Radio, 1992.

Bhabha, Homi K. *Nation and Narration*. London: Routledge, 1990.

Bice, Megan. "Time, Place, & People." In Megan Bice and Sharyn Udall, *The Informing Spirit: Art of the American Southwest and the West Coast of Canada 1925–1945*. Toronto: McMichael Canadian Art Collection, 1993.

Blanchard, Paula. *The Life of Emily Carr*. Vancouver: Douglas & McIntyre, 1987.

Bloore, Ron. "In the Mainstream." *Artscanada* (December 1969).

Bodsworth, Fred. *The Pacific Coast: The Illustrated National History of Canada*. Toronto: NSL Ltd., 1970.

———. *Last of the Curlews*, Toronto: McClelland & Stewart, 1963.

Bohan, Ruth. *The Société Anonyme's Brooklyn Exhibition: Katherine Dreier and Modernism in America*. Ann Arbor, Michigan: U M I Press, 1982.

Brabant, Father. "Mission to Nootka, 1874–1900: Reminiscences of the West Coast of Vancouver Island." Edited by Charles Lillard. Gray's Publishing, 1977.

Bradley, Jessica, and Lesley Johnstone, eds. *Sightlines: Reading Contemporary Canadian Art*. Montreal, Artextes Editions, 1994.

Braid, Kate. *Inward to the Bones: Georgia O'Keeffe's Journey with Emily Carr.* Victoria: Polestar, 1998.

———. *To this Cedar Fountain.* Victoria: Polestar, 1995.

Breen-Needham, Howard, Sandy Frances Duncan, Deborah Ferens, Phyllis Reeve, Susan Yates. *Witness to Wilderness: The Clayoquot Sound Anthology.* Vancouver: Arsenal Pulp Press, 1994.

Breuer, Michael, and Kerry Mason Dodd. *Sunlight in the Shadows: The Landscape of Emily Carr.* Toronto: Oxford University Press, 1984.

Brody, Hugh. *Maps and Dreams.* Vancouver: Douglas & McIntyre, 1981.

Brooker, Bertram. "Canada's Modern Art Movement." *Canadian Forum* 6, no. 69 (June 1926).

———. *Yearbook of the Arts in Canada 1928/9.* Toronto: Macmillan, 1929. (See articles by Marius Barbeau, Lawren Harris, and Bertram Brooker.)

Brown, Gordon, and Hamish Keith. *Introduction to New Zealand Painting.* London: Collins, 1969.

Brown, Jennifer. *Strangers in Blood: Fur Trade Company Families in Indian Country.* Vancouver: University of British Columbia Press, 1980.

Brown, F. Maud. *Breaking Barriers: Eric Brown and the National Gallery.* Toronto: The Society for Art Publications, 1964.

Buchanan, Ian, et al. *Frances Hodgkins: Paintings and Drawings.* London: Thames & Hudson, 1995.

———. "Emily Carr." In *The Clear Spirit,* edited by Mary Q. Innis. Toronto: University of Toronto Press, 1966.

Burns, Flora Hamilton. "Emily Carr and the Newcombe Collection." In *The World of Emily Carr,* exhibition catalogue for the Hudson's Bay Company, Victoria and Vancouver, 1962.

Bus, Helen. "Canadian Women's Autobiography: Some Critical Direction." In *Amazing Spaces: Canadian Women's Writing,* edited by Shirley Newman and Smaro Kamboureli. Edmonton: Longspoon, 1986.

Campbell, Bruce F. *Ancient Wisdom Revived: A History of the Theosophic Movement.* Berkeley: University of California Press, 1980.

Canadian Forum, editorial. "West Coast Indian Art." *Canadian Forum* (February 1928).

Cardinal, Harold. *The Unjust Society: the Tragedy of Canada's Indians.* Edmonton: Hurtig, 1969.

Carpenter, Edward. "Collecting Northwest Coast Art, Introduction to Bill Holm and Bill Reid, Indian Art of the North West Coast: A Dialogue of Craftsmanship and Aesthetics." Seattle: Institute of Art, Washington University Press, 1975.

Carr, Emily. "Modern and Indian Art of the West Coast." *The Supplement to the McGill News* (June 1929):18–22.

———. *Pause: A Sketch Book.* Toronto: Clarke Irwin, 1953.

———. *The Book of Small.* Toronto: Clarke Irwin, 1966.

———. *Hundreds and Thousands.* Toronto: Clarke Irwin, 1966.

·———. *Klee Wyck*. Toronto: Clarke Irwin, 1971.

———. *The House of All Sorts*. Toronto: Clarke Irwin, 1971.

———. *Growing Pains*. Toronto: Irwin, 1971.

———. *Fresh Seeing: Two Addresses by Emily Carr*. Toronto: Clarke Irwin, 1972.

Cassidy, Frank, ed. *Reaching Just Settlements: Land Claims in British Columbia*. Lantzville, BC: Oolican Books, 1991.

———. ed. *Aboriginal Title in British Columbia: Delgamuuk v. the Queen*. Lantzville, BC: Oolican Books, 1992.

Cassidy, Maureen. *From Mountain to Mountain: A History of the Gitksan Village of Ans'payaxw*. Kispiox: Ans'payaxw School Society, 1984.

Clay, Margaret. "Emily Carr as I Knew Her." *The Business and Professional Woman* 26, no. 9 (November/December 1959).

Coburn, Kathleen. "Emily Carr: In Memoriam." *Canadian Forum* (April 1946).

Cole, Douglas. *Captured Heritage—the Scramble for Northwest Coast Artifacts*. Vancouver: Douglas & McIntyre, 1985.

———. *Franz Boas: The Early Years, 1858–1906*. Vancouver: Douglas & McIntyre, 1999.

———. "The Origins of Canadian Anthropology, 1850–1910." *Journal of Canadian Studies* (February 1973).

Cole, Douglas, and Ira Chaikin. *An Iron Hand Upon the People: The Law Against the Potlatch on the Northwest Coast*. Vancouver: Douglas & McIntyre, 1990.

Coleman, M.E. "Emily Carr and Her Sisters." *The Dalhousie Review* 27, no. 1 (April 1947): 29–32.

Cook, Ramsay. "Cultural Nationalism in Canada: An Historical Perspective." In *Canadian Cultural Nationalism*, the Fourth Lester B. Pearson Conference on the Canada–United States Relationship. New York: New York University Press, 1977.

———. "Landscape Painting and National Sentiment in Canada." *Historical Reflections* 1, no. 2 (Winter 1974): 263–285.

Coull, Cheryl. *Traveller's Guide to Aboriginal B.C.* Vancouver: Whitecap Books, 1996.

Crean, Susan. "Notes From the Language of Emotion." *Canadian Art* (Spring 1987).

———. "Standing Up for Canada." *This Magazine* 21, no. 4 (September 1987).

———. *Who's Afraid of Canadian Culture?* Toronto: General Publishing, 1976.

Crosby, Marcia. "Construction of the Imaginary Indian." In *Vancouver Anthology: The Institutional Politics of Art*, edited by Stan Douglas. Vancouver: Talonbooks, 1991.

Culhane, Dara. *The Pleasure of the Crown: Anthropology, Law and First Nations*. Burnaby: Talonbooks, 1997.

Daniels, Roy. "*Emily Carr*." Pure Living Heritage, 4th Series, edited by R.L. McDougall. Toronto: Carleton University Press and University of Toronto Press, 1962.

Daniels, Stephen, and Denis Cosgrove. "Introduction: Iconography and Landscape." In *The Iconography of Landscape*, edited by Stephen Daniels and Denis Cosgrove. Cambridge: Cambridge University Press, 1988.

Darling, David, and Douglas Cole. "Totem Pole Restoration on the Skeena, 1925–1930: An Early Exercise in Heritage Conservation." *B.C. Studies* 47 (Autumn 1980).

Davidson, Margaret. "A New Approach to the Group of Seven." *Journal of Canadian Studies* 4, no. 4 (November 1969).

Davis, Ann. "Emily Carr's Mystic Soul." *The Literary Review of Canada* (February 1993).

———. *The Logic of Ecstasy: Canadian Mystical Painting, 1920–1940*. Toronto: University of Toronto Press, 1992.

———. "Missing Links." In Megan Bice and Sharyn Udall. *The Informing Spirit: Art of the American Southwest and the West Coast of Canada, 1925–1945*. Toronto: McMichael Canadian Art Collection, 1993.

Deacon, William Arthur, and Wilfred Reeves. *Open House*. Ottawa: Graphic Publishers, 1931.

Delbee, Anne. *Camille Claudel, une Femme*. San Francisco: Mercury, 1992.

Dickason, Olive Patricia. *Canada's First Nations: A History of Founding Peoples from Earliest Times*. Toronto: McClelland & Stewart, 1992.

Dilworth, Ira. "Emily Carr: Canadian Artist-Author." *Saturday Night* 57, no. 1 (November 1941).

Docking, Gill. *Two Hundred Years of New Zealand Art*. Melbourne, Australia: Landsdown Press, 1971.

Dragland, Stan. *Floating Voice: Duncan Campbell Scott and the Literature of Treaty 9*. Toronto: Anansi, 1994.

———. ed. *Duncan Campbell Scott: A Book of Criticism*. Ottawa: Tecumseh Press, 1974.

Dreier, Katherine S. *Western Art and the New Era: An Introduction to Modern Art*. New York: Brentano's, 1923.

Duff, Wilson. "Histories, Territories and Laws of the Kitwancool." *Anthropology in B.C. Memoir No. 4*. Victoria: British Columbia Provincial Museum, 1959.

———. "The Indian History of British Columbia." *The Impact of the White Man*, vol. 1, Anthropology in British Columbia, Memoir No. 5 Victoria: Provincial Museum of British Columbia, 1964.

———. "Contribution of Marius Barbeau to West Coast Ethnology." *Anthropologica* 6 (1964): 63–96.

———. "The Fort Victoria Treaties." *B.C. Studies* 3 (Fall 1969).

———. *Images Stone B.C.: Thirty Centuries of Northwest Coast Indian Sculpture*. Toronto: Oxford University Press, 1975.

Dyck, Sandra. "These Things Are Our Totems: Marius Barbeau and the Indigenization of Canadian Art and Culture in the 1920s." M.A. thesis, Carleton University, 1995.

Elderkin, Susan Huntley. "Recovering the Fictions of Emily Carr." *Studies in Canadian Literature* 17 no. 2 (1993).

Eisler, Benita. *O'Keeffe & Stieglitz: An American Romance*. New York: Doubleday, 1991.

Elliott, Bridget, and Jo-Ann Wallace. *Women Artists and Writers: Modernist (im)positionings*. London: Routledge, 1994.

Emberley, Julie. *Thresholds of Difference: Feminist Critique, Native Women's Writings, Postcolonial Theory*. Toronto: University of Toronto Press, 1993.

Endicott, Marion. *Emily Carr: The Story of an Artist*. Toronto: Women's Press, 1981.

Esquimalt Silver Threads Writers Group. *Seafarers, Saints and Sinners: Tales of Esquimault and Victoria West People*. Victoria: Desktop Publishing Ltd., Esquimalt Silver Threads Writers Group, c. 1994.

Evans, Myfanwy. *Frances Hodgkins*. London: Penguin Books, 1948.

———. *"Memorial Exhibition of the Works of Frances Hodgkins 1869–1947*, London: The Arts Council, 1952.

———. "The Life & Art of Frances Hodgkins." *Listener* (21 November 1946).

Fairley, Barker. "What's Wrong with Canadian Art?" *Canadian Art* (Autumn 1948).

Farrell, Alish. "Emily Carr's Vision of the Real." *Queen's Quarterly* 90:3 (Fall 1983).

———. "Signs of Reform: Aspects of a Protestant Iconography." *Religion/Culture Comparative Canadian Studies*, Conference Proceedings, Toronto: Association for Canadian Studies, 1985.

Fenton, Terry, and Karen Wilkin. "Two Isolated Modernists." In *Modern Painting in Canada: Major Movements in Twentieth Century Canadian Art*. Edmonton: Hurtig, 1978.

Ferguson, Russel, Martha Gever, Trinh T. Minh-ha and Cornel West, eds. *Out There: Marginalization and Contemporary Culture*. New York: The New Museum of Contemporary Art; Cambridge, Mass: The MIT Press, 1990.

Fisher, Robin. *Contact and Conflict: Indian-European Relations in British Columbia, 1774–1890*. Vancouver: University of British Columbia Press, 1977.

Flanagan, Sabina. *Hildegard of Bingen 1098–1179: A Visionary Life*. New York and London: Routledge, 1989.

Fletcher, Allan J. "Industrial Algoma and the Myth of Wilderness: Algoma Landscape and the Emergence of the Group of Seven." M.A. thesis, University of British Columbia, 1989.

Forbes, Elizabeth. *Wild Roses at Their Feet: Pioneer Women of Vancouver Island*. Vancouver: Evergreen Press, 1971.

Ford, Clelland, ed. *Smoke from Their Fires: Life of a Kwatkiutl Chief*. New Haven: Institute of Human Relations, Yale University Press, 1961.

Fox, Matthew. *The Coming of the Cosmic Christ*. San Francisco: Harper & Row, 1980.

———. *Illumination of Hildegard of Bingen*. Santa Fe, New Mexico: Bear & Co., 1985.

Francis, Daniel. *The Imaginary Indian: The Image of the Indian in Canadian Culture*. Vancouver: Arsenal Pulp Press, 1993.

————. "Re-hanging the National Wallpaper: the Group of Seven and the Public Mind" *Geist* 5 (Spring 1996).

Freedman, Adele. "Art: The Disturbing Complexity of Emily Carr: The Dark Side of the Legend." *Toronto Life* (February 1980).

Frye, Marilyn. *On Being White*. Trumansburg, New York: Crossing Press, 1983.

Fulford, Robert. "The Trouble with Emily." *Canadian Art* (Winter 1993): 33–39.

Gablik, Suzy. *Has Modernism Failed?* New York: Thames & Hudson, 1984.

————. *The Re-enchantment of Art*. London: Thames & Hudson, 1991.

Galipeau, Pascale. *Les Paradis du Monde: Quebec Folk Art*. Ottawa: Canadian Museum of Civilization, 1995.

Gawthrop, Daniel. *Vanishing Halo: Saving the Boreal Forest*. Vancouver: David Suzuki Foundation/Greystone Books, 1999.

Gill, Linda. *The Letters of Frances Hodgkins*. Auckland: Auckland University Press, 1993.

Glavin, Terry. *Death Feast in Dimlahmid*. Vancouver: New Star, 1990.

Goldie, Terry. *Fear and Temptation: The Image of the Indigene in Canadian, Australian and New Zealand Literatures*. Montreal/Kingston: McGill–Queen's University Press, 1989.

Gough, Barry. *Gunboat Frontier: British Marine Authority and Northwest Coast Indians 1846–1890*. Vancouver: University of British Columbia Press, 1984.

————. "A Priest Versus the Potlatch: The Reverend Alfred James Hall and the Fort Rupert Kwakiutl, 1878–1880." *Journal of Canadian Church Historical Society* 24, no. 2 (1982).

Gould, Jan. *Women of British Columbia*. Saanichton: Hancock House, 1975.

Gowers, Ruth. *Emily Carr*. Berg Women's Series. New York: Leamington Spa, 1987.

Graham, Gwethalyn, and Solange Chaput Rolland. *Dear Enemies*. Toronto: Macmillan, 1963.

Grant, John Webster. *Moon of Wintertime: Missionaries and the Indians of Canada in Encounter since 1534*. Toronto: University of Toronto Press, 1984.

Greenberg, Clement. "Art." *The Nation*, June 15, 1946.

Greer, Germaine. *Obstacle Race: The Fortunes of Women Painters and Their Work*. London: Picador, 1979.

Gregson, Harry. *A History of Victoria, 1842–1970*. Victoria: Victoria Observer Publishing, 1970.

Griffin, Susan. *Woman and Nature: The Roaring Inside Her*. New York: Harper & Row, 1978.

Haftman, Werner. *Painting in the Twentieth Century*. London: Lund Humphries, 1965.

Halliday, William. *Potlatch and Totem and the Recollections of an Indian Agent*. Toronto: Dent, 1934.

Harris, Bess, and R.G.P. Colgrove. *Lawren Harris 1885–1970*. Toronto: Macmillan, 1969.

Harris, Cole. "The Myth of the Land in Canadian Nationalism," in Peter Russell, ed. *Nationalism in Canada*. Toronto: McGraw-Hill Ryerson, 1966.

Harris, Lawren. *Emily Carr: Her Paintings and Sketches*, 1945 (Catalogue). Ottawa: National Gallery of Canada, 1945.

———. "Emily Carr and Her Work." *Canadian Forum* 21 (December 1941).

———. "Modern Art and Aesthetic Reaction: An Appreciation." *Canadian Forum* (May 1927).

———. "Revelation of Art in Canada." *The Canadian Theosophist* 14, no. 5 (7 July 1926).

———. "Theosophy and Art." *The Canadian Theosophist* 14, no. 6 (15 July 1926):

Hay, Elizabeth. *Captivity Tales*. Vancouver: New Star, 1993.

Healey, Elizabeth. *The History of Alert Bay*. Vancouver: Alert Bay Centennial Committee, 1958.

Hembroff-Schleicher, Edythe. "A Cluster of Sunburst: Our Emily." Provincial Archives of British Columbia, Ministry of the Provincial Secretary, July 1977.

———. *Emily Carr: The Untold Story*. Saanichton: Hancock House, 1978.

———. *M.E. Portrait of Emily Carr*. Toronto: Clarke Irwin, 1969.

Hill, Beth. "If Such a Frightful Appendage Can Be Called Ornamental." *Raincoast Chronicles* 8 (1980).

Hill, Charles. *Art for a Nation*. Ottawa: National Gallery of Canada, 1995.

Hiller, Susan, ed. *The Myth of Primitivism*. London: Routledge, 1991.

Hills, Emily-Jane. "Emily Carr . . . in France." *Times Colonist* (9 December 1979).

———. "Emily Carr and Frances Hodgkins." *Times Colonist* (16 December 1979).

Hogref, Jeffrey. *O'Keeffe: The Life an American Legend*. New York: Bantam, 1992.

Holm, Bill. *Smoky-Top: The Art and Times of Willie Seaweed*. Vancouver: Douglas & McIntyre, 1983.

Housser, F.B. *A Canadian Art Movement: The Story of the Group of Seven*. Toronto: Macmillan, 1926.

———. "Some Thoughts on National Consciousness." *Canadian Theosophist* 8, no. 5 (15 July 1927).

———. "Walt Whitman & North American Idealism." *Canadian Theosophist* 11, no. 5 (15 July 1930):

Howell, Arthur. *Frances Hodgkins: Four Vital Years*. London: 1951.

Hubbard, R.H. "Biographies of Artists: M. Emily Carr." In *An Anthology of Canadian Art*. Toronto: University of Toronto Press, 1960.

Humphrey, Ruth. "Emily Carr: An Appreciation." *Queen's Quarterly* (Summer 1958).

———. "Letters from Emily Carr." *Queen's Quarterly* 41, no. 2 (Winter 1972).

Hutcheon, Linda. "Incredulity Toward Meta-narrative: Negotiating Post-Modernism and Feminism." *Tessera* 7 (Fall 1989).

Irigaray, Luce. *This Sex Which Is Not One*. New York: Cornell University Press, 1977.

Innis, Harold. "The Church in Canada." *Essays in Canadian Economic History*, edited by Mary Q. Innis. Toronto: University of Toronto Press, 1956.

Jackson, A.Y. "Artists in the Mountains." *Canadian Forum* (January 1925).

———. *A Painter's Country: An Autobiography of A.Y. Jackson*. Toronto: Clarke Irwin, 1958.

James, Merlin. "Manchester, Influence and Originality: Ivon Hitchens, Frances Hodgkins, Winifred Nicholson." *The Burlington Magazine* 138, no. 1118 (May 1996).

Jensen, Doreen, and Polly Sargent. *Robes of Power*. Vancouver: University of British Columbia Press, 1986.

Jensen, Philip. "A Passage from India." *The Beaver* (June/July 2000).

Jewitt, John R. *White Slaves of the Nootka* [1815], Surrey: Heritage House Publishers, 1987.

Johnson, Peter. *Glyphs and Gallows: The Rock Art of Clo-oose and the Wreck of the John Bright*. Surrey: Heritage House, 1999.

Johnston, Basil. *Indian School Days*. Toronto: Key Porter Books, 1986.

———. *The Manitous: The Spiritual World of the Ojibway*. New York: Harper-Collins, 1995.

Johnston, Franz. "An Objection." *Canadian Forum* (May 1927).

Johnston, Hugh J.M. *Pacific Province: A History of British Columbia*. Vancouver: Douglas & McIntyre, 1996.

Jolicoeur, Nicole. "La Riposte d'Emily Carr." In *Emily Carr*, edited by Judith Mastai. Vancouver: Vancouver Art Gallery, 1991.

Jonaitis, Aldona. *Chiefly Feasts: The Enduring Kwakiutl*. Portland: American Museum of Natural History, 1991.

Julian, Terry. *A Capital Controversy*. New Westminster: Signature Publishing, 1994.

Kanakos, Jeannie L. "The Negotiations to Relocate the Songhees Indians, 1843–1911." M.A. thesis, Simon Fraser University, 1982.

Kandinsky, Wassily. *Concerning the Spiritual in Art*. New York: G. Wittenborn, 1955.

Kellor, Betty. *Pauline: A Biography of Pauline Johnson*. Halifax: Goodread, 1981.

Kelly, Mary. "Re-viewing Modernist Criticism." *Screen* 22, no. 3 (1981).

Kirk, Heather. "Will the Real Emily Carr Please Stand Up?" *The Literary Review of Canada* (June 1994).

Klein, Marcia B. *Beyond the Land Itself: Views of Nature and Canada and the United States*. Cambridge: Harvard University Press, 1970.

Knight, Rolf. *Indians at Work: An Informal History of Native Labour in B.C., 1851–1930*. Vancouver: New Star, 1996.

Kristeva, Julia. *Black Sun: Depression and Melancholia*. New York: Columbia University Press, 1989.

———. "Women's Time." *Signs* (1981).

Kritzwizer, Kay. "Carr: The Angry Artists in Retrospect." *The Globe and Mail* (13 December 1971).

Kroller, Eva-Marie. "Literary Versions of Emily Carr." *Canadian Literature* 109 (Summer 1986).

———. "Resurrections: Susanna Moodie, Catherine Parr Traill and Emily Carr in Contemporary Canadian Literature." *Journal of Popular Culture* 15:3 (Winter 1981).

Krotz, Larry. *Indian Country: Inside Another Canada*. Toronto: McClelland & Stewart, 1992.

Lacombe, Michele. "Theosophy and the Canadian Idealist Tradition." *Journal of Canadian Studies* (Summer 1982).

Landauer, Susan. "Searching for Selfhood: Women Artists of Northern California." In *Independent Spirits: Women Painters of the American West, 1890–1945*, edited by Patricia Trenton. Berkeley: University of California Press, 1995.

Larisey, Peter. *Light for a Cold Land*. Toronto: Dundurn Press, 1993.

Latham, Barbara K., and Roberta J. Pazdro, eds. *Not Just Pin Money: Selected Essays on the History of Women's Work in B.C.* Victoria: Camosun College, 1984.

Laurence, Robin. *Beloved Land: The World of Emily Carr*. Vancouver: Douglas & McIntyre, 1996.

Laviolette, Forest. *The Struggle for Survival, Indian Culture and the Protestant Ethic in British Columbia*. Toronto: University of Toronto Press, 1961.

Lay, Jackie. "To Columbia on the Tynemouth: The Emigration of Single Women and Girls in 1862." In *In Her Own Right: Selected Essays on Women's History in B.C.* Barbara Latham and Cathy Kess, eds; Victoria: Camosun College, 1980.

LeGates, Marlene. *Making Waves: A History of Feminism in Western Society*. Mississauga: Copp Clark, 1996.

Lévesque, Andrée. *Scènes de la vie en rouge: L'époque de Jeanne Corbin, 1906–1944*. Montréal: les éditions du remue-ménage, 1999.

Lévi-Strauss, C. *The Way of the Masks*. Vancouver: Douglas & McIntyre, 1982.

Lillard, Charles. *Seven Shillings a Year: The History of Vancouver Island*. Ganges, B.C.: Horsdale & Shubart, 1986.

Linsley, Robert. "Painting and Social History of British Columbia." In *The Vancouver Anthology: Institutional Politics of Art*, edited by Stan Douglas. Vancouver: Talonbooks, 1991.

———. "Landscapes in Motion: Lawren Harris, Emily Carr and the Heterogeneous Modern Nation." *The Oxford Art Journal* 19, no. 1 (1996): 91.

Lippard, Lucy. "Body, Nature and Ritual in Women's Art." *Chrysalis* no. 2 (1977).

———. *Overlay: Contemporary Art and the Art of Prehistory*. New York: The New Press, 1983.

Lisle, Laurie. *Portrait of an Artist: A Biography of Georgia O'Keeffe*. New York: Washington Square Press, 1980.

Livesay, Dorothy. "Carr & Livesay." *Canadian Literature* 84 (Spring 1980).

Loeb, Susy, ed. *Feminist Collage: Educating Women in the Visual Arts*. New York: Columbia University, 1979.

Loo, Tina. "Dan Cranmer's Potlatch: Law, Coercion, Symbol, and Rhetoric in

British Columbia, 1884–1951." *The Canadian Historical Review* 73, no. 2 (1992).

Lord, Barry. *Towards a People's Art: A History of Painting in Canada*. Toronto: N.C. Press, 1974.

Low, Jean. "Dr. Charles Frederick Newcombe." *The Beaver* (Spring 1982).

Lowe, Sue Davidson. *Stieglitz: A Memoir/Biography*. New York: Farrar, Straus and Giroux, 1983.

Lugrin, N. de Bertrand. *The Pioneer Women of Vancouver Island 1843–1866*. Victoria: The Women's Canadian Club of Victoria, 1928.

Lynch, Gerald. "An Endless Flow: D.C. Scott's Indian Poems." *Studies in Canadian Literature* 7, no. 1 (1982).

Lynes, Barbara Buhler. *O'Keeffe, Stieglitz and the Critics, 1916–1929*. Ann Arbor: University of Michigan Press, 1989.

McCormick, E.H. *The Expatriate*. Wellington: New Zealand University Press, 1954.
———. *Works of Frances Hodgkins in New Zealand*. London: Oxford University Press, 1954.
———. "Frances Hodgkins, a Pictorial Biography." *Ascent* (December 1969).
———. "The Path to Impressionism: 1892–1912." *Art New Zealand* 16 (1980): 28–35.
———. *Portrait of Frances Hodgkins*. Auckland: University of Auckland Press, 1981.

McDonald, Robert A.J. *Making Vancouver: 1863–1913*. Vancouver: University of British Columbia Press, 1996.

McDowell, Jim. *Hamatsa: The Enigma of Cannibalism on the Pacific Northwest Coast*. Vancouver: Ronsdale Press, 1997.

McGregor, Gaile. *The Wacousta Syndrome: Exploration in the Canadian Landscape*. Toronto: University of Toronto Press, 1985.

McInnes, T.R.L. "History of Indian Administration in Canada." *The Canadian Journal of Economic & Political Science* 12 (Feb.–Nov. 1946).

McKinnon, Avenal. *Frances Hodgkins 1869–1947* exhibition catalogue. London: Whitford and Hughes, 1990.

McLaren, Jean. *It's Worth a Try*. Gabriola Island: Potluck Press, 1999.

McLoughlin, John. *Fort Vancouver Letters: First Series 1825–1838*. Edited by W. Kaye Lamb. The Champlain Society, 1941. Kraus reprint, 1968.

McMaster, Gerald, and Lee-Ann Martin. *Indigena: Contemporary Native Perspectives*, with essays by Gloria Cranmer Webster, Alootook Ipellie, George E. Sioui Wendayete, Loretta Todd, Alfred Young Man, and Lenore Keeshig-Tobias. Vancouver: Douglas & McIntyre, 1992.

McNair, Peter. "From Kwakiutl to Kwakwaka'wakw." In *Native Peoples: The Canadian Experience*, edited by Bruce Morrison and C. Roderick Wilson. Toronto: McClelland & Stewart, 1986.

McNeil, Florence. *Emily*. Toronto: Clarke Irwin, 1975.

Mallory, Catherine E. *The Victorian and Canadian Worlds of Emily Carr: The Study of a Divided Imagination*. Ph.D. thesis, Dalhousie University, 1979.

Maracle, Brian. *Back on the Rez: Finding the Way Home*. Toronto: Viking, 1996.

Maracle, Lee. *Bobbi Lee, Indian Rebel*. Toronto: Women's Press, 1990.

———. *Ravensong*. Vancouver: Press Gang, 1993.

———. *I Am a Woman*. Vancouver: Press Gang, 1996.

Marchak, Patricia. *Green Gold*. Vancouver: University of British Columbia Press, 1983.

Marchessault, Jovette. *Le Voyage Magnifique d'Emily Carr*. Quebec: Lemeac, 1990.

Marlatt, Daphne, Sky Lee et. al. *Telling It: Women and Language Across Cultures*. Vancouver: Press Gang, 1990.

———. "Some Notes on the Narcissism of the Viewers with Respect to the Work of Emily Carr, Hildegard of Bingen and Julia Kristeva." Emily Carr Symposium, Vancouver Art Gallery, August 1991.

Mastai, Judith. "Abjection and Politics: The Work of Canadian Modernist Emily Carr." Paper delivered at The Fourth World: America 1492–1992 Conference, University of Essex, 1992.

———. "Excerpts from an Invitation Seminar on the Life and Work of Emily Carr." *Collapse* no. 2 (1992): 79–121.

———. "Hysterical Histories: Emily Carr and the Canadian West." In *Inside the Visible*, edited by M. Catherine de Zegher, 1996.

Maud, Ralph. *Transmission Difficulties: Franz Boas and Tsimshian Mythology*. Vancouver: Talonbooks, 2000.

May, Elizabeth. *At the Cutting Edge: The Crisis in Canada's Forests*. Toronto: Key Porter Books, 1998.

Meilleur, Helen. *A Pour of Rain: Stories from a West Coast Fort*. Victoria: Sono Nis, 1980.

Merchant, Carolyn. *The Death of Nature*. San Francisco: HarperSan Francisco, 1976.

Merrill, Christopher, and Ellen Bradbury, eds. *From the Faraway Nearby: Georgia O'Keeffe as Icon*. Reading, Mass.: Addison Wesley, 1992.

Miki, Roy. *Broken Entries: Race, Subjectivity, Writing*. Toronto: Mercury, 1998.

Miller, J.R. *Skyscrapers Hide the Heavens*. Toronto: University of Toronto Press, 1989.

Morang, Alfred. *Transcendental Painting*. Santa Fe: American Foundation for Transcendental Painting Inc., 1940.

Moray, Gerta. "Northwest Coast Native Culture and the Early Indian Paintings of Emily Carr, 1899–1913." Ph.D. thesis, University of Toronto, 1993.

———. "Wilderness, Modernity and Aboriginality in the Paintings of Emily Carr." *Journal of Canadian Studies* 33, no. 2 (Summer 1998).

Morrison, Ann. "Canadian Art and Cultural Appropriation: Emily Carr and the 1927 Exhibition of Canadian West Coast Art—Native and Modern." M.A. thesis, University of British Columbia, 1991.

Morrison, Toni. *Playing in the Dark: Whiteness and the Literary Imagination*. Cambridge: Harvard University Press, 1992.

Mortimer-Lamb, Harold. "A British Columbia Painter." *Saturday Night* (14 January 1933).

Moses, Daniel David, and Terry Goldie, eds. *An Anthology of Canadian Native Literature*. Toronto: Oxford University Press, 1998.

———. *Almighty Voice and His Wife*. Toronto: Exile Editions, 1998.

Murray, Joan. "The Passion of Emily Carr." *Journal of Canadian Studies* 25, no. 3 (Autumn 1990).

Murray, Peter. *The Devil and Mr. Duncan*. Victoria: Sono Nis, 1985.

Nadel, Ira B. "Canadian Biography and Literary Form." *Essays on Canadian Writing* 33 (Fall 1986).

Nasgaard, Roald. *The Mystic North: Northern Symbolist Landscape in Northern Europe and North America 1890–1940*. Toronto: University of Toronto Press/Art Gallery of Ontario, 1984.

Neering, Rosemary. *Emily Carr*. Toronto: Fitzhenry & Whiteside, 1975.

Nelson, Joyce. "Culture and Agriculture—the Ultimate Simulacrum." *Border/Lines* (Spring 1990).

Newcombe, C.F. "Miss Carr's Collection of Paintings of Indian Totem Poles," a report to Francis Fermode, curator of the Provincial Museum, 17 January 1918. Newcombe Papers, British Columbia Archives.

Newman, Barbara. *Sister of Wisdom: St. Hildegard's Theology of the Feminine*. Berkeley: University of California Press, 1987.

Nochlin, Linda. *Women, Art and Power and Other Essays*. New York: Harper & Row, 1988.

Nowry, Laurence. *Marius Barbeau: Man of Mana*. Toronto: N.C. Press, 1995.

Nunn, Pamela Gerrish. "Frances Hodgkins, 'The Arrival' in Context." *Art in New Zealand* 56 (Spring 1990).

———. "Frances Hodgkins: A Question of Identity." *Women's Art Journal* (Fall/Winter 1994/5).

O'Brien, John. *Gasoline, Oil and Paper: The 1930s Oil-on-Paper Paintings of Emily Carr*. Saskatoon: Mendel Art Gallery, 1995.

O'Keeffe, Georgia. *Georgia O'Keeffe*. New York: Viking Press, 1976.

O'Meara, Walter. *Daughters of the Country: The Women of the Fur Trade and Mountain Men*. New York: Harcourt Brace, 1968.

Ondaatje, Michael. *From Ink Lake*. Toronto: Lester & Orpen Dennys, 1991.

Opie, June. "The Quest for Frances Hodgkins." *Ascent* (1969): 61.

Ormsby, Margaret. *British Columbia: A History*. Toronto: Macmillan, 1976.

Osborne, Brian S. "The Iconography of Nationhood in Canadian Art." In *The Iconography of Landscape*, edited by Denis Cosgrove and Stephen Daniels. Cambridge: Cambridge University Press, 1988.

Pagh, Nancy. "Emily Carr: The Silent, Awe-filled Spaces." *ISLE (Interdisciplinary Studies in Literature and the Environment)* 2:1 (Spring 1994).

———. "Passing Through the Jungle: Emily Carr and Theories of Women's Autobiography." *Mosaic* 25, no. 4 (Fall 1992): 63–79.

Paris, Reine-Marie. *Camille: The Life of Camille Claudel, Rodin's Muse and Mistress*. New York: Seaver, 1984.

Parker, Rozsika, and Griselda Pollock. *Old Mistresses, Women, Art and Ideology*. New York: Pantheon, 1985.

Parkinson, John Edward. "Reading and Writing Emily Carr." M.A. thesis, McMaster University, 1988.

Patterson, Nancy Lou. "Emily Carr's Forest." Exhibition catalogue, University of Waterloo Art Gallery, 1967.

Pearson, Carol. *Emily Carr as I Knew Her*. Toronto: Clarke Irwin, 1954.

Peters, Sarah Whitaker. *Becoming O'Keeffe: The Early Years*. New York: Abbeville Press, 1991.

Pethick, Derek. *James Douglas: Servant of Two Empires*. Vancouver: Mitchell Press, 1969.

Pfaff, L.R. "Lawren Harris and the International Exhibition of Modern Art: Rectification to the Toronto Catalogue (1927) and Some Critical Comments." *RACAR* 11 (1984).

Philip, M. Nourbese. *Frontiers: Essays and Writings on Racism and Culture*. Toronto: Mercury, 1992.

Piaget, Amelia. *People of the Plains*. Toronto: William Briggs, 1909.

Piper, John. "Frances Hodgkins." *Horizon* 4, no. 24 (December 1941).

Pollock, Griselda. "A Politics of Art or an Aesthetic for Women?" *Feminist Art News* 5 (1981).

———. "Vision, Voice and Power: Feminist Marxism and Art History." *Block* 6 (1982).

———. "Women, Art, Art School and Culture." *Block* 6, 11 (1985).

———. "Feminism and Modernism." In *Framing Feminism*, edited by Griselda Pollock and Rozsika Parker, New York: Pandora, 1987.

———. *Vision and Difference: Femininity, Feminism and the Histories of Art*. London: Routledge, 1988.

———. *Generation and Geographies in the Visual Arts: Feminist Readings*. London: Routledge, 1996.

Powe, Bruce. *The Solitary Outlaw*. Toronto: Lester & Orpen Dennys, 1987.

Pratt, Annis. "Affairs with Bears: Some Notes Towards Feminist Archetypal Hypotheses for Canadian Literature." *Gynocritics: Feminist Approaches to Canadian and Quebec Women's Writing*, edited by Barbara Goddard. Toronto: ECW Press, 1987.

Preston, Richard J. "C. Marius Barbeau and the History of Canadian Anthropology." In *The History of Canadian Anthropology*, edited by Jim Freedman. Canadian Ethnology Society, 1976.

Pritchard, Allan. "West of the Great Divide: A View of the Literature of British Columbia." *Canadian Literature* 94 (Summer 1982).

Pullinger, Kate. *The Last Time I Saw Jane*. New York: Little Brown, 1997.

Raunet, Daniel. *Without Surrender, Without Consent: A History of the Nisga Land Claims*. Vancouver: Douglas & McIntyre, 1984.

Raven, Arlene, Cassandra Langer, and Joanna Frueh, eds. *Feminist Art Criticism*. New York: HarperCollins, 1988.

Reid, Dennis. "Lawren Harris." *Artscanada* 25 (December 1968).

———. *The Group of Seven*. Ottawa: National Gallery of Canada, 1970.

———. *A Concise History of Canadian Painting*. Toronto: Oxford University Press, 1973.

———. *Atma Buddhi Manas: The Later Work of Lawren S. Harris*. Toronto: Art Gallery of Ontario, 1985.

———. "Marcel Duchamp in Canada." *Canadian Art* (Winter 1987): 52–54.

Rhoades, Guy E. "West Coast Indian Art." *Saturday Night* 18 (December 1927).

Richardson, Boyce. *People of Terra Nullius: Betrayal and Rebirth in Aboriginal Canada*. Vancouver: Douglas & McIntyre, 1993.

Ricou, Laurie. "Echoes of the Indigenous Voice in the Literature of British Columbia." Unpublished paper, no date (circa 1982). UBC Special Collections.

———. "Everyday Magic: Child Languages in Canadian Literature." Vancouver: University of British Columbia Press, 1987.

Rimstead, Roxanne. "Klee Wyck: Redefining Region through Marginal Realities." *Canadian Literature* 130 (Autumn 1991).

Rioux, Marcel. *Les Québécois*. Paris: Seuil, 1975.

Rioux, Marcel, and Susan Crean. *Two Nations: An Essay on the Culture and Politics of Canada and Quebec in a World of American Preeminence*. Toronto: Lorimer, 1983.

Ritchie, Andrew C. "Introduction." British Contemporary Painters exhibition at Albright Art Gallery. Buffalo: The Holling Press, 1946.

Robertson, Heather. "Totem Poles and Tall Tales." *Canadian Forum* (August 1996).

———. *Reservations Are for Indians*. Toronto: James, Lewis and Samuel, 1970.

Robinson, Roxana. *Georgia O'Keeffe*. New York: HarperCollins, 1989.

Root, Deborah. *Cannibal Culture: Art Appropriation and the Commodification of Difference*. Boulder: Westview Press, 1996.

Ross, Catherine Sheldrick. "A Singing Spirit: Female Rites of Passage in *Klee Wyck*, *Surfacing* and *The Diviners*." *Atlantis* 4, no. 1 (Fall 1978).

Roy, Patricia E. *White Man's Province: British Columbia Politicians and Chinese and Japanese Immigrants 1856–1914*. Vancouver: University of British Columbia Press, 1989.

Ryan, Maureen. "Picturing Canada's Native Landscape: Colonial Expansion, Native Identity and the Image of a Dying Race." *RACAR* 17, no. 2 (1990).

Ryerson, Stanley B. *The Founding of Canada: Beginning to 1815*. Toronto: Progress Books, 1960.

Salem, Lisa. "'Her Blood Is Mingled with Her Ancient Foes': The Concepts of Blood, Race, and 'Miscegenation' in the Poetry and Short Fiction of Duncan Campbell Scott." *Studies in Canadian Literature* 18, no. 1 (1993).

Sanders, Doug. "The Nisga'a Case." *B.C. Studies* 19 (Autumn 1973).

Sanger, Peter. "Finding D'Sonoqua's Child: Myth, Truth and Lies in the Prose of Emily Carr." *Antigonish Review* 69–70 (1987).

Scott, D.C. "The Administration of Indian Affairs in Canada" for the Canadian Institute of International Affairs. Toronto, 1931.

———. "The Last of the Indian Treaties." In *Circle of Affection: and other pieces in Prose and Verse.* Toronto: McClelland and Stewart, 1947.

———. *Selected Poetry.* Toronto: Ryerson Press, 1951.

Sewid-Smith, Daisy (My-Yah-Nelth). *Prosecution or Persecution?* Cape Mudge: Nu-Yum-Baylees Society, 1979.

Shadbolt, Doris. *The Art of Emily Carr.* Toronto: Clarke Irwin, 1979.

———. *Emily Carr.* Vancouver: Douglas & McIntyre, 1990.

Shaul, Sandra. "Lawren Harris and the Dilemma of Nationalism vs. Abstraction." *The Modern Image: Cubism and the Realist Tradition.* Edmonton: Edmonton Art Gallery, 1982.

Shein, Brian. "Playing, Pretending, Being Real." *Canadian Art* (Spring 1987).

Showalter, Elaine. *The Female Malady: Women, Madness, and English Culture, 1830–1980.* New York: Pantheon, 1985.

Siggins, Maggie. *Riel: A Life of Revolution.* Toronto: HarperCollins, 1994.

Simpson, Byrne Hope. *Canadian Portraits.* Toronto: Clarke Irwin, 1958.

Skogan, Joan. *Skeena: A River Remembered.* Vancouver: B.C. Packers, Raincoast, 1983.

Smith, Peter L. "Emily Carr: A Review Article." *B.C. Studies* no. 45 (Spring 1980).

Smyly, John and Carolyn Smyly. *Those Born at Koona.* Vancouver: Hancock House, 1973.

Spradley, James. *Guests Never Leave Hungry.* New Haven: Yale University Press, 1985.

Sproat, Gilbert. *The Nootka: Scenes and Studies of Savage Life*, edited by Charles Lillard. Victoria: Sono Nis, 1987.

Sproxton, Birk. *Mysticism Debunked: Poetry of Bertram Brooker.* Winnipeg: Turnstone Press, 1980.

Stacton, David D. "The Art of Emily Carr." *Queen's Quarterly* 57, no. 4 (1950/1).

Stewart, Wallace. *The Growth of Canadian National Feeling.* Toronto: Macmillan, 1927.

Stich, K.P., ed. *The D.C. Scott Symposium.* Toronto: University of Toronto Press, 1979.

———. "Painters' Words: Personal Narratives of Emily Carr and William Kurelek." *Essays in Canadian Writing* 29 (Summer 1984).

Street, Linda. *Lawren Harris and Theosophy.* M.A. thesis, Carleton University, 1979.

Strong-Boag, Veronica, and Carole Gerson. *Paddling Her Own Canoe: The Times and Texts of E. Pauline Johnson.* Toronto: University of Toronto Press, 2000.

Suttles, Wayne. "Affinal Ties, Subsistence and Prestige among Coast Salish." *American Anthropologist* 62, no. 2 (1960).

———. "Central Coast Salish." in Wayne Suttles, ed. and William C. Sturtevant, series ed. *Handbook of North American Indians* Volume 7, Northwest Coast. Washington, D.C.: Smithsonian Institution.

———. *Coast Salish Essays.* Vancouver: Talonbooks, 1977.

Tator, Carol, et al. *Challenging Racism in the Arts: Case Studies of Controversy and Conflict.* Toronto: University of Toronto Press, 1998.

Taylor, Charles. *Six Journeys: A Canadian Pattern: Brigadier James Sutherland Brown, Bishop William White, James Houston, Herbert Norman, Emily Carr, Scott Simons.* Toronto: Anansi, 1977.

Teitlebaum, Matthew. "Sighting the Single Tree, Sighting the New Found Land." In *Eye of Nature*, Banff: Walter Phillips Gallery, 1991.

Tennant, Paul. *Aboriginal People and Politics: The Indian Land Question in British Columbia 1849–1989.* Vancouver: University of British Columbia Press, 1990.

Thom, William Wylie. "The Fine Arts in Vancouver." M.A. thesis, University of British Columbia, 1969.

Thomas, Hilda. "Klee Wyck: The Eye of the Other." *Canadian Literature* 136 (Spring 1993).

Thornton, Mildred. *Indian Lives and Legends.* Vancouver: Mitchell, 1966.

Tippett, Maria. "Emily Carr's Forest." *Journal of Forest History* 18, no. 4 (October 1973).

———. "Who Discovered Emily Carr?" *Journal of Canadian Art History* 1, no. 2 (Fall 1974).

———. "Emily Carr's Klee Wyck." *Canadian Literature* 72 (Spring 1977).

———. *Emily Carr: A Biography.* Toronto: Oxford University Press, 1979.

———. *By a Lady: Celebrating Three Centuries of Art by Canadian Women.* Toronto: Viking, 1992.

Tippett, Maria, and Douglas Cole. *From Desolation to Splendour: Changing Perceptions of B.C. Landscape.* Toronto: Clarke Irwin, 1977.

Titley, E. Brian. *A Narrow Vision: Duncan Campbell Scott and the Administration of Indian Affairs in Canada.* Vancouver: UBC Press, 1986.

Tobey, Mark. "Reminiscence and Reverie." *Magazine of Art* (October 1951): 228.

Todd, Loretta. "Notes on Appropriation." In *Sightlines: Reading Contemporary Canadian Art*, edited by Jessica Bradley and Lesley Johnstone. Montreal: Artextes Editions, 1994.

Trigger, Bruce G. *Natives and Newcomers: Canada's "Heroic Age" Reconsidered.* Montreal: McGill-Queen's Press, 1985.

Trinh T., Minh-ha, *Woman, Native, Other.* Bloomington: Indiana University Press, 1989.

Tuer, Dot. "To Speak Difference." *Parachute* 43 (June/July/August 1986).

———. "The Art of Nation Building: Constructing a 'Cultural Identity' for Post-War Canada." *Parallelogramme* 17, no. 4 (1992).

Udall, Sharyn R. *Contested Terrain: Myth and Meanings in Southwest Art.* Albuquerque, N.M.: University of New Mexico Press, 1996.

Unwin, Peter. "The Mohawk Princess." *Beaver* (October/November 1999).

Van Kirk, Sylvia. *Many Tender Ties: Women in Fur-Trade Society 1670–1870*. Winnipeg: Watson & Dwyer, 1980.

Vipond, Mary. "The Nationalist Network: English Canada's Intellectuals and Artists in the 1920s." *Canadian Review of Studies in Nationalism* 7, no. 1 (Spring 1980).

————. "Nationalism and Nativism: The Native Sons of Canada in the 1920s." *Canadian Review of Studies in Nationalism* 9, no. 1 (Spring 1982).

Wa, Gisday, and Delgam Uukw. *The Spirit of the Land*. Gabriola, B.C.: Reflections, 1989.

Walker, Barbara G. *The Crone: Woman of Age, Wisdom, and Power*. San Francisco: Harper & Row, 1985.

Walker, Doreen, ed. *Dear Nan: Letters of Emily Carr, Nan Cheney, and Humphrey Toms*. Vancouver: University of British Columbia Press, 1990.

Wachtel, Eleanor. "Review: Maria Tippett, *Emily Carr: A Biography*." *Branching Out* 7, no. 2 (1980).

Walker, Stephanie Kirkwood. *This Woman in Particular: Contexts for the Biographical Image of Emily Carr*. Waterloo: Wilfrid Laurier University Press, 1996.

Wallace, Stewart. *The Growth of Canadian National Feeling*. Toronto: Macmillan, 1927.

Walton, Paul H. "The Group of Seven and Northern Development." *RACAR* 17, no. 2 (1990).

Ward, W. Peter, and Robert A.J. McDonald. *British Columbia Historical Readings*. Vancouver: Douglas & McIntyre, 1981.

Warner, Janet. "Emily Carr's Tennyson." *Canadian Literature* 113–114 (Summer 1987).

Watmough, Don. *West Coast Vancouver Island Cape Scott to Sooke, Including Barkley Sound*. Vancouver: Special Interest Publication, McLean-Hunter, 1984.

Watson, Scott. "Disfigured Nature: The Origins of the Modern Canadian Landscape." In *Eye of Nature*. Banff: Walter Phillips Gallery, 1991.

————. "Race, Wilderness, Territory and the Origins of Modern Canadian Landscape Painting." In *Semiotext(e) Canada* 6, no. 2 (1994).

Weir, Joan. *Catalysts and Watchdogs: B.C.'s Men of God, 1836–1871*. Victoria: Sono Nis, 1995.

Weis, L.P. "D.C. Scott's View of History and the Indians." *Canadian Literature* 3 (1986).

Wertheim, Lucy. *Adventure in Art*. London: Nicholson & Watson, 1947.

White, Howard. "William Duncan and the Miracle of Metlakatla." In *Writing in the Rain*. Vancouver: Harbour, 1990.

Wilken, Karen. "Maple-leaf Modernist: The Case of Emily Carr." *The New Criterion* (December 1993).

Bibliography

Wilson, Alexander. *The Culture of Nature: North American Landscape from Disney to the Exxon Valdez*. Toronto: Between the Lines, 1991.

Women's Missionary Society of the Presbyterian Church of Canada. *The Story of Our Mission*. University of British Columbia Library, ca. 1915.

Woodcock, George. "Nationalism and the Canadian Genius." *artscanada* 36, no. 4 (1979/80).

Wright, Ronald. *Stolen Continents: The "New World" Through Indian Eyes Since 1492*. Toronto: Viking, 1992.

York, Geoffrey. *The Dispossessed*. Toronto: Lester & Orpen Dennys, 1989.

Zemans, Joyce. "Jock Macdonald: The Inner Landscape." *Retrospective*. Toronto: Art Gallery of Ontario, 1981.

———. "First Fruits: The World and Spirit Paintings." *Provincial Essays* 7 (1989).

———. "Establishing the Canon: Nationhood, Identity and the National Gallery's First Reproduction Programme of Canadian Art." *The Journal of Canadian Art History* 16, no. 2 (1995).

Index

Index

Index